Lecture Notes in Computer Science 2372

Edited by G. Goos, J. Hartmanis, and J. van Leeuwen

T0215985

Springer
Berlin
Heidelberg
New York
Barcelona
Hong Kong
London
Milan
Paris
Tokyo

Alberto Pettorossi (Ed.)

Logic Based Program Synthesis and Transformation

11th International Workshop, LOPSTR 2001
Paphos, Cyprus, November 28-30, 2001
Selected Papers

 Springer

Series Editors

Gerhard Goos, Karlsruhe University, Germany
Juris Hartmanis, Cornell University, NY, USA
Jan van Leeuwen, Utrecht University, The Netherlands

Volume Editor

Alberto Pettorossi
University of Rome Tor Vergata
Via del Politecnico 1, 00133 Rome, Italy
E-mail: adp@iasi.rm.cnr.it

Cataloging-in-Publication Data applied for

Die Deutsche Bibliothek - CIP-Einheitsaufnahme

Logic based program synthesis and transformation : 11th international
workshop ; selected papers / LOPSTR 2001, Paphos, Cyprus, November
28 - 30, 2001. Alberto Pettorossi (ed.). - Berlin ; Heidelberg ; New York ;
Barcelona ; Hong Kong ; London ; Milan ; Paris ; Tokyo : Springer, 2002
    (Lecture notes in computer science ; Vol. 2372)
    ISBN 3-540-43915-3

CR Subject Classification (1998): F.3.1, D.1.1, D.1.6, I.2.2, F.4.1

ISSN 0302-9743
ISBN 3-540-43915-3 Springer-Verlag Berlin Heidelberg New York

Springer-Verlag Berlin Heidelberg New York
a member of BertelsmannSpringer Science+Business Media GmbH

http://www.springer.de

© Springer-Verlag Berlin Heidelberg 2002
Printed in Germany

Typesetting: Camera-ready by author, data conversion by PTP-Berlin, Stefan Sossna e.K.
Printed on acid-free paper   SPIN: 10883696   06/3142   5 4 3 2 1 0

Preface

This volume contains the papers from LOPSTR 2001, the 11th International Workshop on Logic-based Program Synthesis and Transformation. Topics of interest to LOPSTR cover all aspects of logic-based program development and, in particular, specification, synthesis, verification, transformation, specialization, analysis, optimization, composition, reuse, component-based software development, and software architectures.

LOPSTR 2001 took place in the Coral Beach Hotel in Paphos (Cyprus) from November 28–30, 2001. Past LOPSTR workshops were held in Manchester, UK (1991, 1992, 1998), Louvain-la-Neuve, Belgium (1993), Pisa, Italy (1994), Arnhem, The Netherlands (1995), Stockholm, Sweden (1996), Leuven, Belgium (1997), Venice, Italy (1999), and London, UK (2000).

LOPSTR 2001 was co-located with the 17th International Conference on Logic Programming (ICLP 2001)[1] and the 7th International Conference on Principles and Practice of Constraint Programming (CP 2001)[2]. The LOPSTR community profited a lot from the scientific discussions, the lectures of the invited speakers, and the various sessions of ICLP and CP.

I would like to express my gratitude to all the authors of the submitted papers and all the attendees for their commitment and cooperation. Among the submitted papers, the Program Committee selected 13 papers for presentation. After the workshop, the authors were asked to submit improved versions of their papers which were then reviewed by the Program Committee. The final versions have been collected in this volume, which also includes the paper by our invited speaker, Natarajan Shankar (Stanford Research Institute, Menlo Park, USA), on the generation of efficient programs from logic.

My warmest thanks also go to all the members of the Program Committee and the additional reviewers for their diligent work and invaluable help. I would like to thank Fabio Fioravanti (IASI-CNR of Rome, Italy), Maurizio Proietti (IASI-CNR of Rome, Italy), and Antonis Kakas (University of Cyprus, Cyprus), who worked with me with great enthusiasm and dedication as members of the Organizing Committee.

The pre-proceedings of LOPSTR 2001 were printed by the IASI Institute of the National Research Council of Rome, Italy, and the Department of Computer Science of the University of Cyprus in Nicosia. I also thank Springer for accepting to publish these final proceedings in the LNCS series. The LOPSTR 2001 home page is: http://www.iasi.rm.cnr.it/~adp/lopstr01_cfp.html.

April 2002   Alberto Pettorossi

---

[1] Codognet, Ph., editor, *Logic Programming — ICLP 2001, Lecture Notes in Computer Science* 2237, Springer-Verlag, 2001.

[2] Walsh, T., editor, *Principles and Practice of Constraint Programming — CP 2001, Lecture Notes in Computer Science* 2239, Springer-Verlag, 2001.

Table of Contents

Invited Speaker

Program Transformation and Equivalence

Program Verificaion

Program Analysis

Program Development

Program Synthesis

Static Analysis for Safe Destructive Updates in a Functional Language*

Natarajan Shankar

Computer Science Laboratory
SRI International
Menlo Park CA 94025 USA
shankar@csl.sri.com
http://www.csl.sri.com/~shankar/
Phone: +1 (650) 859-5272 Fax: +1 (650) 859-2844

Abstract. Functional programs are more amenable to rigorous mathematical analysis than imperative programs, but are typically less efficient in terms of execution space and time. The update of aggregate data structures, such as arrays, are a significant source of space/time inefficiencies in functional programming. Imperative programs can execute such updates in place, whereas the semantics of functional languages require aggregate data structures to be copied and updated. In many functional programs, the execution of aggregate updates by copying is redundant and could be safely implemented by means of destructive, in-place updates. We describe a method for analyzing higher-order, eager functional programs for safe destructive updates. This method has been implemented for the PVS specification language for the purpose of animating or testing specifications to check if they accurately reflect their intended function. We also give a careful proof of correctness for the safety of the destructive update optimization.

1 Introduction

Unlike imperative programming languages, pure functional languages are referentially transparent so that two occurrences of the same expression evaluate to the same value in the same environment. The execution semantics of functional languages are therefore nondestructive since variables representing aggregate data structures such as arrays cannot be destructively updated. Pure functional

* Funded by NSF Grants CCR-0082560 and CCR-9712383, DARPA/AFRL Contract F33615-00-C-3043, and NASA Contract NAS1-20334. The author is deeply grateful to the programme committee of the 11th International Workshop on Logic-based Program Synthesis and Transformation, LOPSTR 01, for the opportunity to present this work. The LOPSTR 01 programme chair, Professor Alberto Pettorossi, made several excellent suggestions, and Pavol Cerny (visiting SRI from ENS Paris) corrected numerous typographical errors in earlier drafts of this paper.

A. Pettorossi (Ed.): LOPSTR 2001, LNCS 2372, pp. 1–24, 2002.
© Springer-Verlag Berlin Heidelberg 2002

languages do not admit constructs for performing in-place modifications of aggregate data structures. The aggregate update problem for functional programs is that of statically identifying those array updates in a program that can be executed destructively while preserving the semantics of the program. This problem has been widely studied but none of the previously proposed techniques appear to have actually been implemented in any widely used functional language. We present a simple, efficient, and effective method for the static detection of safe destructive updates in a functional language. The method has been implemented for the functional fragment of the specification language PVS [ORS92].[1] This fragment is essentially a strongly typed, higher-order language with an eager order of evaluation. The method can be easily adapted to other functional languages, including those with a lazy evaluation order. The analysis method is *interprocedural*. Each function definition is analyzed solely in terms of the *results* of the analysis of the previously defined functions and not their actual definitions. We also outline a proof of the correctness for the introduction of destructive updates.

PVS is a widely used framework for specification and verification. By optimizing functions defined in the PVS specification language with safe destructive updates, specifications can be executed for the purposes of animation, validation, code generation, and fast simplification. The technique is presented for a small functional language fragment of PVS.

The concepts are informally introduced using a first-order functional language with booleans, natural numbers, subranges, *flat* (unnested) arrays over subranges, application, conditionals, and array updates. A flat array maps an index type that is a subrange type $[0..n]$ to an members of an element type that is either a boolean, natural number, or subrange type. The range type of the mapping cannot be a function or array type.

The full analysis given in Section 2 is for a higher-order language that includes lambda-abstractions. A function is defined as $f(x_1, \ldots, x_n) = e$ where e contains no free variables other than those in $\{x_1, \ldots, x_n\}$. A few simple examples serve to motivate the ideas. Let `Arr` be an array from the subrange `[0..9]` to the integers. Let A and B be variables of type `Arr`. An array lookup is written as $A(i)$ for $0 \leq i \leq 9$. An array update has the form $A[(i) := a]$ and represents a new array A' such that $A'(i) = a$ and $A'(j) = A(j)$ for $j \neq i$. Pointwise addition on arrays $A + B$ is defined as the array C such that $C(i) = A(i) + B(i)$ for $0 \leq i \leq 9$. Now consider the function definition

$$f_1(A) = A + A[(3) := 4].$$

When executing $f_1(A)$, the update to A cannot be carried out destructively since the original array is an argument to the $+$ operation. The evaluation of

---

[1] The PVS system and related documentation can be obtained from the URL `http://pvs.csl.sri.com`. The presentation in this paper is for a generic functional language and requires no prior knowledge of PVS. The notation used is also somewhat different from that of PVS.

$A[(3) := 4]$ must return a reference to a new array that is a suitably modified copy of the array A.

The implementation of array updates by copying can be expensive in both space and time. In many computations, copying is unnecessary since the original data structure is no longer needed in the computation that follows the update. Consider the definition

$$f_2(A, i) = A(i) + A[(3) := 4](i).$$

Given an eager, left-to-right evaluation order (as defined in Section 3), the expression $A(i)$ will be evaluated prior to the update $A[(3) := 4]$. Since the original value of A is no longer used in the computation, the array can be updated destructively.[2] The optimization assumes that array A is not referenced in the context where $f_2(A, i)$ is evaluated. For example, in the definition

$$f_3(A) = A[(4) := f_2(A, 3)],$$

it would be unsafe to execute f_2 so that A is updated destructively since there is a reference to the original A in the context when $f_2(A, 3)$ is evaluated.

Next, consider the function definition

$$f_4(A, B) = A + B[(3) := 4].$$

Here, the update to array B can be executed destructively provided A and B are not bound to the same array reference. This happens, for instance, in the definition

$$f_5(C) = f_4(C, C).$$

In such a situation, it is not safe to destructively update the second argument C of f_4 when evaluating the definition of f_4 since the reference to C from the first argument is live, i.e., appears in the context, when the update is evaluated.

The task is that of statically analyzing the definitions of programs involving function definitions such as those of f_1, f_2, f_3, f_4, and f_5, in order to identify those updates that can be executed destructively. Our analysis processes each definition of a function f, and generates the definition for a (possibly) destructive analogue f^D of f that contains destructive updates along with the conditions $LA(f^D)$ under which it is safe to use f^D instead of f. The analysis $LA(f^D)$ is a partial map of the form $\langle x_1 \mapsto X_1, \ldots, x_n \mapsto X_n \rangle$ where $\langle \rangle$ is the empty map. The analysis when applied to a definition $f(x_1, \ldots, x_n) = e$ produces a definition of the form $f^D(x_1, \ldots, x_n) = e^D$, where some occurrences of *nondestructive* updates of the form $e_1[(e_2) := e_3]$ in e have been replaced by *destructive* updates of the form $e_1[(e_2) \leftarrow e_3]$. The analysis of the examples above should therefore yield

---

[2] With a lazy order of evaluation, the safety of this optimization depends on the order in which the arguments of $+$ are evaluated.

$$f_1^D(A) = A + A[(3) := 4] \qquad LA(f_1^D) = \langle \rangle$$
$$f_2^D(A, i) = A(i) + A[(3) \leftarrow 4](i) \quad LA(f_2^D) = \langle A \mapsto \emptyset \rangle$$
$$f_3^D(A) = A[(4) \leftarrow f_2(A, 3)] \qquad LA(f_3^D) = \langle A \mapsto \emptyset \rangle$$
$$f_4^D(A, B) = A + B[(3) \leftarrow 4] \qquad LA(f_4^D) = \langle B \mapsto \{A\} \rangle$$
$$f_5^D(C) = f_4(C, C) \qquad LA(f_5^D) = \langle \rangle$$

Observe that when the array referenced by B is destructively updated in f_4^D, the variable A is live, and hence $LA(f_4^D) = \langle B \mapsto \{A\} \rangle$. The information in $LA(f_4^D)$ is used to reject $f_4^D(C, C)$ as unsafe in the definition of f_5^D. In general, this kind of interprocedural analysis can be too coarse. definition. For example, the definition $f_6(A, B, C) = (A + B[(3) := 4] + C[(4) := 3])$ can be safely mapped to either $f_6^D(A, B, C) = (A + B[(3) \leftarrow 4] + C[(4) \leftarrow 3])$, where $LA(f_6^D) = \langle B \mapsto \{A\}, C \mapsto \{A, B\} \rangle$. The update analysis rejects $f_6^D(A, A, B)$ as unsafe, even though this would have been safe had $f_6^D(A, B, C)$ been defined as $(A + B[(3) := 4] + C[(4) \leftarrow 3])$.

We now informally describe the conditions under which $f^D(x_1, \ldots, x_n) = e$ together with the liveness analysis $LA(f^D)$, is a safe, destructive counterpart of the definition $f(x_1, \ldots, x_n) = e$. The liveness analysis table $LA(f^D)$ as a partial map from the set of variables $\{x_1, \ldots, x_n\}$ to its powerset such that $x_j \in LA(f^D)(x_i)$ if x_j is live in the context (as defined below) of a destructive update applied to (the value bound to) x_i. The table $LA(f^D)$ can be used to determine whether it is safe to replace $f(a_1, \ldots, a_n)$ by $f^D(a_1, \ldots, a_n)$ in another function definition.

Given a definition $f^D(x_1, \ldots, x_n) = e$, where e contains an occurrence of a destructive update operation of the form $e_1[(e_2) \leftarrow e_3]$, the task is to identify if this is a safe destructive update. The crucial idea here is that when the destructive update expression $e_1[(e_2) \leftarrow e_3]$ is evaluated, the array reference for the value of e_1 is modified. This array reference is either freshly created within e_1, in which case the destructive update is safe, or it appears in the binding of some *free* variable in e_1. In the latter case, the update is unsafe if such a variable in e_1 is *live* in the *context* when the update $e_1[(e_2) \leftarrow e_3]$ is being evaluated. More strongly, the analysis must ensure that the value of e_1 does not have any array references in common with its context as it appears when the update is evaluated. Such an analysis can be carried out by examining the *mutable* variables that occur in the body of a function definition. A *mutable type* is a type whose values can contain references. For a first-order language, only array types are mutable. A *mutable variable* is a variable of mutable type.

A specific occurrence of a destructive update u of the form $e_1[(e_2) \leftarrow e_3]$ in an expression e can be identified by decomposing e as $U\{u\}$, where U is an *update context* containing a single occurrence of the *hole* $\{\}$, and $U\{u\}$ is the result of filling the hole with the update expression u. In order to determine if u is a safe destructive update, we compute

1. The set $Lv(U)$ of *live* mutable variables in the update context U. When the expression $U\{u\}$ is evaluated, the free variables in it are bound to val-

ues through some substitution σ, and the free mutable variables are bound to values containing references. The set $Lv(U)$ calculates those variables x such that $\sigma(x)$ is present in the partially evaluated context U' when the subexpression u is evaluated. This is a subset of the mutable variables in U.

2. The set $Ov(e_1)$ of the output array variables in e_1 contains those array variables x such that the reference $\sigma(x)$ is a possible value of $\sigma(e_1)$.

A destructive update expression $e_1[(e_2) \leftarrow e_3]$ occurring in an update context U, where $e \equiv U\{e_1[(e_2) \leftarrow e_3]\}$ in a definition $f^D(x_1, \ldots, x_n) = e$, is *safe* if $Lv(U) \cap Ov(e_1) = \emptyset$. Informally, this means that when some instance $\sigma(e)$ of e is evaluated, the array references that are possible values of $\sigma(e_1)$ do not occur in the context derived from $\sigma(U)$ when the destructive update $e_1[(e_2) \leftarrow e_3]$. However, we are assuming that whenever $x_i \not\equiv x_j$, then $\sigma(x_i) \neq \sigma(x_j)$. This assumption is violated when *aliasing* occurs, i.e., when $\sigma(x_i) = \sigma(x_j)$ for $x_i \not\equiv x_j$, as is the case in the evaluation of $f_4(C, C)$ in the definition of f_5. To account for the possibility aliasing, a table $LA(f^D)$ is constructed so that $Lv(U) \subseteq LA(f^D)(x)$ for each x in $Ov(e_1)$, i.e., $LA(f^D)(x)$ is the set of variables that must not be aliased to x in any invocation of f^D.

The analysis can use the table $LA(g^D)$ to determine when it is safe to invoke a destructive function application $g^D(a_1, \ldots, a_m)$ within the definition of f^D. An application occurrence $g^D(a_1, \ldots, a_m)$ in an update context U, where $U\{g^D(a_1, \ldots, a_m)\} \equiv e$, is safe iff $Ov(a_i) \cap (Lv(U) \cup Ov(a_j)) = \emptyset$ for each x_i in the domain of $LA(g^D)$ and x_j in $LA(g^D)(x_i)$. Why does this condition ensure the safety of the given occurrence of $g^D(a_1, \ldots, a_m)$? If $\sigma(e)$ is the instance of e that is being evaluated, the references that are destructively updated in evaluating $\sigma(g^D(a_1, \ldots, a_m))$ are from the values of $\sigma(a_i)$ for x_i in the domain of $LA(g^D)$. During the evaluation of the body of the definition of g^D, there can be a destructive update to a reference in the value of $\sigma(a_i)$ for x_i in the domain of $LA(g^D)$. The references in the context of this destructive update are either those from the context $\sigma(Lv(U))$ or from $\sigma(Ov(a_j))$ for $x_j \in LA(g^D)(x_i)$. The mapping $LA(f^D)$ must then be defined to satisfy the constraint $Lv(U) \cup Ov(a_j) \subseteq LA(f)(x)$ for each x in $Ov(a_i)$ such that x_i is in the domain of $LA(g^D)$ and x_j in $LA(g^D)(x_i)$.

Thus in the examples f_1 to f_5, we have

1. f_1: If e^D is $A + A[(3) \leftarrow 4]$, then $Ov(A)$ is $\{A\}$, the update context is $(A + \{\})$, and $Lv(A + \{\})$ is $\{A\}$. Since $Ov(A)$ has a nonempty intersection with the live variables in the context, the update is not safe.

2. f_2: If e^D is $A(i) + A[(3) \leftarrow 4](i)$, $Ov(A)$ is $\{A\}$, then the update context is $(A(i) + \{\}(i))$, and $Lv(A(i) + \{\}(i))$ is $\emptyset$. Since the updated variable A is not live in the update context, the update is safe. Note that $LA(f_2^D)(A) = \emptyset$.

3. f_3: If e^D is $A[(4) \leftarrow f_2^D(A, 3)]$. Here, the update context for $f_2^D(A, 3)$ is $(A[(4) \leftarrow \{\}])$, where $Lv(A[(4) \leftarrow \{\}])$ is $\{A\}$. Since A is in the domain of $LA(f_2^D)$ and there is a nonempty intersection between $Ov(A)$ and the live variable set $\{A\}$, the occurrence of $f_2^D(A, 3)$ is unsafe. The update $A[(4) \leftarrow$

$f_2(A, 3)$)] can be executed destructively, since there are no live references to A in the update context $\{\}$. We then have $LA(f_3^D)(A) = \emptyset$.

4. f_4: If e^D is $A + B[(3) \leftarrow 4]$, then $Ov(B)$ is $\{B\}$, the update context is $(A + \{\})$, and $Lv(A + \{\})$ is $\{A\}$. Since $\{B\} \cap \{A\} = \emptyset$, the update is safe, but $LA(f_4^D)(B) = \{A\}$.

5. f_5: If e^D is $f_4^D(C, C)$, then the update context is $\{\}$ with $Lv(\{\})$ equal to $\emptyset$. Since $LA(f_4^D)$ maps B to $\{A\}$ and $Ov(C) = \{C\}$, the analysis detects the aliasing between the binding C for A and C for B. The occurrence of $f_4^D(C, C)$ is therefore unsafe.

The formal explanation for the destructive update analysis and optimization is the topic of the remainder of the paper. A similar analysis and transformation for safe destructive updates was given independently and earlier by Wand and Clinger [WC98] for a first-order, eager, functional language with flat arrays. Their work is in turn based on a polynomial-time, interprocedural analysis given by Shastry, Clinger, and Ariola [SCA93] for determining safe evaluation orders for destructive updates. In this paper, we go beyond the treatment of Wand and Clinger by

1. Employing a notion of update contexts in presenting the analysis.
2. Simplifying the proof of correctness through the use of evaluation contexts.
3. Applying the optimization to a richer language with higher-order operations.
4. Carrying out a complexity analysis of the static analysis procedure.

These extensions are the novel contributions of the paper. We have also implemented our method as part of a code generator for an executable functional fragment of the PVS specification language which generates Common Lisp programs. It was released with PVS 2.3 in the Fall of 1999. Functional programs, such as sorting routines, written in this fragment of PVS execute at speeds that are roughly a factor of five slower than the corresponding programs written in C, and with comparable space usage. The slowness relative to C is primarily due to the overhead of dealing dynamically with multiple array representations.

Clean [vG96] is a lazy functional language where a destructive update optimization has been implemented. The Clean optimization scheme requires programmer annotations to ensure safe destructive updates. Other annotation schemes for expressing destructive updates in functional languages include the use of state monads [Wad97] and various linear type systems [Wad90]. The method presented here does not rely on any programmer annotations.

There is a large body of work on static analysis applied to the destructive array update problem including that of Hudak [Hud87], Bloss and Hudak [BH87], Bloss [Blo94], Gopinath and Hennessy [GH89], and Odersky [Ode91]. Draghicescu and Purushothaman [DP93] introduce the key insight exploited here that in a language with flat arrays, the sharing of references between a term and its context can only occur through shared free variables, but their update analysis for a lazy language has exponential complexity. Laziness complicates the analysis since there is no fixed order of evaluation on the terms as is the case with eager evaluation. Goyal and Paige [GP98] carry out a copy optimization that works together with reference counting to reduce the need for copying data structures in the set-based language SETL. The *destructive evaluation* of recursive programs studied by Pettorossi [Pet78] and Schwarz [Sch82], employs annotations to construct an intermediate form that explicitly reclaims storage cells during evaluation. This is a slightly different problem from that of destructive array updates, but their annotations are obtained through a similar live variable analysis.

In comparison to previous approaches to update analyses, the method given here is simple, efficient, interprocedural, and has been implemented for an expressive functional language. The implementation yields code that is competitive in performance with efficient imperative languages. The proof of correctness is simple enough that the method can be adapted to other languages with only modest changes to the correctness argument.

2   Update Analysis

We describe a small functional language and an update analysis procedure for this language that generates a destructive counterpart to each function definition. The language is strongly typed. Each variable or function has an associated type. Type rules identify the well-typed expressions. The type of a well-typed expression can be computed from the types of its constituent subexpressions. Types are exploited in the analysis, but the principles apply to untyped languages as well.

The base types consist of bool, integer, and *index types* of the form $[0 < \kappa]$, where κ is a numeral. The only type constructor is that for function types which are constructed as $[T_1, \ldots, T_n \rightarrow T]$ for types $T, T_1, \ldots, T_n$. The language admits subtyping so that $[0 < i]$ is a subtype of $[0 < j]$ when $i \leq j$, and these are both subtypes of the type integer. A function type $[S_1, \ldots, S_n \rightarrow S]$ is a subtype of $[T_1, \ldots, T_n \rightarrow T]$ iff $S_i \equiv T_i$ for $0 < i \leq n$, and S is a subtype of T. We do not explain more about the type system and the typechecking of expressions. Readers are referred to the formal semantics of PVS [OS97] for more details. An array type is a function type of the form $[[0 < i] \rightarrow W]$ for some numeral i and base type W, so that we are, for the present, restricting our attention to flat arrays. The language used here is similar to that employed by Wand and Clinger [WC98], but with the important inclusion of higher-order operations and lambda-abstraction. We allow arrays to be built by lambda-abstraction, whereas Wand and Clinger use a NEW operation for constructing arrays.

The metavariable conventions are that W ranges over base types, S and T range over types, x, y, z range over variables, p ranges over primitive function symbols, f and g range over defined function symbols, a, b, c, d, and e range over expressions, L, M, N range over sets of array variables.

The expression forms in the language are

1. Constants: Numerals and the boolean constants TRUE and FALSE.
2. Variables: x
3. Primitive operations p (assumed to be nondestructive) and defined operations f.
4. Abstraction: $(\lambda(x_1 : T_1, \ldots, x_n : T_n) : e)$, is of type $[T_1, \ldots, T_n \rightarrow T]$, where e is an expression of type T given that each x_i is of type T_i for $0 < i \leq n$. We often omit the types $T_1, \ldots, T_n$ for brevity.
5. Application: $e(e_1, \ldots, e_n)$ is of type T where e is an expression of type $[T_1, \ldots, T_n \rightarrow T]$ and each e_i is of type T_i.
6. Conditional: IF e_1 THEN e_2 ELSE e_3 is of type T, where e_1 is an expression of type bool, and e_2, and e_3 are expressions of type T.
7. Update: A nondestructive update expression $e_1[(e_2) := e_3]$ is of type $[[0 < i] \rightarrow W]$, where e_1 is of array type $[[0 < i] \rightarrow W]$, e_2 is an expression of type $[0 < i]$, and e_3 is an expression of type W. A destructive update expression $e_1[(e_2) \leftarrow e_3]$ has the same typing behavior as its nondestructive counterpart.

A program is given by a sequence of function definitions where each function definition has the form $f(x_1 : T_1, \ldots, x_n : T_n) : T = e$. The body e of the definition of f cannot contain any functions other than the primitive operations, the previously defined functions in the sequence, and recursive occurrences of f itself. The body e cannot contain any free variables other than those in $\{x_1, \ldots, x_n\}$.

A variable of array type is bound to an array reference, i.e., a reference to an array location in the store, as explicated in the operational semantics (Section 3). A type is *mutable* if it is an array or a function type. A type is *updateable* if it is an array type or a function type whose range type is updateable. A variable is mutable if its type is mutable, and updateable if its type is updateable. $Mv(a)$ is the set of all mutable free variables of a, $Ov(a)$ is the set of updateable output variables in a, and $Av(a)$ is the set of active mutable variables in the value of a. These will be defined more precisely below so that $Ov(a) \subseteq Av(a) \subseteq Mv(a)$.

Output Analysis. In order to analyze the safety of a destructive update, we need to compute the set of variables whose references could be affected by the update. For an update expression $e_1[(e_2) \leftarrow e_3]$, this is just the set of variables in e_1 that might potentially propagate array references to the value. $Mv(a)$ is defined as the set of mutable free variables of a. The set of output variables of an expression a of array type is computed by $Ov(a)$. Thus $Ov(a)$ could be conservatively approximated by the set of *all* updateable variables in a, but the analysis below is more precise. The auxiliary function $Ovr(a)$ computes a lambda-abstracted set of variables $(\lambda(x_1, \ldots, x_n) : S)$ for a defined function or a lambda-abstraction in the function position of an application. This yields a more precise estimate of the set of output variables. For example, if the array addition operation $+$ is defined as $(\lambda X, Y : (\lambda(x : [0 < i]) : X(x) + Y(x)))$, then $Ovr(X + Y) = (\lambda(X, Y) : \emptyset)(\{X\}, \{Y\}) = \emptyset$.

Given a sequence of definitions of functions $f_1, \ldots, f_m$, the table OA is a map from the function index i to the output analysis for the definition of f_i, i.e., $Ovr(f_i) = OA(i)$. A map such as OA from an index set I to some range type T is represented as $\langle i_1 \mapsto t_1, \ldots, i_n \mapsto t_n \rangle$. The domain of a map OA is represented as $dom(OA)$. The result of applying a map OA to a domain element i is represented as $OA(i)$. The update of a map OA as $OA\langle i \mapsto t \rangle$ returns t when applied to i, and $OA(j)$ when applied to some j different from i. The empty map is just $\langle \rangle$. For a sequence of definitions of functions $f_1, \ldots, f_m$, the output analysis table OA is defined as OA_m, where OA_0 is the empty map $\langle \rangle$, and $OA_{i+1} = OA_{i+1}^k$ for the least k such that $OA_{i+1}^k = OA_{i+1}^{k+1}$. The map OA_i^j for the definition $f_i(x_1, \ldots, x_n) = e$, is computed iteratively as

$$OA_i^0 = OA_{i-1}\langle i \mapsto (\lambda x_1, \ldots, x_n : \emptyset) \rangle$$
$$OA_i^{k+1} = OA_i^k \langle i \mapsto Ovr(OA_i^k)(\lambda(x_1, \ldots, x_n) : e) \rangle.$$

The over-approximation of the output variables, $Ov(a)$, is defined below in terms of the auxiliary function $Ovr(a)$. The defining equations have to be read in order so that the first equation, when applicable, supersedes the others. The case of destructive updates $e_1[(e_2) \leftarrow e_3]$ in the definition of Ovr is counterintuitive. $Ovr(F)(e_1[(e_2) \leftarrow e_3])$ is defined to return $\emptyset$ instead of $Ovr(F)(e_1)$. This is because the destructive update overwrites the array reference corresponding to the value of e_1, and does not propagate the original array to the output.

$$Ovr(F)(a) = \emptyset, \text{ if } a \text{ is not of updateable type}$$
$$Ovr(F)(x) = \{x\}, \text{ if } x \text{ is of updateable type}$$
$$Ovr(F)(f_i) = F(i)$$
$$Ovr(F)(a(a_1, \ldots, a_n)) = Ovr(F)(a)(Ov(F)(a_1), \ldots, Ov(F)(a_n))$$
$$Ovr(F)(\lambda(x : [0 < i]) : e) = \emptyset$$
$$Ovr(F)(\lambda(x_1, \ldots, x_n) : e) = (\lambda(x_1, \ldots, x_n) : Ov(F)(e))$$
$$Ovr(F)(\text{IF } e_1 \text{ THEN } e_2 \text{ ELSE } e_3) = Ov(F)(e_2) \cup Ov(F)(e_3)$$
$$Ovr(F)(a_1[(a_2) := a_3]) = \emptyset$$
$$Ovr(F)(a_1[(a_2) \leftarrow a_3]) = \emptyset$$
$$Ov(F)(a) = S - \{x_1, \ldots, x_n\}, \text{ if }$$
$$Ovr(F)(a) = (\lambda(x_1, \ldots, x_n) : S)$$
$$Ov(F)(a) = Ovr(F)(a), \text{ otherwise}$$

When F is fixed to be OA, we just write $Ovr(e)$ for $Ovr(OA)(e)$, and $Ov(e)$ for $Ov(OA)(e)$. Note that $Ovr(e)$ can return either a lambda-abstraction $(\lambda x_1, \ldots, x_n : S)$ or a set of variables S. The definition above uses the application form

$$Ovr(F)(a)(Ov(F)(a_1), \ldots, Ov(F)(a_n))$$

which is defined below.

$$(\lambda(x_1, \ldots, x_n) : S)(S_1, \ldots, S_n) = (S - \{x_1, \ldots, x_n\}) \cup \bigcup \{S_i | x_i \in S\}$$

$$S(S_1, \ldots, S_n) = S \cup S_1 \cup \ldots \cup S_n$$

As an example, we extract the output variables returned by the definition

$$f_1(x, y, z, i) = \text{IF}(x(i) < y(i), x, f_1(y, z, x, i)).$$

The iterations then proceed as

$$OA_1^0(1) = (\lambda x, y, z, i : \emptyset)$$
$$OA_1^1(1) = (\lambda x, y, z, i : \{x\})$$
$$OA_1^2(1) = (\lambda x, y, z, i : \{x, y\})$$
$$OA_1^3(1) = (\lambda x, y, z, i : \{x, y, z\})$$
$$OA_1^4(1) = (\lambda x, y, z, i : \{x, y, z\})$$

The complexity of computing the output variables of an expression e with n updateable variables is at most $n * |e|$ assuming that the set operations can be performed in linear time by representing the sets as bit-vectors. If the size of these bit-vectors fits in a machine word, then the set operations take only constant time and the complexity is just $|e|$. Since the cardinality of the output variables of an expression is bounded by the number n of updateable variables in the expression, the fixed point computation of the table entry OA has at most n iterations. The complexity of computing the table entry for a function definition is therefore at most $n^2 * |e|$.

Active Variables. The set $Av(a)$ of variables returns the active variables in an expression. It is used to keep track of the variables that point to active references in already evaluated expressions. The set $Av(a)$ includes $Ov(a)$ but additionally contains variables that might be trapped in closures. We already saw that $Ov(\lambda(x : [0 < i]) : X(x) + Y(x)) = \emptyset$ since this returns a new array reference. Also, $Ov(\lambda(x : \texttt{integer}) : X(i) + x)$ (with free variables X and i) is $\emptyset$ because the lambda-abstraction is not of updateable type. However, the evaluation of $(\lambda(x : \texttt{integer}) : X(i) + x)$ yields a value that traps the reference bound to X. This means that X is live in a context that contains $(\lambda(x : \texttt{integer}) : X(i) + x)$. On the other hand, $Av(a)$ is more refined than $Mv(a)$ since $Av(X(i))$ is $\emptyset$, whereas $Mv(X(i))$ is X.

As with the output variables, the active variable analysis for the defined operations $f_1, \ldots, f_m$, are computed and stored in a table VA, where $VA = VA_m$, $VA_0 = []$, and $VA_{i+1} = VA_{i+1}^k$ for the least k such that $VA_{i+1}^{k+1} = VA_{i+1}^k$. The computation of VA_i^j is given by

$$VA_i^0 = VA_{i-1}\langle i \mapsto (\lambda(x_1, \ldots, x_n) : \emptyset)\rangle$$
$$VA_i^{j+1} = VA_i^j\langle i \mapsto Avr(VA_i^j)((\lambda(x_1, \ldots, x_n) : e))\rangle$$

The operation $Av(F)(e)$ of collecting the active variables in an expression e relative to the table F is defined in terms of the auxiliary operation $Avr(F)(e)$ as

$$Avr(F)(a) = \emptyset, \text{ if } a \text{ is not of mutable type}$$
$$Avr(F)(x) = \{x\}, \text{ if } x \text{ is of mutable type}$$
$$Avr(F)(f_i) = F(i)$$
$$Avr(F)(a(a_1, \ldots, a_n)) = Avr(F)(a)(Av(F)(a_1), \ldots, Av(F)(a_n))$$
$$Avr(F)((\lambda(x : [0 < i]) : e)) = \emptyset$$
$$Avr(F)((\lambda(x_1, \ldots, x_n) : e)) = (\lambda(x_1, \ldots, x_n) : Av(F)(e))$$
$$Avr(F)(\text{IF } e_1 \text{ THEN } e_2 \text{ ELSE } e_3) = Av(F)(e_2) \cup Av(F)(e_3)$$
$$Avr(F)(a_1[(a_2) := a_3]) = \emptyset$$
$$Avr(F)(a_1[(a_2) \leftarrow a_3]) = \emptyset$$
$$Av(F)(f_i) = \emptyset$$
$$Av(F)((\lambda(x_1, \ldots, x_n) : e)) = Mv((\lambda(x_1, \ldots, x_n) : e))$$
$$Av(F)(a) = Avr(F)(a), \text{ otherwise}$$

For example, if f_2 is defined as

$$f_2(x, y, z) = \text{IF}(z = 0, (\lambda(u : \text{integer}) : x(u + u)), f_2(y, x, z - 1)),$$

then $VA_2 = \lambda x, y, z : \{x, y\}$. Given the table VA, we abbreviate $Av(VA)(e)$ as $Av(e)$, and $Avr(VA)(e)$ as $Avr(e)$.

Lemma 1. $Ov(e) \subseteq Av(e)$.

Proof. This is easily established since $Ov(e)$ and $Av(e)$ have similar definitions but the latter collects both updateable and mutable variables, whereas the former collects only the updateable variables. For the case of lambda-abstractions e occurring in non-function positions $Av(e)$ collects all the mutable variables, whereas $Ov(e)$ collects only those variables that might be propagated to the output when the lambda-abstraction is actually applied. ∎

The complexity analysis for the computation of the active variables is similar to that for output variables but with n representing the number of mutable variables in the expression.

Update Contexts. An *update context* U is an expression containing a single occurrence of a hole $\{\}$. An update context U has one of the forms

1. $\{\}$.
2. $\{\}(e_1, \ldots, e_n)$.
3. $e(e_1, \ldots, e_{j-1}, \{\}, e_{j+1}, \ldots, e_n)$.
4. $\text{IF}(\{\}, e_2, e_3)$, $\text{IF}(e_1, \{\}, e_3)$, or $\text{IF}(e_1, e_2, \{\})$.
5. $\{\}[(e_2) := e_3]$, $e_1[(\{\}) := e_3]$, or $e_1[(e_2) := \{\}]$.
6. $\{\}[(e_2) \leftarrow e_3]$, $e_1[(\{\}) \leftarrow e_3]$, or $e_1[(e_2) \leftarrow \{\}]$.
7. $U\{V\}$ for update contexts U and V.

The primary observation about update contexts is that the hole {} can occur anywhere except within a lambda-abstraction. Note that the context of evaluation of an update expression within a lambda-abstraction is not easily calculated. For ease of explanation, the definition of update contexts above is conservative in not allowing holes {} to occur within lambda-abstractions that occur in function positions of beta-redexes, e.g., let-expressions, even though the context of evaluation for the hole can be exactly determined.

Live Variables. The key operation over update contexts is that of calculating the *live* variables $Lv(U)$. Since the order of evaluation is known, it is easy to determine exactly which subexpressions in the context U will have already been evaluated before the expression in the hole. The live variables in U must contain the active variables $Av(a)$ for those subexpressions a that are evaluated before the hole, and $Mv(b)$ for the subexpressions b that are evaluated subsequent to the hole. More precisely,

$$Lv(\{\}) = \emptyset$$
$$Lv(\{\}(e_1, \ldots, e_n)) = \bigcup_i Mv(e_i)$$
$$Lv(e(e_1, \ldots, e_{j-1}, \{\}, \ldots, e_n)) = Av(e) \cup \bigcup_{i<j} Av(e_i) \cup \bigcup_{i>j} Mv(e_i)$$
$$Lv(\mathtt{IF}(\{\}, e_2, e_3)) = Mv(e_2) \cup Mv(e_3)$$
$$Lv(\mathtt{IF}(e_1, \{\}, e_3)) = \emptyset$$
$$Lv(\mathtt{IF}(e_1, e_2, \{\})) = \emptyset$$
$$Lv(\{\}[(e_2) := e_3]) = \emptyset$$
$$Lv(e_1[(\{\}) := e_3]) = Mv(e_1) \cup Mv(e_3)$$
$$Lv(e_1[(e_2) := \{\}]) = Mv(e_1)$$
$$Lv(\{\}[(e_2) \leftarrow e_3]) = \emptyset$$
$$Lv(e_1[(\{\}) \leftarrow e_3]) = Mv(e_1) \cup Mv(e_3)$$
$$Lv(e_1[(e_2) \leftarrow \{\}]) = Mv(e_1)$$
$$Lv(U\{V\}) = Lv(U) \cup Lv(V)$$

The complexity analysis for the live variables computation is at most that of computing the active variables of the expression, i.e., $n * |e|$, since this includes the computation of the active variables of the relevant subexpressions as well.

Liveness Analysis.   Given a definition of the form $f^D(x_1, \ldots, x_n) = e^D$, $LA(f^D)$ is a partial map from the updateable variables in $\{x_1, \ldots, x_n\}$ so that $LA(f^D)(x_i)$ is the set of variables that must not aliased to x_i whenever f^D is invoked. The set $LA(f^D)(x_i)$ contains those variables in e^D that are live in some update context U of a destructive update $e_1[(e_2) \leftarrow e_3]$, i.e., $e^D \equiv U\{e_1[(e_2) \leftarrow e_3]\}$, and $x_i \in Ov(e_1)$. The liveness analysis $LA(f^D)$ can be calculated by means of a fixed point computation on the definition so that $LA(f^D) = LA^k(f^D)$ for the least k such that $LA^{k+1}(f^D) = LA^k(f^D)$.

$LA^0(f^D)(x_i) = \bot$, if

$\qquad x_i$ is not updateable, or

$\qquad \forall U, e_1, e_2, e_3 : e \equiv U\{e_1[(e_2) \leftarrow e_3]\} \Rightarrow x_i \notin Ov(e_1)$, and

$\qquad \forall U, g^D, a_1, \ldots, a_n : \quad e \equiv U\{g^D(a_1, \ldots, a_m)\}$
$\qquad\qquad\qquad\qquad\qquad \Rightarrow \forall j : x_j \in dom(LA(g^D)) : x_i \notin Ov(a_j)$

$LA^0(f^D)(x_i) = L_1 \cup L_2$, otherwise, where

$\qquad L_1 = \{y \mid \exists U, e_1, e_2, e_3 : \quad e^D \equiv U\{e_1[(e_2) \leftarrow e_3]\},$ and
$\qquad\qquad\qquad\qquad\qquad \wedge x_i \in Ov(e_1)$
$\qquad\qquad\qquad\qquad\qquad \wedge y \in Lv(U)\}$

$\qquad L_2 = \{y \mid \exists \quad U, g^D, a_1, \ldots, a_m :$
$\qquad\qquad\qquad e^D \equiv U\{g^D(a_1, \ldots, a_m)\}$
$\qquad\qquad\qquad \wedge (\exists j, l : \quad x_j \in dom(LA(g^D))$
$\qquad\qquad\qquad\qquad\qquad \wedge x_i \in Ov(a_j)$
$\qquad\qquad\qquad\qquad\qquad \wedge x_l \in LA(g^D)(x_j)$
$\qquad\qquad\qquad\qquad\qquad \wedge y \in Av(a_l) \cup Lv(U))\}$

$LA^{k+1}(f^D)(x_i) = LA^k(f^D)(x_i)$, if

$\qquad \forall U, a_1, \ldots, a_n : \quad e^D \equiv U\{f^D(a_1, \ldots, a_n)\}$
$\qquad\qquad\qquad\qquad\qquad \Rightarrow \forall j : x_j \in dom(LA^k(f^D)) \wedge x_i \notin Ov(a_j)$

$LA^{k+1}(f^D)(x_i) = L \cup LA^k(f^D)(x_i)$ where

$\qquad L = \{y \mid \exists U, a_1, \ldots, a_n : \quad e^D \equiv U\{f^D(a_1, \ldots, a_n)\}$
$\qquad\qquad\qquad\qquad \wedge (\exists j, l : \quad x_j \in dom(LA^k(f^D))$
$\qquad\qquad\qquad\qquad\qquad\qquad \wedge x_l \in LA^k(f^D)(x_j)$
$\qquad\qquad\qquad\qquad\qquad\qquad \wedge x_i \in Ov(a_j)$
$\qquad\qquad\qquad\qquad\qquad\qquad \wedge y \in Av(a_l) \cup Lv(U))\}$

An entry in the liveness analysis table is a partial map from the set of variables $\{x_1, \ldots, x_n\}$ to subsets of this set. The number of iterations in the fixed point computation of a liveness analysis entry is at worst n^2. Each iteration is itself of complexity at worst $n * |e^D|$, yielding a complexity of $O(n^3 * |e^D|)$ for a definition of the form $f^D(x_1, \ldots, x_n) = e^D$. In recent work, Pavol Cerny has simplified the definitions of these analyses so that the program e is examined only once to compute an abstract flow analysis table. In practice, only a small fraction of the variables in a function definition are mutable, so this complexity is unlikely to be a significant bottleneck.

Safe Updates. Let $\gamma(e)$ represent the result of repeatedly replacing destructive updates $e_1[(e_2) \leftarrow e_3]$ in e by corresponding nondestructive updates $e_1[(e_2) := e_3]$, and destructive applications $g^D(a_1, \ldots, a_n)$ by $g(a_1, \ldots, a_2)$. It is easy to see that if $e = \gamma(e')$, then $Ov(e) = Ov(e')$ and $Av(e) = Av(e')$.

To obtain the destructive definition $f^D(x_1, \ldots, x_n) = e^D$ and the liveness table $LA(f^D)$, from the definition $f(x_1, \ldots, x_n) = e$, we construct e^D so that $\gamma(e^D) \equiv e$ and e^D is safe. An expression e^D is *safe* if

1. Every occurrence of $e_1[(e_2) \leftarrow e_3]$ in e^D within an update context U (i.e., $e^D \equiv U\{e_1[(e_2) \leftarrow e_3]\}$), satisfies $Ov(e_1) \cap Lv(U) = \emptyset$ and $Lv(U) \subseteq LA(f^D)(x)$ for each variable x in $Ov(e_1)$.
2. Every occurrence of a destructive function application $g^D(a_1, \ldots, a_n)$ in e within an update context U (i.e., $e^D \equiv U\{g^D(a_1, \ldots, a_n)\}$) satisfies $Ov(a_i) \cap (Lv(U) \cup Av(a_j)) = \emptyset$ for each x_i in the domain of $LA(g^D)$ and $y_i \in LA(g^D)(x_i)$. Furthermore, $Lv(U) \cup Av(a_j) \subseteq LA(f^D)(x)$ for each variable x in $Ov(a_i)$ for x_i in the domain of $LA(g^D)$ and $x_j \in LA(g^D)(x_i)$.

There are several different strategies for identifying safe destructive updates in order to obtain the definition $f^D(x_1, \ldots, x_n) = e^D$ from $f(x_1, \ldots, x_n) = e$. We present one such strategy that is quite conservative. The choice of different strategies does not affect the underlying theory and correctness argument. We first compute e^+ from e by converting all occurrences of safe updates in e to destructive form, all recursive function calls $f(a_1, \ldots, a_n)$ to $f^+(a_1, \ldots, a_n)$, and all safe occurrences of other function calls $g(a_1, \ldots, a_m)$ to $g^D(a_1, \ldots, a_m)$. This yields a definition $f^+(x_1, \ldots, x_n) = e^+$ that might be overly aggressive in its recursive calls. Since the liveness analysis for updates and function calls is unaffected by the transition from e to e^+, the only unsafe subterms in the definition e^+ are the recursive calls of the form $f^+(a_1, \ldots, a_n)$. The next step is to recognize and eliminate the unsafe recursive calls from the definition of f^+. Using $LA(f^+)$, we construct e^D by replacing the unsafe recursive calls $f^+(a_1, \ldots, a_n)$ by $f(a_1, \ldots, a_n)$, and the safe recursive calls by $f^D(a_1, \ldots, a_n)$. This yields the definition $f^D(x_1, \ldots, x_n) = e^D$.

Theorem 1 (Safe Definition). *The destructive definition $f^D(x_1, \ldots, x_n) = e^D$ obtained from the nondestructive definition $f(x_1, \ldots, x_n) = e$, is safe.*

Proof. In the definition $f^+(x_1, \ldots, x_n) = e^+$, the destructive updates and the function calls other than f^+ are safe because they depend only on the output variable analysis $Ov(d)$, the active variable analysis $Av(d)$ for subterms d of e, and the liveness analysis $LA(g)$ for functions g other than f or f^+. These update terms therefore continue to remain safe in the definition of f^+.

For each x_i, $LA(f^D)(x_i)$ is $\perp$ or $LA(f^D)(x_i) \subseteq LA(f^+)(x_i)$. Since the definition e^D is constructed from e^+ by replacing the unsafe destructive recursive calls by safe ones with respect to $LA(f^+)$, the definition $f^D(x_1, \ldots, x_n) = e^D$ is safe with respect to $LA(f^D)$.   ∎

3 Operational Semantics

We present operational semantics for the languages with destructive updates. We then exhibit a bisimulation between evaluation steps on a nondestructive expression e and its safe destructive counterpart e^D. The concepts used in defining the operational semantics are quite standard, but we give the details for the language used here.

The expression domain is first expanded to include

1. Explicit arrays: $\#(e_0, \ldots, e_{n-1})$ is an expression representing an n-element array.
2. References: $ref(i)$ represents a reference to reference number i in the store. Stores appear in the operational semantics.

A *value* is either a boolean constant, integer numeral, a closed lambda-abstraction $(\lambda x_1, \ldots, x_n : e)$ or a reference $ref(i)$. The metavariable v ranges over values.

An *evaluation context* [Fel90] E is an expression with an occurrence of a hole [] and is of one of the forms

1. $[]$
2. $[](e_1, \ldots, e_n)$
3. $v(v_1, \ldots, v_{j-1}, [], e_{j+1}, \ldots, e_n)$
4. $\mathtt{IF}([], e_2, e_3)$, $\mathtt{IF}(\mathtt{TRUE}, [], e_3)$, or $\mathtt{IF}(\mathtt{FALSE}, e_2, [])$.
5. $e_1[([]) := e_3]$, $e_1[(v_2) := []]$, or $[][(v_2) := v_3]$.
6. $e_1[([]) \leftarrow e_3]$, $e_1[(v_2) \leftarrow []]$, or $[][(v_2) \leftarrow v_3]$.
7. $E_1[E_2]$, if E_1 and E_2 are evaluation contexts.

A *redex* is an expression of one of the following forms

1. $p(v_1, \ldots, v_n)$.
2. $f(v_1, \ldots, v_n)$.
3. $(\lambda(x : [0 < n]) : e)$.
4. $(\lambda(x_1, \ldots, x_n) : e)(v_1, \ldots, v_n)$.
5. $\#(v_0, \ldots, v_{n-1})$.
6. $\mathtt{IF\ TRUE\ THEN}\ e_1\ \mathtt{ELSE}\ e_2$.
7. $\mathtt{IF\ FALSE\ THEN}\ e_1\ \mathtt{ELSE}\ e_2$.
8. $ref(i)[(v_2) := v_3]$.
9. $ref(i)[(v_2) \leftarrow v_3]$.

A *store* is a mapping from a reference number to an array value. A store s can be seen as a list of array values $[s[0], s[1], \ldots,]$ so that $s[i]$ returns the $(i+1)$'th element of the list. Let $s[i]\langle i \mapsto v_i \rangle$ represent the array value $\#(w_0, \ldots, v_i, \ldots, w_{n-1})$, where $s[i]$ is of the form $\#(w_0, \ldots, w_i, \ldots, w_{n-1})$. List concatenation is represented as $r \circ s$.

A *reduction* transforms a pair consisting of a redex and a store. The reductions corresponding to the redexes above are

1. $\langle p(v_1, \ldots, v_n), s \rangle \to \langle v, s \rangle$, if the primitive operation p when applied to arguments $v_1, \ldots, v_n$ yields value v.
2. $\langle f(v_1, \ldots, v_n), s \rangle \to \langle [v_1/x_1, \ldots, v_n/x_n](e), s \rangle$, if f is defined by $f(x_1, \ldots, x_n) = e$.
3. $\langle (\lambda(x : [0 < n]) : e), s \rangle \to \langle \#(e_0, \ldots, e_{n-1}), s \rangle$, where $e_i \equiv (\lambda(x : [0 < n]) : e)(i)$, for $0 \le i < n$.
4. $\langle (\lambda(x_1 : T_1, \ldots, x_n : T_n) : e)(v_1, \ldots, v_n), s \rangle \to \langle [v_1/x_1, \ldots, v_n/x_n](e), s \rangle$.
5. $\langle \#(v_0, \ldots, v_{n-1}), s \rangle \to \langle ref(m), s' \rangle$, where $s \equiv [s[0], \ldots, s[m-1]]$ and $s' \equiv s \circ [\#(v_0, \ldots, v_{n-1})]$.
6. $\langle \text{IF TRUE THEN } e_1 \text{ ELSE } e_2, s \rangle \to \langle e_1, s \rangle$.
7. $\langle \text{IF FALSE THEN } e_1 \text{ ELSE } e_2, s \rangle \to \langle e_2, s \rangle$.
8. $\langle ref(i)[(v_2) := v_3], s \rangle \to \langle ref(m), s' \rangle$, where

$$s \equiv [s[0], \ldots, s[i], \ldots, s[m-1]]$$
$$s' \equiv [s[0], \ldots, s[i], \ldots, s[m]]$$
$$s[m] = s[i]\langle v_2 \mapsto v_3 \rangle.$$

9. $\langle ref(i)[(v_2) \leftarrow v_3], s \rangle \to \langle ref(i), s' \rangle$, where $s_1 \equiv [s[0], \ldots, s[i], \ldots, s[m-1]]$ and $s_2 \equiv [s[0], \ldots, s[i]\langle v_2 \mapsto v_3 \rangle, \ldots, s[m-1]])$.

An evaluation *step* operates on a pair $\langle e, s \rangle$ consisting of a closed expression and a store, and is represented as $\langle e, s \rangle \longrightarrow \langle e', s' \rangle$. If e can be decomposed as a $E[a]$ for an evaluation context E and a redex a, then a step $\langle E[a], s \rangle \longrightarrow \langle E[a'], s' \rangle$ holds if $\langle a, s \rangle \to \langle a', s' \rangle$. The reflexive-transitive closure of $\longrightarrow$ is represented as $\langle e, s \rangle \overset{*}{\longrightarrow} \langle e', s' \rangle$. If $\langle e, s \rangle \overset{*}{\longrightarrow} \langle v, s' \rangle$, then the result of the computation is $s'(v)$, i.e., the result of replacing each reference $ref(i)$ in v by the array $s'[i]$. The computation of a closed term e is initiated on an empty store as $\langle e, [] \rangle$. The value $eval(e)$ is defined to be $s(v)$, where $\langle e, [] \rangle \overset{*}{\longrightarrow} \langle v, s \rangle$.

4   Correctness

The correctness proof demonstrates the existence of a bisimulation between evaluations of the unoptimized nondestructive program and the optimized program. The key ideas in the proof are:

1. The safe update analysis is lifted from variables to references since the expressions being evaluated do not contain free variables.
2. The safety of an expression is preserved by evaluation.
3. Given a nondestructive configuration $\langle e, s \rangle$ and its destructive counterpart $\langle d, r \rangle$, the relation $s(e) = \gamma(r(d))$ between the two configurations is preserved by evaluation. Recall that the operation $\gamma(a)$ transforms all destructive updates $a_1[(a_2) \leftarrow a_3]$ in a to corresponding nondestructive updates $a_1[(a_2) := a_3]$, and all destructive applications $g^D(a_1, \ldots, a_n)$ to the corresponding nondestructive applications $g(a_1, \ldots, a_n)$.

4. When e and d are values, then the bisimulation ensures that the destructive evaluation returns the same result as the nondestructive evaluation.

The intuitive idea is that the destructive optimizations always occur safely within update contexts during evaluation. When an update context coincides with an evaluation context U, the references accessible in the context are a subset of $Lv(U)$. The safety condition on the occurrences of destructive operations within an update context then ensures that a reference that is updated destructively does not occur in the context. The observation that all destructive operations occur safely within update contexts can be used to construct a bisimulation between a nondestructive configuration $\langle e, s \rangle$ and a destructive configuration $\langle d, r \rangle$ that entails the invariant $s(e) = \gamma(r(d))$. This invariant easily yields the main theorem

$$eval(e) = eval(e^D)$$

for a closed, reference-free expression e.

The application of a store s of the form $[s[0], \ldots, s[n-1]]$ to an expression e, written as $s(e)$, replaces each occurrence of $ref(i)$ in e by $s[i]$, for $0 \le i < n$.

The definition of safety for an expression e has been given in Section 2 (page 14). A destructive expression is either a destructive update of the form $e_1[(e_2) \leftarrow e_3]$ or a destructive function invocation of the form $g^D(a_1, \ldots, a_n)$. An expression is safe if all destructive expressions occur safely within update contexts. In the update analysis in Section 2, the expressions being analyzed contained variables but no references, but the expressions being evaluated contain references and not variables. The definitions of Ovr, Mv, and Av have to be extended to include references so that

$$Ovr(ref(i)) = Mv(ref(i)) = Av(ref(i)) = \{ref(i)\}.$$

With this change, for a closed term e, the sets returned by $Ov(e)$, $Mv(e)$, and $Av(e)$, consist entirely of references. Recall that $Ov(e) \subseteq Av(e) \subseteq Mv(e)$.

A closed expression d is *normal* if every occurrence of a destructive expression u in d occurs within an update context, i.e., there is some update context U such that $d \equiv U\{u\}$.

Lemma 2. *Normality is preserved during evaluation: if d is a normal, closed term and $\langle d, r \rangle \Longrightarrow \langle d', r' \rangle$, then so is d'.*

Proof. Essentially, U is an update context if the hole $\{\}$ in U does not occur within a lambda-abstraction. Any evaluation context E can be turned into an update context as $E[\{\}]$, but not necessarily vice-versa. It is easy to see that none of the reductions causes a destructive term to appear within a lambda-abstraction. ∎

Let $dom(r)$ for a store r be the set $\{ref(i) | i < |r|\}$. A configuration $\langle d, r \rangle$ is called *well-formed* if d is a normal, closed term and each reference $ref(i)$ occurring in e is in the domain of r, $dom(r)$.

Lemma 3. *The well-formedness of configurations is preserved during evaluation.*

Proof. By Lemma 2, if $\langle d, r \rangle \longrightarrow \langle d', r' \rangle$ and d is a normal, closed term, then so is d'. The only redexes that introduce new references are $\#(v_0, \ldots, v_{n-1})$ and $ref(i)[(v_2) := v_3]$. In either case, the reduction step ensures that the store is updated to contain an entry for the newly introduced reference. ∎

Since we are dealing with flat arrays, the expression $r(d)$ contains no references when $\langle d, r \rangle$ is a well-formed configuration.

Let $\rho(d)$ be the operation of collecting all the references occurring in the expression d.

Lemma 4. *For every reduction $\langle a, r \rangle \to \langle a', r' \rangle$, $\rho(a') \cap dom(r) \subseteq \rho(a)$. Hence, for each evaluation step $\langle d, r \rangle \longrightarrow \langle d', r' \rangle$, $\rho(d') \cap dom(r) \subseteq \rho(d)$.*

Proof. Any references $ref(i)$ in r that are unreachable in a, i.e., $ref(i) \notin \rho(a)$, are also unreachable in a'. This is because for each of the reductions $\langle a, r \rangle \to \langle a', r' \rangle$, the only references in a' that are not in a are those that are also not in r. ∎

Lemma 5. *If a is a normal, safe, closed expression, $\langle E[a], s \rangle$ is a well-formed configuration, $\langle E[a], s \rangle \longrightarrow \langle E[a'], s' \rangle$, and $Ov(a') - Ov(a)$ is nonempty, then $Ov(a') \cap Lv(E[\{\}])$ and $Av(a') \cap Lv(E[\{\}])$ are both empty.*

Proof. For a redex a and its residual a', $(Ov(a') - Ov(a))$ (alternately, $(Av(a') - Av(a))$) is nonempty only if a is either an array of the form $\#(v_0, \ldots, v_{n-1})$, an update expression $ref(i)[(v_2) := v_3]$, or a destructive update $ref(i)[(a_2) \leftarrow a_3]$. In the first two cases, the reference in the singleton set $Ov(a')$ is fresh and does not occur in $E[\{\}]$. In the third case, since a' is a destructive subexpression of a safe expression $ref(i) \notin Lv(E[\{\}])$. Since $Ov(a') = Av(a') = \{ref(i)\}$, $Ov(a') \cap Lv(E[\{\}])$ and $Av(a') \cap Lv(E[\{\}])$ are both empty. ∎

Lemma 6. *If E is an evaluation context, then $Lv(E[\{\}]) = Mv(E)$.*

Proof. By induction on the structure of an evaluation context. If $E \equiv []$, then $Lv(E[\{\}]) = Mv(E[\{\}]) = \emptyset$. If $E \equiv [](e_1, \ldots, e_n)$, then $Lv(E[\{\}]) = Mv(E)$. When $E \equiv v(v_1, \ldots, v_{j-1}, [], e_{j+1}, \ldots, e_n)$, we use the observation that for any value v, $Mv(v) = Av(v)$, to conclude that $Lv(E[\{\}]) = Mv(E)$. If $E \equiv \mathtt{IF}([], e_2, e_3)$, then $Lv(E[\{\}]) = Mv(e_2) \cup Mv(e_3) = Mv(E)$. The remaining cases for conditional expressions and update expressions can be similarly examined. The final case when $E \equiv E_1[E_2]$, we can assume that E_1 is one of the above cases but not the empty context. We know that $Lv(E_1[E_2[\{\}]]) = Lv(E_1[\{\}]) \cup Lv(E_2[\{\}])$, which by the induction hypothesis is just $Mv(E)$. ∎

Theorem 2. *If $\langle d, r \rangle$ is a well-formed configuration, $\langle d, r \rangle \longrightarrow \langle d', r' \rangle$, and d is safe, then d' is safe.*

Proof. We have to show that every occurrence of a destructive expression u' in d' is safe. Let d be of the form $E[a]$ for some evaluation context E and redex a. Then, d' is of the form $E[a']$ where $\langle a, r \rangle \to \langle a', r' \rangle$. Given any occurrence of an update expression u' in an update context U' in d', the residual a' either occurs within u', u' occurs within a', or a' occurs within U. This is because none of the redexes can partially overlap a destructive expression.

If a' occurs properly in u', then $d' \equiv U'\{u'\}$, and the following cases arise:

1. u' is of the form $d_1'[d_2' \leftarrow d_3']$: Then, if a' occurs in either d_2' or d_3', we have that $d_1' \equiv d_1$, where $u \equiv d_1[(d_2) \leftarrow d_3]$ and $d \equiv U'\{u\}$. Therefore, $Ov(d_1') = Ov(d_1)$ and u' occurs safely within the update context U' since u occurs safely within U'.
   If a' occurs in d_1', then $(Ov(d_1') - Ov(d_1)) \subseteq (Ov(a') - Ov(a))$. Since every evaluation context is an update context, we have an update context V' such that $d_1' \equiv V'\{a'\}$, $d_1 \equiv V'\{a\}$, and $d \equiv U'\{V'\{a\}\}$. By Lemma 5, if $(Ov(a') - Ov(a))$ is nonempty, then $Lv(U'\{V'\}) \cap (Ov(a') - Ov(a))$ is empty. Since $Lv(U'\{V'\}) = Lv(U') \cup Lv(V')$, it follows that u' is safe in the update context U'.
2. u' is of the form $g^D(b_1', \ldots, b_n')$, where a' occurs in b_i for some i, $1 \le i \le n$. Then, $u \equiv g^D(b_1, \ldots, b_n)$, where $b_j \equiv b_j'$ for j, $1 \le j \le n$ and $i \ne j$. Since, $\langle d, r \rangle$ is a well-formed configuration, $Lv(U') \subseteq dom(r)$. By Lemma 5, we have that $(Ov(b_i') - Ov(b)) \cap Lv(U')$ is empty, as is $(Ov(b_i') - Ov(b_i)) \cap Lv(g^D(\ldots, b_{i-1}, \{\}, b_{i+1}, \ldots)))$, and similarly for $Av(b_i') - Av(b_i)$. In order to ensure that $g^D(b_1', \ldots, b_n')$ occurs safely within U', we have to check that for any x_j in $dom(LA(g^D))$, $Ov(b_j') \cap Lv(U')$ is empty, and for $k \ne j$ and x_k in $LA(g^D)x_j$, $Av(b_k') \cap Ov(x_j)$ is empty. Since $U\{g^D(b_1, \ldots, b_n)\}$ is safe, if $j \ne i$, then clearly $Ov(b_j') = Ov(b_j)$ and $Ov(b_j') \cap Lv(U')$ is empty. If additionally, $k \ne i$, then $Av(b_k') = Av(b_k)$ and $Av(b_k') \cap Av(b_j)$ is also empty. If $j = i$, then we know that $Ov(b_j') \cap Lv(U')$ is empty. If $k = i$, then $Av(b_j') \cap Lv(g^D(\ldots, b_{i-1}', \{\}, b_{i+1}', \ldots))$ is empty, and since $Ov(b_j') \subseteq Lv(g^D(\ldots, b_{i-1}', \{\}, b_{i+1}', \ldots))$, we have that $Av(b_k') \cap Ov(b_j')$ is empty.

If u' occurs (properly or not) within a', then by the syntax of a redex a, one of the following two cases is possible:

1. Redex a is a conditional expression and a' must be either the THEN or ELSE part of a. Since the argument is symmetrical, we consider the case when u' occurs in the THEN part. Then U is of the form $U_1\{IF(b_1, \{U_2\{\}\}, b_3)\}$ and U' is then of the form $U_1\{U_2\{\}\}$. Since $Lv(U_1) \cup Lv(U_2) \subseteq Lv(U)$. Therefore, u' occurs safely in U'.

2. Redex a is of the form $g^D(v_1, \ldots, v_n)$ and is reduced to a' of the form $\sigma(b^D)$, where g^D is defined as $g^D(x_1 \ldots, x_n) = b^D$ and substitution σ is of the form $\langle x_1 \mapsto v_1, \ldots, x_n \mapsto v_n \rangle$. We have to ensure that any update expression u' occurring in b^D is safe within the update context U' where $d' \equiv U'\{u'\}$. Note that we have already checked the safety of b^D during the generation of the definition of g^D.

If u' is of the form $\sigma(b_1[(b_2) \leftarrow b_3])$, we have $b^D \equiv V\{b_1[(b_2) \leftarrow b_3]\}$ where $Ov(b_1) \cap Lv(V) = \emptyset$. Since b^D does not contain any references, the result of applying substitution σ to b^D is just $\sigma(V)\{\sigma(e_1)[\sigma(e_2) \leftarrow \sigma(e_3)]\}$. It is easy to check that $Lv(\sigma(V)) = \rho(Lv(V))$. Note that for a value v, $Ov(v) \subseteq Av(v) \subseteq Mv(v) = \rho(v)$. From the update analysis of g, we know that $Ov(b_1) \cap Lv(V) = \emptyset$ and $Lv(V) \subseteq LA(g^D)(x)$ for $x \in Ov(b_1)$. Note that $Ov(\sigma(b_1)) \subseteq \rho(\sigma(Ov(b_1)))$. Since the occurrence of $g^D(v_1, \ldots, v_n)$ is safe with respect to the update context U, and $U' = U\{V\}$,

a) $Ov(\sigma(b_1)) \cap Lv(U) = \emptyset$

b) $Ov(\sigma(b_1)) \cap \sigma(Lv(V)) = \emptyset$

Therefore, the destructive update $\sigma(b_1)[(\sigma(b_2)) \leftarrow \sigma(b_3)]$ is safe with respect to the update context U'.

A similar argument can be used to show that if u' is of the form $f^D(b_1, \ldots, b_n)$ in b^D, it occurs safely within the update context U', where $d' \equiv U'\{u'\}$.

The final case is when u' and a' do not overlap, then a' occurs in U'. Except for the case where a is a destructive update, every other instance of a reduction of a from a redex a in U yielding U', we can check that $(Lv(U') \cap dom(r)) \subseteq Lv(U)$. Clearly, then u' occurs safely in U' since it occurs safely in U. When redex a is a destructive update of the form $ref(i)[(b_2) \leftarrow b_3]$, then by Lemma 6, $ref(i) \notin Lv(E[\{\}])$. If u' occurs in E, then $Mv(u') \subseteq Lv(E[\{\}])$, and hence u' again occurs safely in U'.   ∎

The significance of the safety invariant established in Theorem 2 should be obvious. It shows that whenever a destructive update redex $ref(i)[(v_2) \leftarrow v_3]$ is evaluated, it occurs within a context that is both an evaluation context $E[]$ and an update context $E[\{\}]$. Since by Lemma 6, $Lv(E[\{\}]) = Mv(E)$ and by Theorem 2, $ref(i) \notin Lv(E[\{\}])$, the destructive update can be executed safely without any unintended side-effects.

Given that all configurations are well-formed and safe, it is easy to establish the bisimulation between destructive and nondestructive execution. The bisimulation R between a nondestructive configuration $\langle e, s \rangle$ and a destructive configuration $\langle d, r \rangle$ is given by $\exists \pi : e = \gamma(\pi(d)) \wedge (\forall\, j \in dom(r) : s[\pi(j)] = r[j])$, where π is a permutation from $dom(r)$ to $dom(s)$ and $\pi(d)$ is the result of replacing each occurrence of $ref(i)$ in d by $ref(\pi(i))$.

Theorem 3. *If $\langle e, s \rangle$ is a well-formed configuration where e is a nondestructive expression, and $\langle d, r \rangle$ is a well-formed configuration with a safe destructive ex-*

pression d, *then the relation* R *given by* $\lambda \langle e, s \rangle, \langle d, r \rangle : \exists \pi : e = \gamma(\pi(d)) \wedge (\forall j \in dom(r) : s[\pi(j)] = r[j])$ *is a bisimulation with respect to evaluation.*

Proof. By Lemma 2 we already have that for a safe, well-formed configuration $\langle d, r \rangle$, whenever $\langle d, r \rangle \longrightarrow \langle d', r' \rangle$ then $\langle d', r' \rangle$ is a safe, well-formed configuration. If $R(\langle e, s \rangle, \langle d, r \rangle)$ holds, $\langle e, s \rangle \longrightarrow \langle e, s' \rangle$, and $\langle d, r \rangle \longrightarrow \langle d', r' \rangle$, then we can show that $R(\langle e', s' \rangle, \langle d', s' \rangle)$ holds. First note that if there is a π such that $e = \gamma(\pi(d))$, then if $e = E[a]$ and $d = D[b]$, then $E = \gamma(\pi(D))$ and $a = \gamma(\pi(b))$. We also have that $\langle a, s \rangle \rightarrow \langle a', s' \rangle$ where $e' \equiv E[a']$, and $\langle b, r \rangle \rightarrow \langle b', r' \rangle$, where $d' \equiv D[b']$.

If a is a redex of the form $ref(i)[(v_2) := v_3]$ and b is of the form $ref(j)[(v_2) \leftarrow v_3]$, then we know that $\pi(j) = i$. Since $D[b]$ is safe, $ref(j) \notin Mv(D[\{\}])$, and b' is $ref(j)$, while $r'[j]$ is $r[j]\langle v_2 \mapsto v_3 \rangle$ and $r'[k] = r[k]$ for $k \neq j$. On the nondestructive side, a' is $ref(m)$, where s' is $s \circ [s(i)\langle v_2 \mapsto v_3 \rangle]$. If we let π' be $\pi \langle j \mapsto m \rangle$, then since $s[i] = r[j]$, we also have $s'[m] = r'[j]$. Since $ref(j) \notin Mv(D)$ and $ref(m) \notin Mv(E)$, $\gamma(\pi'(D)) = \gamma(\pi(D)) = E$.

In every other case for the redexes a and b, the destructive and nondestructive evaluation steps are essentially identical, and $\gamma(\pi(b')) = a'$, and hence $\gamma(r'(b')) = s'(a')$. ∎

The main correctness theorem easily follows from the bisimulation proof.

Theorem 4. *If e and d are closed, reference-free terms such that $\gamma(d) \equiv e$, then*

$$eval(d) \equiv eval(e).$$

5   Observations

As already mentioned, our analysis is essentially similar to one given independently and earlier by Wand and Clinger [WC98], but our presentation is based on update contexts, and the correctness proof here is more direct, due to the use of evaluation contexts. Wand and Clinger use an operational semantics based on an abstract machine with a configuration consisting of a label, an environment, a return context, and a continuation.

The worst-case complexity of analyzing a definition $f(x_1, \ldots, x_n) = e$ as described here is $n^3 * |e|$. Our definitions for the various analyses used here, are quite naive, and their efficiency can be easily improved. The procedure requires n^2 iterations in the fixed point computation since $LA(f)$ is an n-element array consist of at most $n - 1$ variables. The complexity of each iteration is at worst $n * |e|$. In practice, this complexity is unlikely to be a factor since only a few variables are mutable. If n is smaller than the word size, then the set operations can be executed in constant time yielding a complexity $n^2 * |e|$.

We have used a simple core language for presenting the ideas. The method can be adapted to richer languages, but this has to be done carefully. For example, nested array structures introduce the possibility of structure sharing within an array where, for example, both $A(1)$ and $A(2)$ reference the same array. Such internal structure sharing defeats our analysis. For example, the update of index 3 of the array at index 2 of A might have the unintended side-effect of updating a shared reference at index 1 of array A. The analysis has to be extended to rule out the nested update of nested array structures. Non-nested updates of nested arrays, such as $A(2)[(3) := 4]$, are already handled correctly by the analysis since we check that A is not live in the context, and the result returned is the updated inner array $A(2)$ and not the nested array A. Other nested structures such as records and tuples also admit similar structure sharing, but type information could be used to detect the absence of sharing.

Allowing array elements to be functional is only mildly problematic. Here, it is possible for references to the original array to be trapped in a function value (closure) as in $A[(2) := (\lambda(x) : x + A(2)(2))]$. It is easy to modify the notion of an update context and the accompanying definitions to handle functional values in arrays.

The analysis method can be adapted to lazy functional languages. Here, an additional analysis is needed to determine for a function $f(x_1, \ldots, x_n) = e$ if an argument x_j might be evaluated after an argument x_i in the body e of f.

PVS functions are translated to destructive Common Lisp operations that are then compiled and executed. We omit performance information due to lack of space. A draft report with performance results for PVS can be obtained from the URL www.csl.sri.com/shankar/PVSeval.ps.gz.

Since functional programs require nondestructive arrays for correct operation, we have carried out some experiments with good data structures for this case. The results here are encouraging but outside the scope of this paper.

6   Conclusions

Experience has shown that the semantic simplicity of functional programming can be used to derive efficient and easily optimizable programs. Optimizations arising from the static analysis for destructive updates presented in this paper enables functional programs to be executed with time and space efficiencies that are comparable to low-level imperative code. The update analysis has been implemented within a code generator for the functional fragment of the specification language PVS. An efficient execution capability for this fragment is useful for validating specifications and in fast simplification of executable terms arising in a proof.

A common criticism of specification languages is that there is a duplication of effort since the design is described in a specification language as well as an implementation language. As a result, the verified design is different from the implemented one, and these two designs evolve separately. Through the generation of efficient code from logic, it is possible to unify these designs so that the implementation is generated systematically from its description in a logic-based specification language. Systematic logic-based transformations [PP99] can be used to obtain more efficient algorithms and better resource usage. Such transformations can also lead to programs that are more optimizable, as is needed for the update analysis given here to be effective. The target of the transformation can then be subjected to static analysis (e.g., update analysis) to support the generation of efficient, possibly destructive, code in a programming language. The target programming language, in our case, Common Lisp, bridges the gap between the logic-based program and the target machine. The programming language compiler then handles the machine-specific optimizations.

There is a great deal of work to be done before such code generation from a specification language can match or surpass the efficiency of custom code written in a low-level programming language like C. Most of the remaining work is in implementing other forms of analyses similar to the update analysis described in this paper. The C language allows various low-level manipulations on pointers and registers that cannot be emulated in a high-level language, but the vast majority of programs do not exploit such coding tricks. For these programs, we believe that it is quite feasible to generate code from a high-level logic-based specification language that matches the efficiency of the best corresponding C programs.

References

[BH87]   A. Bloss and P. Hudak. Path semantics. In *Proceedings of the Third Workshop on the Mathematical Foundations of Programming Language Semantics*, number 298 in Lecture Notes in Computer Science, pages 476–489. Springer-Verlag, 1987.

[Blo94]   Adrienne Bloss. Path analysis and the optimization of nonstrict functional languages. *ACM Transactions on Programming Languages and Systems*, 16(3):328–369, 1994.

[DP93]   M. Draghicescu and S. Purushothaman. A uniform treatment of order of evaluation and aggregate update. *Theoretical Computer Science*, 118(2):231–262, September 1993.

[Fel90]   M. Felleisen. On the expressive power of programming languages. In *European Symposium on Programming*, number 432 in Lecture Notes in Computer Science, pages 35–75. Springer-Verlag, 1990.

[GH89]   K. Gopinath and John L. Hennessy. Copy elimination in functional languages. In *16th ACM Symposium on Principles of Programming Languages*. Association for Computing Machinery, January 1989.

[GP98]   Deepak Goyal and Robert Paige. A new solution to the hidden copy problem. In *Static Analysis Symposium*, pages 327–348, 1998.

[Hud87]   P. Hudak. A semantic model of reference counting and its abstraction. In S. Abramsky and C. Hankin, editors, *Abstract Interpretation of Declarative Languages*. Ellis Horwood Ltd., 1987. Preliminary version appeared in Proceedings of 1986 ACM Conference on LISP and Functional Programming, August 1986, pages 351–363.

[Ode91] Martin Odersky. How to make destructive updates less destructive. In *Proc. 18th ACM Symposium on Principles of Programming Languages*, pages 25–26, January 1991.

[ORS92] S. Owre, J. M. Rushby, and N. Shankar. PVS: A prototype verification system. In Deepak Kapur, editor, *11th International Conference on Automated Deduction (CADE)*, volume 607 of *Lecture Notes in Artificial Intelligence*, pages 748–752, Saratoga, NY, June 1992. Springer-Verlag.

[OS97] Sam Owre and Natarajan Shankar. The formal semantics of PVS. Technical Report SRI-CSL-97-2, Computer Science Laboratory, SRI International, Menlo Park, CA, August 1997.

[Pet78] A. Pettorossi. Improving memory utilization in transforming recursive programs. In J. Winkowski, editor, *Proceedings of MFCS 1978*, pages 416–425, Berlin, Germany, 1978. Springer-Verlag.

[PP99] Alberto Pettorossi and Maurizio Proietti. Synthesis and transformation of logic programs using unfold/fold proofs. *Journal of Logic Programming*, 41(2-3):197–230, 1999.

[SCA93] A. V. S. Sastry, William Clinger, and Zena Ariola. Order-of-evaluation analysis for destructive updates in strict functional languages with flat aggregates. In *Conference on Functional Programming Languages and Computer Architecture*, pages 266–275, New York, 1993. ACM Press.

[Sch82] Jerald Schwarz. Using annotation to make recursion equations behave. *IEEE Transactions on Software Engineering*, 8(1):21–33, 1982.

[vG96] John H. G. van Groningen. The implementation and efficiency of arrays in Clean 1.1. In *Proc. 8th International Workshop on Implementation of Functional Languages, IFL'96*, number 1268 in Lecture Notes in Computer Science, pages 105–124. Springer-Verlag, 1996.

[Wad90] P. Wadler. Linear types can change the world! In M. Broy and C. Jones, editors, *Programming Concepts and Methods*. North-Holland, Amsterdam, 1990.

[Wad97] P. Wadler. How to declare an imperative. *ACM Computing Surveys*, 29(3):240–263, September 1997.

[WC98] Mitchell Wand and William D. Clinger. Set constraints for destructive array update optimization. In *Proc. IEEE Conf. on Computer Languages '98*, pages 184–193. IEEE, April 1998.

A Transformation Technique for Datalog Programs Based on Non-deterministic Constructs*

Petros Potikas[1], Panos Rondogiannis[1], and Manolis Gergatsoulis[2]

[1] Department of Informatics & Telecommunications,
University of Athens, Panepistimiopolis, 157 84 Athens, Greece,
ppotik@cs.ntua.gr, prondo@di.uoa.gr
[2] Institute of Informatics & Telecommunications, N.C.S.R. 'Demokritos',
153 10 Aghia Paraskevi Attikis, Greece
manolis@iit.demokritos.gr

Abstract. Recently, a novel transformation technique for Datalog programs, called the *branching-time transformation*, was introduced by the authors. In this paper we propose a significant extension of the branching-time transformation which we believe opens up a promising new direction of research in the area of value-propagating Datalog optimizations. One of the novel characteristics of the proposed approach is that the target language is $Datalog_{nS}$ extended with *choice predicates*, a form of non-deterministic construct that was originally introduced in the area of *intensional logic programming*.

Keywords: Logic Program Transformations, Deductive Databases.

1 Introduction

An important class of transformation techniques for Datalog programs is based on the idea of propagating the input values of the top level goal of the source program in order to restrict the generation of atoms in the bottom-up computation. Such techniques include the *counting transformation* [SZ88], the *magic sets* [BR91,SSS96], the *pushdown approach* [GSZ99], and so on. A novel transformation that also belongs to this category, is the *branching-time transformation* [RG98,RG01], that was recently proposed by the authors for the class of Chain Datalog programs. The branching-time transformation was inspired by a similar technique that has been proposed for functional programming languages [Yag84,Wad91,RW97,RW99].

In this paper, we extend the branching approach so as that it can handle a significantly broader class of well-moded Datalog programs. One of the

---

* This work has been partially supported by the University of Athens under the project "Design, Implementation and Applications of Intensional Programming Languages" (grant no 70/4/5827).

A. Pettorossi (Ed.): LOPSTR 2001, LNCS 2372, pp. 25–45, 2002.

novel characteristics of the new branching approach is that the target language is $Datalog_{nS}$ [CI93,Cho95] extended with choice predicates [OW94], a non-deterministic construct that was originally introduced in intensional logic programming [OW92]. The use of choice predicates allows the transformation of clauses containing multiple consumptions of variables. We believe that the use of non-deterministic constructs opens up a promising direction of research in the area of Datalog optimizations. The main contributions of the paper can be summarized as follows:

- We propose an extension of $Datalog_{nS}$ with choice predicates and demonstrate that it is a suitable target language for query optimization.
- We propose a new value-propagating transformation technique for a class of moded Datalog programs. Actually, the class of programs that we consider is broader than those considered by other related transformations.
- We demonstrate that non-deterministic constructs can prove especially useful for defining new powerful transformations for Datalog programs (and possibly for more general logic programs). In particular, we demonstrate that multiple consumptions of variables in Datalog programs can be treated effectively using choice predicates.

The rest of this paper is organized as follows: Section 2 gives an outline of the proposed transformation technique. Sections 3 and 4 introduce the source and the target languages of the transformation, while section 5 introduces the transformation algorithm itself. Section 6 discusses related transformation techniques, and section 7 discusses possible future extensions. Finally, in the Appendix, a detailed proof of the correctness of the algorithm is presented.

2   An Outline of the Technique

In the area of deductive databases, Datalog and bottom-up fixpoint computation are favored. The effectiveness of bottom-up execution for Datalog programs is based on optimization techniques, often referred as *query optimization techniques*. A query optimization is a transformation of a query (program and goal) to a new query, that is semantically equivalent to the initial one, in a form suitable for bottom-up evaluation. A known family of query optimizations is the value-propagating techniques, that treat queries in which goals have some bound arguments.

The branching-time transformation was recently introduced by the authors in the area of value-propagating Datalog optimizations, and applies (in its initial form) to the class of Chain Datalog programs [RG98,RG01]. The branching transformation is applied on all clauses of the initial program, and for each one of them produces a set of new clauses (each one of which contains at most one IDB predicate in its body). Intuitively, the resulting clauses reflect in a more direct way the flow of the argument values that takes place when the initial program is executed.

In the branching transformation, for every predicate in the initial program two new predicates are introduced; each one of them has two arguments, a control one (in the form of a list of natural numbers) and a data one which encodes the argument being passed. The intuition behind the control argument is that it "links" the two new predicates and coordinates them so as that the correct answers will be produced.

To illustrate the branching transformation in its initial form, consider the following Chain Datalog program (in which p is an IDB predicate while e an EDB one):

$$\leftarrow p(a, Y).$$
$$p(X, Z) \leftarrow e(X, Z).$$
$$p(X, Z) \leftarrow p(X, Y), p(Y, Z).$$

In the class of chain programs that we consider, the first argument of each predicate is considered as an input one while the second as an output (this is due to the fact that we consider goal atoms with their first argument bound). The new predicates p1 and p2 introduced by the transformation for a program predicate p, correspond to the calls (inputs) and the answers (outputs) respectively for the predicate p in the top-down computation.

We demonstrate the transformation by considering in turn each clause of the initial program. The transformation of the goal clause results in:

$$\leftarrow p2([\,],Y).$$
$$p1([\,],a).$$

Notice that the bound argument of the initial goal clause has become an argument of a unit clause in the transformed program. As a result, the bottom-up evaluation of the resulting program would use this unit clause in its first step in order to restrict the set of atoms produced in subsequent steps.

The transformation of the first clause of the source program results in:

$$p2(L,Z) \leftarrow e2([1|L],Z).$$
$$e1([1|L],X) \leftarrow p1(L,X).$$

Notice the label 1 that appears in both e2([1|L],Z) and e1([1|L],X). The basic idea is that this label relates the two atoms that have resulted from the same call in the initial program (namely the call e(X,Z)). It is important to note that *any* label can be used instead of 1, as long as this label is different from the ones that are assigned to other calls of the initial program.

The second clause of the initial program is transformed as follows:

$$p2(L,Z) \leftarrow p2([3|L],Z).$$
$$p1([3|L],Y) \leftarrow p2([2|L],Y).$$
$$p1([2|L],X) \leftarrow p1(L,X).$$

Finally, the branching transformation also introduces the clause:

$$e2(L,Y) \leftarrow e(X,Y), e1(L,X).$$

which plays the role of an interface to the database atoms whose predicate is e.

Notice that the program obtained by the transformation is not a Datalog one. In fact, it is a Datalog$_{nS}$ program [CI93,Cho95]. We should also note that in the original papers defining the branching transformation [RG98,RG01], sequences of temporal operators are used instead of lists of natural numbers, and the resulting program is a *Branching Datalog* one (Branching Datalog is the function-free subset of the branching-time logic programming language *Cactus* [RGP98]). It is however easy to show that the two approaches are equivalent.

Notice also that the Herbrand base of the programs resulting from the transformation is not finite due to the lists that have been introduced. However, as we have demonstrated in [RG01] (based on the results in [Cho95]) there exists a terminating bottom-up computation that produces all the answers to the goal clause.

For a more detailed description of the branching transformation, the interested reader should consult [RG01,RG98].

However, the branching technique in the form described above, does not apply to Datalog programs in which there exist multiple consumptions of variables. The following example demonstrates the issues that arise in such a case. Consider a Datalog program that contains the clause:

$$p(X,Z) \leftarrow q(X,W), r(X,W,Z).$$

The problem with the above clause, arises from the fact that X appears twice in the body of the clause. When attempting to apply the branching technique to the above program, the relationship between the two different occurrences of X is lost, and the resulting program is no longer semantically equivalent to the initial one. More specifically, a naive translation of the above clause would produce (among others) the two following clauses:

$$q1([11|L],X) \leftarrow p1(L,X).$$
$$r1([12|L],X) \leftarrow p1(L,X).$$

where 11 and 12 are natural numbers. Notice that the two occurrences of X in the body of the initial clause have been separated from each other as they have been placed in different clauses in the target program, and it is therefore possible for them to instantiate to different values (something which was not the case in the original clause). In this way the resulting program may produce answers which are not included in the set of answers of the initial program.

In this paper, we propose a solution to the above problem based on *choice predicates* [OW94], a form of non-deterministic construct that has been proposed in the area of *intensional logic programming* [OW92] (similar non-deterministic constructs have also been considered in other forms in [GGSZ97,GPZ01]). Choice predicates are declarative in nature and have a well-defined and elegant semantics [OW94]. The basic idea behind choice predicates is that under a given context (represented by the list L in the above example), a predicate can only be true of a unique value. Therefore, the above two clauses can be instead written as:

$$q1([11|L],X) \leftarrow \#p1(L,X).$$
$$r1([12|L],X) \leftarrow \#p1(L,X).$$

where #p1 is the choice version of the predicate p1, which at any given L can be true of only one value X. This restores the connection between the two occurrences of X, resulting in a target program equivalent to the source one.

3   The Source Language of the Transformation

In the following, we assume familiarity with the basic notions of logic programming [Llo87].

A set D of ground facts (or unit clauses) without function symbols is often referred as an *extensional database* or simply a *database*. The predicates of the atoms in a database are called *EDB predicates*. A *Datalog program* P consists of a finite set of clauses without function symbols. Predicates that appear in the heads of clauses of P are called *intensional* or *IDB predicates* (IDBs). We assume that EDB predicates do not appear in the head of program clauses; moreover, we assume that predicates appearing only in the bodies of the clauses of a Datalog program are EDB predicates. A Datalog program P together with a database D is denoted by P_D.

In the rest of this paper we adopt the following notation: *constants* are denoted by a, b, c and vectors of constants by e; *variables* by uppercase letters such as X, Y, Z and vectors of variables by v; predicates by p, q, r, s; also subscripted versions of the above symbols will be used.

The class of programs on which the proposed transformation applies is a subclass of Datalog.

Definition 1. *A clause*
$$p_0(v_0, Z_n) \leftarrow p_1(v_1, Z_1), p_2(v_2, Z_2), \ldots, p_n(v_n, Z_n).$$
with $n > 0$, is called consecutive consumption clause *(or cc-clause for short) if:*

1. *Each v_i, for $i = 0, \ldots, n$ is a nonempty vector of distinct variables, and $Z_1, \ldots, Z_n$ are distinct variables.*
2. *$vars(v_0) = vars(v_1)$ and $vars(v_i) = \{Z_{i-1}\} \cup u_{i-1}$, for $i = 2, \ldots, n$, where $u_{i-1} \subseteq vars(v_{i-1})$.*
3. *$Z_i \notin \bigcup_{j \le i} vars(v_j)$, for $i = 1, \ldots, n$.*

A program P is said to be a consecutive consumption Datalog program *(or cc-Datalog program) if all its clauses are cc-clauses. A goal G is of the form $\leftarrow q(e, Z)$, where e is a nonempty vector of constants, Z is a variable and q is an IDB predicate. A query Q is a pair $\langle G, P \rangle$, where G is a goal and P is a program. A query Q is said to be* consecutive consumption query, *or cc-query if the program P and the goal G are of the aforementioned form.*

It should be mentioned here that cc-Datalog clauses are moded; the terms v_i of the above definition correspond to input arguments while each Z_i corresponds to the single output argument of each atom. An occurrence of a variable in an input argument of the head or in the output argument of an atom in the body will be called *productive*; otherwise it will be called *consumptive*.

Example 1. The following clause is a cc-clause:

$$p(\overset{+}{X}, \overset{+}{Y}, \overset{-}{Z}) \leftarrow q(\overset{+}{Y}, \overset{+}{X}, \overset{-}{W}), r(\overset{+}{X}, \overset{+}{W}, \overset{-}{R}), s(\overset{+}{W}, \overset{+}{R}, \overset{-}{Z}).$$

where the $+$ and $-$ signs above the variables denote the input and output arguments respectively.

The intuition behind the class of cc-Datalog programs is that each value produced by an atom can only be consumed in a sequence of (one or more) consecutive atoms immediately following the atom that produced it. Many natural Datalog programs belong to this class; for example, the class of Chain Datalog programs is a proper subset of this class.

Definition 2. *A simple cc-Datalog program is a cc-Datalog program in which every clause has at most two atoms in its body.*

The semantics of cc-Datalog programs can be defined in accordance to the semantics of classical logic programming. The notions of *minimum model* M_{P_D} of P_D, where P_D is a cc-Datalog program P together with a database D, and *immediate consequence operator* T_{P_D}, transfer directly [Llo87].

The following proposition (which can be proved using unfold/fold transformations [TS84,GK94,PP97]) establishes the equivalence between cc-Datalog programs and simple cc-Datalog ones. Notice that by $M(p, P_D)$ we denote the set of atoms in the minimal model of P_D whose predicate symbol is p.

Proposition 1. *Every cc-Datalog program P can be transformed into a simple cc-Datalog program P' such that for every predicate symbol p appearing in P and for every database D, $M(p, P_D) = M(p, P'_D)$.*

In the presentation of the proposed transformation algorithm we use simple cc-Datalog programs as the source language. Because of the above proposition this is not a restriction of the power of the algorithm. Moreover, the transformation could be easily formulated so as to apply directly to cc-Datalog clauses with more than two body atoms (but this could imply a more complicated presentation and correctness proof).

4 The Target Language of the Transformation

The target language of the transformation is the language Datalog$_{nS}$ [CI93, Cho95] extended with choice predicates [OW94].

4.1 Datalog$_{nS}$

Datalog$_{nS}$ is an extension of Datalog in which atoms and terms may have a single distinguished argument, which is said to be *functional,* in addition to the usual *data arguments* (the structure of the functional terms is not however arbitrary, see [Cho95] for details). Datalog$_{nS}$ has as a special case a language which is exactly like Datalog but in which *the first argument of every predicate is a list of natural numbers.* In the rest of this paper when we refer to Datalog$_{nS}$ we will mean this particular subset.

4.2   Choice Predicates

Choice predicates [OW94] were initially introduced in the area of temporal logic programming as a means for ensuring that a given predicate is single-valued at a particular moment in time (or more generally at a particular context). Actually, with every predicate symbol p of a given program, a predicate $\#p$ (called the *choice version* of p), is associated. Choice predicates can only appear in the bodies of program clauses (their axiomatization is implicit, see [OW94] for details).

To motivate choice predicates consider writing a program whose purpose is to assign a classroom to persons (teachers) over different moments in time. The problem is to find all different such assignments in such a way that at every different moment only a single person occupies a classroom. The EDB predicate requests_class(Time, Person) expresses the fact that Person requests the particular classroom at time Time. The IDB predicate uses_class(Time, Person) expresses the fact that Person *actually* uses the classroom at time Time.

```
requests_class(0,tom).
requests_class(0,nick).
requests_class(1,mary).
uses_class(Time,Person) ← #requests_class(Time,Person).
```

In the above program, #requests_class is the choice predicate that corresponds to the (classical) predicate requests_class. The crucial property of a choice predicate is that it is single-valued for any given time-point. This means that either #requests_class(0,tom) or #requests_class(0,nick) but not both, will be considered as true at time-point 0. Therefore, the above program does not have a unique minimum model (as is the case in classical logic programming); instead, it has a set of minimal models, one for every different possible (functional) assignment of persons over the moments in time. More specifically, if we denote by D the database of the above program (corresponding to the three facts), the two minimal models of the program are the following:

$$M_1 = \{\#uses\_class(0, tom), \#uses\_class(1, mary), uses\_class(0, tom),$$
$$uses\_class(1, mary), \#requests\_class(0, tom),$$
$$\#requests\_class(1, mary)\} \cup D$$

and

$$M_2 = \{\#uses\_class(0, nick), \#uses\_class(1, mary), uses\_class(0, nick),$$
$$uses\_class(1, mary), \#requests\_class(0, nick),$$
$$\#requests\_class(1, mary)\} \cup D$$

Choice predicates are not necessarily restricted to apply to simple temporal logic programming languages such as the one used in the above example (in which time is linear); they are also applicable to more general intensional programming languages [OW92] that include the language Datalog$_{nS}$ which we have adopted for defining the proposed transformation. More specifically, in [OW94], Orgun and Wadge develop a general semantic framework for choice predicates that can apply to a wide class of intensional logic programming languages.

The language we will be using in the rest of this paper as the target language of the transformation, is Datalog$_{nS}$ extended with choice predicates.

Notice that for every predicate symbol p (either IDB or EDB) a predicate $\#p$ is associated.

Definition 3. *A Choice Datalog$_{nS}$ program is a Datalog$_{nS}$ program which may contain choice atoms in the bodies of its clauses.*

An exposition of the formal semantics of Choice Datalog$_{nS}$ is given in the Appendix of the paper.

5   The Transformation Algorithm

In this section we provide a formal definition of the transformation algorithm. The algorithm is subsequently illustrated by a representative example.

The algorithm: Let P be a given simple cc-Datalog program and G a given goal clause. For each $(n + 1)$-ary predicate p in P, we introduce $n + 1$ binary IDB predicates $p_1^+, \ldots, p_n^+, p^-$ together with their choice versions $\#p_1^+, \ldots, \#p_n^+, \#p^-$, where p_i^+ corresponds to the i-th input argument of p and p^- to the $(n+1)$-th argument of p (which is the output one). The transformation processes each clause in P and the goal clause G and gives as output a Choice Datalog$_{nS}$ program P^* together with a new goal clause G^*. We assume the existence of a labeling function which assigns different labels to atoms that appear in the bodies of clauses of P. Labels are natural numbers and are denoted by $l_1, l_2, \ldots$. The algorithm is defined by a case analysis, depending on the form of the clause being processed every time:

Case 1: Let C be a clause of the form:

$$p(\boldsymbol{v}_0, Z) \leftarrow q(\boldsymbol{v}_1, Y), r(\boldsymbol{v}_2, Z).$$

and let l_1, l_2 be the labels of $q(\boldsymbol{v}_1, Y)$ and $r(\boldsymbol{v}_2, Z)$ respectively. Then C is transformed in the following way:

1. The following clause is added to P^*:

$$p^-(L, Z) \leftarrow \#r^-([l_2|L], Z).$$

2. Let X be a variable that appears in the k-th position of $\boldsymbol{v}_0$ and also in the m-th position of $\boldsymbol{v}_1$. Then, the following clause is added to P^*:

$$q_m^+([l_1|L], X) \leftarrow \#p_k^+(L, X).$$

The case of a variable appearing in $\boldsymbol{v}_0$ and also in $\boldsymbol{v}_2$, is treated analogously.

3. If the output variable Y of q appears in the m-th position of $\boldsymbol{v}_2$, then the following clause is added to P^*:

$$r_m^+([l_2|L], Y) \leftarrow \#q^-([l_1|L], Y).$$

Case 2: Let C be a clause of the form:

$$p(v_0, Z) \leftarrow q(v_1, Z).$$

and let l_3 be the label of $q(v_1, Z)$. Then C is transformed as follows:

1. The following clause is added to P^*:

$$p^-(L, Z) \leftarrow \#q^-([l_3|L], Z).$$

2. Let X be a variable that appears in the k-th position of v_0 and also in the m-th position of v_1. Then, the following clause is added to P^*:

$$q_m^+([l_3|L], X) \leftarrow \#p_k^+(L, X).$$

Case 3: For every EDB predicate p of P with n input variables and one output variable, a new clause of the following form is added to P^*:

$$p^-(L, Y) \leftarrow p(X_1, \ldots, X_n, Y), \#p_1^+(L, X_1), \ldots, \#p_n^+(L, X_n).$$

Case 4: The transformation of the goal clause:

$$\leftarrow p(a_1, \ldots, a_n, Y).$$

results to a set of n new facts, which are added to P^*:

$$p_i^+([\,], a_i).$$

for $i = 1, \ldots, n$. The new goal clause G^* is:

$$\leftarrow p^-([\,], Y).$$

We give an example to show the application of the algorithm and the need for choice predicates.

Example 2. Let P be the cc-Datalog program that follows, where q, p are IDB predicates and e, f, g are EDB predicates:

```
← q(a1,Z).
q(X,Z) ← f(X,Z).
q(X,Z) ← e(X,Y),p(Y,Z).
p(X,Z) ← q(X,W),g(X,W,Z).
```

The program (together with a new goal clause) obtained by applying the transformation algorithm to $P \cup \{\leftarrow q(a1, Z)\}$ is:

```
← q2([],Z).
q1([],a1).
q2(L,Z) ← #f2([1|L],Z).
f1([1|L],X) ← #q1(L,X).
q2(L,Z) ← #p2([3|L],Z).
p1([3|L],Y) ← #e2([2|L],Y).
e1([2|L],X) ← #q1(L,X).
p2(L,Z) ← #g3([5|L],Z).
g2([5|L],W) ← #q2([4|L],W).
g1([5|L],X) ← #p1(L,X).
q1([4|L],X) ← #p1(L,X).
e2(L,Y) ← e(X,Y), #e1(L,X).
f2(L,Y) ← f(X,Y), #f1(L,X).
g3(L,Z) ← g(X,Y,Z), #g1(L,X), #g2(L,Y).
```

Consider now the following database D:

```
e(a1,a2).        f(a2,a).        g(a2,a,b3).
e(a1,b1).        f(b1,b).        g(b1,a,a3).
```

Both the initial and the final program have the single answer $Z = b3$. However, if we replace the choice predicates with the corresponding classical ones, then the resulting program will have an extra (incorrect) answer, namely $Z = a3$.

The correctness of the transformation algorithm is demonstrated by the following theorem (whose proof, which is given in the Appendix, is based on fixpoint induction).

Theorem 1. *Let P be a simple cc-Datalog program, D a database and $\leftarrow p(a_1, \ldots, a_n, Y)$ be a goal clause. Let P^* be the Choice Datalog$_{nS}$ program obtained by applying the transformation algorithm to $P \cup \{\leftarrow p(a_1, \ldots, a_n, Y)\}$. Then there exists a limit interpretation M of P_D^* such that $\#p^-([\,\,], b) \in M$ iff $p(a_1, \ldots, a_n, b) \in T_{P_D} \uparrow \omega$.*

The notion of limit interpretations used in the above theorem is also formally defined in the Appendix.

6 Related Work

In this paper we have introduced a transformation technique for query optimization in the area of deductive databases. More specifically, the proposed method belongs to a well-known class of techniques, which is based on the propagation of the input values of the query-goal in order to restrict the generation of atoms for the efficient bottom-up computation of the final answers. Related techniques are the *counting method* [SZ88], the *pushdown approach* [GSZ99] and the *magic sets transformation* [BR91,SSS96]. A detailed comparison of the proposed transformation with these other approaches is clearly outside the scope of this paper. Instead, we provide certain preliminary indications that the proposed technique offers certain benefits when compared to these other approaches.

The most widely known technique in the area of value propagating Datalog optimizations, is the magic sets transformation. In this approach, for each IDB predicate of the source program a new predicate, called magic predicate, is introduced. The arguments of a magic predicate are the bound arguments of the corresponding IDB predicate of the initial program and the aim is to push selections into rules. The magic sets can be applied on general Datalog [BR91, SSS96] programs, therefore it is the most widely applicable among all similar techniques. The generality, however, of the magic sets can prove a disadvantage in certain cases. As discussed in [RG01], the output code produced by the magic approach is often much less efficient than the one produced by the branching transformation in its initial form (and therefore also in its extension introduced in this paper).

In the counting method integer indices are introduced to encode two fixpoint computations, one for the propagation of the bindings in the top-down phase and the other for the generation of the desired result in the bottom-up computation. In its initial form, counting was applicable only to a restricted class of queries [Ull89,HN88]. Later, it was extended to *generalized counting*, which applies to the class of queries with the *binding-passing property (BPP)*[SZ88], a significantly broader class in which many natural programs belong. Intuitively, BPP guarantees that "bindings can be passed down to any level of recursion". However, the class of BPP queries does not include all the Chain Datalog ones and hence not all the cc-Datalog ones. For an example, consider the traversal of a graph using double recursion (the program in section 2). The generalized counting method can not treat this case, since the corresponding program does not have the BPP; but this program is actually a chain one, and therefore it can be easily transformed by the branching transformation.

The pushdown method is based on the relationship between chain queries and context-free languages. Moreover, the context-free language corresponding to a query is associated to a pushdown automaton; in this way the initial query is rewritten in a more suitable form for efficient bottom-up execution. The *pushdown method* applies to all chain queries [GSZ99], and generally it covers a subclass of the proposed technique, as it cannot treat the case of multiple consumptions of variables.

The proposed technique is also related to certain approaches that aim at transforming non-linear into linear Datalog programs [AGK96]. However, it is known that the whole class of chain queries cannot be linearized if the target language is just Datalog [AC89].

7 Discussion

In this paper, we introduce a transformation algorithm from a subclass of moded Datalog programs to Choice Datalog$_{nS}$ ones. The programs obtained have the following interesting properties:

- Every clause contains at most one IDB atom in its body.
- Every clause in the resulting program corresponding to an IDB predicate in the source program, uses only a single data variable.
- Every IDB predicate in the resulting program is binary, its first argument actually being a control argument in the form of a list.

We believe that the work presented in this paper can be extended in various ways. We are currently investigating possible extensions of the source language, perhaps allowing more than one output arguments, as well as more general patterns of consumptions. In particular, we believe that the restriction to consecutive consumption of the input arguments is not essential but lifting this restriction seems to require a more involved correctness proof. Another point for further research is the use of non-deterministic constructs that are more appropriate for deductive databases, like these proposed in [GPZ01]. Apart from its theoretical interest, the transformation algorithm can be viewed as the basis of new evaluation strategies for a class of moded Datalog programs. It would therefore be interesting to carry out a careful performance comparison with related optimization techniques, which would reveal the strong and weak points of each approach.

References

[AC89]   F. Afrati and S. Cosmadakis. Expressiveness of restricted recursive queries. In *Proc. 21st ACM Symp. on Theory of Computing*, pages 113–126, 1989.

[AGK96]   F. Afrati, M. Gergatsoulis, and M. Katzouraki. On transformations into linear database logic programs. In D. Bjørner, M. Broy, and I. Pottosin, editors, *Perspectives of Systems Informatics (PSI'96), Proceedings*, Lecture Notes in Computer Science (LNCS) 1181, pages 433–444. Springer-Verlag, 1996.

[BR91]   C. Beeri and R. Ramakrishnan. On the power of magic. *The Journal of Logic Programming*, 10(1,2,3 & 4):255–299, 1991.

[Cho95]   Jan Chomicki. Depth-bounded bottom-up evaluation of logic programs. *The Journal of Logic Programming*, 25(1):1–31, 1995.

[CI93]   J. Chomicki and T. Imielnski. Finite representation of infinite query answers. *ACM Transaction of Database Systems*, 18(2):181–223, June 1993.

[GGSZ97]   F. Giannotti, S. Greco, D. Saccà, and C. Zaniolo. Programming with non-determinism in deductive databases. *Annals of Mathematics and Artificial Intelligence*, 19(1–2):97–125, 1997.

[GK94]   M. Gergatsoulis and M. Katzouraki. Unfold/fold transformations for definite clause programs. In M. Hermenegildo and J. Penjam, editors, *Programming Language Implementation and Logic Programming (PLILP'94), Proceedings*, Lecture Notes in Computer Science (LNCS) 844, pages 340–354. Springer-Verlag, 1994.

[GPZ01]   F. Giannotti, D. Pedreschi, and C. Zaniolo. Semantics and expressive power
          of non-deterministic constructs in deductive databases. *Journal of Com-
          puter and Systems Sciences*, 62(1):15–42, 2001.

[GSZ99]   S. Greco, D. Saccà, and C. Zaniolo. Grammars and automata to optimize
          chain logic queries. *International Journal on Foundations of Computer
          Science*, 10(3):349–372, 1999.

[HN88]   R. W. Haddad and J. F. Naughton. Counting methods for cyclic relations.
          In *Proc. 7th ACM SIGACT-SIGMOD-SIGART Symposium on Principles
          of Database Systems*, pages 333–340. ACM Press, 1988.

[Llo87]   J. W. Lloyd. *Foundations of Logic Programming*. Springer-Verlag, 1987.

[OW92]   M. A. Orgun and W. W. Wadge. Towards a unified theory of intensional
          logic programming. *The Journal of Logic Programming*, 13(4):413–440,
          1992.

[OW94]   M. A. Orgun and W. W. Wadge. Extending temporal logic programming
          with choice predicates non-determinism. *Journal of Logic and Computa-
          tion*, 4(6):877–903, 1994.

[PP97]   A. Pettorossi and M. Proietti. Transformation of logic programs. In D. M.
          Gabbay, C. J. Hogger, and J. A. Robinson, editors, *Handbook of Logic in
          Artificial Intelligence and Logic Programming*, volume 5, pages 697–787.
          Oxford University Press, 1997.

[RG98]   P. Rondogiannis and M. Gergatsoulis. The intensional implementation
          technique for chain datalog programs. In *Proc. of the 11th International
          Symposium on Languages for Intensional Programming (ISLIP'98), May
          7-9, Palo Alto, California, USA*, pages 55–64, 1998.

[RG01]   Panos Rondogiannis and Manolis Gergatsoulis. The branching-time trans-
          formation technique for chain datalog programs. *Journal of Intelligent
          Information Systems*, 17(1):71–94, 2001.

[RGP98]   P. Rondogiannis, M. Gergatsoulis, and T. Panayiotopoulos. Branching-
          time logic programming: The language Cactus and its applications. *Com-
          puter Languages*, 24(3):155–178, October 1998.

[RW97]   P. Rondogiannis and W. W. Wadge. First-order functional languages and
          intensional logic. *Journal of Functional Programming*, 7(1):73–101, 1997.

[RW99]   P. Rondogiannis and W. W. Wadge. Higher-Order Functional Languages
          and Intensional Logic. *Journal of Functional Programming*, 9(5):527–564,
          1999.

[SSS96]   S. Sippu and E. Soisalon-Soininen. An analysis of magic sets and related
          optimization strategies for logic queries. *Journal of the ACM*, 43(6):1046–
          1088, 1996.

[SZ88]   D. Saccà and C. Zaniolo. The generalized counting method for recursive
          logic queries. *Theoretical Computer Science*, 4(4):187–220, 1988.

[TS84]   H. Tamaki and T. Sato. Unfold/fold transformations of logic programs. In
          Sten-Åke Tarnlund, editor, *Proc. of the Second International Conference
          on Logic Programming*, pages 127–138, 1984.

[Ull89]   Jeffrey D. Ullman. *Principles of Database and Knowledge-Base Systems*,
          volume I & II. Computer Science Press, 1989.

[Wad91]   W. W. Wadge. Higher-Order Lucid. In *Proceedings of the Fourth Interna-
          tional Symposium on Lucid and Intensional Programming*, 1991.

[Yag84]   A. Yaghi. *The intensional implementation technique for functional lan-
          guages*. PhD thesis, Dept. of Computer Science, University of Warwick,
          Coventry, UK, 1984.

Appendix A: The Correctness of the Transformation

A.1. Semantics of Choice Datalog$_{nS}$

The Herbrand base B_{P_D} of a Choice Datalog$_{nS}$ program P along with a database D, includes all those ground atomic formulas constructed using constants from the Herbrand universe U_{P_D} of P_D and predicates from P_D or choice versions of predicates from P_D. A Herbrand interpretation I of P_D is (as usual) a subset of its Herbrand base B_{P_D}. We can define a T_{P_D} operator in the usual way. However, we need something stronger than the usual T_{P_D} in order to define the semantics of Choice Datalog$_{nS}$ programs. We therefore define the operator NT_{P_D} that works exactly like T_{P_D} but does not throw away any choice atoms [OW94]. More formally:

Definition 4. *Let P be a Choice Datalog$_{nS}$ program, D a database, and I a Herbrand interpretation of P_D. Then $NT_{P_D}(I)$ is defined as follows:*

$$NT_{P_D}(I) = T_{P_D}(I) \cup choices(I)$$

where $choices(I)$ is the set of the choice atoms belonging to I.

Furthermore, the semantics of Choice Datalog$_{nS}$ programs require another operator, namely the C_{P_D} operator, which returns all possible immediate extensions of a given Herbrand interpretation of P_D, determined by arbitrary choices (as will be further explained below).

Let I be a Herbrand interpretation of a Choice Datalog$_{nS}$ program and let p be a predicate symbol that appears in program P_D. Define:

$$E_{p,L}(I) = \{e \mid p(L,e) \in I\}$$

and also:

$$E_{\#p,L}(I) = \{e \mid \#p(L,e) \in I\}$$

Also let:

$$S_I = \{\langle p, L, e \rangle \mid E_{p,L}(I) \neq \emptyset \text{ and } E_{\#p,L}(I) = \emptyset \text{ and } e \in E_{p,L}(I)\}$$

In other words, S_I is a set such that $\langle p, L, e \rangle \in S_I$, if no choice has been made for p at the context L and e is a possible candidate for this choice. The formal definition of C_{P_D} is given below:

Definition 5. *Let P be a Choice Datalog$_{nS}$ program, D a database and I an interpretation of P_D. Then, $C_{P_D}(I)$ is defined as follows:*

$$C_{P_D}(I) = \{I \cup \{\#p(L,e)\} \mid \langle p, L, e \rangle \in S_I\}$$

Some observations can be made about the C_{P_D} operator. The first one is that C_{P_D} preserves the previous computed atoms (it does not reject anything). The next thing is that C_{P_D} when applied to an interpretation I, chooses *exactly* one among all the possible $\langle p, L, e \rangle$ triples in S_I, and returns the atom $\#p(L, e)$. In other words, given an interpretation I, $C_{P_D}(I)$ is a set of interpretations each one corresponding to a different choice atom being added to I.

We now define the notion of P-chain which intuitively describes a bottom-up computation of a given program P. During the bottom-up computation the operators $NT_{P_D} \uparrow \omega$ and C_P alternate as shown in the following definition:

Definition 6. *Let P be a Choice Datalog$_{nS}$ program and D a database. A P-chain is a sequence $\langle M_0, M_1, M_2, \ldots \rangle$ satisfying the following conditions:*

$$M_0 = \emptyset$$

and

$$M_{i+1} \in C_{P_D}(NT_{P_D} \uparrow \omega(M_i)), \quad i \geq 0.$$

The least upper bound of a P−chain $\langle M_0, M_1, M_2, \ldots \rangle$ is $M = \bigcup_{i < \omega} M_i$. Then $M_0, M_1, \ldots$ will be called *approximations* of M and M is called a *limit interpretation* of P.

The lemma stated below will be used in the proofs that follow.

Lemma 1. *Let P be a Choice Datalog$_{nS}$ program, D be a database and let $\langle M_0, M_1, \ldots \rangle$ be a P-chain. Then, for all $L \in List(\mathcal{N})$, all predicate symbols p and for all vectors of constants e from U_{P_D}, if $\#p(L, e) \in M_i$ then $\#p(L, e) \in M_{i+1}$, $i \geq 0$.*

Proof. An easy consequence of the definition of a P-chain.

Finally, the following definitions will be required in the proof of the correctness of the transformation:

Definition 7. *Let P be a program and D a database. Then, the depends on relation on B_{P_D} is the least relation on B_{P_D} such that:*

1. *A depends on A for all $A \in B_{P_D}$.*
2. *$\#A$ depends on A for all non-choice atoms $A \in B_{P_D}$.*
3. *If $A \leftarrow B$ is a ground instance of a clause in P then A depends on B.*
4. *If A depends on B and B depends on C then A depends on C.*

Let $A, B \in B_{P_D}$ such that A depends on B. We define the *distance* between A and B to be the minimum number of ground instances of program rules used in order to establish the dependence of A from B. When the distance is greater than 0 we say that A *depends essentially* on B.

Definition 8. *Let P be a Choice Datalog$_{nS}$ program, D a database and let $\langle M_0, M_1, \ldots \rangle$ be a P-chain. Then, M_i will be called minimal with respect to a set S of choice atoms if M_i contains exactly the choice atoms on which the atoms in S depend on.*

A.2. Correctness Proof

The following definition will be used in order to simplify the notation that appears in the proofs.

Definition 9. *Let C be a simple cc-Datalog clause and p, q two predicate symbols that appear in C. Then, $S_{p^+q^+}$ is the set of positions of input variables of p that are also input variables of q. Moreover, $f_{p^+q^+} : S_{p^+q^+} \to S_{q^+p^+}$ is the function that takes the position where an input variable appears in predicate p and returns its position in predicate q.*

Example 3. Consider the following cc-clause:
$$p(\overset{+}{X}, \overset{+}{Y}, \overset{-}{W}) \leftarrow q(\overset{+}{Y}, \overset{+}{X}, \overset{-}{Z}), r(\overset{+}{X}, \overset{+}{Z}, \overset{-}{W}).$$
In this clause, $S_{p^+q^+} = \{1,2\}$, $S_{q^+r^+} = \{2\}$, $S_{r^+q^+} = \{1\}$, and $f_{q^+r^+}(2) = 1$.

Let P be a simple cc-Datalog program, D a database and $\leftarrow p(a_1, \dots, a_n, Y)$ a goal clause. The correctness proof of the transformation proceeds as follows: at first we show (see Lemma 4 below) that if a ground instance $p(a_1, \dots, a_n, b)$ of the goal clause is a logical consequence of P_D then $\#p^-([\,], b)$ belongs to a limit interpretation M of P_D^*, where $P^* \cup \{\leftarrow p^-([\,], Y)\}$ is obtained by applying the transformation algorithm to $P \cup \{\leftarrow p(a_1, \dots, a_n, Y)\}$. In order to prove this result we establish a more general lemma (Lemma 3 below).

The inverse of Lemma 4 is given as Lemma 6. More specifically, we prove that whenever $\#p^-([\,], b)$ belongs to a limit interpretation of P_D^* then $p(a_1, \dots, a_n, b)$ is a logical consequence of P_D. Again, we establish this result by proving the more general Lemma 5. Combining the above results we get the correctness proof of the transformation algorithm. The correctness proof requires the following lemma:

Lemma 2. *Let P be a simple cc-Datalog program, G a goal clause and D a database. Let P^* and G^* be the Choice Datalog$_{nS}$ program and the goal clause that result from the transformation. For all predicates p defined in P_D^*, all $L \in List(\mathcal{N})$, and all constants $a, b \in U_{P_D^*}$:*

1. *$p^-(L, b)$ does not essentially depend on $p^-(L, a)$.*
2. *$p^+(L, b)$ does not depend on $p^-(L, a)$.*
3. *$p_j^+(L, b)$ does not essentially depend on $p_i^+(L, a)$.*

The proof of the above lemma can be easily established by induction on the distance of the atoms.

Lemma 3. *Let P be a simple cc-Datalog program, G a goal clause and D a database. Let P^* and G^* be the Choice Datalog$_{nS}$ program and the goal clause that result from the transformation. For all predicates p defined in P_D, all $L \in List(\mathcal{N})$, and all constants $a_1, \dots, a_n, b \in U_{P_D}$, if $p(a_1, \dots, a_n, b) \in T_{P_D} \uparrow \omega$ and there exists an approximation I to a limit interpretation of P_D^* that is minimal with respect to the set $S = \{\#p_1^+(L, a_1), \dots, \#p_n^+(L, a_n)\}$, then there exists an approximation J, where $I \subset J$ that is minimal with respect to the set $\{\#p^-(L, b)\}$.*

Proof. We show the above by induction on the approximations of $T_{P_D} \uparrow \omega$.

Induction Basis:

The induction basis trivially holds because $T_{P_D} \uparrow 0 = \emptyset$ and thus $p(a_1, \ldots, a_n, b)$ $\in T_{P_D} \uparrow 0$ is false.

Induction Hypothesis:

We assume that: for all predicates p defined in P_D, all $L \in List(\mathcal{N})$, and all constants $a_1, \ldots, a_n, b \in U_{P_D}$, if $p(a_1, \ldots, a_n, b) \in T_{P_D} \uparrow k$ and there exists an approximation I to a limit interpretation of P_D^* that is minimal with respect to the set $S = \{\#p_1^+(L, a_1), \ldots, \#p_n^+(L, a_n)\}$, then there exists an approximation J, where $I \subset J$ that is minimal with respect to the set $\{\#p^-(L, b)\}$.

Induction Step:

We demonstrate the desired result for the $k+1$ iteration of the T_{P_D} operator. We will therefore prove that: if $p(a_1, \ldots, a_n, b) \in T_{P_D} \uparrow (k + 1)$ and there exists an approximation I to a limit interpretation of P_D^* that is minimal with respect to the set $S = \{\#p_1^+(L, a_1), \ldots, \#p_n^+(L, a_n)\}$, then there exists an approximation J, where $I \subset J$ that is minimal with respect to the set $\{\#p^-(L, b)\}$.

We use a case analysis on the way that $p(a_1, \ldots, a_n, b)$ has been introduced into $T_{P_D} \uparrow (k + 1)$.

Case 1: Assume that $p(a_1, \ldots, a_n, b)$ has been added to $T_{P_D} \uparrow (k + 1)$ because it is a fact in D. According to the transformation algorithm, in P^* there exists a rule of the form:

$$p^-(L, Y) \leftarrow p(X_1, \ldots, X_n, Y), \#p_1^+(L, X_1), \ldots, \#p_n^+(L, X_n).$$

Since I is minimal with respect to $S = \{\#p_1^+(L, a_1), \ldots, \#p_n^+(L, a_n)\}$, I does not contain any atom of the form $p^-(L, e)$ because such an atom could only have been added using the above clause. Now since $p(a_1, \ldots, a_n, b) \in T_{P_D} \uparrow (k + 1)$, using the clause above we conclude that $p^-(L, b) \in NT_{P_D^*} \uparrow \omega(I)$. Consider the interpretation $J = NT_{P_D^*} \uparrow \omega(I) \cup \{\#p^-(L, b)\}$. Clearly, $J \in C_{P_D^*}(NT_{P_D^*} \uparrow \omega(I))$. Moreover, J is minimal with respect to $\{\#p^-(L, b)\}$ because I is minimal with respect to S.

Case 2: Assume that $p(a_1, \ldots, a_n, b)$ has been added to $T_{P_D} \uparrow (k + 1)$ using a rule of the form:

$$p(\ldots) \leftarrow q(\ldots), r(\ldots). \tag{1}$$

and suppose that the arities of p, q and r are $n+1$, $n+1$ (because of condition 2 of Definition 1) and $m+1$ respectively. Then, there exists a constant c instantiating the output variable of $q(\ldots)$ such that the corresponding instances of $q(\ldots)$ and $r(\ldots)$ in clause (1) are in $T_{P_D} \uparrow k$.

Consider now an input argument of q (say the t-th one) which shares its variable with an input argument of p (say the s-th one). Then a rule of the form:

$$q_t^+([l_1|L], X) \leftarrow \#p_s^+(L, X). \tag{2}$$

where $s = f_{q+p+}(t)$, has been added to P^* by the transformation algorithm. Moreover, for each input argument of r which shares its variable with an input argument of p, we have in P^* a clause of the form:

$$r_t^+([l_2|L], X) \leftarrow \#p_s^+(L, X). \tag{3}$$

where $s = f_{r+p+}(t)$. Consider now $I' = NT_{P_D^*} \uparrow \omega(I)$. Using clause (2), we derive that $q_t^+([l_1|L], a_s) \in I'$, for all $t = 1, \ldots, n$ and $s = f_{q+p+}(t)$. Notice that for every t there is exactly one a_s such that $q_t^+([l_1|L], a_s) \in I'$, due to the fact that in clause (2) there exists a choice atom in the right hand side. Moreover, from clause (3), we derive that $r_t^+([l_2|L], a_s) \in I'$, for all $t \in S_{r+p+}$ and $s = f_{r+p+}(t)$. Again, notice that for every t there is exactly one a_s such that $r_t^+([l_2|L], a_s) \in I'$, due to the fact that in clause (3) there exists a choice atom in the right hand side.

Starting from I' and alternating $C_{P_D^*}$ and $NT_{P_D^*} \uparrow \omega$ we can construct an approximation I'' whose choice atoms are exactly those of I' together with the choice atoms of the set $\{\#q_1^+([l_1|L], a_{f_{q+p+}(1)}), \ldots, \#q_n^+([l_1|L], a_{f_{q+p+}(n)})\}$. It is easy to see that I'' is minimal with respect to $\{\#q_1^+([l_1|L], a_{f_{q+p+}(1)}), \ldots, \#q_n^+([l_1|L], a_{f_{q+p+}(n)})\}$, because *all* choice atoms regarding input arguments of p that belong to I' are used for the production of the choice atoms regarding the input arguments of q. Therefore we can apply the induction hypothesis on q under the list $[l_1|L]$, and on approximation I'', which gives:

> Since the approximation I'' is minimal with respect to the set $S' = \{\#q_1^+([l_1|L], a_{f_{q+p+}(1)}), \ldots, \#q_n^+([l_1|L], a_{f_{q+p+}(n)})\}$ and $q(a_{f_{q+p+}(1)}, \ldots, a_{f_{q+p+}(n)}, c) \in T_{P_D} \uparrow k$ then there exists an aproximation J', where $I'' \subset J'$ which is minimal with respect to $\{\#q^-([l_1|L], c)\}$.

Since for the input argument of r which shares its variable with the output argument of q there is a clause in P^* of the form:

$$r_w^+([l_2|L], X) \leftarrow \#q^-([l_1|L], X). \tag{4}$$

it follows that $r_w^+([l_2|L], c) \in NT_{P_D^*} \uparrow \omega(J')$. Notice now that J' can not contain any choice atoms regarding the remaining input arguments of r at context $[l_2|L]$: if any such choice atom existed, then by the minimality of J' with respect to $\{\#q^-([l_1|L], c)\}$ we get that the production of $\#q^-([l_1|L], c)$ depends on this atom; but then, the production of $r_w^+([l_2|L], c)$ also depends on this atom (which is impossible from Lemma 2).

Now, iterating $C_{P_D^*}$ and $NT_{P_D^*} \uparrow \omega$ we can create an interpretation J'' whose choice atoms are those of J' plus the choice atoms that correspond to all the input arguments of r at context $[l_2|L]$. Then J'' is minimal with respect to all choice atoms that correspond to the input arguments of r under the context $[l_2|L]$ (because J' is minimal with respect to $\{\#q^-([l_1|L], c)\}$). Therefore, we can apply the induction hypothesis on r under the list $[l_2|L]$ and on approximation J'', getting:

> Since $\#r_w^+([l_2|L], c) \in J''$ and $\#r_t^+([l_2|L], a_s) \in J''$, for all $t \in S_{r+p+}$, $s = f_{r+p+}(t)$, and $r(a_{r_1}, \ldots, a_{r_m}, b) \in T_{P_D} \uparrow k$ where $a_{r_l} = c$, if $l = w$, otherwise $a_{r_l} = a_s$, where $s = f_{r+p+}(l)$, then there exists J''' such that $J'' \subset J'''$, and J''' is minimal with respect to the set $\{\#r^-([l_2|L], b)\}$.

Finally, using the fact that $\#r^-([l_2|L], b) \in J'''$ together with clause:

$$p^-(L, Y) \leftarrow \#r^-([l_2|L], Y). \tag{5}$$

we conclude that $p^-(L, b) \in NT_{P_D^*} \uparrow \omega(J''')$. Notice that there is no other atom of the form $\#p^-(L, e)$ in J''' since otherwise either $p^-(L, b)$ would depend on $\#p^-(L, e)$, but this is not possible because of lemma 2, or the production of $p^-(L, b)$ is completely independent from $\#p^-(L, e)$, but then J''' would not be minimal with respect to $\{\#r^-([l_2|L], b)\}$. We can thus construct an approximation $J = NT_{P_D^*} \uparrow \omega(J''')) \cup \{\#p^-(L, b)\}$, which is minimal with respect to the set $\{\#p^-(L, b)\}$.

Case 3: Assume that $p(a_1, \ldots, a_n, b)$ has been added to $T_{P_D} \uparrow (k + 1)$ using a rule of the form:

$$p(\ldots) \leftarrow q(\ldots). \tag{6}$$

The proof for this case is a simplified version of Case 2.

Lemma 4. *Let P be a simple cc-Datalog program, D be a database and $\leftarrow p(a_1, \ldots, a_n, Y)$ be a goal clause. Let P^* be the Choice Datalog$_{nS}$ program obtained by applying the transformation algorithm to $P \cup \{\leftarrow p(a_1, \ldots, a_n, Y)\}$. If $p(a_1, \ldots, a_n, b) \in T_{P_D} \uparrow \omega$ then there is a limit interpretation M of P_D^* such that $\#p^-([\,], b) \in M$.*

Proof. Since by transforming the goal clause, the facts $p_i^+([\,], a_i)$, for $i = 1, \ldots, n$, are added to P^*, this lemma is a special case of Lemma 3.

Lemma 5. *Let P be a simple cc-Datalog program, D a database and P^* be the Choice Datalog$_{nS}$ program that results from the transformation. Let M be a limit interpretation of P_D^*. Then for all predicates p defined in P_D^*, for all $L \in List(\mathcal{N})$ and for $b \in U_{P_D}$, if $\#p^-(L, b) \in M$, then there exist constants $a_1, \ldots, a_n \in U_{P_D}$ such that $p(a_1, \ldots, a_n, b) \in T_{P_D} \uparrow \omega$ and $\#p_i^+(L, a_i) \in M$, for $i = 1, \ldots, n$.*

Proof. We show the above by induction on the approximations of M.

Induction Basis:

It is convenient to show the induction basis for both M_0 and M_1. We therefore will show that: (a) if $\#p^-(L, b) \in M_0$, then there exist constants $a_1, \ldots, a_n \in U_{P_D}$ such that $p(a_1, \ldots, a_n, b) \in T_{P_D} \uparrow \omega$ and $\#p_i^+(L, a_i) \in M_0$, for $i = 1, \ldots, n$ and (b) if $\#p^-(L, b) \in M_1$, then there exist constants $a_1, \ldots, a_n$ in U_{P_D} such that $p(a_1, \ldots, a_n, b) \in T_{P_D} \uparrow \omega$ and $\#p_i^+(L, a_i) \in M_1$, for $i = 1, \ldots, n$.

The statement (a) vacuously holds because $M_0 = \emptyset$. The statement (b) also holds because $NT_{P_D^*} \uparrow \omega(M_0)$ contains only facts of the form $p_i^+([\,], a_i)$, for $i = 1, \ldots, n$ (i.e. non-choice predicates); there are no other atoms in $NT_{P_D^*} \uparrow \omega(M_0)$ because all atoms in the bodies of clauses in P^* are choice atoms. So, applying the $C_{P_D^*}$ operator on it, we get one of the $\#p_i^+$ atoms (and not any $\#p^-$ atom). Thus $\#p^-(L, b) \in M_1$ is false.

Induction Hypothesis:
If $\#p^-(L, b) \in M_k$, then there exist constants $a_1, \ldots, a_n$ in U_{P_D} such that $p(a_1, \ldots, a_n, b) \in T_{P_D} \uparrow \omega$ and $\#p_i^+(L, a_i) \in M_k$, for $i = 1, \ldots, n$.

Induction Step: We will prove that:
If $\#p^-(L, b) \in M_{k+1}$, then there exist constants $a_1, \ldots, a_n$ in U_{P_D} such that $p(a_1, \ldots, a_n, b) \in T_{P_D} \uparrow \omega$ and $\#p_i^+(L, a_i) \in M_{k+1}$, for $i = 1, \ldots, n$.

Case 1: Assume that $\#p^-(L, b)$ has been introduced in M_{k+1} by a clause of the form:

$$p^-(L, Y) \leftarrow p(X_1, \ldots, X_n, Y), \#p_1^+(L, X_1), \ldots, \#p_n^+(L, X_n). \tag{1}$$

Then p is an EDB predicate in D and there exist constants $a_1, \ldots, a_n$ in U_{P_D} such that $p(a_1, \ldots, a_n, b) \in T_{P_D} \uparrow 1$ and $\#p_i^+(L, a_i) \in M_k$, for $i = 1, \ldots, n$.

Case 2: Assume now that there exists in P a clause of the form:

$$p(\ldots) \leftarrow q(\ldots), r(\ldots). \tag{2}$$

such that the arities of p, q and r are $n + 1$, $n + 1$ (because of condition 2 of Definition 1) and $m + 1$ respectively, and the labels of $q(\ldots)$ and $r(\ldots)$ are l_1 and l_2 respectively. The translation of the above clause results in clauses of the form:

$$p^-(L, Y) \leftarrow \#r^-([l_2|L], Y). \tag{3}$$
$$r_t^+([l_2|L], Y) \leftarrow \#q^-([l_1|L], Y). \tag{4}$$
$$r_t^+([l_2|L], Y) \leftarrow \#p_s^+(L, Y). \tag{5}$$
$$q_t^+([l_1|L], Y) \leftarrow \#p_s^+(L, Y). \tag{6}$$

in P^* (where the range of the indices t and s in the above clauses can be easily derived from the description of the transformation algorithm). Assume now that $\#p^-(L, b) \in M_{k+1}$ and $p^-(L, b)$ has been introduced in M_{k+1} by using a clause of the form (3) above. Therefore, $\#r^-([l_2|L], b) \in M_k$ (and also in M_{k+1} from lemma 1).

We can now apply the induction hypothesis on r, and we get that:

Since $\#r^-([l_2|L], b) \in M_k$, then there exist constants $c_1, \ldots, c_m$ such that $r(c_1, \ldots, c_m, b) \in T_{P_D} \uparrow \omega$ and $\#r_j^+([l_2|L], c_j) \in M_k$, for $j = 1, \ldots, m$.

Notice now that the only way that $\#r_t^+([l_2|L], c_t)$, for all input argument positions t of r, can have been introduced in M_k, is by using either a clause of the form (4) or a clause of the form (5) above (all other clauses defining r_t^+, have a different head in the list and can not be used). We have two cases:

Subcase 2.1: If $r_t^+([l_2|L], c_t)$, with $t \in S_{r+p^+}$ has been introduced in M_k using clause (5) above then[1] $\#p_s^+(L, c_{f_{p+r+}(s)}) \in M_{k-1}$, for all $s \in S_{p+r+}$, which also means from Lemma 1 that $\#p_s^+(L, c_{f_{p+r+}(s)}) \in M_k$.

---

[1] It can be easily seen that Case 2 of the induction step is only applicable for values of k which are greater than 2.

Subcase 2.2: If $r_t^+([l_2|L], c_t)$, where t is the input position of r which shares its variable with the output position of q in clause (2), has been introduced using clause (4), we conclude that $\#q^-([l_1|L], c_t) \in M_{k-1}$, which also means from Lemma 1 that $\#q^-([l_1|L], c_t) \in M_k$.

Using the induction hypothesis on q, we get that:

Since $\#q^-([l_1|L], c_t) \in M_k$, then there exist constants $a_1, \ldots, a_n$ in U_{P_D} such that $q(a_1, \ldots, a_n, c_t) \in T_{P_D} \uparrow \omega$ and $\#q_j^+([l_1|L], a_j) \in M_k$, for $j = 1, \ldots, n$.

Now, as the set of input arguments of q is the same as the set of input arguments of p (see the condition 2 in the definition of cc-clauses), using clauses of the form (6) above as before we get that $\#p_s^+(L, a_{f_{p+q+}(s)}) \in M_{k-1}$, for all $s \in S_{p+q+}$, which implies from Lemma 1 that $\#p_s^+(L, a_{f_{p+q+}(s)}) \in M_k$.

Therefore, we have that $q(a_1, \ldots, a_n, c_t) \in T_{P_D} \uparrow \omega$ and $r(c_1, \ldots, c_m, b) \in T_{P_D} \uparrow \omega$. In order for these two ground atoms to be combined using clause (2) to obtain an atom for p, we have to make sure that if an a_i and a c_j correspond to input argument positions of q and r which in clause (2) share the same variable, then $a_i = c_j$. But it is easy to see that this is ensured because both values are obtained from the same $\#p_s^+$ (which holds because the choice predicates have a unique value under a given context).

Therefore, $q(a_1, \ldots, a_n, c_t)$ and $r(c_1, \ldots, c_m, b)$ can be combined using clause (2) to give $p(a_1, \ldots, a_n, b) \in T_{P_D} \uparrow \omega$.

Case 3: Assume that in P there exists a clause of the form:

$$p(\ldots) \leftarrow q(\ldots). \tag{7}$$

The proof of this case is similar (and actually simpler) to that for Case 2.

Lemma 6 is a special case of Lemma 5.

Lemma 6. *Let P be a simple cc-Datalog program, D be a database and $\leftarrow p(a_1, \ldots, a_n, Y)$ be a goal clause. Let P^* be the Choice Datalog$_{nS}$ program obtained by applying the transformation algorithm to $P \cup \{\leftarrow p(a_1, \ldots, a_n, Y)\}$. If there exists a limit interpretation M of P_D^* such that $\#p^-([\ ], b) \in M$ then $p(a_1, \ldots, a_n, b) \in T_{P_D} \uparrow \omega$.*

Proof. As $\#p^-([\ ], b) \in M$, from Lemma 5 we have that there are constants $c_1, \ldots, c_n \in U_{P_D}$ such that $p(c_1, \ldots, c_n, b) \in T_{P_D} \uparrow \omega$ and $\#p_i^+([\ ], c_i) \in M$, for $i = 1, \ldots, n$. But as the only instances of $p_i^+([\ ], X)$ in M, are $p_i^+([\ ], a_i)$, we conclude that $c_i = a_i$, for $i = 1, \ldots, n$.

Theorem 2. *Let P be a simple cc-Datalog program, D a database and $\leftarrow p(a_1, \ldots, a_n, Y)$ be a goal clause. Let P^* be the Choice Datalog$_{nS}$ program obtained by applying the transformation algorithm to $P \cup \{\leftarrow p(a_1, \ldots, a_n, Y)\}$. Then there exists a limit interpretation M of P_D^* such that $\#p^-([\ ], b) \in M$ iff $p(a_1, \ldots, a_n, b) \in T_{P_D} \uparrow \omega$.*

Proof. It is an immediate consequence of Lemmas 4 and 6.

On Deforesting Parameters of Accumulating Maps

Kazuhiko Kakehi[1], Robert Glück[2*], and Yoshihiko Futamura[3]

[1] Graduate School of Information Science and Technology, The University of Tokyo
& Institute for Software Production Technology, Waseda University
Tokyo 113-8656, Japan, kaz@ipl.t.u-tokyo.ac.jp
[2] PRESTO, JST & Institute for Software Production Technology
Waseda University, School of Science and Engineering
Tokyo 169-8555, Japan, glueck@acm.org
[3] Institute for Software Production Technology
Waseda University, School of Science and Engineering
Tokyo 169-8555, Japan, futamura@futamura.info.waseda.ac.jp

Abstract. Deforestation is a well-known program transformation technique which eliminates intermediate data structures that are passed between functions. One of its weaknesses is the inability to deforest programs using accumulating parameters.
We show how intermediate lists built by a selected class of functional programs, namely 'accumulating maps', can be deforested using a single composition rule. For this we introduce a new function `dmap`, a symmetric extension of the familiar function `map`. While the associated composition rule cannot capture all deforestation problems, it can handle accumulator fusion of functions defined in terms of `dmap` in a surprisingly simple way. The rule for accumulator fusion presented here can also be viewed as a restricted composition scheme for attribute grammars, which in turn may help us to bridge the gap between the attribute and functional world.

1 Introduction

Deforestation [24] is a well-known program transformation technique which can eliminate intermediate data structures that are passed between functions. *Shortcut deforestation* [9], the most successful variant of deforestation, restricts the optimization to lists that are created with `build` and consumed by `foldr`. This exploits the fact that many list consuming functions are easily expressed in terms of these two higher-order functions. Compared to deforestation, shortcut deforestation has the advantage that a single, local transformation rule suffices to optimize a large class of programs which makes it well suited as compiler optimization (*e.g.*, it is used in the Glasgow Haskell compiler).

One of the weaknesses [2] of such transformations is the inability to deforest programs using accumulating parameters. This is not just a deficiency of these techniques, for other program transformers suffer from the same weakness (*e.g.*,

---

* On leave from DIKU, Dept. of Computer Science, University of Copenhagen.

A. Pettorossi (Ed.): LOPSTR 2001, LNCS 2372, pp. 46–56, 2002.
© Springer-Verlag Berlin Heidelberg 2002

supercompilation [22][1], *calculational methods* [10]). When composing a consumer of lists with a producer of lists, where the producer is written using an accumulating parameter, the intermediate list cannot be removed. For example, the expression `rev (rev xs)` cannot be fused into a single `copy xs` (let alone identity) when `rev` is the fast version of list reversal.

Clearly, this situation is not satisfactory for program composition. While accumulating parameters often let functions be naturally expressed (*e.g.*, `rev`) and generally improve efficiency, they disable deforestation. As it turns out, the problem of accumulator deforestation is harder to solve in an automatic fashion than one might expect.

We show how intermediate lists built by 'accumulating maps' can be deforested using a single composition rule. For this, we introduce a new function `dmap`, a symmetric extension of the familiar function `map`, and study the composition of list producers and consumers defined in terms of `dmap`. Since `dmap` is a generalization of the map function, our transformations cannot solve all deforestation problems shortcut deforestation can (the latter is based on `foldr`). However, we can handle accumulator fusion in a surprisingly simple and easy way (such as the composition of fast reverses), an optimization which shortcut deforestation cannot do. This is due to the restriction to map-style list producers and consumers. In fact, the laws for `dmap` exhibit some interesting combinatorics.

Recently, composition methods using results of *attribute grammars* have been proposed [4,13,14,16] which allow transformations not possible by ordinary deforestation. The problem of accumulator composition studied in this paper is a restricted instance of the more powerful *composition of attribute grammars* (or also *tree transducers* [6]) [5,7,8]. While our class is very limited compared to the general method, it can successfully compose programs with an accumulating parameter, and importantly, *simply*. It also highlights some key features of attribute compositions, in the *functional* world. This in turn may help us to bridge the gap between the functional and the attribute world.

The paper is organized as follows. First we introduce `dmap` and show examples of functions defined using `dmap` (Sect. 2). Then we state the main rule for accumulator fusion and discuss important instances of the rule (Sect. 3), and show several deforestation examples (Sect. 4). After comparing our idea to related works, especially to the theory of attribute grammars (Sect. 5), we conclude with mentioning open problems and limitations (Sect. 6).

Preliminaries. In this paper, we borrow the notation of Haskell to describe programs and transformation rules. The syntax of the language is not defined explicitly in this paper; the transformation rules apply to a function skeleton `dmap`. The semantics can be either call-by-need or call-by-value. An important restriction is that the length of input lists is finite. This will be discussed in Sect. 4.5. We assume that there are no side-effects in the functions used in this paper.

---

[1] The relation between supercompilation and deforestation is discussed in [21].

Definition of dmap

$$\begin{array}{ll}
\text{dmap f g }[\,] & \text{ys} = \text{ys} \\
\text{dmap \# \# }(x : xs) \text{ ys} = \text{ys} \\
\text{dmap \# g }(x : xs) \text{ ys} = & \text{dmap \# g xs }(g\ x : ys) \\
\text{dmap f \# }(x : xs) \text{ ys} = (f\ x) : (\ \text{dmap f \# xs ys }) \\
\text{dmap f g }(x : xs) \text{ ys} = (f\ x) : (\ \text{dmap f g xs }(g\ x : ys)\ )
\end{array}$$

Examples

$$\begin{array}{ll}
\text{copy xs} = \text{dmap id \# xs }[\,] & \text{fba xs} = \text{dmap \# f xs }[\,] \\
\text{rev xs} = \text{dmap \# id xs }[\,] & \text{where f a} = b,\ f\ b = b,\ f\ c = c \\
\text{app xs ys} = \text{dmap id \# xs ys} & \text{fcb xs} = \text{dmap \# g xs }[\,] \\
\text{map f xs} = \text{dmap f \# xs }[\,] & \text{where g a} = a,\ g\ b = c,\ g\ c = c \\
\text{mir xs} = \text{dmap id id xs }[\,]
\end{array}$$

Fig. 1. Definition of dmap and examples

2   Accumulating Map

In order to perform accumulator fusion of map-style functions, we introduce a higher-order function skeleton dmap ('double map') which extends function map in two respects: (1) by an additional function parameter g building the elements of an accumulator; (2) by a list parameter ys that terminates the list constructed by applying f and g to the elements of xs. Informally, dmap is defined by

$$\text{dmap f g }[x_1, ..., x_n]\ [y_1, ..., y_m] = [\underbrace{f\ x_1, ..., f\ x_n}_{\text{apply f}},\ \underbrace{g\ x_n, ..., g\ x_1}_{\text{apply g}},\ \underbrace{y_1, ..., y_m}_{\text{'zero'}}]\ .$$

A definition of dmap is shown in Fig. 1. The application of g to $[x_1, ..., x_n]$ in reverse order is implemented by an accumulating parameter. In addition, we define that the corresponding sublist is dropped from the output if function f or g is not present, for notational convenience expressed by a special symbol # ('null function'). For example, when g is not present, we have the identity:

$$\text{dmap f \# xs }[\,] = \text{map f xs} . \tag{1}$$

Figure 1 shows several familiar list processing functions defined in terms of dmap (*e.g.*, reverse, append, map). Here dmap serves as a primitive for the recursion scheme. Functions rev, mir, fba and fcb are implementations using accumulators. The asymptotic complexity of a function is not changed by defining it in a direct way using dmap.

It should be noted that we use the special symbol # as syntactic sugar and that we assume dmap with # is implemented in a suitable form in order not to

$$\text{dmap f g (dmap h k xs ys) zs}$$
$$= \text{dmap (f.h) (f.k) xs} \tag{3}$$
$$\text{(dmap f g ys}$$
$$\text{(dmap (g.k) (g.h) xs zs))}$$

Fig. 2. Composition of dmap over dmap

reexamine function parameters or produce unused lists. Though all four combinations can be defined separately, use of this notation simplifies the composition rule. This will be demonstrated in Sect. 4.

Remark. From an attribute grammar perspective, we can say that dmap, while performing a recursive descent over the input list xs, computes an *inherited attribute* with g (passed downwards) and a *synthesized attribute* with f (passed upwards). At the end of the recursion, the value of the inherited attribute is passed upwards as the synthesized attribute. We will discuss this connection in more detail in Sect. 5.

3   Fusion of Accumulating Maps

The composition of two functions defined by map is given by the familiar rule

$$\text{map g (map f xs)} = \text{map (g.f) xs} \tag{2}$$

where dot (.) denotes function composition. The expression on the *rhs* avoids the construction of an intermediate list and the composition of the functions f and g may enable further optimizations.

The composition of two functions defined by dmap, which has an accumulating parameter ys, is shown in Fig. 2. It can be justified as follows. Let $xs = [x_1, ..., x_n]$, $ys = [y_1, ..., y_m]$, and $zs = [z_1, ..., z_l]$ $(n, m, l \geq 0)$. Then using the definition of dmap and list properties we have:

$$\text{dmap f g (dmap h k } [x_1, ..., x_n]\ [y_1, ..., y_m])\ [z_1, ..., z_l]$$
$$= \text{dmap f g } [(h\ x_1), ..., (h\ x_n), (k\ x_n), ..., (k\ x_1), y_1, ..., y_m]\ [z_1, ..., z_l]$$
$$= [\,(f.h\ x_1), ..., (f.h\ x_n), (f.k\ x_n), ..., (f.k\ x_1),$$
$$(f\quad y_1), ..., (f\quad y_m), (g\quad y_m), ..., (g\quad y_1),$$
$$(g.k\ x_1), ..., (g.k\ x_n), (g.h\ x_n), ..., (g.h\ x_1), z_1, ..., z_l\,]$$
$$= \text{dmap (f.h) (f.k) } [x_1, ..., x_n]$$
$$\text{(dmap f g } [y_1, ..., y_m]$$
$$\text{(dmap (g.k) (g.h) } [x_1, ..., x_n]\ [z_1, ..., z_l]))$$

The *rhs* of (3) in Fig. 2 has the advantage that it is more efficient than the *lhs* in that it avoids the construction of an intermediate list. The compositions of the function parameters (f.h, f.k, g.h, g.k) may enable further optimizations. Note that the *rhs* applies h and k twice to the input xs which may degrade performance in case these functions are expensive to calculate and their compositions cannot be optimized.

4   Using the Fusion Rule

When composing functions defined by dmap, we will make use of several simplifications of the fusion rule (3) in Fig. 2. An important case is when some of the parameters of dmap are initialized to fixed values, for example, to the empty list ([]) or to the null function (#). We will now discuss the most interesting cases.

1) It is not uncommon that the last parameter of dmap is initialized to the empty list (*e.g.*, see the definitions of copy, rev, map, mir in Fig. 1), and we can immediately simplify the fusion rule:

$$
\begin{aligned}
&\text{dmap f g (dmap h k xs [\,]) zs} \\
&= \text{dmap (f.h) (f.k) xs (dmap (g.k) (g.h) xs zs)} \quad (4)
\end{aligned}
$$

2) Another important simplification occurs when function parameters are initialized to the null function (#). For example, take the case when two of the four function parameters are the null function. Then we obtain the following four fusion rules. They tell us that an entire class of two-pass compositions can be simplified into a single pass. Note that none of the list parameters appears twice on the *rhs*, and that h and k are computed only once for the elements of xs.

$$
\text{dmap f \# (dmap h \# xs ys) zs} = \text{dmap (f.h) \# xs (dmap f \# ys zs)} \quad (5)
$$
$$
\text{dmap f \# (dmap \# k xs ys) zs} = \text{dmap \# (f.k) xs (dmap f \# ys zs)} \quad (6)
$$
$$
\text{dmap \# g (dmap h \# xs ys) zs} = \text{dmap \# g ys (dmap \# (g.h) xs zs)} \quad (7)
$$
$$
\text{dmap \# g (dmap \# k xs ys) zs} = \text{dmap \# g ys (dmap (g.k) \# xs zs)} \quad (8)
$$

3) Both cases may occur at the same time, which drastically simplifies the fusion rule. Take the four equations (5– 8) and let ys = [ ]. Then we obtain four simple fusion rules (after renaming the function parameters):

$$
\text{dmap f \# (dmap g \# xs [\,]) zs} = \text{(dmap (f.g) \# xs zs)} \quad (9)
$$
$$
\text{dmap f \# (dmap \# g xs [\,]) zs} = \text{(dmap \# (f.g) xs zs)} \quad (10)
$$
$$
\text{dmap \# f (dmap g \# xs [\,]) zs} = \text{(dmap \# (f.g) xs zs)} \quad (11)
$$
$$
\text{dmap \# f (dmap \# g xs [\,]) zs} = \text{(dmap (f.g) \# xs zs)} \quad (12)
$$

The reader may have spotted that the well-known composition of map (2) is an instance of (9) where zs = [ ], and recalling equality (1) between map and dmap.

4) Two algebraic properties are handy for further simplifications: (i) The identity function id works as a *unit element* for all functions f: id.f = f.id = f; (ii) the special symbol # is a *zero element* for all functions f: #.f = f.# = # . In fact, we used the last property to obtain rules (5–12).

Using the fusion rule and the simplifications above, we can enjoy several interesting optimizations. We show some of them using the programs defined in Fig. 1. When accumulation is involved, deforestation techniques fail to optimize the programs.

4.1 Example: app over app

This is a classical example of deforestation that composes two app functions. In our framework app is defined as app xs ys = dmap id # xs ys. Rule (5) applies directly:

$$
\begin{aligned}
\text{app (app xs ys) zs} &= \text{dmap id \# (dmap id \# xs ys) zs} \\
&= \text{dmap (id.id) \# xs (dmap id \# ys zs)} \quad — (5) \\
&= \text{dmap id \# xs (dmap id \# ys zs))} \qquad — \textit{simplification}
\end{aligned}
$$

This result can be translated, for readability, to app xs (app ys zs). This example shows that our idea achieves the same transformation as deforestation if functions are defined with dmap.

4.2 Example: rev over rev

This example cannot be fused by ordinary deforestation, but is straightforward with our fusion rule. rev xs is defined as dmap # id xs []. Since rev has an operation only on its accumulator, (12) applies for this composition.

$$
\begin{aligned}
\text{rev (rev xs)} &= \text{dmap \# id (dmap \# id xs []) []} \\
&= \text{dmap (id.id) \# xs []} \qquad\quad — (12) \\
&= \text{dmap id \# xs []} \qquad\qquad\quad — \textit{simplification}
\end{aligned}
$$

We can easily derive the equation rev (rev xs) = copy xs. As in deforestation, the optimized program does not produce an intermediate list.

4.3 Example: mir over mir

This example fused by the powerful attribute grammar method, is also in our scope. mir xs is defined as dmap id id xs []. The original rule (3) is required.

$$
\begin{aligned}
\text{mir (mir xs)} &= \text{dmap id id (dmap id id xs []) []} \\
&= \text{dmap (id.id) (id.id) xs (dmap id id []} \\
&\qquad\qquad \text{(dmap (id.id) (id.id) xs []))} \quad — (3) \\
&= \text{dmap id id xs (dmap id id xs []))} \qquad — \textit{simplification}
\end{aligned}
$$

This can be folded into mir' xs (mir xs), where mir' xs ys = dmap id id xs ys. The intermediate result is eliminated by this composition and runs efficiently.

4.4 More Examples

As previous examples show, the transformation is straightforward. Table 1 summarizes the results of other transformations. They show that our method easily derives rev (mir xs) = mir xs. As for composition of fcb and fba, while the original definitions are iterative and use an accumulator, the resulting definition is recursive. This is a tradeoff of the transformation: while the original program traverses the list twice in an iterative manner, the transformed program traverses the list only once, but does so in a recursive manner.

Table 1. Transformation results

source program	result of composition	note
rev (mir xs)	dmap id id xs []	equal to mir xs
map f (app xs ys)	dmap f # xs (dmap f # ys [])	
map f (rev xs)	dmap # f xs []	equal to rev (map f xs)
dmap f g (rev xs) ys	dmap # f xs (dmap g # xs ys)	
fcb (fba xs)	dmap h # xs [], where h a = c, h b = c, h c = c	

4.5 Termination

All transformation rules preserve the semantics under a call-by-value semantics, and under a lazy semantics if we assume the length of the input lists is finite. When infinite lists are involved under a lazy semantics, the *rhs* of an equation may terminate and deliver a result, while the *lhs* does not.

Table 2 illustrates this for the rules (5–8) where, for simplicity, we assume the function parameters (f, g, h, k) are id. There are two cases in which the outputs differ (marked with '!'). While the *lhs* whose outer dmap has the second function parameter accumulates the result traversing an input lists of infinite length, the *rhs* produces a partial result.

As an example consider the case rev (rev (x : $\perp$)). When rev is defined by dmap where the first function parameter is absent (Fig. 1), fusion rule (12) applies. While the *lhs* of (12) does not return a result, namely $\perp$, the *rhs*, a function equivalent to copy (x : $\perp$), reduces to head-normal form x : $\perp$.

5 Related Work

This section gives a comparison to related works on composing functions.

Table 2. Nested **dmaps** (*lhs*) and their fused version (*rhs*) under lazy evaluation

	input		output		
	xs	ys	*lhs*	*rhs*	Remark
(5)	x1 : ⊥	[y1, y2]	x1 : ⊥	x1 : ⊥	
	[x1, x2]	y1 : ⊥	x1 : x2 : y1 : ⊥	x1 : x2 : y1 : ⊥	
(6)	x1 : ⊥	[y1, y2]	⊥	⊥	
	[x1, x2]	y1 : ⊥	x2 : x1 : y1 : ⊥	x2 : x1 : y1 : ⊥	
(7)	x1 : ⊥	[y1, y2]	⊥	y2 : y1 : ⊥	!
	[x1, x2]	y1 : ⊥	⊥	⊥	
(8)	x1 : ⊥	[y1, y2]	⊥	y2 : y1 : x1 : ⊥	!
	[x1, x2]	y1 : ⊥	⊥	⊥	

5.1   Attribute Grammar Composition

We extended **map** with an accumulating parameter **ys** and a function **g** computing its elements. Function **g** is similar to function **f**, which is also applied to the elements of **xs**, except that **g** computes information flowing downwards to the end of the list, while **f** computes information flowing upwards as the list is traversed. In terms of attribute grammars, we speak of computing *inherited* and *synthesized attributes*, respectively. At first, attribute grammars are very loosely connected to functional programs, but it was already pointed out [11] that they can be seen as special functional programs. In fact, restricted functional programs can be translated into attribute grammars and vice versa.

Moreover, since there are also composition techniques for attribute grammars, we can use these techniques to eliminate intermediate results of functional programs. In [5,7,8] powerful methods for composing attribute grammars are presented. Indeed, function **dmap** represents a class of attributed tree transducers [6] restricted to one inherited and one synthesized attribute, and lists as data structure. The computation of both attributes is 'regular' in the sense that functions **f** and **g** are applied to each element of the input list, and the computation of both attributes is strictly separated. Thus, **dmap** falls into the class of *single-use* attributed tree transducers. The operations on inherited or synthesized attribute can be present or not (expressed by the null function).

The fusion rule presented here captures some of these ideas, but for a selected case. Two attributes of the same kind are fused into a synthesized attribute, and the rest turn into an inherited attribute. The four fusion rules in (9–12) display these properties. The main advantages of our fusion rule are the simplicity of transformation and the elegant elimination of copy rules. Attribute grammars composition is a powerful technique, and it can handle wider range of problems than ordinary deforestation or our techniques do. In order to enjoy this benefit, however, we have first to translate functions into attribute grammars, then compose, and finally translate back again into the functional world. As another drawback, attribute grammars sometimes suffer from copy rules [4] which just pass the information intact to other attributes. With our composition rule, the handling and elimination of copy rules are straightforward.

A related technique [15], based on the composition of attribute grammars but without transforming functions into the attribute world, can also compose functions for which ordinary deforestation fails. It realizes the composition of producers with accumulation and consumers without accumulation. It differs from our idea in that the producer can have more than one accumulating parameter, but this comes at the expense of no accumulating parameter in the consumer.

5.2 Using Abstraction

Another way is to use abstraction of expressions, namely *lambda abstraction* or *continuation*. Lambda abstraction enables a subexpression including an accumulating parameter to be taken out of an expression and it often helps program optimization, like deriving accumulative reverse from naive reverse which uses append, or tupling to avoid multiple traversals over inputs (*e.g.*, [19,25]; the latter also points out the relation of continuation or accumulation to attribute grammars). Lambda abstraction and composition strategy is presented in [18]. However, it does not show how the composition of two nested expressions with lambda abstraction is treated. It seems they will not always be easy to compose. To examine this, let us examine shortcut deforestation.

In shortcut deforestation the function `dmap` can be defined with `foldr` with the help of continuation. For example,

dmap f g xs ys = (foldr (\ a e b → (f a) : e ((g a) : b)) id xs) ys

holds. Through properly abstracting constructors with `build`, function fusion is possible by the `foldr/build` rule (or `foldr/augment` if need be).

This fusion, which replaces occurrences of (abstracted) constructors in the input expression with the parameters of `foldr`, however, does not produce the simple result as `dmap` derives when continuations are involved. The benefit of `dmap` fusion is its simplicity.

6 Conclusion and Future Work

We presented the composition of a selected, restricted class of functional programs using `dmaps`, which enables the deforestation of a certain kind of accumulating parameters. This idea is not only related to the theory of attribute grammars, as explained above, but also to `foldr/build`. Both `foldr/build` and `dmap` share the same advantages compared to unfold/fold-transformation techniques [1]. There is no risk of performing an infinite transformation and there is no need to keep track of previous function calls to perform fold and generalization steps, since a single, local rule is sufficient.

The composition of two `dmap` functions both wins and loses in comparison with `foldr/build`. We win because functions can be deforested by `dmap`-fusion which cannot be optimized by foldr/build (*e.g.*, mir over mir); we lose because not all functions definable as foldr/build can be expressed as dmap. One example is filter. This does not fit into the format of dmap.

It is an open question how to transform programs in a dmap representation automatically. The same problem arise in shortcut deforestation and there are some suggestions [17,3] how to derive the desired representation by foldr and build. The latter automatically realizes function fusion through type inference without explicitly introducing build. This idea does not apply to our framework, however: while foldr and build only matters *where* proper constructors appear, dmap defines *how* constructors are produced.

It is well-known [26] that an optimization can enable certain optimizations, while disabling others. It is a task for future work to determine the order of deforestation-like optimizations as to achieve the best overall optimization effect. Since dmap can be expressed using other, simpler list processing functions, it will be an interesting task to redefine functions in the manner of 'concatenate vanishes' [23,20]. Finally, we note that the laws for dmap can be proven using the standard properties of append, reverse, and map.

We have not yet taken the detailed benchmarks of the composition. We expect better performance by composition in most examples, though there are two possible cases of degradation. The function dmap works under both of eager and lazy evaluation. As the first case of degradation, it is possible that two dmaps only with an accumulative function parameter (*e.g.*, rev) run faster than their composed result in eager evaluation. This is because *dmap* benefits from running as tail recursion. The other case of degradation occurs, as was explained in Sect. 3, when expensive function parameters are copied by dmap composition.

Using dmap, compositions of functions with recursion and accumulating parameters become quite simple and easy to optimize. As is demonstrated in Sect. 5.2, indeed dmap can also be defined in the framework of foldr and build, but they are not fused in a simpler form under shortcut deforestation. We have formalized an idea of function fusion by introducing an accumulating variant of foldr and giving its fusion rule [12]. We hope this will enlarge the applicability of function composition in the presence of accumulating parameters.

Acknowledgments. The authors would like to thank Alberto Pettorossi and the anonymous reviewers for providing many helpful and detailed comments.

References

1. R. Burstall and J. Darlington. A transformation system for developing recursive programs. *J. ACM*, 24(1): 44–67, 1977.
2. W.-N. Chin. Safe fusion of functional expressions II: Further improvements. *J. Funct. Prog.*, 4(4): 515–555, 1994.
3. O. Chitil. Type inference builds a short cut to deforestation. *Proc. of the International Conference on Functional Programming*, 249–260, ACM Press 1999.
4. L. Correnson, E. Duris, D. Parigot, and G. Roussel. Declarative program transformation: A deforestation case-study. In G. Nadathur (ed.), *Principles and Practice of Declarative Programming*, LNCS 1702, 360–377, Springer-Verlag 1999.

5. Z. Fülöp. On attributed tree transducers. *Acta Cybern.*, 5: 261–279, 1981.
6. Z. Fülöp and H. Vogler. *Syntax-directed semantics: Formal models based on tree transducers.* EATCS Monographs Theoret. Comp. Sci., Springer-Verlag 1998.
7. H. Ganzinger. Increasing modularity and language-independency in automatically generated compilers. *Sci. Comput. Prog.*, 3: 223–278, 1983.
8. R. Giegerich. Composition and evaluation of attribute coupled grammars. *Acta Inf.*, 25(4): 355–423, 1988.
9. A. Gill, J. Launchbury, and S. Jones. A short cut to deforestation. In *Proc. Conference on Functional Programming Languages and Computer Architecture*, 223–232, ACM Press 1993.
10. Z. Hu, H. Iwasaki, and M. Takeichi. Calculating accumulations. *New Gener. Comput.*, 17(2): 153–173, 1999.
11. T. Johnsson. Attribute grammars as a functional programming paradigm. In G. Kahn (ed.), *Functional Programming Languages and Computer Architecture*, LNCS 274, 154–173, Springer-Verlag 1987.
12. K. Kakehi, R. Glück, and Y. Futamura. An Extension of Shortcut Deforestation for Accumulative List Folding. *IEICE Trans. on Inf. & Syst.*, to appear.
13. A. Kühnemann. *Berechnungsstärken von Teilklassen primitiv-rekursiver Programmschemata.* Ph.D thesis, Technical University of Dresden, 1997. In German.
14. A. Kühnemann. Benefits of tree transducers for optimizing functional programs. In V. Arvind and R. Pamanujan (eds.), *Foundations of Software Technology and Theoretical Computer Science*, LNCS 1530, 146–157, Springer-Verlag 1998.
15. A. Kühnemann. Comparison of deforestation techniques for functional programs and for tree transducers. In A. Middeldorp and T. Sato (eds.), *Functional and Logic Programming*, LNCS 1722, 114–130, Springer-Verlag 1999.
16. A. Kühnemann, R. Glück, and K. Kakehi. Relating accumulative and non-accumulative functional programs. In A. Middeldorp (ed.), *Rewriting Techniques and Applications*, LNCS 2051, 154–168, Springer-Verlag 2001.
17. J. Launchbury and T. Sheard. Warm fusion: Deriving build-catas from recursive definitions. In *Proc. International Conference on Functional Programming Languages and Computer Architecture*, 314–323, ACM Press 1995.
18. A. Pettorossi. Program development using lambda abstraction. In K. Nori (ed.), *Foundations of Software Technology and Theoretical Computer Science*, LNCS 287, 420–434, Springer-Verlag 1987.
19. A. Pettorossi and A. Skowron. The lambda abstraction strategy for program derivation. *Fund. Inform.*, 12(4): 541–561, 1989.
20. D. Sands. Total correctness by local improvement in the transformation of functional programs. *ACM TOPLAS*, 18(2): 175–234, 1996.
21. M. H. Sørensen, R. Glück, and N. D. Jones. A positive supercompiler. *J. Funct. Prog.*, 6(6): 811–838, 1996.
22. V. Turchin. The concept of a supercompiler. *ACM TOPLAS*, 8(3): 292–325, 1986.
23. P. Wadler. *The concatenate vanishes.* Internal report, Dept. of Comp. Sci., Univ. of Glasgow, 1987.
24. P. Wadler. Deforestation: transforming programs to eliminate trees. *Theoret. Comput. Sci.*, 73(2): 231–248, 1990.
25. M. Wand. Continuation-based program transformation strategies. *J. ACM*, 27(1): 164–180, 1980.
26. D. Whitfield and M. Soffa. An approach for exploring code-improving transformations. *ACM TOPLAS*, 19(6): 1053–1084, 1997.

Equivalence in Answer Set Programming

Mauricio Osorio, Juan A. Navarro, and José Arrazola

Universidad de las Américas, CENTIA
Sta. Catarina Mártir, Cholula, Puebla
72820 México
josorio, ma108907, arrazola@mail.udlap.mx

Abstract. We study the notion of strong equivalence between two Answer Set programs and we show how some particular cases of testing
strong equivalence between programs can be reduced to verify if a formula is a theorem in intuitionistic or classical logic. We present some
program transformations for disjunctive programs, which can be used to
simplify the structure of programs and reduce their size. These transformations are shown to be of interest for both computational and theoretical reasons. Then we propose how to generalize such transformations
to deal with free programs (which allow the use of default negation in
the head of clauses). We also present a linear time transformation that
can reduce an augmented logic program (which allows nested expressions
in both the head and body of clauses) to a program consisting only of
standard disjunctive clauses and constraints.

1 Introduction

Answer Set Programming (ASP), also known as Stable Logic Programming
[12] or A-Prolog, is an important outcome of the theoretical work on Non-
monotonic Reasoning and AI applications of Logic Programming in the last
15 years. The main syntactic restriction needed is to eliminate function symbols from the language, because using infinite domains the answer sets are
no longer necessarily recursively enumerable. There are two popular software
implementations for computing answer sets, DLV and SMODELS, that are
available online at the addresses http://www.dbai.tuwien.ac.at/proj/dlv/ and
http://saturn.hut.fi/pub/smodels/ respectively.

One important issue to determine is when two programs are 'equivalent'.
Two notions of equivalence with respect to ASP are defined in [15]. We define
two programs to be *equivalent* if both have exactly the same answer sets. Two
programs P_1 and P_2 are said to be *strongly equivalent* if, for every program P,
the programs $P_1 \cup P$ and $P_2 \cup P$ are equivalent. Notice, if we are able to determine
that two different codings for some part of a program are strongly equivalent,
then we can safely replace one by the other without changing the declarative
semantics of the program.

Often, in applications of Logic Programming, we are interested in computing
answer sets for several different programs $P_1, P_2, \ldots, P_n$ containing a large common part P. The same conclusions are redundantly calculated each time from

A. Pettorossi (Ed.): LOPSTR 2001, LNCS 2372, pp. 57–75, 2002.

the same rules when computing these answer sets. Examples of such applications are found in answer set planning [7] where the method of finding a plan reduces to compute answer sets for several programs containing the knowledge of an agent and its planning strategy at each instant in time.

Similar algorithms are suggested for diagnostic reasoning from authors in [11,3] where the knowledge of an agent at two consecutive moments of time is represented by logic programs P_n and P_{n+1} that differ from each other only by some rules about the current observations and goals. To determine its next action the agent needs to compute answer sets for P_n and P_{n+1} which, again, share a large common part. The transformations discussed in this paper can be used to simplify and reduce this large common part and optimize then the computation of answer sets for each individual program.

It has been shown that both Jankov and HT logics characterize the class of strongly equivalent augmented logic programs [15,13]. Augmented programs allow nested expressions using conjunction, disjunction and default negation in both the body and head of clauses. Here we present some results that relate strong equivalence of augmented programs with intuitionistic and classical logic. These relations to intuitionistic and classical logic turn out to be very useful because in these last two logics many results are available.

In particular we prove that, given two augmented programs, it is possible to construct in linear time a propositional formula F, of linear size with respect to the programs, such that these two programs are strongly equivalent if and only if F is a theorem in intuitionistic logic. We also show that if a program P can prove, in the sense of classical logic, a negated atom $\neg a$ then we can add this fact to the program preserving strong equivalence. Similarly, for a disjunctive program P, if using only its positive fragment it is possible to obtain an intuitionistic proof for an atom a then we can safely add this fact to the program. In general it is shown that the answer set semantics satisfies negative cumulativity, namely a literal $\neg a$ can be added to a program preserving equivalence if $\neg a$ is true in every answer set of the given program.

It is also interesting to study some program transformations that preserve these equivalence notions. Some basic transformation rules for logic programs were defined in [19] and shown to be of great interest for several theoretical and practical reasons. Theoretical achievements are presented in [10] where a combination of transformation methods with logic programming technology created a powerful framework for investigating the semantics of logic programs. It was proved that most of the popular semantics, including the well-founded semantics WFS, can be defined as confluent transformation systems in a natural way. A polynomial time computable approximation of the answer set semantics for normal programs using this approach is defined in [10]. It has also been proved how program transformations can, in certain cases, transform programs into *tight* ones [17]. Tight programs have the desirable property that a satisfiability solver can be used to efficiently compute answer sets.

We propose and study some other transformations in the context of answer sets. We point out some possible applications as described above and stress the use of such transformations for theoretical purposes. Some popular transformations for normal programs (**RED$^+$**, **RED$^-$**, **SUC**, **Failure**, **Contra**) had been generalized to disjunctive programs and proved to preserve equivalence. We present here a generalization of the **Loop** transformation, defined in [9], and prove that it also preserves equivalence. We also continue and generalize some of these transformations to free programs (which allow default negation in the head of clauses) and prove that they preserve strong equivalence.

We also show a theoretical application of such transformations. They are used, in particular, to prove and construct a linear time computable transformation of free programs (with negation in the head) to disjunctive ones. This simple transformation allows us to compute answer sets for programs up to the augmented type (with nested expressions) using current software implementations, which can deal with disjunctive clauses and constraints only. Of course they also propose a way to implement new software capable to compute answer sets in more general circumstances. We think our results will contribute to a better understanding of the notion of ASP in general propositional theories.

It is a standard procedure in answer set programming to work with finite propositional theories. Variables are removed from programs with predicates by grounding. As Lifschitz noted in [14] "We treat programs as propositional objects; rules with variables are viewed as *schemata* that represent their ground instances." Function symbols are not allowed so that the ground instance of a program is always finite. This is why our attention is mainly restricted to finite propositional theories. However, it is also discussed how some of our results can be applied to programs with predicates before making these programs ground.

Our paper is structured as follows: in Section 2 we present the syntax of disjunctive, general, free and augmented programs, we also include the official definition of answer sets for augmented logic programs. In Section 3 we present the definition of some si-logics and our results for relations between Jankov and Intuitionistic logics. In Section 4 we present an application of our results to ASP. We prove some results on strong equivalence. Some transformations for disjunctive and free programs are discussed. Also reductions of programs to simplify their structure are proposed. In Section 6 we present our conclusions. Finally in Section 7 we give the proofs of our results.

2   Background

A *signature* $\mathcal{L}$ is a finite set of elements that we call *atoms*, or *propositional symbols*. The language of propositional logic has an alphabet consisting of

> proposition symbols: $p_0, p_1, \ldots$
> connectives: $\wedge, \vee, \leftarrow, \perp$ auxiliary symbols: (,).

Where $\wedge$, $\vee$, $\leftarrow$ are 2-place connectives and $\perp$ is a 0-place connective. Formulas are built up as usual in logic. If F is a formula we will refer to its signature $\mathcal{L}_F$ as the set of atoms that occur in F. The formula $\neg F$ is introduced as an abbreviation for $\perp \leftarrow F$ (default negation), and $F \equiv G$ as an abbreviation for

$(F \leftarrow G) \wedge (G \leftarrow F)$, also $\top$ abbreviates $\neg\bot$. Observe that $\top$ can be equivalently defined as $a \leftarrow a$ where a is any atom. A *literal* is either an atom a, or the negation of an atom $\neg a$. The *complement* of a literal is defined as $(a)^c = \neg a$ and $(\neg a)^c = a$, analogously given $\mathcal{M}$ a set of literals $\mathcal{M}^c = \{(a)^c \mid a \in \mathcal{M}\}$.

Given a set of formulas $\mathcal{F}$, we define the set $\neg\mathcal{F} = \{\neg F \mid F \in \mathcal{F}\}$. Also, for a finite set of formulas $\mathcal{F} = \{F_1, \ldots, F_n\}$, we define $\bigwedge \mathcal{F} = F_1 \wedge \cdots \wedge F_n$ and $\bigvee \mathcal{F} = F_1 \vee \cdots \vee F_n$. If $\mathcal{F} = \emptyset$ then we define $\bigwedge \mathcal{F} = \top$ and $\bigvee \mathcal{F} = \bot$.

When a formula is constructed as a conjunction (or disjunction) of literals, $F = \bigwedge \ell$ (or $F = \bigvee \ell$) with ℓ a set of literals, we denote by $Lit(F)$ such set of literals ℓ. *Elementary formulas* are atoms and the connectives $\bot$ and $\top$ [22], and an $\wedge\vee\neg$ formula is a formula constructed by using (only) the logical connectives $\{\wedge, \vee, \neg\}$ arbitrarily nested. For instance $\neg(a \wedge b) \vee (\neg c \wedge (p \vee \neg q))$ is an $\wedge\vee\neg$ formula.

A *clause* is a formula of the form $H \leftarrow B$ where H and B, arbitrary formulas in principle, are known as the *head* and *body* of the clause respectively. If $H = \bot$ the clause is called a *constraint* and may be written as $\leftarrow B$. When $B = \top$ the clause is known as a *fact* and can be noted just by H.

An *augmented* clause is a clause where H and B are any $\wedge\vee\neg$ formulas. A *basic formula* is either $\top$ or an $\wedge\vee\neg$ formula, which does not contain the negation as failure operator ($\neg$). Note that a broader form of this type of clauses is considered in [22] where they also include two kinds of negation as well as implications in the body. We only include one kind of negation that corresponds to their default negation, however they use the symbol *not* for our negation $\neg$.

A *free* clause is a clause of the form $\bigvee(\mathcal{H}^+ \cup \neg\mathcal{H}^-) \leftarrow \bigwedge(\mathcal{B}^+ \cup \neg\mathcal{B}^-)$ where $\mathcal{H}^+, \mathcal{H}^-, \mathcal{B}^+, \mathcal{B}^-$ are, possibly empty, sets of atoms. Sometimes such clause might be written as $\mathcal{H}^+ \vee \neg\mathcal{H}^- \leftarrow \mathcal{B}^+, \neg\mathcal{B}^-$ following typical conventions for logic programs. When $\mathcal{H}^- = \emptyset$, there is no negation in the head, the clause is called a *general* clause. If, moreover, $\mathcal{H}^+ \neq \emptyset$ (i.e. it is not a constraint) the clause is called a *disjunctive* clause. When the set $\mathcal{H}^+$ contains exactly one element the clause is called *normal*.

Finally, a *program* is a finite set of clauses. If all the clauses in a program are of a certain type we say the program is also of this type. For instance a set of augmented clauses is an *augmented program*, a set of free clauses is a *free program* and so on.

For general programs, and proper subclasses, we will use $HEAD(P)$ to denote the set of all atoms occurring in the head of clauses in P.

2.1   Answer Sets

We now define the background for *answer sets*, also known as *stable models*. This material is taken from [22] with minor modifications since we do not consider their classical negation.

Definition 2.1. *[22] We define when a set X of atoms satisfies a basic formula F, denoted by $X \models F$, recursively as follows:*

for elementary F, $X \models F$ if $F \in X$ or $F = \top$.

$X \models F \wedge G$ if $X \models F$ and $X \models G$.
$X \models F \vee G$ if $X \models F$ or $X \models G$.

Definition 2.2. *[22] Let P be a basic program. A set of atoms X is* closed under *P if, for every clause $H \leftarrow B$ in P, $X \models H$ whenever $X \models B$.*

Definition 2.3. *[22] Let X be a set of atoms and P a basic program. X is called an* answer set *for P if X is minimal among the sets of atoms closed under P.*

Definition 2.4. *[22] The* reduct *of an augmented formula or program, relative to a set of atoms X, is defined recursively as follows:*

for elementary F, $F^X = F$.
$(F \wedge G)^X = F^X \wedge G^X$.
$(F \vee G)^X = F^X \vee G^X$.
$(\neg F)^X = \bot$ *if* $X \models F^X$ *and* $(\neg F)^X = \top$ *otherwise.*
$(H \leftarrow B)^X = H^X \leftarrow B^X$.
$P^X = \{(H \leftarrow B)^X \mid H \leftarrow B \in P\}$

Definition 2.5 (Answer set). *[22] Let P be an augmented program and X a set of atoms. X is called an* answer set *for P if it is an answer set for the reduct P^X.*

As can be seen, answer sets are defined for propositional logic programs only. However this definition can be extended to *predicate programs*, which allow the use of predicate symbols in the language, but without function symbols to ensure the ground instance of the program to be finite. So a *term* can only be either a variable or a constant symbol.

A *substitution* is a mapping from a set of variables to a set of terms. The symbol θ is used to denote a substitution. The application of a substitution θ over an atom p will be denoted as $p\theta$. For more formal definitions and discussions related to substitutions we refer to [16]. Suppose for example we have a substitution θ where $\theta := [X/a, Y/b, Z/a]$. Then $p(X, Y, Z, c)\theta$ is the ground instance $p(a, b, a, c)$.

The ground instance of a predicate program, $Ground(P)$, is defined in [14] as the program containing all ground instances of clauses in P. Then M is defined as an answer set of a predicate program P if it is an answer set for $Ground(P)$.

We want to stress the fact that the general approach for calculating answer sets of logical programs is to work with their ground instances. However we will see that some of our proposed transformations can be applied to programs before grounding, so that less computational effort might be required.

3   Results on Logic

A si-logic is any logic stronger (or equal) than intuitionistic (I) and weaker than classical logic (C). For an axiomatic theory, like I, we also use its name to denote the set of axioms that define it. Jankov Logic (Jn) is the si-logic

$Jn = I \cup \{\neg p \vee \neg\neg p\}$, where the axiom schema $\neg p \vee \neg\neg p$ characterizing it is also called *weak law of excluded middle*. The HT logic (or G_3) can be defined as the multivalued logic of three values as defined by Gödel, or axiomatically as $I \cup \{(\neg q \rightarrow p) \rightarrow (((p \rightarrow q) \rightarrow p) \rightarrow p)\}$.

We write $\vdash_X$ to denote the provability relation in a logic X. Two formulas F and G are said to be equivalent under a given logic X if $\vdash_X F \equiv G$, also denoted as $F \equiv_X G$.

We present now several results on intuitionistic and Jankov logics, which will be used later to prove and construct other properties and transformations related to Answer Set Programming. However notice that the following results and definitions in this section are not restricted to the syntax of clauses or logical programs. Formulas are as general as they can be built typically in logic.

Lemma 3.1. *Let T be any theory, and let F, G be a pair of equivalent formulas under any si-logic X. Any theory obtained from T by replacing some occurrences of F by G is equivalent to T (under X).*

Definition 3.1. *The set $\mathbf{P}$ of positive formulas is the smallest set containing all formulas that do not contain the $\bot$ connective.*

The set $\mathbf{N}$ of two-negated formulas is the smallest set $\mathbf{X}$ with the properties:

1. *If a is an atom then $(\neg\neg a) \in \mathbf{X}$.*
2. *If $A \in \mathbf{X}$ then $(\neg\neg A) \in \mathbf{X}$.*
3. *If $A, B \in \mathbf{X}$ then $(A \wedge B) \in \mathbf{X}$.*
4. *If $A \in \mathbf{X}$ and B is any formula then $(A \vee B), (B \vee A), (A \leftarrow B) \in \mathbf{X}$.*

For a given set of formulas Γ, the positive subset of Γ, denoted as $\mathrm{Pos}(\Gamma)$, is the set $\Gamma \cap \mathbf{P}$.

Proposition 3.1. *Let Γ be a subset of $\mathbf{P} \cup \mathbf{N}$, and let $A \in \mathbf{P}$ be a positive formula. If $\Gamma \vdash_I A$ iff $\mathrm{Pos}(\Gamma) \vdash_I A$.*

Proposition 3.2. *Let $a_1, \ldots, a_n$ be all the atoms occurring in a formula A. Then $\vdash_{Jn} A$ iff $(\neg a_1 \vee \neg\neg a_1), \ldots, (\neg a_n \vee \neg\neg a_n) \vdash_I A$.*

Lemma 3.2. *Let A be a positive formula and Γ be a subset of $\mathbf{P} \cup \mathbf{N}$. $\Gamma \vdash_{Jn} A$ iff $\mathrm{Pos}(\Gamma) \vdash_I A$.*

4   Applications to ASP

In this section we return to the context of Answer Set Programming. So far we can define several types of equivalence between programs. For example, two logic programs P_1 and P_2 are said to be equivalent under stable, denoted $P_1 \equiv_{\mathrm{stable}} P_2$, if they have the same answer sets. Similarly P_1 and P_2 are equivalent under logic X if the formula $\vdash_X \bigwedge P_1 \equiv \bigwedge P_2$ is provable.

Another useful definition of equivalence, known as strong equivalence, can be defined in terms of any equivalence relation for logic programs.

Definition 4.1 (Strong equivalence). *Two programs P_1 and P_2 are said to be* strongly equivalent *(under X) if for every program P, $P_1 \cup P$ and $P_2 \cup P$ are equivalent (under X).*

This definition is given in [15] in the context of stable semantics where it is found to be particularly useful. The main purpose of our paper is now to stand some relations between these different types of equivalence.

In general, it is clear that strong equivalence implies equivalence. But the converse is not always true.

Example 4.1. Consider the programs $P_1 = \{a \leftarrow \neg b\}$ and $P_2 = \{a\}$. They are equivalent in stable because $\{a\}$ is the unique stable model for both programs. However $P_1 \cup \{b \leftarrow a\}$ has no stable models, while $P_2 \cup \{b \leftarrow a\}$ has $\{a, b\}$ as a stable model.

One first important connection of Answer Set Programming with Logic is given in the following theorem.

Theorem 4.1 ([15]). *Let P_1 and P_2 be two augmented programs. Then P_1 and P_2 are strongly equivalent under stable iff P_1 and P_2 are equivalent under G_3 logic.*

In [13] a different version of this theorem is proved using Jankov Logic instead of the G_3 logic.

Theorem 4.2 ([13]). *Let P_1 and P_2 be two augmented programs. Then P_1 and P_2 are strongly equivalent under stable iff P_1 and P_2 are equivalent in Jankov logic.*

Using the machinery of logic and results from previous section we can propose alternative ways of testing whether two programs are strong equivalent, and some simple transformations that preserve strong equivalence.

Lemma 4.1. *Let P_1 and P_2 be two augmented programs, and let $\{a_1, \dots, a_n\}$ be the atoms in $\mathcal{L}_{P_1 \cup P_2}$. Then the programs P_1 and P_2 are strongly equivalent iff $(\neg a_1 \vee \neg \neg a_1), \dots, (\neg a_n \vee \neg \neg a_n) \vdash_I \bigwedge P_1 \equiv \bigwedge P_2$.*

Consider the following program P_1 that shows that intuitionistic logic cannot be used in theorem 4.2 (the program, as well as the observation, was given in [15]).

$P_1:$ $q \leftarrow \neg p.$
       $p \leftarrow \neg q.$
       $r \leftarrow p \wedge q.$
       $s \leftarrow p.$
       $s \leftarrow q.$

Let P_2 be $P_1 \cup \{s \leftarrow \neg r\}$. We can show, by Theorem 4.2, that they are strongly equivalent by showing that they are equivalent in Jankov logic. Note that by using our lemma 4.1 we can use intuitionistic logic to get the desired result.

Furthermore, it is possible to use an automatic theorem prover, like *porgi* implemented in standard ML and available at http://cis.ksu.edu/~allen/porgi.html, to help us to solve our task.

We can also use lemma 3.2 to reduce a proof of strong equivalence to a proof in intuitionistic logic without having to add the extra assumptions $(\neg a_i \vee \neg\neg a_i)$. Of course, we need the hypothesis of the lemma to hold. An interesting case is the following.

Lemma 4.2. *Let P be a disjunctive program and a an atom. P is strongly equivalent to $P \cup \{a\}$ iff $Pos(P) \vdash_I a$.*

Lemma 4.3. *Given an augmented program P and a negated atom $\neg a$, then P is strongly equivalent to $P \cup \{\neg a\}$ iff $P \vdash_C \neg a$*

The above two lemmas allow us to add known or provable facts to programs in order to simplify them and make easier the computation of answer sets.

Lemma 4.4 (Negative Cumulativity). *Stable satisfies negative cumulativity, namely: for every atom a, if $\neg a$ is true in every stable model of P, then P and $(P \cup \{\neg a\})$ have identical stable models.*

5   Program Transformations

In this section we will study some transformations that can be applied to logic programs. We verify some properties and applications, and stress the use of such transformations for theoretical reasons. We show how they can be used to define semantics and impose desirable properties to them.

5.1   Disjunctive Programs

We will first discuss some transformations defined for disjunctive programs. Given a clause $C = \mathcal{A} \leftarrow \mathcal{B}^+, \neg\mathcal{B}^-$, we write *dis-nor(C)* to denote the set of normal clauses $\{a \leftarrow \mathcal{B}^+, \neg(\mathcal{B}^- \cup (\mathcal{A} \setminus \{a\})) \mid a \in \mathcal{A}\}$. This definition is extended to programs as usual, applying the transformation to each clause.

For a normal program P, we write *Definite(P)* to denote the definite program obtained from P removing every negative literal in P. For a disjunctive program, *Definite(P) = Definite(dis-nor(P))*. And given a definite program P, by $MM(P)$ we mean the unique minimal model of P (which always exists for definite programs, see [16]).

The following transformations are defined in [4] for disjunctive programs.

Definition 5.1 (Basic Transformation Rules). *A transformation rule is a binary relation on the set of all programs defined within the signature $\mathcal{L}$. The following transformation rules are called* basic. *Let a disjunctive program P be given.*

RED⁺: *Replace a rule $\mathcal{A} \leftarrow \mathcal{B}^+, \neg\mathcal{B}^-$ by $\mathcal{A} \leftarrow \mathcal{B}^+, \neg(\mathcal{B}^- \cap HEAD(P))$.*

RED⁻: *Delete a clause* $\mathcal{A} \leftarrow \mathcal{B}^+, \neg \mathcal{B}^-$ *if there is a clause* $\mathcal{A}' \leftarrow \top$ *in P such that* $\mathcal{A}' \subseteq \mathcal{B}^-$.

SUB: *Delete a clause* $\mathcal{A} \leftarrow \mathcal{B}^+, \neg \mathcal{B}^-$ *if there is another clause* $\mathcal{A}' \leftarrow \mathcal{B}'^+, \neg \mathcal{B}'^-$ *such that* $\mathcal{A}' \subseteq \mathcal{A}$, $\mathcal{B}'^+ \subseteq \mathcal{B}^+$ *and* $\mathcal{B}'^- \subseteq \mathcal{B}^-$.

Example 5.1. Let P be the program:

$$P: \quad a \vee b \leftarrow c \wedge \neg c \wedge \neg d.$$
$$a \vee c \leftarrow b.$$
$$c \vee d \leftarrow \neg e.$$
$$b \leftarrow \neg c \wedge \neg d \wedge \neg e.$$

then $HEAD(P) = \{a, b, c, d\}$ and we can apply **RED⁺** on the 4th clause to get the program

$$P_1: \quad a \vee b \leftarrow c \wedge \neg c \wedge \neg d.$$
$$a \vee c \leftarrow b.$$
$$c \vee d \leftarrow \top.$$
$$b \leftarrow \neg c \wedge \neg d \wedge \neg e.$$

If we apply **RED⁺** again we will obtain

$$P_2: \quad a \vee b \leftarrow c \wedge \neg c \wedge \neg d.$$
$$a \vee c \leftarrow b.$$
$$c \vee d \leftarrow \top.$$
$$b \leftarrow \neg c \wedge \neg d.$$

And now we can apply **SUB** to get the program

$$P_3: \quad a \vee c \leftarrow b.$$
$$c \vee d \leftarrow \top.$$
$$b \leftarrow \neg c \wedge \neg d.$$

Finally we can remove the third clause using **RED⁻**

$$P_4: \quad a \vee c \leftarrow b.$$
$$c \vee d \leftarrow \top.$$

We observe that the transformations just mentioned above are among the minimal requirements a *well-behaved* semantics should have (see [8]). The following are two other transformations as defined in [4].

GPPE$_a$: *(Generalized Principle of Partial Evaluation)* If P contains a clause $\mathcal{A} \leftarrow \mathcal{B}^+, \neg \mathcal{B}^-$, $\mathcal{B}^+ \neq \emptyset$, and B^+ contain a distinguished atom a, where $a \notin (\mathcal{A} \cap \mathcal{B}^+)$, replace such clause by the following n clauses ($i = 1, \ldots, n$):

$$\mathcal{A} \cup (\mathcal{A}_i \setminus \{a\}) \leftarrow (\mathcal{B}^+ \setminus \{a\}) \cup \mathcal{B}_i{}^+, \neg(\mathcal{B}^- \cup \mathcal{B}_i{}^-),$$

where $\mathcal{A}_i \leftarrow \mathcal{B}_i{}^+, \neg \mathcal{B}_i{}^-$ are all clauses with $a \in \mathcal{A}_i$. If no such clauses exist, we simply delete the former clause. If the transformation cannot be applied then GPPE$_a$ behaves as the identity function over $\mathcal{A} \leftarrow \mathcal{B}^+, \neg \mathcal{B}^-$.

TAUT$_a$: *(Tautology)* If there is a clause $\mathcal{A} \leftarrow \mathcal{B}^+, \neg\mathcal{B}^-$ such that $\mathcal{A} \cap \mathcal{B}^+ \neq \emptyset$ and $\mathcal{A} \cap \mathcal{B}^+$ contain a distinguished atom a then remove such clause. If the transformation cannot be applied then TAUT$_a$ behaves as the identity function over $\mathcal{A} \leftarrow \mathcal{B}^+, \neg\mathcal{B}^-$.

The rewriting system that contains, besides the basic transformation rules, the rules **GPPE** and **TAUT** is introduced in [4] and denoted as $\mathcal{CS}_1$. This system is also used in [5] to define a semantic known as the disjunctive well-founded semantics or D-WFS.

However, the computational properties of the $\mathcal{CS}_1$ system are not very good. In fact, computing the normal form of a program is exponential, whereas it is known that the WFS can be computed in quadratic time. Some other transformations need to be defined in order to solve this computational problem.

Definition 5.2 (Dsuc). *If P contains the clause $a \leftarrow \top$ and there is also a clause $\mathcal{A} \leftarrow \mathcal{B}^+, \neg\mathcal{B}^-$ such that $a \in \mathcal{B}^+$, then replace it by $\mathcal{A} \leftarrow (\mathcal{B}^+ \setminus \{a\}), \neg\mathcal{B}^-$.*

It is not hard to verify that the transformations **RED$^-$, DSuc, TAUT** and **SUB** preserve strong equivalence, while **RED$^+$** and **GPPE** preserve equivalence only.

The transformation **Dloop** is defined in [9] with the purpose of generalizing the useful **Loop** transformation [6]. Recall that the well-founded model computation of SMODELS can be considered as an efficient implementation of a specific strategy where the use of **Dloop** is essential [6]. The authors in [17] claimed that **Dloop** preserves equivalence under stable, but they only provided a vague hint for the proof. We formally prove that indeed **DLoop** preserves equivalence. Our proof follows the spirit of the proof of this proposition in the case of normal programs [6], but more technical difficulties are now involved.

Definition 5.3 (Dloop). *Let $unf(P) = \mathcal{L}_P \setminus MM(Definite(P))$. Then we define* $\mathbf{Dloop}(P) = \{\mathcal{A} \leftarrow \mathcal{B}^+, \neg\mathcal{B}^- \in P \mid \mathcal{B}^+ \cap unf(P) = \emptyset\}.$

Proposition 5.1. *Let P be a disjunctive program. If $a \in unf(P)$ is an atom and P_1 is obtained from P by an application of **TAUT$_a$**, then $unf(P) = unf(P_1)$ and $\mathbf{Dloop}(P) = \mathbf{Dloop}(P_1)$.*

Let **TAUT$_a^+$** denote the transitive closure of **TAUT$_a$**. Thus, **TAUT$_a^+$**(P) is the program obtained by the application 'as long as possible' of the transformation **TAUT$_a$** to P. The next corollary follows immediately.

Corollary 5.1. *Let P be a program. If $a \in unf(P)$ and $P_1 = \mathbf{TAUT}_a^+(P)$ then $unf(P) = unf(P_1)$ and $\mathbf{Dloop}(P) = \mathbf{Dloop}(P_1)$.*

Similarly we will now prove that, if the program does not contain any more tautologies with respect to a, then *unf* and **Dloop** does not change after a single application of **GPPE$_a$**. This result will also extend immediately for **GPPE$_a^+$** which is the transitive closure of **GPPE$_a$**.

Proposition 5.2. *Let P be a disjunctive program such that $P = \mathbf{TAUT}_a^+(P)$. If $a \in unf(P)$ and P_1 is obtained from P by an application of $\mathbf{GPPE}_a$, then $unf(P) = unf(P_1)$ and $\mathbf{Dloop}(P) = \mathbf{Dloop}(P_1)$.*

Corollary 5.2. *Let P be a disjunctive program such that $P = \mathbf{TAUT}_a^+(P)$. If $a \in unf(P)$ let $P_1 = \mathbf{GPPE}_a^+(P)$, then $unf(P) = unf(P_1)$ and $\mathbf{Dloop}(P) = \mathbf{Dloop}(P_1)$.*

Theorem 5.1 (Dloop preserve stable). *Let P_1 be a disjunctive program. If $P_2 = \mathbf{Dloop}(P_1)$ then P_1 and P_2 are equivalent under the stable semantics.*

If we consider $\mathcal{CS}_2$ as the rewriting system based on the transformations $\mathbf{SUB}, \mathbf{RED}^+, \mathbf{RED}^-, \mathbf{Dloop}, \mathbf{Dsuc}$ as defined in [1], it is possible to define a semantic called D1-WFS [18].

Consider again example 5.1. As we noticed before program P reduces to P_4. Observe $unf(P_4) = \{a, b\}$, and by an application of **Dloop** we can obtain P_5, which contains the single clause: $c \lor d \leftarrow \top$.

For normal programs both systems D-WFS and D1-WFS are equivalent since they define WFS. However the residual programs w.r.t $\mathcal{CS}_1$ and $\mathcal{CS}_2$ are not necessarily the same, and for disjunctive programs they may give different answers. An advantage of $\mathcal{CS}_2$ over $\mathcal{CS}_1$ is that residual programs are polynomial-time computable, as it can be easy seen by the definition of the tranformations.

We will show also how to generalize the **Dloop** transformation to work with predicate programs. The definitions of $MM(P)$ and $Definite(P)$ are generalized for predicate programs applying corresponding definitions to the ground instance of P. Recall that θ denotes a substitution of variables over terms.

Definition 5.4 (Predicate Dloop). *Let P be a disjunctive predicate program, and let $\mathcal{L}$ be the language of $Ground(P)$. We define:*

$unf(P) = \mathcal{L} \setminus MM(Definite(P))$.
$P_1 = \{\mathcal{A} \leftarrow \mathcal{B}^+, \neg \mathcal{B}^- \in P \mid \forall \theta, \forall p \in unf(P), \forall b \in \mathcal{B}^+ \text{ we have } b\theta \neq p\}$.
$P_2 = \{\mathcal{A} \leftarrow \mathcal{B}^+, \neg \mathcal{B}^- \in Ground(P) \setminus Ground(P_1) \mid \mathcal{B}^+ \cap unf(P) = \emptyset\}$.

*The transformation **Dloop** reduces a program P to $\mathbf{Dloop}(P) := P_1 \cup P_2$.*

Theorem 5.2 (Dloop preserves stable). *Let P and P' be two disjunctive predicate programs. If P' is obtained of P by an application of **Dloop** then P and P' are equivalent under stable.*

Example 5.2. We illustrate a Dloop reduction for a disjunctive predicate program P:

$$m(b).$$
$$h(a).$$
$$p(X) \lor q(X) \leftarrow f(X). \qquad\qquad m(b).$$
$$f(X) \leftarrow q(X). \qquad\qquad h(a).$$
$$r(X) \leftarrow k(X) \land \neg p(X). \quad\Longrightarrow\quad r(X) \leftarrow k(X) \land \neg p(X).$$
$$k(X) \leftarrow m(X). \qquad\qquad k(b) \leftarrow m(b).$$
$$k(X) \leftarrow h(X). \qquad\qquad k(a) \leftarrow h(a).$$
$$w(X) \leftarrow m(X). \qquad\qquad w(b) \leftarrow m(b).$$

Also observe that $unf(P) = \{m(a), h(b), p(a), p(b), q(a), q(b), f(a), f(b), w(a)\}$.

5.2   Free Programs

Now we propose a set of Basic Transformation Rules for free programs, which defines a rewriting system that we will call $CS++$. These transformations are generalizations of notions already given for disjunctive programs.

Definition 5.5. *A transformation rule is a binary relation on free programs over $\mathcal{L}$. The following transformation rules are called basic. Let P be a program.*

(a) *Delete a clause $H \leftarrow B$ if there is another clause $H' \leftarrow \top$ in P such that $(Lit(H'))^c \subset Lit(B)$.*

(b) *Delete a clause $H \leftarrow B$ if there is another clause $H' \leftarrow B'$ in P such that $Lit(H') \subseteq Lit(H)$ and $Lit(B') \subseteq Lit(B)$.*

(c) *If there is a clause of the form $l \leftarrow \top$ where l is a literal, then in all clauses of the form $H \leftarrow B$ such that $l \in Lit(B)$ delete l from B.*

(d) *If there is a clause of the form $l \leftarrow \top$ where l is a literal, then in all clauses of the form $H \leftarrow B$ such that $l^c \in Lit(H)$ delete l^c from H.*

(e) *Delete a clause $H \leftarrow B$ if it is a simple theorem in Jn. By definition, $H \leftarrow B$ is a simple Jn theorem only if: $Lit(H) \cap Lit(B) \neq \emptyset$ or $Lit(B)$ is inconsistent (it contains both b and $\neg b$ for some atom b).*

Lemma 5.1 ($CS++$ is closed under Jn Logic). *Let P_1 and P_2 be two programs related by any transformation in $CS++$. Then $P_1 \equiv_{Jn} P_2$.*

It has been found that $CS++$ is very useful in ASP. The transformations proposed for this rewriting system can be applied without much computational effort. They are also generalizations of transformations given for normal programs. In the case of normal programs $CS++$, without reducing inconsistency in the body as a theorem and plus two more transformations (**Loop** and **Failure**), is strong enough to compute the WFS semantics efficiently, see [6]. In many useful cases the stable semantics has only one model that corresponds to the WFS semantics. Moreover, sometimes these transformations can transform a program to a tight one [17]. For tight programs the stable semantics corresponds to the supported semantics. Recent research [2] has shown that, in this case, a satisfiability solver (e.g. SATO [24]) can be used to obtain stable models. Interestingly, some examples are presented in [2] where the running time of SATO is approximately ten times faster than SMODELS, one of the leading stable model finding systems [21].

Example 5.3. Consider the following example that illustrates some reductions obtained applying $CS++$ transformations to a program:

$$
\begin{array}{l}
\neg a \vee b \leftarrow c \wedge d \\
\neg a \leftarrow c \wedge t \\
\neg k \vee p \leftarrow p \wedge q \\
t \leftarrow \top
\end{array}
\qquad \Longrightarrow \qquad
\begin{array}{l}
\neg a \leftarrow c \\
t \leftarrow \top
\end{array}
$$

5.3 Transformations

Finally we would like to present some other transformations that can be used to simplify the structure of programs. The concept of an answer set for a program has been generalized to work with augmented programs, however current popular software implementations do not support more than disjunctive programs. These transformations will allow us to compute answer sets for programs with more complicated logical constructions.

Lifschitz, Tang and Turner offered [22] a generalization of stable semantics for augmented programs. They also showed that it is possible to transform an augmented program into a free one without altering the resulting stable models.

Theorem 5.3 ([22]). *Any augmented program is strongly equivalent under stable to a free program.*

Inoue and Sakama showed [20] that every free program P can be transformed into disjunctive one P' such that P' is a conservative extension of P. We say that P' is a *conservative extension* of P to denote the fact that M is a stable model of P iff M' is a stable model of P' such that $M = M' \cap \mathcal{L}_P$. However their transformation is very expensive and involves a cubic increase in the size of programs.

We show this same goal can be achieved with a linear time computable transformation whose increase of program's size is also linear.

Lemma 5.2. *Let P be a free program. For a given set $S \subseteq \mathcal{L}_P$ let $\varphi \colon S \to \Sigma$ be a bijective function, where Σ is a set of atoms such that $\Sigma \cap \mathcal{L}_P = \emptyset$. Let $\Delta_S = \bigcup_{a \in S} \{\varphi(a) \leftarrow \neg a., \bot \leftarrow a \wedge \varphi(a).\}$. Then $P \cup \Delta_S$ is a conservative extension of P.*

If we take S as the set of atoms appearing negated in the head of clauses in P, lemma 5.2 can allow us to eliminate such negations building a general program. Formally:

Theorem 5.4. *Let P be a free program and let S be the set containing all atoms a such that $\neg a$ appears in the head of some clause in P. Let φ and Δ_S be defined as in lemma 5.2. Let P' be the general program obtained from P by replacing each occurrence of $\neg a$ with $\varphi(a)$ for all $a \in S$. Then $P' \cup \Delta_S$ is a general program that is a conservative transformation of P. In particular M is stable model of P iff M_S is a stable model of $P' \cup \Delta_S$, where $M_S = M \cup \varphi(S \setminus M)$.*

It is well known that a general program P is equivalent to a disjunctive program under a simple translation. Namely, replace every constraint clause $\bot \leftarrow A$ by $p \leftarrow A \wedge \neg p$, where p is an atom not in $\mathcal{L}_P$.

Notice that Theorem 5.3 together with Theorem 5.4 stand an equivalence between programs that shows augmented programs are not more expressive than disjunctive ones with respect to the stable semantics.

This transformation can be applied also to logical programs with predicates before grounding.

Theorem 5.5. *Let P be a free predicate program. Obtain P' by replacing every literal $\neg p(X_1, \ldots, X_n)$ appearing in the head of some clause in the program with the atom $notp(X_1, \ldots, X_n)$, where notp is a new predicate symbol. Also add the clauses $notp(X_1, \ldots, X_n) \leftarrow \neg p(X_1, \ldots, X_n)$, $\bot \leftarrow p(X_1, \ldots, X_n) \wedge notp(X_1, \ldots, X_n)$. The program P' is a conservative extension of P.*

6   Conclusions

No much research has been done on answer set programming for free or augmented programs. Interesting new connections between logic and logic programming are beginning to arise. It is important to obtain and generalize results that can be used for designing software to help the programmer write correct programs and compute answer sets for free or augmented programs. Our paper provides initial results on this direction.

We presented several results that relate provability in Jankov logic to provability in Intuitionistic logic. Based on our results we proposed several ideas that can help to decide if two theories are strongly equivalent. Some transformations for disjunctive and free programs are studied and we have shown that they preserve equivalence. We also presented a simple transformation from free programs to disjunctive ones that preserves the stable semantics. Our results are given for propositional theories, but it is shown how some of them can be generalized to be applied to programs with predicates. Another problem, left for future research, will be to generalize other transformations, such as **Loop**, to free programs.

Acknowledgements. The authors thank Michael Gelfond for suggesting that our results could be applied on answer set planning and diagnostic reasoning. This research is sponsored by the Mexican National Council of Science and Technology, CONACyT (project 35804-A).

References

1. J. Arrazola, J. Dix and M. Osorio. Confluent term rewriting systems for non-monotonic reasoning. *Computación y Sistemas*, II(2-3):299–324, 1999.
2. Y. Babovich, E. Erdem, and V. Lifschitz. Fages' theorem and answer set programming. In *Proceedings of the 8th International Workshop on Non-Monotonic Reasoning*, 2000.
3. C. Baral and M. Gelfond. Reasoning agents in dynamic domain. In J. Minker, editor, *Logic Based Artificial Intelligence*, pages 257–279. Kluwer, 2000.
4. S. Brass and J. Dix. Characterizations of the Disjunctive Stable Semantics by Partial Evaluation. *Journal of Logic Programming*, 32(3):207–228, 1997.
5. S. Brass and J. Dix. Characterizations of the Disjunctive Well-founded Semantics: Confluent Calculi and Iterated GCWA. *Journal of Automated Reasoning*, 20(1):143–165, 1998.
6. S. Brass, J. Dix, B. Freitag and U. Zukowski. Transformation-based bottom-up computation of the well-founded model. *Theory and Practice of Logic Programming*, 1(5):497–538, 2001.

7. Y. Dimopoulos, B. Nebel and J. Koehler. Encoding planning problems in non-monotonic logic programs. In *Proceedings of the Fourth European Conference on Planning*, pages 169–181. Springer-Verlag, 1997.

8. J. Dix. A Classification-Theory of Semantics of Normal Logic Programs: II. Weak Properties. *Fundamenta Informaticae*, XXII(3):257–288, 1995.

9. J. Dix, J. Arrazola and M. Osorio. Confluent rewriting systems in non-monotonic reasoning. *Computación y Sistemas*, Volume II, No. 2-3:104–123, 1999.

10. J. Dix, M. Osorio and C. Zepeda. A General Theory of Confluent Rewriting Systems for Logic Programming and its Applications. *Annals of Pure and Applied Logic*, Volume 108, pages 153–188, 2001.

11. M. Gelfond, M. Balduccini and J. Galloway. Diagnosing Physical Systems in A-Prolog. In T. Eiter, W. Faber and M. Truszczynski, editors, *Proceedings of the 6th International Conference on Logic Programming and Nonmonotonic Reasoning*, pages 213-226, Vienna, Austria, 2001.

12. M. Gelfond and V. Lifschitz. The Stable Model Semantics for Logic Programming. In R. Kowalski and K. Bowen, editors, *5th Conference on Logic Programming*, pages 1070–1080. MIT Press, 1988.

13. D. Jongh and A. Hendriks. Characterization of strongly equivalent logic programs in intermediate logics. *http://turing.wins.uva.nl/ lhendrik/*, 2001.

14. V. Lifschitz. Foundations of logic programming. In *Principles of Knowledge Representation*, pages 69-127. CSLI Publications, 1996.

15. V. Lifschitz, D. Pearce and A. Valverde. Strongly equivalent logic programs. *ACM Transactions on Computational Logic*, 2:526–541, 2001.

16. J. Lloyd. *Foundations of Logic Programming*. Springer, Berlin, 1987. 2nd edition.

17. M. Osorio, J. Nieves and C. Giannella. Useful transformation in answer set programming. In A. Provetti and T. Son, editors, *Answer Set Programming: Towards Efficient and Scalable Knowledge Representation and Reasoning*, pages 146–152. AAAI Press, Stanford, USA, 2001.

18. M. Osorio and F. Zacarias. High-level logic programming. In B. Thalheim and K.-D. Schewe, editors, *FolKS*, LNCS 1762, pages 226–240. Springer Verlag, Berlin, 2000.

19. A. Pettorossi and M. Proietti. Transformation of Logic Programs. In D. Gabbay, C. Hogger and J. Robinson, editors, *Handbook of Logic in Artificial Intelligence and Logic Programming*, Vol. 5, pages 697–787. Oxford University Press, 1998.

20. C. Sakama and K. Inoue. Negation as Failure in the Head. *Journal of Logic Programming*, 35(1):39–78, 1998.

21. P. Simons. Towards constraint satisfaction through logic programs and the stable model semantics. Technical Report 47, Helsinki University of Technology, Digital Systems Laboratory, August 1997.

22. L. Tang, V. Lifschitz and H. Turner. Nested expressions in logic programs. *Annals of Mathematics and Artificial Intelligence*, 25:369–389, 1999.

23. P. Taylor, J. Girard and Y. Lafont. *Proofs and types*. Cambridge University Press, 1989.

24. H. Zhang. Sato: A decision procedure for propositional logic. *Association for Automated Reasoning Newsletter*, 22:1–3, March 1993.

7 Appendix: Proofs.

Proof of Proposition 3.1.

The proof is by induction on the length of the deduction for $\Gamma \vdash_I A$ using the sequent calculus defined in [23].

If $\Gamma \vdash_I A$ is an axiom, the base of induction, then $\Gamma = \{A\}$ and the proposition is trivial.

If the last rule in the deduction of $\Gamma \vdash_I A$ is a left structural rule $\mathcal{L}X$, $\mathcal{L}W$, $\mathcal{L}C$ or one of the logical rules $\mathcal{L}i\wedge$, $\mathcal{R}\wedge$, $\mathcal{L}\vee$, $\mathcal{R}i\vee$, $\mathcal{L}\rightarrow$, $\mathcal{R}\rightarrow$, the inductive hypothesis can be applied to the previous sequent(s) in the deduction. And since taking positive subsets in the premises of this rules preserves "provability" it is possible to prove $\text{Pos}(\Gamma) \vdash_I A$.

Consider the case when the last rule is $\mathcal{L}\vee$

$$\frac{\Gamma_1, B \vdash_I A \qquad \Gamma_2, C \vdash_I A}{\Gamma_1, \Gamma_2, B \vee C \vdash_I A} \mathcal{L}\vee$$

where $\Gamma = \Gamma_1, \Gamma_2, B \vee C$.

If $B \vee C \in \mathbf{P}$ then also B and A are in $\mathbf{P}$, so by the inductive hypothesis we have proofs for $\text{Pos}(\Gamma_1, B) \vdash_I A$ and $\text{Pos}(\Gamma_2, C) \vdash_I A$. Using again rule $\mathcal{L}\vee$ now we prove

$$\frac{\text{Pos}(\Gamma_1), B \vdash_I A \qquad \text{Pos}(\Gamma_2), C \vdash_I A}{\text{Pos}(\Gamma_1, \Gamma_2), B \vee C \vdash_I A}$$

which finally leads to $\text{Pos}(\Gamma) \vdash_I A$.

If $B \vee C \in \mathbf{N}$ then either B or C are in $\mathbf{N}$. Suppose that $B \in \mathbf{N}$, the other case is analogous. Applying the inductive hypothesis on $\Gamma_1, B \vdash_I A$ we have a proof for $\text{Pos}(\Gamma_1) \vdash_I A$. Now, using the weakening rule $\mathcal{L}W$, it is possible to prove $\text{Pos}(\Gamma_1), \text{Pos}(\Gamma_2) \vdash_I A$ or, equivalently, $\text{Pos}(\Gamma) \vdash_I A$.

The proof of all the other cases mentioned above follow similarly.

Note that the last rule cannot be a negation rule since $\mathcal{L}\neg$ will need A to be empty, and $\mathcal{R}\neg$ implies $A \notin \mathbf{P}$ contradicting the hypothesis of the proposition. The last rule is also not $\mathcal{R}W$ since it will assert $\Gamma \vdash_I$ or, equivalently, $\vdash_I \neg(\bigwedge \Gamma)$. But $\vdash_C \neg(\bigwedge \Gamma)$ is not even provable since there is an interpretation, which assigns *true* to each atom, that evaluates the formula to *false*.

Proof of Proposition 3.2.

It suffices to show that any instance of the axiom scheme $\neg A \vee \neg\neg A$ can be proved from the set of hypothesis $\{\neg a_1 \vee \neg\neg a_1, \ldots, \neg a_m \vee \neg\neg a_m\}$, where $a_1, \ldots, a_m$ are all the atoms occurring in A.

The proof is by induction on the size of A. For the base case we assume that $A \in \{a_1, \ldots, a_m, \bot\}$. If $A \in \{a_1, \ldots, a_m\}$ the statement is true by hypothesis. If $A = \bot$ then the result is true since $\neg\bot \vee \neg\neg\bot$ is a theorem. For the induction step we assume that $(\neg a_1 \vee \neg\neg a_1), \ldots, (\neg a_m \vee \neg\neg a_m) \vdash_I \neg F_1 \vee \neg\neg F_1$ and similarly for $F_2 \vee \neg\neg F_2$.

Now it is not hard to prove that $(\neg F_1 \vee \neg\neg F_1), (\neg F_2 \vee \neg\neg F_2) \vdash_I \neg(F_1 \odot F_2) \vee \neg\neg(F_1 \odot F_2)$, where $\odot$ represents any binary connective, and then the result follows immediately. Recall that $\neg A$ abbreviates the formula $\bot \leftarrow A$ and so we do no have to consider this case in the proof.

Proof of Lemma 3.2.

Proposition 3.2 states $\Gamma \vdash_{Jn} F$ is equivalent to $\Gamma, (\neg a_1 \vee \neg\neg a_1), \ldots, (\neg a_m \vee \neg\neg a_m) \vdash_I F$. Now Proposition 3.1 will allow us to remove the instances of axioms

$\neg a_i \vee \neg\neg a_i$ together with all other formulas containing negation connectives. That is $Pos(\Gamma) \vdash_I F$.

7.1 Proofs about Equivalence

Proof of Lemma 4.1.

Direct by theorem 4.2 and proposition 3.2.

Proof of Lemma 4.2.

For a disjunctive clause C of the form $\bigvee H_p \leftarrow \bigwedge(B_p \cup \neg B_n)$, we will write $tr(C)$ to denote the augmented clause $\bigvee(H_p \cup \neg\neg B_n) \leftarrow \bigwedge B_p$. For a disjunctive program P the program $tr(P)$ is obtained just applying the transformation on each clause. Some simple, easy to verify, properties of this transformation are: $P \equiv_{\text{Jn}} tr(P)$, $tr(P) \subset \mathbf{P} \cup \mathbf{N}$ and $Pos(tr(P)) = Pos(P)$.

Now P is strongly equivalent to $P \cup \{a\}$ iff, by theorem 4.2, $P \equiv_{\text{Jn}} P \cup \{a\}$ iff $P \vdash_{\text{Jn}} a$ iff, since $P \equiv_{\text{Jn}} tr(P)$, $tr(P) \vdash_{\text{Jn}} a$ iff, by lemma 3.2, $Pos(tr(P)) \vdash_I a$ iff $Pos(P) \vdash_I a$.

Proof of Lemma 4.3.

It is an easy, and well known, result that $P \vdash_C \neg a$ if and only if $P \vdash_{\text{Jn}} \neg a$. But $P \vdash_{\text{Jn}} \neg a$ iff $P \cup \{\neg a\} \equiv_{\text{Jn}} P$ and, by theorem 4.2, iff these two programs are strongly equivalent.

Proof of Lemma 4.4.

The proof is by contradiction. Suppose there is a model M that is a stable model of P, but M is not a stable model of $P \cup \{\neg a\}$ (or vice versa). In either case we have $a \notin M$, since by hypothesis a does not appear in stable models of P and, on the other hand, models for $P \cup \{\neg a\}$ cannot contain a. It follows $(P \cup \{\neg a\})^M = P^M$ and therefore stable models of the two programs are the same.

Proof of Proposition 5.1.

Suppose $b \in unf(P)$ then $b \notin MM(Definite(P)) \supseteq MM(Definite(P_1))$ thus $b \in unf(P_1)$.

To prove the other contention take $b \in unf(P_1)$ and suppose P contains a rule $\mathcal{A} \leftarrow \mathcal{B}^+, \neg\mathcal{B}^-$ such that $a \in \mathcal{A} \cap \mathcal{B}^+$. Since $unf(P) \subseteq unf(P_1)$ then $\{a, b\} \subseteq unf(P_1)$, so $\{a, b\}$ is not contained in $M := MM(Definite(P_1))$. Furthermore M is a model of each clause $b \leftarrow a \wedge \alpha$ in $Definite(P) \setminus Definite(P_1)$, so M is a model of $Definite(P)$. Thus $b \notin MM(Definite(P))$ and $b \in unf(P)$.

Now we know that $unf(P) = unf(P_1)$ and so $\mathbf{Dloop}(P) = \{\mathcal{A} \leftarrow \mathcal{B}^+, \neg\mathcal{B}^- \in P \mid \mathcal{B}^+ \cap unf(P) = \emptyset\} = \mathbf{Dloop}(P_1)$.

Proof of Corollary 5.1.

Follows immediately applying proposition 5.1 to each $a \in \mathcal{L}$.

Proof of Proposition 5.2.

By hypothesis of a $\mathbf{GPPE}_a$ application, there exist clauses in P, namely $\mathcal{A} \leftarrow \mathcal{B}^+, \neg\mathcal{B}^-$ and $\mathcal{A}_1 \leftarrow \mathcal{B}_1^+, \neg\mathcal{B}_1^-$, such that $a \in \mathcal{B}^+ \cap \mathcal{A}_1$.

Let $b \in unf(P)$, by hypothesis we have that $\{a, b\} \subseteq unf(P)$, so $\{a, b\}$ is not contained in $M := MM(Definite(P))$. Furthermore M is a model of each clause $x \leftarrow \mathcal{B}^+ \setminus \{a\}$ in $Definite(P_1) \setminus Definite(P)$, because we have $x \neq a$ and there exists $d \in (\mathcal{B}^+ \setminus \{a\}) \cap unf(P)$, thus M is a model for $Definite(P_1)$, but M is not a model for $\{a, b\}$, so $b \in unf(P_1)$.

For the other contention, we suppose that $b \in unf(P)$ and, since $a \in unf(P)$, then $\{a, b\}$ is not subset of I, where $I := MM(Definite(P_1))$. Also I is a model of every clause $x \leftarrow \mathcal{B}^+$ in $Definite(P) \setminus Definite(P_1)$, because $a \in \mathcal{B}^+$. Thus I is a model for $Definite(P_1)$; nevertheless I is not model for $\{a, b\}$, so $b \in unf(P)$.

We have that $unf(P) = unf(P_1)$ so $\mathbf{Dloop}(P) = \{\mathcal{A} \leftarrow \mathcal{B}^+, \neg\mathcal{B}^- \in P \mid \mathcal{B}^+ \cap unf(P) = \emptyset\} = \mathbf{Dloop}(P_1)$.

Proof of Corollary 5.2.

Follows immediately applying proposition 5.2 to each $a \in \mathcal{L}$.

Proof of Theorem 5.1.

Let $B_{P_1} \subset unf(P_1)$ be the set of elements in $unf(P_1)$ such that they appear in the body of some clause in P. The proof is by induction over n, the number of elements in B_{P_1}. If $n = 0$ the result follows immediately, since it implies $P_1 = \mathbf{Dloop}(P_1)$. Now suppose the result holds for all programs P where $|B_P| < n$. Let $b \in B_{P_1}$, if we take $P' = \mathbf{TAUT}_b^+(P_1)$ then, by corollary 5.1, $\mathbf{Dloop}(P') = \mathbf{Dloop}(P_1)$ and now P' has no tautologies with respect to b. Let $P'' = \mathbf{GPPE}_b^+(P')$ so, by corollary 5.2, $\mathbf{Dloop}(P'') = \mathbf{Dloop}(P')$. Observe that b does not appear in any body of clauses in P'', furthermore there are not new atoms, so $|B_{P''}| < |B_{P_1}|$. By inductive hypothesis we have $P'' \equiv_{\text{stable}} \mathbf{Dloop}(P'')$, but $\mathbf{Dloop}(P'') = \mathbf{Dloop}(P_1) = P_2$ and since $\mathbf{TAUT}$ and $\mathbf{GPPE}$ preserve stable, proved in [4], $P_1 \equiv_{\text{stable}} P' \equiv_{\text{stable}} P''$. Thus $P_1 \equiv_{\text{stable}} P_2$.

Proof of Theorem 5.2.

We already know that $P \equiv_{\text{stable}} Ground(P)$ by the definition of stable. Also $Ground(P) \equiv_{\text{stable}} \mathbf{Dloop}(Ground(P))$ by theorem 5.1. It is easy to verify that $\mathbf{Dloop}(Ground(P)) = Ground(\mathbf{Dloop}(P))$. So we can finally obtain as desired that $P \equiv_{\text{stable}} Ground(\mathbf{Dloop}(P))$.

Proof of Lemma 5.1.

Let P_1 and P_2 be two programs related by any transformation in $\mathcal{CS}++$ but (e). Then it is easy to check that $P_1 \equiv_I P_2$ (note that we used intuitionistic logic). The case (e) is direct.

Proof of Lemma 5.2.

First we will prove that if M is an answer set of P then $M^* = M \cup \varphi(S \setminus M)$ is an answer set of $P \cup \Delta_S$. According to the definition of answer sets given in section 2 we must show M^* is closed under the reduct $(P \cup \Delta_S)^{M^*}$ and minimal among the sets with this property.

By construction M^* is closed under $(\Delta_S)^{M^*}$ and also M is closed under P^M, since it is an answer set of P, therefore we have M^* is closed under $(P \cup \Delta_S)^{M^*}$. Just note both the *reduct operator* and the *closure condition* can be distributed among clauses. Also extra atoms in M^* not in $\mathcal{L}_P$ (not in M) are not significant while calculating the reduct of the program P.

Now we will check M^* is minimal. Suppose there is another set of atoms N^* closed under $(P \cup \Delta_S)^{M^*}$ and $N^* \subset M^*$. Write N^* as the disjoint union $N^* = N \cup N'$ where $N = N^* \cap \mathcal{L}_P$ and $N' = N^* \setminus \mathcal{L}_P$. Note $M^* = M \cup \varphi(S \setminus M)$ is also written in such form. Observe N^* is closed under P^{M^*} and thus N is closed under P^M. Since $N^* \subset M^*$ we have $N \subseteq M$ and, on the other hand, since M is minimal among the sets of atoms closed under P^M we have $M \subseteq N$. So $N = M$.

Then if $N^* \neq M^*$ there must be an atom $x \in \varphi(S \setminus M)$ such that x is not in N', also not in N^*. Let $a \in S$ be the atom such that $\varphi(a) = x$. We also have, since $x \in \varphi(S \setminus M)$, a is not in M, and also not in N^* or M^*. But now neither a nor x are in N^* so this set does not satisfy the clause $(x \leftarrow \neg a)^{M^*} = x \leftarrow \top$ contained in $(\Delta_S)^{M^*}$. So N^* is not closed under $(P \cup \Delta_S)^{M^*}$ arising contradiction.

For the converse we have to prove that if M^* is an answer set of $P \cup \Delta_S$ then $M = M^* \cap \mathcal{L}_P$ is an answer set of P. Decompose, as done before, $M^* = M \cup M'$. It is immediate M^* is closed under P^{M^*} and therefore M is closed under P^M.

Before we can finish observe that given an atom $a \in S$ and $x = \varphi(a)$, we have $a \in M$ if and only if $x \notin M'$. This is easy to verify since having both atoms (or none) in M^* will make it impossible for M^* to be closed under $(\Delta_S)^{M^*}$.

Finally we can check M is minimal. Suppose there is N closed under P^M and $N \subset M$. Construct $N^* = N \cup M'$, so $N^* \subset M^*$. Previous notes makes it easy to verify that N^* is closed under $(\Delta_S)^{M^*}$, therefore N^* is closed under $(P \cup \Delta_S)^{M^*}$ contradicting the fact that M^* is the minimal set with such property.

Proof of Theorem 5.4.

First, by lemma 5.2, we know $P \cup \Delta_S$ is a conservative extension of P. Note that $\Delta_S \vdash_{G_3} \varphi(a) \equiv \neg a$ for each $a \in S$, then by lemma 3.1, $P \cup \Delta_S \equiv_{G_3} P' \cup \Delta_S$ where P' is obtained from P replacing each occurrence of $\neg a$ with $\varphi(a)$ for all $a \in S$. This equivalence in G_3 logic is, from theorem 4.1, the same as strong equivalence with respect to stable semantics. Thus, $P' \cup \Delta_S$ is a general program that is a conservative transformation of P.

Proof of Theorem 5.5.

Let $\mathbf{T}$ be such transformation. Now it is easy to verify that $\mathbf{T}(Ground(P)) = Ground(\mathbf{T}(P))$, and by theorem 5.4 it follows $\mathbf{T}(Ground(P))$ is a conservative extension of $Ground(P)$. Thus, by definition of answer sets, $\mathbf{T}(P)$ is a conservative extension of P.

Proof Theory, Transformations, and Logic Programming for Debugging Security Protocols

Giorgio Delzanno[1] and Sandro Etalle[2]

[1] Dipartimento di Informatica e Scienze dell'Informazione
Università di Genova, via Dodecaneso 35, 16146 Italy
giorgio@disi.unige.it
[2] CWI, Amsterdam and Faculty of Computer Science,
University of Twente, P.O.Box 217, 7500AE Enschede, The Netherlands
etalle@cs.utwente.nl

Abstract. In this paper we define a sequent calculus to formally specify, simulate, debug and verify security protocols. In our sequents we distinguish between the *current knowledge* of principals and the *current global state* of the session. Hereby, we can describe the operational semantics of principals and of an intruder in a simple and modular way. Furthermore, using proof theoretic tools like the analysis of *permutability* of rules, we are able to find efficient proof strategies that we prove complete for special classes of security protocols including Needham-Schroeder. Based on the results of this preliminary analysis, we have implemented a Prolog meta-interpreter which allows for rapid prototyping and for checking safety properties of security protocols, and we have applied it for finding error traces and proving correctness of practical examples.

1 Introduction

Cryptographic protocols are the essential means for the exchange of confidential information and for authentication. Their correctness and robustness are crucial for guaranteeing that a hostile intruder can not get hold of secret information (e.g. a private key) or to force unjust authentication. Unfortunately, the design of cryptographic protocols appears to be rather error-prone. This gave impulse to research on the formal verification of security protocols see e.g. [13,6,20,23, 18,28,29]. In this setting several approaches are based on Dolev and Yao's [13], where it is proposed to test a protocol explicitly against a hostile intruder who has complete control over the network, can intercept and forge messages. By an exhaustive search, one can establish whether the protocol is flawed or not as shown, e.g., in [23,21,8,16]. Clearly, a crucial aspect in this approach is try to limit the search space explosion that occurs when modelling the intruder's behaviour . To this end, many solutions have been employed, ranging from human intervention to the use of approximations. In recent work [15,30,22], this problem has also been tackled by reducing the intruder's action to a constraint solving problem.

A. Pettorossi (Ed.): LOPSTR 2001, LNCS 2372, pp. 76–90, 2002.
© Springer-Verlag Berlin Heidelberg 2002

The origin of this paper was our intention to investigate the possible application of existing logic programming systems for debugging and verification of security protocols. Logic programming tools provide natural built-in mechanisms like backtracking to explore the search space generated by a transition system. A direct implementation of a protocol simulator, however, would suffer from problems like state explosion, infinite-derivations, etc. To tackle these problems, in this paper we use a combination of techniques stemming from proof theory and program transformation. Proof theory allows us to formally specify the protocol and intruder behaviours. Here, a systematic study of the structure of the resulting proofs serves as formal justification for an interesting series of optimizations. Via sound and complete transformation, we will derive specialised rules that form the core of the simulator we implemented in Prolog. Our techniques also allows us to isolate a class of protocols, we called *fully-typed* for which, in case of finite-number of sessions, forward exploration is guaranteed to terminate.

The reason we have chosen to specify protocols using sequent calculus is based on the following observation. During the execution of a protocol stage two kind of changes take place: a change in *knowledge* that is monotonic, as it is not modified during later stages, and a change of *state* that is non-monotonic (e.g. the presence of messages on the network). In our approach the knowledge is modelled by a first-order theory, and the state by a multiset of first order atoms. A protocol can be specified in a natural way by a *multi-conclusion proof system* in which every proof rule corresponds uniquely to a legal protocol action. In this setting a proof corresponds to a *protocol trace*. In addition to this, the proof system allows to model a potential intruder by adding few rules modelling its behaviour. It is then possible to check if the intruder has a way of breaking the protocol.

Via a natural translation of our specialised proof system into Horn clauses, we obtained a working prototype that we used in some practical experiments. The prototype is written in Prolog, and allows the user to formally specify a cryptographic protocol, by writing Prolog rules defining it. We want to mention that the Prolog prototype employs in a crucial way the notion of *delay* declarations. Specifically, delay declaration are used to make the *intruder* generate *on-demand* messages that are partially instantiated: only the pattern expected by one of the other principals must be explicitly generated, the remaining part of the message can be represented via existentially quantified variables.

Plan of the paper. In Section 2, we present the language (formulae and sequents) used to describe security protocols and safety properties. In Section 3, we present additional proof rules for modelling the intruder. In Section 4, we analyse the resulting proof system, and we introduce the notion of fully-typed protocols. In Section 7, we briefly describe our Prolog implementation of a automated prover for our logic, some experimental results, and, finally, address related works.

2   Proof Theoretic Specification of Security Protocols

The Needham-Schroeder Protocol. As a working example, we will consider the security protocol based on public-key cryptography proposed by Needham and Schroeder in [25]. The protocol allows two *principals*, say Alice and Bob, to exchange two *secret numbers*, that might be used later for *signing* messages. At first, Alice creates a *nonce* N_a and sends it to Bob, together with its identity. A nonce is a randomly generated value. The message is encrypted with Bob's public key, so that only Bob will be able to decipher the message. When Bob receives the message, he creates a new nonce N_b. Then, he sends the message $\langle N_a, N_b \rangle$ encrypted with the public key of Alice. Alice deciphers the message, and sends back the nonce N_b encrypted with the public key of Bob. At this point, Alice and Bob know both N_a and N_b. Following the notation commonly used to describe security protocol [6], the protocol has the following rules.

1. $A \to B : \{A, N_a\}_{K_b}$ 2. $B \to A : \{N_a, N_b\}_{K_a}$ 3. $A \to B : \{N_b\}_{K_b}$

2.1   The Proof System

Using a proof system for representing a protocol is natural if one considers that at each protocol transaction two kind of changes occur in the system: First, a change in the *knowledge* of the agents involved in the transaction, that is typically persistent and thus *monotonic*; secondly, a change in the *state* of the agents and of the network, that is typically *non-monotonic*. In our approach, *knowledge* (which includes the specification of the protocol rules) is modelled by a first order theory, denoted by Δ, and *states* are modelled via multisets of atomic formulae, denoted by S. We then define multi-conclusion sequents having the form $\Delta \longrightarrow S$, that will be used to represent *(instantaneous) configurations* during a protocol execution. The advantage of this approach wrt either coding immediately the whole system in Prolog (as in the NRL analyser [21]), is that in this way we can more easily prove properties of the whole system such as Theorems 4, 5 and 7. We will use *compound proof rules* to specify the behaviour of the principals. A *compound proof rule* has the form

$$\frac{\Delta \vdash \phi \quad \Delta, \Delta' \longrightarrow S'}{\Delta \longrightarrow S}$$

where S and S' are multisets, Δ and Δ' are first-order theories, ϕ is a first-order formula and $\vdash$ is a given provability operator. When $\Delta, \Delta' \longrightarrow S'$ is absent from the premise we call it a *closing* rule. Here, Δ, Δ' denotes the set $\Delta \cup \Delta'$. Each protocol transaction is modelled via a compound rule where S and Δ are respectively the *global state* and *knowledge before* the transaction is fired; ϕ models the conditions under which the transaction can be fired; S' is the state of the system *after* the transaction is completed; Δ' is the *new knowledge*, acquired during the transaction. In the rest of the paper Δ and Δ' will be sets of *Horn Clauses*, i.e. universally quantified implicational formulae indicated as

$a \leftarrow b_1 \wedge \dots \wedge b_n$ where $a, b_1, \dots, b_n$ are atoms. We allow b_i to be an equality or an inequality $t \neq s$, other than this, negation is not involved, and no other tests are allowed (like $<$, etc.). For the moment, the relation $\vdash$ will denote the provability relation built on top of *ground (variable-free) resolution*. A (partial) protocol execution starting from the state $\mathcal{S}_0$ and knowledge Δ_0 (i.e., in the configuration $\Delta_0 \longrightarrow \mathcal{S}_0$) and ending in the configuration $\Delta_n \longrightarrow \mathcal{S}_n$ is thus represented via a (partial) proof tree (here and in the sequel we omit the proof trees for $\vdash$ when possible) A proof is *successful* if each premise is satisfied. We will use non-closing rules to specify the protocol and the intruder and a closing rule to specify the (reachability) properties we wish to demonstrate or refute. Thus, by modifying the closing rules of the proof system one can modify its meaning.

Knowledge and State Description Language. The *global state* of the system is described via a multiset containing *agent states* and *messages*. A *Agent State* is an atom `agent(ID,Role,Step)` where `ID` is the agent's identifier, `Role` is its role in the protocol (e.g., *initiator* or *responder*), and `Step` is a counter denoting the current step of the protocol the agent is at. In presence of parallel sessions, some agent ID may occur more than once in the global state, in particular, it may occur while having different roles (agent "a" could be at the same time initiator of one protocol session and responder in another session). On the other hand, *Messages* contain lists of objects (keys or nonces), that may in turn be encrypted. We use `enc(K,M)` to represent a message encoded with the (public) key `K`. More precisely, the set $\mathcal{M}$ of messages is defined by the following syntax (symmetric encryption is omitted for brevity): keys and nonces are represented as `key(I)` and `nonce(I)` where `I` is an integer; objects are either keys, nonces or terms like `enc(K,M)`; list of contents are either empty `[]`, or `[O|M]` where `O` is an object, and `M` is a list of contents; finally a message is a term `msg(M)`. *Knowledge* is encoded in *Horn clauses*. Knowledge can be roughly be divided into *global* knowledge, that is common to all principals (like the rules for describing a protocol, explained in the next section) and the agents' *private* knowledge, that is encoded in unit clauses of the form `knows(ID,D)`, where `ID` is the identifier of the agent that possesses it, and `D` is a term such as `keypar(k1,k2)`, `key(k3)`, `nonce(n)` and (overloading the notation) `msg(m)`, where `k1`, `k2`, `k3`, `n` are objects, `m` is a message, and the function symbols `keypar`, `key`, `nonce`, `msg` can be seen as labels, that serve as place-holders for facilitating the retrieval of stored values.

Protocol Specification. A protocol specification allows us to describe all traces starting from a given initial state. Formally, a protocol specification is a pair $\langle \Delta_0, \mathcal{S}_0 \rangle$ consisting of the initial knowledge Δ_0, and the initial global state $\mathcal{S}_0$. In turn, the initial knowledge Δ_0 can be seen as the union of Δ_{rules} (the rules that specify the protocol) and $\Delta_{knowledge}$ (the agents' initial knowledge).

The Protocol Rules, Δ_{rules}. The rules of a generic protocol are always defined according to a fixed pattern: an agent receives a message, removes it from the communication media, composes a new one, and adds it to the communication media. In order to model a protocol rule like $A \rightarrow B : M$, we simply need to specify which messages an agent *expects* or *composes* at a given step of the protocol. For this purpose, we use a special predicate, namely `compose`, to describe the behaviour of the sender A as well as the structure of the message M, and a special predicate, namely `expect`, to describe the behaviour of the receiver B. The *synchronisation* of the agents can be left as part of the *operational* semantics defined via our proof system. `expect` has the following fixed signature: `expect(ID,Role,Step,Message,Knowledge)`. One can think of the first four argument as being *input arguments*, while the last one is an *output* one. The query `expect(ID,Role,Step,Message,Knowledge)` should succeed in the current global knowledge whenever agent having identifier `ID` and role `Role` at step `Step` can receive message `Message`; `Knowledge` is the list of facts the agent learns during the transaction, represented by a list of terms of the form *identifier(value$_1$, ... , value$_n$)*. For instance, Bob's role in the first transaction is specified by:

```
expect(ID,responder,1,msg(enc(key(Pkb),[key(Pka),nonce(Na)]))),Info):-
    knows(ID,keypar(_,Pkb)),knows(ID,key(Pka)),
    Info = [other_nonce(Na),other_key(Pka)].
```

here `Info` is used by the responder to memorise the reception of nonce `Na` from the agent having public key `Pka`. The predicate `compose` is used to compose new messages. In `compose(ID,Role,Step,Nonce,Message,Knowledge)`, one can think of the first four argument as being *input arguments*, while the last two are *output*. The extra input argument `Nonce` is used for passing a fresh nonce to the rule, in case that it is needed for composing a message. The query `compose(ID,Role,Step,Nonce,Message,Knowledge)` succeeds when agent `ID` in role `Role` at step `Step` can produce message `Message`, possibly using the nonce `Nonce`, and `Knowledge` is the list of facts the agent learns during the transaction. In `expect` and `compose` we only allow *equalities* and *inequalities* between free variables but not relations like $>$ (less than). Summarising, Δ_{rules} is the logic program that contains the definitions of `expect` and `compose`.

The Initial Knowledge. It describes the initial knowledge of each agent via a set of *unit clauses*. For a single session of Needham-Schroeder, it can consists of the set of atoms: { `knows(a,keypar(ska,pka)).`, `knows(_,key(pka)).`, `knows(b,keypar(skb,pkb)).`, `knows(_,key(pkb)).`, } where the underscore _ is the anonymous variable: `knows(_,key(pka))` indicates that every agent knows the public key of a; here "a" and "b" are the identifiers of the agents involved.

Initial Global State. $\mathcal{S}_0$ is the multiset of agents in their initial state. It determines which agents are present and their role. Therefore, it determines also how many *parallel sessions* we investigate (by doing so, we allow only a finite number of parallel sessions). For the single session of Needham-Schroeder, the initial global state is $\mathcal{S}_0 = \{agent(a, initiator, 1), agent(b, responder, 1)\}$. If we wanted to analyse two sessions of this protocol, in which agent a has role *initiator* in one session and role *responder* in the other session, all we needed to change is the initial state, which would be: $S_0 = \{agent(a, initiator, 1), agent(b,$ $responder, 1), agent(a, responder, 1), agent(c, initiator, 1)\}$.

Proof Rules. Once we have a protocol specification $\langle \Delta_0, S_0 \rangle$, we need to embed it in a proof system, whose interleaving operational semantics will model the protocol behaviour.

Definition 1 (Proof System for a Protocol Specification). *The* (compound) *proof system derived from a protocol specification* $\langle \Delta_0, S_0 \rangle$, *consists of the following two rules*

$$\frac{\Delta \vdash compose(id, role, st, n, m, \mathbf{K}) \quad \Delta, \Delta' \longrightarrow agent(id, role, st + 1), msg(m), S}{\Delta \longrightarrow agent(id, role, st), S} \; send$$

provided n does not occur in Δ and S; $\Delta' = \{knows(id, k) \mid k \in \mathbf{K}\}$.

$$\frac{\Delta \vdash expect(id, role, step, m, \mathbf{K}) \quad \Delta, \Delta' \longrightarrow agent(id, role, step + 1), S}{\Delta \longrightarrow agent(id, role, step), msg(m), S} \; receive$$

provided that $\Delta' = \{knows(id, k) \mid k \in \mathbf{K}\}$.

Where $agent(id, role, step + 1), msg(m), S$ indicates the multiset consisting of $agent(id, role, step + 1)$, $msg(m)$ and the element of the multiset S. Notice that these rules depend on the predicates **expect** and **compose** that are defined in Δ. The side condition of the *send* requires n to be a fresh nonce. Actually, the above rule applies when **send** needs at most one fresh nonce. Rule for where more nonces are needed are obtained via a straightforward generalisation.

The Safety Property Π. Intuitively, our objective is to answer questions like: *is it possible to reach a final state in which the intruder has got hold of the nonces N_a and N_b?* For this purpose, we interested in *safety* properties that can formulated in terms of reachability properties (if a given unwanted situation is not reachable, then the system satisfies the safety property). To describe the state to be tested for reachability we use a special query $closing(S)$, whose definition is given in a separate program Π (to be added to Δ) and we add to the proof system the following closing rule.

$$\frac{\Delta \vdash closing(S)}{\Delta \longrightarrow S} \; final$$

For instance, to check if two agents can actually reach the end of the protocol while exchanging each others nonces, we need the following program Π

```
closing(S):- subset([agent(ID1,initiator,4),agent(ID2,responder,4)],S),
             knows(ID2,other_nonce(N_a)),knows(ID1,other_nonce(N_b)),
             knows(ID2,my_nonce(N_b)),knows(ID1,my_nonce(N_a)).
```

Proofs as Traces. The proof system allows us to formally describe all possible *traces* of an (interleaving) execution of the principals. A trace can be viewed in fact as a single threaded proof for the $\longrightarrow$-sequents leading to a final state, and in which all auxiliary conditions are satisfied. Formally, a proof is a sequence of sequents $\Delta_0 \longrightarrow S_0, \dots, \Delta_k \longrightarrow S_k$ where $\Delta_i \longrightarrow S_i$ and $\Delta_{i+1} \longrightarrow S_{i+1}$ correspond respectively to the lower and upper sequent of an instance of one of the proof rules *receive*, and *send*, in which all auxiliary sequents of the form $\Phi \vdash \phi$ are provable for each $0 \le i < k$. Finally, $\Delta_k \longrightarrow S_k$ is the lower sequent of an instance of the *final rule* in which all premises are satisfied. The following property then holds.

Proposition 2 (Soundness). *Given a protocol specification* $\langle \Delta_0, S_0 \rangle$, *and a safety property specification* Π, *every proof for the sequent* $\Delta_0, \Pi \longrightarrow S_0$ *corresponds to a trace that from the initial state of the protocol leads to a final configuration* $\Delta \longrightarrow S$ *in which a closing rule of* Π *can be fired.*

3   Modelling an Intruder

In order to test a protocol specification against a malicious intruder, we assume the existence of a new agent, called *Trudy*, that has complete control over the network. The task of Trudy is to get hold of secret information and/or to spoil the communication between the honest principals, for instance by letting them believe they have correctly exchanged nonces, while they have not. Our system can be used for checking if such a malicious intruder is actually able to fulfil its objectives. This is achieved by providing the following fixed rules for specifying Trudy's behaviour

$$\frac{\Delta, \mathcal{T}(\Delta, m) \longrightarrow S}{\Delta \longrightarrow msg(m), S} \; intercept \qquad \frac{\Delta \vdash contrive(m) \quad \Delta \longrightarrow msg(m), \mathcal{R}}{\Delta \longrightarrow \mathcal{R}} \; forge$$

where $\mathcal{T}(\Delta, m) = \{knows(trudy, n) \mid \Delta \vdash decompose(m, n)\}$. In the rule for intercepting a message, the set of facts $\mathcal{T}(\Delta, m)$ represents the *closure* of the knowledge of the intruder with respect to what Trudy can decipher using the predicate **decompose**. Following from this definition, given a message m (i.e. a ground term), $\mathcal{T}(\Delta, m)$ always consists of a finite set of facts. Trudy can also create a message in order to try to cheat the other principals. Starting from her current knowledge, Trudy uses the predicate **contrive** to generate a random message of arbitrary size. This message is placed in the global state via the *forge* rule. Clearly, Trudy has to possess at least a public-private key pair, and a certain number of random numbers (nonces) with which it contrives messages (if the knowledge of Trudy is empty, Trudy is not able to contrive anything). Thus, an *intruder* is a set of clauses containing the rules for **decompose** and **contrive** together with a *set* of facts each one storing a new nonce, $knows(trudy, nonce(n))$, where n is a fresh integer, or a pair of keys, i.e., $knows(trudy, keypar(sk, pk))$ where sk, pk are fresh terms. We can now analyse the protocol traces in presence of Trudy. The *extended proof system* derived from a protocol specification

$\langle \Delta_0, \mathcal{S}_0 \rangle$, a safety property specification Π and combined with an intruder specification Δ_{trudy} consists of the rules *intercept* and *forge*, together with the rules *send, receive* and *final*. Now, we can describe all possible *traces* of an interleaving execution of the principals and of Trudy as stated in the following theorem.

Proposition 3 (Soundness). Given a protocol specification $\langle \Delta_0, \mathcal{S}_0 \rangle$, a safety property specification Π, every proof for the sequent $\Delta_0, \Pi, \Delta_{trudy} \longrightarrow \mathcal{S}_0$ corresponds to a trace of an interleaved execution of the principals and an intruder Δ_{trudy} that from $\mathcal{S}_0$ leads to a final configuration $\Delta \longrightarrow \mathcal{S}$ that satisfies the condition specified by Π.

For example, it is possible that after the protocol has completed Trudy got hold of one of the secret nonces. This is done by taking Π to be the following program.

```
closing(S):- subset([agent(ID1,initiator,4),agent(ID2,responder,4)],S),
             knows(ID2,other_nonce(N_a)), knows(ID1,other_nonce(N_b)),
             knows(ID2,my_nonce(N_b)),    knows(ID1,my_nonce(N_a)),
             (knows(trudy,object(N_a));knows(trudy,object(N_b))).
```

4   Analysis and Tuning of the Proof System

During a protocol execution, Trudy can generate an arbitrary number of messages, and at any step Trudy can generate a message of arbitrary size. Thus, the search space is infinite. In this section we show that by *proof theoretic* analysis we can drastically reduce the search space, and identify a large class of protocol specification for which the search space is finite. First, we have to solve the problem of the initial knowledge of the intruder. In fact Proposition 3 depends on a specific intruder Δ_{trudy}, that can be arbitrarily large. The following (new) result shows that it is possible to build a (small) Δ_{trudy} which suffices:

Theorem 4. *Given a protocol specification $\langle \Delta_0, \mathcal{S}_0 \rangle$, and a safety property specification Π then there exists an intruder $\Gamma_{\Delta_0, \Pi}$ such that for any other intruder Δ_{trudy}: If there exists a proof for $\Delta_0, \Pi, \Delta_{trudy} \longrightarrow \mathcal{S}_0$ then there exists a proof for $\Delta_0, \Pi, \Gamma_{\Delta_0, \Pi} \longrightarrow \mathcal{S}_0$.*

Secondly, we have to avoid possibly infinite branches. It is straightforward to check that this can only be achieved by bounding the number of the forge rule in a proof. We show now that each proof is equivalent to a proof in which the number of forge rules is equal to the number of expect rules (which is bounded by definition). We start by noting that we can move and remove some occurrence of the forge rule, preserving equivalence. Our proof system enjoys, in fact, the following properties. (a) The rule *forge* always permutes up with *send*: e.g. by permuting two adjacent send and forge rule, one obtains an equivalent proof. (b) The rule *forge* permutes up with *intercept* and *receive* whenever the contrived message is different from the intercepted or expected message. (c) An occurrence of the forge rule which is followed by the rule *final* can be removed provided we assume that the presence of messages in $\mathcal{S}$ does not influence the result of the query *closing*($\mathcal{S}$). (d) The rule *forge* and *intercept* cancel each other out whenever they are defined on the same message. In this case Trudy first contrives a new message m using her current knowledge in Δ and then intercepts it and decomposes it using again her current knowledge. It is not difficult to prove that in this case we can prune both rule instances form the proof.

The above properties demonstrate that we can restrict to proofs in which each forge rule is followed by (i.e. is just below) a receive rule, that reads the message generated by `contrive`. Since the description of a protocol is finite, there might be only a finite number of receive rules in a proof. Thus, if we disregard the steps needed to prove $\vdash$, such proofs are of bounded depth; in practice we can now restrict to bounded traces.

The third and last source of nontermination comes from the fact that, declaratively speaking, $\Delta \vdash contrive(m)$ might have an arbitrarily large proof. Operationally, `contrive` might generate an arbitrarily large message. In order to deal with this we need one last transformation operation. Consider the following schema

$$\frac{\Delta \vdash contrive(m) \quad \dfrac{\Delta \vdash expect(i,r,m,s,\mathbf{K}) \quad \Delta, \Delta' \longrightarrow agent(i,r,s'),\mathcal{S}}{\Delta \longrightarrow msg(m), agent(i,r,s),\mathcal{S}}\ receive}{\Delta \longrightarrow agent(i,r,s),\mathcal{S}}\ forge$$

where $s' = s + 1$, $\Delta' = \{knows(id, k) \mid k \in \mathbf{K}\}$. Thus, we derive the rule

$$\frac{\Delta \vdash contrive(m) \wedge expect(i,r,s,m,\mathbf{K}) \quad \Delta, \Delta' \longrightarrow agent(i,r,s'),\mathcal{S}}{\Delta \longrightarrow agent(i,r,s),\mathcal{S}}\ forge\text{-}receive$$

This transformation alone does not guarantee termination: we have to combine it with a suitable search strategy. We do this in the next section. The following property summarises what we achieved so far.

Theorem 5 (Proof Normalisation). Given a protocol $\langle \Delta_0, \mathcal{S}_0 \rangle$, and a property Π, any proof π for the sequent $\Delta_0, \Pi, \Gamma_{\Delta_0,\Pi} \longrightarrow \mathcal{S}_0$ is equivalent to a proof π' that makes use of the derived rule *forge-receive* and in which there are no occurrences of *forge*.

Proofs in which the *forge* rule does not occur are called *normal* proofs.

4.1   Completeness of Normal Proofs for Fully-Typed Protocols

The derived rule *forge-receive* is still nondeterministic and this can be an obstacle when trying to automatically build a proof. The problem is that `contrive` might still generate arbitrarily large messages. We note however that in protocols like Needham-Schroeder the predicate `expect` puts severe limitations to the nondeterminism of `contrive`. The crucial point here is that if `expect(id,r,s,m,k)` succeeds, then the shape of `m` is uniquely determined by `id` and `s`. This inspires the following definition of fully-typed protocol.

Definition 6 (Fully-Typed Protocol). A protocol $\langle \Delta_0, S_0 \rangle$ is *fully-typed* if for any agent knowledge Δ, if $\Delta_0, \Delta \vdash expect(id, r, s, m_1, i_1)$ and if $\Delta_0, \Delta \vdash expect(id, r, s, m_2, i_2)$, then the m_1 is equal m_2 modulo *renaming* of constants terms.

If the protocol is fully typed, given id and s, each expected message has a fixed *term* structure in which only *constant* symbols are allowed to vary. By using abstract interpretation one can effectively check if a protocol is fully typed.

Fully-typed protocols allow for an effective use of the *forge-receive* rule by a guided generation of messages. The idea is to interleave the Prolog execution of `expect` and `contrive`: after extracting the pattern of an expected message using `expect(id,r,s,m,i)`, `contrive` simply has to check whether the message is "contrivable" (e.g., that it is not encrypted using a key that is not known to Trudy) and to fill all remaining holes using new nonces or keys and nonces Trudy has stored in previous steps. This can be naturally done within any Prolog implementation that allows the presence of *delay declarations*. This renders finite the search space, and leads us to the following completeness result.

Theorem 7 (Completeness of Normal Proofs). Given a fully typed protocol specification $\langle \Delta_0, S_0 \rangle$, and a property specification Π, there exists an implementation $\vdash$ such we can decide whether or not there exists a proof for $\Delta_0, \Pi, \Gamma_{\Delta_0, \Pi} \longrightarrow S_0$.

5   Implementation

We now show how we can literally translate the proof system presented in the previous section into Prolog. However, we want to stress that the framework so far developed is amenable to different implementation methodologies (e.g., bottom-up instead of top-down). First, one needs to eliminate functions application in the top-left side of the sequent. Special care has to be taken for mathematical expressions. After this operation, rule *expect* becomes

$$\frac{\Delta \vdash expect(id, r, s, m, \mathbf{K}) \land s' \text{ is } s + 1 \quad \Delta \cup \Delta' \longrightarrow agent(id, r, s'), S}{\Delta \longrightarrow agent(id, r, s), msg(m), S}$$

Where $\Delta' = \{knows(id, k) \mid k \in \mathbf{K}\}$. Then, we have to build a Prolog rule for modelling it. We use lists in order to model multisets, and – in order to benefit from the control predicates offered in Prolog – we decided not to write a meta-interpreter, but to incorporate Δ into the actual program (the same program `expect` and `compose` are defined in), and realise the changes that have to occur in Δ by means of `assert` and `retract` actions. It is worth mentioning that for our first prototype we *did* build a meta-interpreter, but we eventually decided to change methodology mainly for debugging reasons: our system is also meant for simulation and testing of (security) protocols. To this end, it is important that bugs in the protocol be promptly traceable. By avoiding the use of a meta-interpreter, we could benefit directly from the (alas, not astonishing) debugging tools offered by the Prolog implementation. As it turned out, using a non-meta program has another advantage which is invaluable for our purposes: namely the direct use of coroutining tools such as delay declarations.

Each rule of the proof system, once modified according to the first step above is translated into a Prolog clause defining the predicate state/1, according to the following schema: the rule

$$\frac{\Delta \vdash G \quad \Delta \cup \{knows(id, c_1), \dots, knows(id, c_m)\} \longrightarrow s_1, \dots, s_j, \mathcal{S}}{\Delta \longrightarrow t_1, \dots, t_k, \mathcal{S}}$$

is transformed into the clause

```
state(State):- substate([t̄₁, ... ,t̄ₖ], State, Rest_of_state),Ḡ,
    add_knowledge(id̄, [c̄₁, ... ,c̄ₘ]), state([s̄₁, ... ,s̄ⱼ|Rest_of_state]).
```

Where the over-lining is a straightforward mapping that takes care of translating atoms and terms according to Prolog's naming conventions (variables in uppercase, terms in lowercase, etc.). The predicate add_knowledge takes care of adding the appropriate clauses to the program. It has to behave in such a way that the clauses are removed upon backtracking (we need backtracking to be able to explore the search space of the traces in presence of an intruder). Since the clause we need to add are always ground, then we can undo an assert(c) simply by performing a retract(c).

6   Coroutining

As we have seen, the logical nature of Prolog allowed us to find an almost literal translation from the proof system into Prolog. The correctness of such translation is evident. Completeness is guaranteed provided that we avoid non-terminating derivations, which is always a risk, considering that Prolog selection rule is not fair. Fortunately, Prolog allows for a number of control methods; in our particular case, *delay declarations* allow for a very efficient execution, which is terminating for a large class of protocol's specification. We now show why. The crucial rule in this respect is *forge-receive*, which is translated as follows:

```
state(State):-  substate([agent(Id,Role,Step)],State,Rest),
    contrive(M),expect(Id,Role,Step,M,Info),NStep is Step +1,
    add_knowledge(Id,Info),state([agent(Id,Role,NStep)|Rest]).
```

This rule models Trudy forging a message via contrive(M), and trying to send it to the agent whose identifier is Id. If expect(Id,Role,Step,M,Info) succeeds, then the honest principal has accepted the contrived message as a legal one. The problem here is that contrive(M) has an infinite SLD tree (the intruder is allowed to contrive arbitrarily large and random messages). In order to avoid nontermination we can force contrive to generate only those messages that can be accepted by the corresponding expect; for this we can profitably exploit the availability of *logical variables*. For instance, if the definition of expect does not employ negation then we can simply call expect *before* calling `contrive`; `expect` will (partially) instantiate M to the message the agent Id is actually expecting, and `contrive` only needs to check if that message is contrivable, eventually "filling the gaps" that M presents: i.e. instantiating the still free variables appearing in M with values the intruder knows. This makes the rule terminating. More in general, we can enforce an optimal execution strategy also without atom's reordering and without the limitation to specifications that do not employ inequalities. The definition of contrive is

```
contrive(msg(M)) :- contrive_content(M).
```

```
contrive_content([H,H2|T]):- contrive_token(H),contrive_content([H2|T]).
contrive_content([H]):- contrive_token(H).
contrive_content(enc(key(K),M1)):-
  ( knows_object(trudy,K), contrive_content(M1)
  ; knows(trudy,msg(enc(key(K),M1)))).
```

```
contrive_token(M):- (M=nonce(N);M=key(N)), knows_object(trudy,N).
```

Where `knows_object` is an obvious predicate such that `knows_object(trudy,K)` succeeds if K is an object (key or nonce) Trudy is aware of (either because it had invented it in advance, or because it had intercepted it). In order to let it be terminating (and efficient), we simply have to add the declarations

```
delay contrive(X) until nonvar(X)
delay contrive_content(X) until nonvar(X)
delay contrive_token(X) until nonvar(X)
```

With these declarations, `contrive` will only generate messages that are readable by the other agent involved in the communication. It is worth noticing that this optimisation is possible thanks to two factors. The first is that we are not using any longer a ground resolution method. Declaratively, a ground semantics, is perfectly suitable. However, a direct implementation of such a semantics would unavoidably be very inefficient. The second is that we use (bidirectional) logical variables in a non-trivial way.

7   Conclusions

The contribution of this paper is threefold: (1) a proof-theoretic method for specifying security protocols. (2) a proof-theoretic methodology for specialising the proof system wrt the underlying protocol. It is worth mentioning that part of the specialisations we presented in Section 4 and in Section 6, were also present in previous papers, but only as "rule of thumb"; this is the first paper in which such optimizations ore proved correct, by means of rule transformations. (3) An implementation in Prolog of the system, which is now a tool allowing to specify, simulate and thus debug security protocols. In addition, it allows to verify safety properties of protocols, and in this we proved that it achieve completeness when protocols are *fully-typed*.

Theorem 7 applies when we consider a bounded number of parallel execution of the same protocol. The tool we have developed can be easily extended to cover also unbounded number of sessions, but completeness would be lost: if no attack exists the tool might run forever (Durgin et al. showed in [14] that the problem of finding an attack in presence of unbounded number of sessions is undecidable). Our future work focus on finding safe approximations for guaranteeing the termination of the tool also in presence of unbounded number of parallel sessions.

Lowe has tackled this problem in an orthogonal way. In [19] he demonstrates that if the protocol satisfies certain conditions, a parallel attack exists if and only if an attack exists within a single run of the protocol. For such protocols, demonstrating absence of attacks in a single session (which can be done with our tool) is sufficient for demonstrating absence of attacks in parallel sessions.

In [27], Paulson models a protocol in presence of an intruder as an inductively defined sets of traces, and uses Isabelle and HOL to *interactively* prove the absence of attacks. Paulson's approach works on an infinite-state search space. In our approach we use instead proofs structured as *trees* to represent protocol traces. Our approach is closer to Basin's method [3], where *lazy data structures* are used to generate the infinite-search tree representing protocol traces in a *demand-driven* manner. To limit state explosion Basin applies however heuristics that prune the generated tree. In our work we get similar results via a formal analysis of the proof system: in this way we *only* generate proofs without useless steps of the intruder. Trace semantics were also used for model-checking based analysis. In this context, we find the work of Lowe [17,18], who first identified and fixed the flaws in the Needham-Schroeder protocol, and the work of Mitchell et al. [24]. As pointed out e.g., in [16], these approaches require ad-hoc solutions for limiting the search space. In contrast, our approach allows for a finite search space for all *fully-typed* protocols.

Our approach combines aspects related to the multiset rewriting-based approach of [7,8] and the declarative way of specifying protocols using logic programs taken in [2,12]. A multiset rewriting formalism has also been used by Rusinowitch et al. by implementing it in OCAML in the CASRUL system [9], and, in the later [16] by processing the rewrite rules in the theorem-prover daTac. Conceptually, our system shares some features with that developed (independently) by Chevalier and Vigneron [11,10]. As in [11,10], we deal with communication in a constraint-based way, in which the intruder only checks if he is able to generate a certain message. Differently from the previous approaches, we separate in clear way knowledge and state and, thus we reason about knowledge and specify every principal using very simple *Horn programs*. In our opinion, this makes our framework more suitable for a specification tool.

Recently, a few works have appeared that employ constraint-solving techniques, possibly in combination with traces [15,22,30]. Typically, the task of the intruder is brought down to that of checking whether certain messages are *contrivable*. In a way, these work have something in common with our approach in that the transformation we performed by combining the receive and the forge rule aims at reducing the task of the intruder to *check* whether he is able to generate a certain message. Differently from us, [15,22,30] do this in a more radical way, and the checking phase is postponed *after* that the whole trace has been completed (while we check it after the next protocol step has been carried out). An advantage of our approach is that it permits to define a prototype for the simulation and fast prototyping of security protocols. In fact, our model allows to simulate all traces of a protocol, including thus those leading to failure. This is of course crucial when debugging a protocol. Because of their symbolic nature, this would not be possible using the models of [15,22,30].

Logic programming languages have been applied to specify security protocols in several different ways. Meadow's NRL Protocol Analyser [21] performs a reachability analysis using state-enumeration enriched by lemmata proved by induction. This way, NRL can cope with a potential infinite search space. Our approach differs from this previous work firstly in that NRL explores the search space in a backward fashion. Secondly, using proof theory we can formally reason on class of proofs and protocols for which finite-state exploration is both sound and complete. Furthermore, Prolog is used in our approach to *declaratively* specify each principal. In [2], Aiello and Massacci use a logic programming language but using a different perspective, i.e., with *stable semantics*, to specify and debug protocols. In this setting knowledge, protocol rules, intruder capabilities and objectives are specified in a declarative way. Finally, Blanchet [5] uses Prolog to specify *conservative abstractions* that can be used to prove security protocols free from attacks. Intuitively, Horn clauses are used here as *constructors* and *deconstructors* for the messages exchanged on the net and intercepted by the intruder. In [1] Abadi and Blanchet relate this approach to that of using *types* for guaranteeing the secrecy of communication, an approach substantially different from ours. The verification procedure combines aspects of *unfolding* and *bottom-up* evaluation (following, however, a depth-first strategy).

References

1. M. Abadi and B. Blanchet. Analyzing Security Protocols with Secrecy Types and Logic Programs. In *Proc. POPL 2002*, pages 33–44, 2002.
2. L. C. Aiello and F. Massacci. Verifying security protocols as planning in logic programming. *Trans. on Computational Logic*, 2001.
3. D. Basin. Lazy infinite-state analysis of security protocols. Secure Networking — CQRE [Secure] '99", LNCS 1740, pages 30–42, 1999.
4. G. Bella and L. C. Paulson. Kerberos version IV: Inductive analysis of the secrecy goals. In *Proc.5th Symp. on Research in Computer Security*, LNCS 1485, pages 361-375, 1998.
5. B. Blanchet. An efficient cryptographic protocol verifier based on prolog rules. In *Proc. CSFW'01*, 2001.
6. M. Burrows, M. Abadi, and R. Needham. A logic of authentication. *ACM Trans. on Computer Systems*, 8(1):18–36, 1990.
7. I. Cervesato, N. Durgin, P. Lincoln, J. Mitchell, and A. Scedrov. A meta-notation for protocol analysis. In *Proc. CSFW '99*, pages 55–69, 1999.
8. I. Cervesato, N. Durgin, J. Mitchell, Lincoln, and A. Scedrov. Relating strands and multiset rewriting for security protocol analysis. In *Proc. CSFW '00*, pages 35-51, 2000.

9. Y. Chevalier, F. Jacquemard, M. Rusinowitch, M. Turuani, and L. Vigneron. CAS-RUL web site. http://www.loria.fr/equipes/protheo/SOFTWARES/CASRUL/.

10. Y.Chevalier and L.Vigneron. A tool for lazy verification of security protocols. In *Proc. Int'l Conf. Automated Software Engineering*, 2001.

11. Y.Chevalier and L.Vigneron. Towards efficient automated verification of security protocols. In *Proc. VERIF '01*, 2001.

12. G. Delzanno. Specifying and debugging security protocols via hereditary harrop formulas and lambda prolog. In *Proc. FLOPS '01*, pages 123–137, 2001.

13. D. Dolev and A. C. Yao. On the security of public key protocols. *IEEE Trans. on Information Theory*, 29(2):198–208, 1983.

14. N. Durgin, P. Lincoln, J. Mitchell, and A. Scedrov. Undecidability of bounded security protocols. In *Proc. FMSP'99 (FLOC '99)*, 1999.

15. A. Huima. Efficient infinite-state analysis of security protocols. In *Proc. FMSP '99 (FLOC '99)*, 1999.

16. F. Jacquemard, M. Rusinowitch, and L. Vigneron. Compiling and verifying security protocols. In *Proc. LPAR 2000*, LNCS 1995, pages 131-160, 2000.

17. G. Lowe. Breaking and fixing the Needham-Schroeder public-key protocol using FDR. *Software Concepts and Tools*, (17):93–102, 1996.

18. G. Lowe. Casper: A compiler for the analysis of security protocols. In *Proc.CSFW '97*, pages 18–30, 1997.

19. G. Lowe. Towards a completeness result for model checking of security protocols. *J. of Computer Security*, 7(2-3):89–146, 1998.

20. C. Meadows. Formal verification of cryptographic protocols: A survey. In *Proc. ASIACRYPT '94*, pages 133–150, 1995.

21. C. Meadows. The NRL protocol analyzer: An overview. *J. of Logic Programming*, 26(2):113–131, 1996.

22. J. Millen and V. Shmatikov. Constraint solving for bounded-process cryptographic protocol analysis. In *Proc. 2001 ACM Conf. on Computer and Communication Security*, pages 166 – 175, 2001.

23. J. K. Millen, S. C. Clark, and S. B. Freedman. The Interrogator: Protocol security analysis. *IEEE Trans. on Software Engineering*, 13(2):274–288, 1987.

24. J. C. Mitchell, M. Mitchell, and U. Stern. Automated analysis of cryptographic protocols using murφ. In *Proc. Conf. on Security and Privacy*, pages 141–153, 1997.

25. R. M. Needham and M. D. Schroeder. Using encryption for authentication in large networks of computers. *Comm. of the ACM*, 21(12):993–999, 1978.

26. L. C. Paulson. Mechanized proofs of security protocols: Needham-Schroeder with public keys. T.R. 413, Univ. of Cambridge, Computer Laboratory, January 1997.

27. L. C. Paulson. The inductive approach to verifying cryptographic protocols. *J. of Computer Security*, 6:85–128, 1998.

28. A. W. Roscoe. Modelling and verifying key-exchange protocols using csp and fdr. In *IEEE Symp. on Foundations of Secure Systems*, 1995.

29. A. W. Roscoe. *The Theory and Practice of Concurrency*. Prentice-Hall, 1999.

30. M. Rusinowitch and M. Turuani. Protocol insecurity with finite number of sessions is np-complete. In *Proc. CSFW '01*, 2001.

Abstract Conjunctive Partial Deduction Using Regular Types and Its Application to Model Checking

Michael Leuschel and Stefan Gruner

Department of Electronics and Computer Science
University of Southampton
Highfield, Southampton, SO17 1BJ, UK
{mal,sg}@ecs.soton.ac.uk
http://www.ecs.soton.ac.uk/~mal

Abstract. We present an abstract partial deduction technique which uses regular types as its domain and which can handle conjunctions, and thus perform deforestation and tupling. We provide a detailed description of all the required operations and present an implementation within the ECCE system. We discuss the power of this new specialisation algorithm, especially in the light of verifying and specialising infinite state process algebras. Here, our new algorithm can provide a more precise treatment of synchronisation and can be used for refinement checking.

1 Introduction

Program specialisation, also called *partial evaluation* or *partial deduction*, is an automatic technique for program optimisation (see, e.g., [16,24,29]). The central idea is to specialise a given source program for a particular application domain. The main idea of *abstract interpretation* [7,2,22] is to statically analyse programs by interpreting them over some *abstract domain*. This is done in such a way as to ensure termination of the abstract interpretation and to ensure that the so derived results are a *safe approximation* of the programs' concrete runtime behaviour(s).

At first sight *abstract interpretation* and *program specialisation* might appear to be quite different techniques: abstract interpretation focusses on *correct and precise* analysis, while the main goal of program specialisation is to produce more *efficient residual code* (for a given task at hand). Nonetheless, it is often felt that there is a close relationship between abstract interpretation and program specialisation and, recently, there has been a lot of interest in the integration of these two techniques (see, e.g., [6,33,23,44,45,46]).

[28,30] presented a generic framework and algorithm for top-down program specialisation, which supersedes earlier top-down specialisation approaches in generality and power. [28,30] established several *generic correctness results* and have cast several existing techniques in the framework. [28,30] has illustrated on some examples how the additional power can be exploited in practice, for

A. Pettorossi (Ed.): LOPSTR 2001, LNCS 2372, pp. 91–110, 2002.

improved generalisation, unfolding and code-generation. Applications in verification and model checking were also hinted at.

In this paper we present a particular instantiation of the abstract partial deduction framework of [28,30], by using an abstract domain based upon regular types. This instantiation partly resembles the technique of [19,20] (the two techniques were developed more or less independently). However, there are still considerable differences with [19,20]. For example, our approach can handle conjunctions together with the regular type information. This provides advantages for specialisation tasks, such as more tractable local control [32] and enables optimisations such as deforestation and tupling. As we will show in the paper, it also enables new applications in the verification of infinite state systems. In summary, the combined power of conjunctions and regular types enables transformations which cannot be achieved by either approach alone. We describe our implementation, based upon the ECCE system [27]. We also present the very first experiments with this implementation and demonstrate its usefulness for infinite state model checking of process algebras.

2 Preliminaries

In the remainder of this paper we suppose some familiarity with basic notions in logic programming [1,39] as well as some acquaintance with partial deduction [29]. In this paper, we restrict ourselves to definite programs and goals (but possibly with declarative built-in's such as is, call, functor, arg, \==).

We need the following definitions. An *expression* is either a term, an atom or a conjunction. We use $E_1 \preceq E_2$ to denote that the expression E_1 is an instance of the expression E_2. By $vars(E)$ we denote the set of variables appearing in an expression E. By mgu we denote a function which computes an idempotent and relevant[1] most general unifier θ of two expressions E_1 and E_2 (and returns *fail* if no such unifier exists) Also, by $msg(E_1, E_2)$ we denote a most specific generalisation [26] of E_1 and E_2.

Also, as common in partial deduction, the notion of SLD-trees is extended to allow *incomplete* SLD-trees which may contain leaves where no literal has been selected for further derivation. A *resultant* is a formula $H \leftarrow B$ where H and B are conjunctions of literals. The resultant of a SLD-derivation of $P \cup \{\leftarrow Q\}$ with c.a.s. θ leading to the *resolvent* $\leftarrow B$ is the formula $Q\theta \leftarrow B$. We also denote by $\mathcal{Q}$ the set of all conjunctions and by 2^S the power-set of some set S.

Abstract Partial Deduction. In classical partial deduction [40] a program is specialised for a set of ordinary atoms (or conjunctions in the case of conjunctive partial deduction [9]). In abstract partial deduction a program is specialised for a set of abstract conjunctions, defined as follows:

Definition 1. *An* abstract domain $(\mathcal{AQ}, \gamma)$ *is a couple consisting of a set* $\mathcal{AQ}$ *of so-called* abstract conjunctions *and a* total *concretisation function* $\gamma : \mathcal{AQ} \rightarrow$

---

[1] I.e., $\theta\theta = \theta$ and $vars(\theta) \subseteq vars(E_1) \cup vars(E_2)$.

$2^{\mathcal{Q}}$, *providing the link between the abstract and the concrete domain, such that* $\forall \mathbf{A} \in \mathcal{AQ}$ *the following hold:*

1. $\forall Q \in \gamma(\mathbf{A})$ *we have* $\forall \theta : Q\theta \in \gamma(\mathbf{A})$,
2. $\exists Q \in \mathcal{Q}$ *such that* $\forall Q' \in \gamma(\mathbf{A}) : Q' \preceq Q$.

Property (1) expresses the requirement that the image of γ is *downwards closed*, which is vital in correctness proofs [30]. Property (2) expresses the fact that all conjunctions in $\gamma(\mathbf{A})$ have the same number of conjuncts and with the same predicates at the same position. This property is crucial to enable the construction of (correct) residual code.[2]

One particular abstract domain, which arises in the formalisation of classical partial deduction [40] and conjunctive partial deduction [9], is the $\mathcal{PD}$-domain where $\mathcal{AQ} = \mathcal{Q}$ (i.e. the abstract conjunctions are the concrete ones) and $\gamma(Q) = \{Q' \mid Q' \preceq Q\}$ (i.e. an abstract conjunction denotes all its instances). For example, we can use the concrete conjunction $p(X) \wedge q(X)$ as an abstract conjunction in the $\mathcal{PD}$-domain with $p(a) \wedge q(a) \in \gamma(p(X) \wedge q(X))$ as well as $p(X) \wedge q(X) \in \gamma(p(X) \wedge q(X))$, but $p(a) \wedge q(b) \notin \gamma(p(X) \wedge q(X))$.

The main difference of abstract partial deduction [30] over abstract interpretation is that both the concrete and the abstract domain have to be analysed (the residual program has to be expressed in the concrete domain). Concretely, when specialising an abstract conjunction $\mathbf{A}$ we have to generate:

(1) *concrete* resultants $H_i \leftarrow B_i$, which have to be totally correct for all possible calls in $\gamma(\mathbf{A})$,
(2) for each resultant $H_i \leftarrow B_i$ an *abstract* conjunction $\mathbf{A_i}$ approximating all the possible resolvent goals which can occur after resolving an element of $\gamma(\mathbf{A})$ with $H_i \leftarrow B_i$.

Step (1) is called *abstract unfolding* and step (2) *abstract resolution*. The formal definitions can be found in [30]. An abstract partial deduction algorithm can now be obtained [30] by computing the least fixpoint of the operator U : $2^{\mathcal{AQ}} \rightarrow 2^{\mathcal{AQ}}$ defined by $U(S) = \omega(S \cup \{ares(\mathbf{A}, C) \mid \mathbf{A} \in S \wedge C \in aunf(\mathbf{A})\})$, where ω is a widening function ensuring termination. Through this we obtain a set of abstract conjunctions from which we generate residual code using abstract unfolding combined with a renaming operation (which maps conjunctions back to atoms and thus general resultants back to Horn clauses).

3 Limitations of the $\mathcal{PD}$-Domain for Verification

3.1 Verification by Specialisation

[37] established that infinite state model checking can be performed by a combination of partial deduction and abstract interpretation. The contribution of the paper is also the development of a CTL (computation tree logic; see, e.g., [5]) interpreter in logic programming and its use as a sound basis for model checking

---

[2] Observe that property 2. still admits the possibility of a bottom element $\perp$ whose concretisation is empty.

of finite and infinite state systems via program analysis and specialisation in general. The advantage of this approach is its generality. For example, one can change the specification formalism by providing a different interpreter (e.g, for CSP or the B-method or variations thereof, see [31]), one can tune the verification algorithm by tuning the settings of the specialisation algorithm (see [35, 34]), and one can also try to apply the verification approach for systems and properties which are in principle undecidable.

[35] gave a first formal answer about the power of the approach and showed that when we encode ordinary Petri nets as logic programs and use existing program specialisation algorithms, we can decide the so-called "coverability problems" (which encompass quasi-liveness, boundedness, determinism, regularity,...). Recent experiments [38] seem to suggest that this approach fares quite well in practice, compared to some existing verification systems. [34] proved completeness results for another class of infinite state model checking tasks, namely covering problems for reset Petri nets. The latter are particularly interesting as they lie on the "border between decidability and undecidability". These results extend to other Petri net formalisms which can be viewed as so-called Well-Structured Transition Systems (WSTS's), for which certain properties are decidable [12].

All of the results above were obtained in the setting of classical partial deduction. Now, certain process algebras can also be viewed as WSTS's, so one would hope that the approach could handle those as well. Unfortunately, this is not the case, as we will show below. The solution will be moving to a more refined abstract domain.

3.2   Limitation of Classical Partial Deduction

Let us first present a verification example where existing partial deduction techniques, e.g., those based on the $\mathcal{PD}$-domain, fail. This motivates the development of a more precise domain later in the paper.

Example 1. Take the following specification of an agent P expressed using the process algebra CSP [48] (where "$\rightarrow$" denotes the action prefix, and "$|||$" the interleaving operator): $P =_{Def} a \rightarrow (P|||P)$
The operational semantics of CSP tells us that the agent P can perform the action a (leading to the expression $P|||P$). This expression, in turn, can perform a leading to either $(P|||P)|||P$ or $P|||(P|||P)$, and so on. This CSP specification is thus infinite state, in the sense that an infinite number of different expressions can be reached. Infinite state descriptions can be very useful (e.g., to specify protocols with an arbitrary number of connections) but explicit model checking techniques cannot cope with them and are thus, e.g., unable to establish that P cannot deadlock.

Using the method of [37], one would first encode P and the safety property that our system should not deadlock, as a logic program. This can for example be done as follows (where we have also added support for a choice operator and for a parallel composition which synchronises every action; we have also defined a small client-server system in this process algebra, with two clients and a server that can replicate itself at will):

```
unsafe(State) :- deadlock(State).
unsafe(State) :- trans(_Action,State,NewState),unsafe(NewState).

trans(A,prefix(A,X),X).
trans(A,choice(X,_),X1) :- trans(A,X,X1).
trans(A,choice(_,X),X1) :- trans(A,X,X1).
trans(A,interleave(X,Y),interleave(X1,Y)) :- trans(A,X,X1).
trans(A,interleave(X,Y),interleave(X,Y1)) :- trans(A,Y,Y1).
trans(A,par(X,Y),par(X1,Y1)) :- trans(A,X,X1),trans(A,Y,Y1).
trans(tau,agent(X),XDef) :- agent(X,XDef).

deadlock(stop).
deadlock(interleave(X,Y)) :- deadlock(X),deadlock(Y).
deadlock(choice(X,_Y)) :- deadlock(X).
deadlock(choice(_X,Y)) :- deadlock(Y).
deadlock(par(X,Y)) :- \+(trans(_,par(X,Y),_)).

agent(p,prefix(a, interleave(agent(p),agent(p)))).
agent(server,choice(prefix(new_server, interleave(agent(server),
     agent(server))),   prefix(request,prefix(serve,agent(server)))))).
agent(client,prefix(request,prefix(serve,agent(client)))).
agent(system,par(agent(client),par(agent(client),agent(server)))).
```

To prove our safety property, [37] then proposes to use partial deduction combined with abstract interpretation to attempt to transform the above program into the empty program for the query `unsafe(agent(p))`. If this transformation is successful, the infinite state system is safe. This approach can successfully handle [35] various versions and extensions of Petri nets. However, the state expressions of process algebras are more involved and existing partial deduction techniques will not be able to deduce that `unsafe(agent(p))` must fail. Let us examine why this is the case. First, as explained above, the state P leads to the state $P|||P$, and hence the call

$\quad\quad$`unsafe(agent(p))`$\quad$ will lead, e.g., to $\quad$`unsafe(par(agent(p),agent(p)))`.

At that point most partial deduction systems will stop the unfolding[3] and perform generalisation.[4] Now, in the $\mathcal{PD}$-domain the most precise generalisation possible is the *msg* of the two calls which in this case is `unsafe(X)`. In other words, we lose all the information on the system and we cannot prove the safety property. Indeed, the unconstrained call `unsafe(X)` can of course also represent `unsafe(stop)` which *can* deadlock. Hence, it is impossible to transform `unsafe(X)` into *fail*. For a query such as `unsafe(agent(system))` the task is even more complicated (and even existing goal directed abstract interpretation systems, such as the current release of [17], are not able to derive failure of `unsafe(agent(system))`).

---

[3] E.g., ECCE will detect that `agent(p)` $\trianglelefteq$ `par(agent(p),agent(p))`.

[4] A similar situation will arise even if we delay generalisation.

This precision problem did not arise in the context of Petri nets in [35,34]. Indeed, Petri nets have a "fixed structure", which can be captured within the $\mathcal{PD}$-domain. For example, take a Petri net with three places and where markings are encoded as lists of natural numbers. Then the *msg* of, e.g., `unsafe([0,s(0),0])` and `unsafe([s(0),s(0),s(0)])` is `unsafe([X,s(0),X])` and in this case the *msg* is actually quite precise, and the $\mathcal{PD}$-domain is sufficient to decide several interesting problems [35,34].

4   The RUL Domain

To solve the above problem (and many others as well), we propose to move to a more precise abstract domain in which we can implement a more refined generalisation operation. More concretely, we propose to use an abstract domain using regular types encoded as regular unary logic programs [49,18], for which efficient algorithms exist and which is nonetheless a sufficiently expressive domain. This domain also yields improved precision in more "classical" applications of partial deduction (see, e.g., [10]).

4.1   Regular Unary Logic Programs

We will use the following definition, slightly adapted from [20] (we handle the *any* type slightly differently):

Definition 2. *A canonical regular unary clause is a clause of the form:*
$$t_0(f(X_1,\ldots,X_n)) \leftarrow t_1(X_1) \wedge \ldots \wedge t_n(X_n)$$
where $n \geq 0$ and $X_1,\ldots,X_n$ are distinct variables. A regular unary logic (RUL) program is a finite set of regular unary clauses, in which no two different clause heads have a common instance, together with the single fact $any(X) \leftarrow$. Given a (possibly non-ground) conjunction T and a RUL program R, we write $R \models \forall(T)$ iff $R \cup \{\leftarrow T\}$ has an SLD-refutation with the empty computed answer. Finally, the success set of a predicate t in a RUL program R is defined by $success_R(t) = \{s \mid s \text{ is ground} \wedge R \models \forall(t(s))\}$.

Example 2. For example, given the following RUL-program R, we have $R \models \forall(t1([a]))$ and $R \models \forall(t1([X,Y]))$.

```
t1([]).                        any(X).
t1([H|T]) :- any(H),t1(T).
```

Given a RUL-program R and two type predicates t_1 and t_2, there exist efficient procedures for checking inclusion ($success_R(t_1) \subseteq success_R(t_1)$) and computing new type predicates t_3, t_4 and RUL programs R_1, R_2 realising the intersection ($success_{R_1}(t_3) = success_R(t_1) \cap success_R(t_2)$) and an upper bound ($success_{R_2}(t_4) \supseteq success_R(t_1) \cup success_R(t_2)$) respectively.

Definition 3. *We define the RUL-domain* $(\mathcal{AQ}, \gamma)$ *to consist of abstract conjunctions of the form* $\langle Q, T, R \rangle \in \mathcal{AQ}$ *where* Q, T *are concrete conjunctions and* R *is a RUL program such that:* $T = t_1(X_1) \wedge \ldots \wedge t_n(X_n)$, *where* $vars(Q) = \{X_1, \ldots, X_n\}$ *and* t_i *are predicates defined in* R. *The* concretisation function γ *is defined as follows:* $\gamma(\langle Q, T, R \rangle) = \{Q\theta \mid R \models \forall(T\theta)\}$. T *is called a type conjunction.*

Using R from Ex. 2 we have that $\gamma(\langle p(X), t1(X), R \rangle) = \{p([]), p([X]), p([a]), \ldots, p([X, Y]), p([X, X]), p([a, X]), \ldots\}$. Note that abstract conjunctions from our RUL-domain are called R-conjunctions in [20].

4.2 Standard Operations on Abstract Conjunctions

Simplification and Normalisation. The following operation is used to simplify type conjunctions and to detect inconsistencies.

Definition 4. Simplification *of a type conjunction* T *into* T' *within a RUL program* R, *is defined as follows. We build an SLD-tree* τ *for* $R \cup \{\leftarrow T\}$ *by repeatedly selecting literals of the form* $t_i(s_i)$, *where* $t_i \neq any$ *and* s_i *is not a variable, until we only have calls with variables as arguments remaining. Due to the nature of* R *this SLD-tree will have a single branch with the empty computed answer. If this produces a finitely failed SLD-tree* τ, *we write* $T \leadsto_R fail$, *otherwise we write* $T \leadsto_R T'$, *where* T' *is the conjunction in the leaf of* τ.

E.g., using R from Ex. 2, $t1([X, Y|T])) \leadsto_R any(X) \wedge any(Y) \wedge t1(T)$ and $t1(b) \leadsto_R fail$. Note that, by definition, $T \leadsto_R fail$ implies that $\forall \sigma. R \not\models \forall(T\sigma)$.

Definition 5. *A regular type conjunction is said to be* canonical *[20] iff it is a type conjunction of the form* $t_1(X_1) \wedge \ldots \wedge t_k(X_k)$, $k > 0$ *where* $X_1, \ldots, X_k$ *are distinct variables. A regular unary logic program is said to be* canonical *iff for all predicates* t *defined in* R, $R \cup \{\leftarrow t(X)\}$ *has a refutation. An abstract conjunction* $\langle Q, T, R \rangle$ *is said to be* canonical *iff* R *is canonical and either* T *is canonical or* $T = fail$.

Proposition 1. *Every abstract conjunction* $\langle Q, T, R \rangle$ *can be translated into an equivalent canonical abstract conjunction* $\langle Q, T', R' \rangle$. *By* canonical($\langle Q, T, R \rangle$) *we denote one such equivalent abstract conjunction.*

We can compute *canonical*($\langle Q, T, R \rangle$) by first applying the simplification operation from Definition 4 to $T \leadsto_R T_S$. If $T_S = fail$ we set $T_S = fail$ and $R = \emptyset$. Otherwise, for all tuples of atoms in T_S which have the same variable as argument, we replace them by their intersection, yielding T' (unless any type intersection yields an empty type, in which case we set T' to *fail*). In order to obtain R', we add all type intersections to R and we remove all those predicates which are empty (i.e., which cannot reach a fact in the predicate dependency graph). This is very similar to the **simplify** procedure in [20].

Finally, a type conjunction T can be projected on a set of variables V, denoted by $project_V(T)$, by simply removing all those conjuncts in T which do not contain a variable in V.

Instance checking. We will denote the fact that $\gamma(\mathbf{A_1}) \subseteq \gamma(\mathbf{A_2})$ by $\mathbf{A_1} \sqsubseteq \mathbf{A_2}$. For abstract partial deduction, $\mathbf{A_1} \sqsubseteq \mathbf{A_2}$ means that if we have already generated residual code for $\mathbf{A_2}$ then we do not have to generate code for $\mathbf{A_1}$, as we can reuse the code generated for $\mathbf{A_2}$. Below, we discus how one can check $\sqsubseteq$ in practice.

There exist efficient algorithms for deciding whether a regular type is a sub-type of another regular type. Hence, for abstract conjunctions such as $\mathbf{A_1} = \langle p(X), t_1(X), \{t_1(a)\}\rangle$, $\mathbf{A_2} = \langle p(Z), t_2(Z), \{t_2(a), t_2(b)\}\rangle$ it is easy to see that $\mathbf{A_1} \sqsubseteq \mathbf{A_2}$, as t_1 is a strict subtype of t_2. However, when the first components of two abstract conjunctions are not variants of each other, the solution is less obvious and we describe a decision procedure below. Take, for example, $\mathbf{A_3} = \langle p(a, Y), t_1(Y), \{t_1(a), t_1(b)\}\rangle$ $\mathbf{A_4} = \langle p(X, b), t_2(X), \{t_2(a)\}\rangle$. How can we infer that $\mathbf{A_4} \sqsubseteq \mathbf{A_3}$? The first thing we need is to be able to transfer all of the structure information into the type conjunction. This is achieved by the following definition.

Definition 6. *Given an abstract conjunction $\mathbf{A} = \langle Q, T, R \rangle$ we define its rulified form, denoted by rulify($\mathbf{A}$) inductively as follows:*

- *rulify$(\langle A_1 \wedge \ldots \wedge A_n, T_0, R_0\rangle) = \langle B_1 \wedge \ldots \wedge B_n, T_n, R_n\rangle$ where for $1 \leq i \leq n$ we have $\langle B_i, T_i, R_i\rangle = rulify\_atom(\langle A_i, T_{i-1}, R_{i-1}\rangle)$*
- *rulify$\_atom(\langle p(s_1, \ldots, s_n), T_0, R_0\rangle) = \langle p(X_1, \ldots, X_n), T_n, R_n\rangle$ where for $1 \leq i \leq n$ we have $\langle X_i, T_i, R_i\rangle = rulify\_term(\langle s_i, T_{i-1}, R_{i-1}\rangle)$*
- *rulify$\_term(\langle X, T, R\rangle) = \langle X, T, R\rangle$ if X is a variable*
- *rulify$\_term(\langle c, T, R\rangle) = \langle X, t_k(X) \wedge T, R \cup \{t_k(c)\}\rangle$ where X is a fresh variables and t_k a fresh predicate symbol*
- *rulify$\_term(\langle f(s_1, \ldots, s_n), T_0, R_0\rangle) =$ $\langle X, t_k(X) \wedge T_n, R_n \cup \{t_k(f(X_1, \ldots, X_n) \leftarrow t_1(X_1) \wedge \ldots t_n(X_n))\}\rangle$ where $X, X_1, \ldots, X_n$ are fresh variables and t_k a fresh predicate symbol and where for $1 \leq i \leq n$ we have rulify$\_term(\langle s_i, T_{i-1}, R_{i-1}\rangle) = \langle r_i, T_i, R_i\rangle$.*

An abstract conjunction $\mathbf{A}$ such that $\mathbf{A} = rulify(\mathbf{A})$ is called rulified.

Now a first attempt at deciding $\sqsubseteq$ would be to compute $rulify(.)$ for both conjunctions and then use the subtype check on all argument positions. For example, for $\mathbf{A_3} = \langle p(a, Y), t_1(Y), \{t_1(a), t_1(b)\}\rangle$ $\mathbf{A_4} = \langle p(X, b), t_2(X), \{t_2(a)\}\rangle$, we obtain $rulify(\mathbf{A_3}) = \langle p(X, Y), t_3(X) \wedge t_1(Y), \{t_1(a), t_1(b), t_3(a)\}\rangle$ and $rulify(\mathbf{A_4}) = \langle p(X, Y), t_2(X) \wedge t_4(Y), \{t_2(a), t_4(a)\}\rangle$. We have that t_3 and t_2 are equivalent and t_4 is a strict subtype of t_1. Hence we can conclude $\mathbf{A_4} \sqsubseteq \mathbf{A_3}$.

Unfortunately, this procedure is unsound in general! Indeed, take for example $\mathbf{A_5} = \langle p(f(X), X), t_1(X), \{t_1(a).t_1(b).\}\rangle$ and $\mathbf{A_6} = \langle p(Z, X), t_1(X) \wedge t_2(Z), \{t_1(a).t_1(b).t_2(f(V)) \leftarrow t_1(V)\}\rangle$. We can see that $rulify(\mathbf{A_5}) = \mathbf{A_6}$ and hence we would wrongly conclude that $\mathbf{A_6} \sqsubseteq \mathbf{A_5}$. In fact, we have, for example, that $p(f(a), b) \in \gamma(\mathbf{A_6})$ while $p(f(a), b) \notin \gamma(\mathbf{A_5})$.

The problem lies in the fact that, while we have $\mathbf{A} \sqsubseteq rulify(\mathbf{A})$, we do not have $rulify(\mathbf{A}) \sqsubseteq \mathbf{A}$. A simple solution to this problem would be to only consider rulified abstract conjunctions at the global level of the specialisation algorithm (i.e., before specialising an abstract conjunction, it is systematically rulified). Hence, to decide whether a given new abstract conjunction $\mathbf{B}$ which arises during partial deduction is already covered by some existing, rulified abstract conjunction $\mathbf{A}$ we simply check whether $rulify(\mathbf{B}) \sqsubseteq \mathbf{A}$ which is a sound approximation of $\mathbf{B} \sqsubseteq \mathbf{A}$.

Unfortunately, as we have seen on A_5 and A_6 above, this solution implies an inherent precision loss, which can be especially harmful for conjunctive partial deduction, where variable links will often be broken by the $rulify$ procedure. For example, $rulify(\langle p(f(X)) \wedge q(X), any(X), \{\}\rangle = \langle p(Z) \wedge q(X), t_1(Z), \{t_1(f(Z)) \leftarrow any(Z)\}\rangle$, and the link between p and q has been broken and we would no longer get any benefit from conjunctive partial deduction. So, we need a more refined solution, which we present below. We first introduce another operation on abstract conjunctions, which is an extension of the simplification procedure from Def. 4.

Definition 7. Extended Simplification *of a canonical type conjunction T into T' within a canonical RUL program R, is defined as follows. First, we compute $T \leadsto_R T_S$ and then we build a finite SLD-tree τ for $R \cup \{\leftarrow T_S\}$ by repeatedly selecting the leftmost literal which unifies with at most one clause head in R. Also, let θ be the computed answer of the unique branch of τ. If this produces a finitely failed SLD-tree τ, we write $T \leadsto_R^\theta fail$, otherwise we write $T \leadsto_R^\theta T'$, where T' is the conjunction in the leaf of τ.*

We now define extended simplification for canonical abstract conjunctions as follows: $esimplify(\langle Q, T, R \rangle) = \langle Q\theta, T', R \rangle$ where $T \leadsto_R^\theta T'$.

For example, for $R = \{t_1(a), t_1(f(Z)) \leftarrow t_2(Z), t_2(f(V)) \leftarrow t_1(V)\}$, we have $t_1(f(X)) \leadsto_R^{\{X/f(V)\}} t_1(V)$ while $t_1(f(X)) \leadsto_R t_2(X)$.

Note that it is important that both R or T are canonical, otherwise τ can be infinite (for example using $T = t_1(X) \wedge t_2(X)$ and R above, we obtain an infinitely failed, deterministic SLD-tree for $R \cup \{\leftarrow T\}$).

Observe that, $T \leadsto_R^\theta fail$ implies that $\forall \sigma. R \not\models \forall(T\sigma)$.

Proposition 2. *Let $\mathbf{A_1} = \langle Q_1, T_1, R_1 \rangle$ and $\mathbf{A_2} = \langle Q_2, T_2, R_2 \rangle$ be two abstract conjunctions in canonical form such that $\gamma(\mathbf{A_1}) \neq \emptyset$ and $\gamma(\mathbf{A_2}) \neq \emptyset$. Let $T_1 \leadsto_{R_1}^{\theta_1} T_1', T_2 \leadsto_{R_2}^{\theta_2} T_2'$. Then $\mathbf{A_1} \sqsubseteq \mathbf{A_2}$ iff $Q_1\theta_1$ is an instance of $Q_2\theta_2$ and $rulify(\mathbf{A_1}) \sqsubseteq rulify(\mathbf{A_2})$.*

Proof. (Sketch) First, one can establish that $\gamma(esimplify(\mathbf{A})) = \gamma(\mathbf{A})$, $\mathbf{A} \sqsubseteq rulify(\mathbf{A})$, and $rulify(rulify(\mathbf{A})) \sqsubseteq rulify(\mathbf{A})$. One can also prove that if $t \in \gamma(rulify(\langle Q, T, R \rangle))$ and $t \notin \gamma(\langle Q, T, R \rangle)$ then t is not an instance of Q.

Soundness ($\mathbf{A_1} \sqsubseteq \mathbf{A_2}$ if $Q_1\theta_1$ is an instance of $Q_2\theta_2$ and $rulify(\mathbf{A_1}) \sqsubseteq rulify(\mathbf{A_2})$): Suppose that there exists $t_1 \in \gamma(\mathbf{A_1})$ such that $t_1 \notin \gamma(\mathbf{A_2})$. We know that t_1 is an instance of $Q_1\theta_1$. By the above lemmas we also know that t_1 cannot be an instance of Q_2 (nor of $Q_2\theta_2$). We thus have a contradiction, as $Q_1\theta_1$ is an instance of $Q_2\theta_2$.

Completeness (i.e., $\mathbf{A_1} \sqsubseteq \mathbf{A_2}$ only if $Q_1\theta_1$ is an instance of $Q_2\theta_2$ and $rulify(\mathbf{A_1}) \sqsubseteq rulify(\mathbf{A_2})$): Suppose that $\mathbf{A_1} \sqsubseteq \mathbf{A_2}$. First, by montonicity of tuple-distributive closure we have that $rulify$ is monotonic, i.e., we must have $rulify(\mathbf{A_1}) \sqsubseteq rulify(\mathbf{A_2})$. So, suppose that $Q_1\theta_1$ is not an instance of $Q_2\theta_2$. Hence there must be a position in $Q_1\theta$ with subterm t_1 such that either:

- t_1 is a non-variable term and the corresponding subterm t_2 in $Q_2\theta_2$ exists and has no common instance with t_1. This contradicts $\mathbf{A_1} \sqsubseteq \mathbf{A_2}$ as $\gamma(\mathbf{A_1}) \neq \emptyset$.
- or t_1 is a variable, say X, and the corresponding subterm $f(r_1, \ldots, r_n)$ with $n \geq 0$ in $Q_2\theta_2$ exists and is not a variable. However, as $\mathbf{A_1}$ is canonical, this means that T_1' cannot be fully simplified, as the type t_x of X in T_1' must contain a single clause of the form $t_x(f(X_1, \ldots, X_n)) \leftarrow Body$.
- or the corresonding subterm in $Q_2\theta$ is a variable, say X, which also appears at another position p_2 of $Q_2\theta$. The subterm t_1' at that position p_2 within $Q_1\theta_1$ in turn exists and is different from t_1. Again, there are different cases for t_1 and t_1', which all lead to a contradiction. Suppose, for example, that t_1 and t_1' are two different variables, say V and W. Now, as T_1' is fully simplified and as $\mathbf{A_1}$ is canonical, we know that we can find at least two different instances of V which satisfy the type conjunction T_1'. The same holds for W. We can thus chose a concretisation of $\mathbf{A_1}$ which maps V and W to two different terms and hence we cannot have $\mathbf{A_1} \sqsubseteq \mathbf{A_2}$.

As $\gamma(\mathbf{A_1}) \neq \emptyset$ and $\gamma(\mathbf{A_2}) \neq \emptyset$ can be easily decided using the emptiness check for regular types, and since abstract conjunctions can be converted into canonical form, Proposition 2 gives us a decision procedure for $\sqsubseteq$.

Example 3. Let us return to $\mathbf{A_5} = \langle p(f(X), X), t_1(X), R_1 \rangle$ and $\mathbf{A_6} = \langle p(Z, X), t_1(X) \wedge t_2(Z), R_2 \rangle$ from above, where $R_1 = \{t_1(a).t_1(b).\}$ and $R_2 = \{t_1(a).t_1(b). t_2(f(V)) \leftarrow t_1(V)\}$. We have that $t_1(X) \leadsto_{R_1}^\emptyset t_1(X)$ and $t_1(X) \wedge t_2(Z) \leadsto_{R_2}^{\{Z/f(V)\}} t_1(X) \wedge t_1(V)$. We also have that $p(f(X), X)$ is an instance of $p(Z, X)\{Z/f(V)\} = p(f(V), X)$, but not the other way around. We have already seen that $rulify(\mathbf{A_5}) = rulify(\mathbf{A_6}) = \mathbf{A_6}$. Hence, by Proposition 2 we can conclude that $\mathbf{A_5} \sqsubseteq \mathbf{A_6}$ and $\mathbf{A_6} \not\sqsubseteq \mathbf{A_5}$.

For the only-if part of Proposition 2 it is important for $\mathbf{A_1}$ and $\mathbf{A_2}$ to be in canonical form. Take the non-canonical abstract conjunction $\langle p(X), T_1, \{t_1(a), t_1(b), t_2(b), t_2(c)\} \rangle$, with $T_1 = t_1(X) \wedge t_2(X)$. We have $T_1 \leadsto_{R_1}^\emptyset T_1$, while for the canonical abstract conjunction $\langle p(Z), t_3(Z), \{t_3(b)\} \rangle$ we have $t_3(Z) \leadsto_{R_2}^{Z/b} true$ and $p(X)$ is not an instance of $p(b)$ even though both abstract conjunctions are actually equivalent.

Discussion. Note that, while in [20] the authors describe the *rulify_term* procedure (called regular representation of a term) they do not discuss how to decide $\sqsubseteq$ for abstract conjunctions. In fact, the algorithm in [20] does not explicitly check for $\sqsubseteq$: new abstract conjunctions are always added to the old set of abstract conjunctions, an upper bound $\sqcup$ followed by a widening is computed, and the algorithm terminates when the result is the same as the old. Hence, in the absence of widening, this corresponds to implicitly saying that $\mathbf{A_1} \sqsubseteq \mathbf{A_2}$ if $\mathbf{A_1} \sqcup \mathbf{A_2} = \mathbf{A_2}$. This is sound, but not a decision procedure. Take for example, $\mathbf{A_1} = \langle p(X, a, a), t_1(X), R \rangle$ $\mathbf{A_2} = \langle p(a, X, X), t_1(X), R \rangle$, with $R = \{t_1(a).\}$. According to [20] the upper bound of $\mathbf{A_1}$ and $\mathbf{A_2}$ is $\mathbf{A_3} = \langle p(X, Y, Y), t_1(X) \wedge t_1(Y), R \rangle$ and one would fail to spot that $\mathbf{A_1} \sqsubseteq \mathbf{A_2}$ as well as $\mathbf{A_2} \sqsubseteq \mathbf{A_1}$.

Also, to our knowledge, [20] does not use the extended simplification procedure $\leadsto_R^\theta$, which, apart from its use in deciding $\sqsubseteq$, is also useful in making regular type information explicitly visible to other parts of the specialisation procedure, e.g., for specialising built-ins. Take for example, $\mathbf{A} = \langle Y$ is $X *$ $X, t_1(X) \wedge any(Y), R \rangle$ with $R = \{t_1(3).\}$. By looking at Y is $X * X$ a specialiser cannot spot that Y can actually be computed. However, by applying extended simplification, we obtain $esimplify(\mathbf{A}) = \langle Y$ is $3 * 3, any(Y), R \rangle$ as $t_1(X) \wedge any(Y) \leadsto_R^{\{X/3\}} any(Y)$. A specialiser (such as ECCE) can now evaluate the built-in and infer that Y is 9.

4.3 Abstract Unfolding and Resolution

We can now define an abstract unfolding and an abstract resolution in the RUL-domain. In the context of classical partial deduction, an unfolding rule U is a function which, given a program P and a goal $\leftarrow Q$, returns a finite SLD-tree for $P \cup \{\leftarrow Q\}$. Abstract unfolding will be similar to classical unfolding, except that we prune all the branches which are incompatible with the regular type information. We can also (optionally) use the type information to further instantiate the goals using our extended simplification.

Definition 8. *Let U be a classical unfolding rule. We define the* abstract unfolding *function $aunf_U(\mathbf{A})$, mapping abstract conjunctions to sets of resultants, as follows. Given $\mathbf{A} = \langle Q, T, R \rangle$, we compute $aunf_U(\mathbf{A})$ as follows:*
(1) do a classical unfolding of Q in P, using the unfolding rule U, producing an SLD-tree τ for $P \cup \{\leftarrow Q\}$ with resultants $\{Q\theta_1 \leftarrow B_1, \ldots, Q\theta_k \leftarrow B_k\}$.
(2) For every resultant $Q\theta_i \leftarrow B_i$, compute $T\theta_i \leadsto_R T'$. If $T' = fail$ then we remove the resultant, otherwise we keep it as an element of $aunf_U(\mathbf{A})$. Finally, assuming that T' and R are canonical,[5] we compute $T \leadsto_R^\theta T'$ and replace the resultant $Q\theta_i \leftarrow B_i$ by $(Q\theta_i \leftarrow B_i)\theta$.

Take for example an abstract goal $\mathbf{A} = \langle p(X), t_1(X), R \rangle$ with R from Ex. 2:

```
t1([]).
t1([H|T]) :- any(H),t1(T).
any(X).
```

Now take the following program P:

```
p(a).
p([]).
p([H|T]) :- p(H),p(T).
```

Classical unfolding of $p(X)$ could give us (depending on the unfolding rule) the original program P back. As we have $t_1(a) \leadsto_R fail$ the first resultant will be pruned by the abstract unfolding of $\mathbf{A}$, which thus returns:

```
p([]).
p([H|T]) :- p(H),p(T).
```

---

[5] If T' and R are not canonical we can always convert them into equivalent canonical ones.

Definition 9. *To compute the* abstract resolution *of an abstract conjunction* $\mathbf{A} = \langle Q, T, R \rangle$ *and a particular resultant* $Q\theta_i \leftarrow B_i$, *denoted by* $ares(\mathbf{A}, Q\theta_i \leftarrow B_i)$, *we do the following:*

- *We compute* $\langle B_i, T_c, R_c \rangle = canonical(\langle B_i, T\theta, R \rangle)$
- *We compute* $T_c' = project_{vars(B_j)}(T_c)$
- *Finally, we compute* T_c'' *by adding* $any(Y)$ *to* T_c' *for any fresh, existential variable* Y *in* B_i *for which no conjunct* $t(Y)$ *exists in* T_c'.

We return the abstract conjunction $\langle B_i, T_c'', R_c \rangle$.

Let us return to our small example above, involving the abstract goal $\mathbf{A} = \langle p(X), t_1(X), R \rangle$, and let us compute $ares(\mathbf{A}, C)$, where $C = p([H|T]) \leftarrow p(H) \wedge p(T)$ is the second clause of the abstract unfolding. We have that $t_1([H|T]) \rightsquigarrow_R any(H) \wedge t_1(T)$ and thus $ares(\mathbf{A}, C) = \langle p(H) \wedge p(T), any(H) \wedge t_1(T), R \rangle$. The framework of [30] allows us to split this abstract conjunction into two abstract conjunctions $\mathbf{A_1} = \langle p(H), any(H), R \rangle$ and $\mathbf{A_2} = \langle p(T), t_1(T), R \rangle$, which can be specialised separately. We have that $\mathbf{A_2} \sqsubseteq \mathbf{A}$, and it does not have to be specialised, while $\mathbf{A_1} \not\sqsubseteq \mathbf{A}$ and we thus do have to specialise it. The final specialised program could thus look like (where renaming has mapped $\mathbf{A}$ to p_1 and $\mathbf{A_2}$ to p_2):

```
p_1([]).                        p_2(a).
p_1([H|T]) :- p_2(H),p_1(T).    p_2([]).
                                p_2([H|T]) :- p_2(H),p_2(T).
```

The next step is now to see whether the above approach can be fully automated. The difficult part will of course be handling the control, in particular the generalisation operation ($aunf(.)$ and $ares(.)$ have already been fully defined above). We describe our first attempts and our first implementation below.

5   An Algorithm for Abstract Partial Deduction

In this section we present a procedure for performing abstract, conjunctive partial deduction within the RUL domain. This procedure also performs a bottom-up success information propagation.

The procedure is parametrised by the following: an unfolding rule U, a predicate $covered(L, \gamma)$, a whistle function $whistle(L, \gamma)$, a generalisation function $generalise(L, W, \gamma)$, and finally a bottom-up success information propagation $bottom\_up_P(\mathbf{A})$.

Intuitively, $covered(L, \gamma)$ is a way of checking whether L or a generalisation of L has already been treated in the global tree γ. Formally, $covered(L, \gamma) = true$ must imply that $label(L)$ can be split up into subconjunctions (see [28,30]) such that for every subconjunction $\mathbf{L_i}$: $\exists M \in \gamma$ such that M is processed and $\mathbf{L_i} \sqsubseteq label(M)$. A particular implementation can decide to be more demanding.

The function $bottom\_up_P$ maps a given abstract conjunction $\mathbf{A}$ to an instance $\mathbf{A}'$ of it (i.e., $\mathbf{A}' \sqsubseteq \mathbf{A}$), such that all the computed instances of elements of $\gamma(\mathbf{A})$ are contained in $\gamma(\mathbf{A}')$. In our first implementation, we simply re-used the top-down, goal-directed analysis from [17], as distributed with the SP system [15].

Procedure 5.1 (*generic partial deduction procedure*)

Input: a program P and a goal $\leftarrow Q$
Output: a set of abstract conjunctions $\mathcal{A}$ and a global tree γ
Initialisation: $\gamma :=$ a "global" tree with one unmarked node, labelled by $\langle Q, true, \emptyset \rangle$
repeat
    pick an unmarked leaf node L in γ
    if $covered(L, \gamma)$ **then**   mark L as processed
    else
        $W = whistle(L, \gamma)$
        if $W \neq fail$ **then**
            mark L as generalised
            for all abstract conjunctions $\mathbf{A} \in generalise(L, W, \gamma)^6$**do**
                add a new unmarked child C of L to γ ; $label(C) := \mathbf{A}$
        else
            mark L as processed
            for all resultants $C \in aunf_U(label(L))$ **do**
                for all abstract conjunctions $\mathbf{A} \in ares(label(L), R)$ **do**
                    add a new unmarked child C of L to γ ; $label(C) := bottom\_up_P(\mathbf{A})$
until all nodes are processed or generalised
output $\mathcal{A} := \{ label(A) \mid A \in \gamma \wedge A$ is marked processed $\}$ and γ

The other two parameters are used to ensure termination. Intuitively, the $whistle(L, \gamma)$ is used to detect whether the branch of γ ending in L is "dangerous", in which case it returns a value different from $fail$ (i.e., it "blows"). This value should be an ancestor W of L compared to which L looked dangerous (e.g., L is bigger than W in some sense). The generalisation operation will then compute a generalisation of L and W, less likely to lead to non-termination.

Formally, $generalise(L, W, \gamma)$ must return a set of abstract conjunctions which is more general than both $label(L)$ and $label(W)$ (i.e., they an both be split up into subconjunctions such that for every subconjunction $\mathbf{A}_i$ we have $\exists \mathbf{M} \in generalise(L, W, \gamma)$ such that $\mathbf{A}_i \sqsubseteq \mathbf{M}$; see [28,30]). This generalisation will replace $label(W)$ in the global tree γ.

For the $whistle(L, \gamma)$ we can try to apply the whistles discussed in [25,9]. We propose to use whistles that also take the characteristic trees into account, as those will be influenced by the regular type information. This is probably the easiest way to take the regular type information into account, especially since an in-depth inspection of the associated RUL programs might be prohibitively expensive. In our first experiments we have used whistles which "blow" if a growing characteristic tree is detected ([36]) and if the structure of the concrete conjunction part grows according to some measure (e.g., the homeomorphic embedding or just term-size). It is easy to see that these whistles are well-quasi orders ([9]) on abstract conjunctions and hence are still sufficient to ensure termination, provided the generalisation operation cannot be applied infinitely often.

---

^{6} Alternatively one can try to replace W by a generalisation. This is controlled by the *parent_abstraction* switch in ECCE.

Our generalisation operation is a strict improvement of the generalisation for conjunctive partial deduction from [9] and the generalisation operation for abstract R-conjunctions in [19,20].[7]

In essence, $generalise(\langle Q_1, T_1, R_1 \rangle, \langle Q_2, T_2, R_2 \rangle, \gamma)$ is computed as follows:
- we compute the *best matching conjunction* [9] BMC within Q_1 wrt Q_2
- we split Q_1 into Q_1', BMC, Q_1'' (i.e., $Q_1 = Q_1' \wedge BMC \wedge Q_1''$)
- we compute the generalisation $\mathbf{G}$ of $\langle BMC, project_{vars(BMC)}(T_1), R_1 \rangle$ and $\langle Q_2, T_2, R_2 \rangle$ as described in [19,20] (i.e., we compute the *msg* of Q_2 and BMC and we compute the upper bound of the regular type information followed by a "shortening")
- we return the set of abstract conjunctions $\{ \langle Q_1', project_{vars(Q_1')}(T_1), R_1 \rangle,$ $\langle Q_1'', project_{vars(Q_1'')}(T_1), R_1 \rangle, \mathbf{G} \}$.

6 Implementation in ECCE

The ECCE system [27] provides a highly parametric partial deduction procedure where one can dynamically change the parameters and even provide his own code. We have used this aspect of ECCE to encode an abstract conjunction $\mathbf{A} = \langle Q, T, R \rangle$ as a concrete conjunction $Q, rul\_constraint(T, R)$ and provided special support for the predicate $rul\_constraint/1$ using the toolkit [17,18] by John Gallagher. For example, the *covered* check was re-implemented to take the type information into account. For this, goals are put into a normal form where all the syntactic information is put in the regular types. E.g., $p(a)$ is normalised into $p(X), t_1(X)$ with RUL theory $t_1(a) \leftarrow$. This allows *covered* to be implemented using the inclusion test on regular types of [17].

For local control, we use determinate unfolding and the homeomorphic embedding $\trianglelefteq$ augmented with a satisfiability check on the type information (which is currently applied after every unfolding step). Otherwise, no special treatment for regular types has to be provided as they will never be unfolded by ECCE directly.

Finally, a (relatively minor) rewrite of ECCE itself was required. In fact, we had to extend ECCE to be able to handle two kinds of predicates: ordinary predicates for which code has to be generated and constraint predicates (such as $rul\_constraint/1$) for which no code has to be generated but which can be duplicated or removed "at will".

First Experiments. We have run our new technique on the *specialisation* benchmarks from [27], confirming that our technique is precise enough to perform both deforestation and tupling. Most of the current benchmarks in [27] can be handled by conjunctive partial deduction alone, hence for most benchmarks we noticed only minor differences with conjunctive partial deduction (e.g., a 17% improvement for *liftsolve.lmkng*). For several of the benchmarks (e.g., *liftsolve.db2*), we

---

[7] This generalisation operation is no longer a widening in the context of conjunctive abstract partial deduction as it never splits conjunctions.

also stumbled upon a relatively unexpected problem, namely that the bottom-up analysis [17], which we used to compute *bottom_up$_P$* in Procedure 5.1, did not terminate. Possible non-termination of [17] was already discovered in [42], but up until now it was believed that this would rarely occur in practice.

Fortunately, for one benchmark at least, we noticed a considerable improvement. In fact, for the *model_elim* benchmark (originally from [10]) the new procedure provided an extra speedup of 9.3 over conjunctive partial deduction (the total speedup is now 33.5 compared to 3.6 with just conjunctive partial deduction; this is much better than any of the systems used in [25]).

For *verification*, we managed to tackle the example from Subsection 3.2, to show that both unsafe(agent(p)) and unsafe(agent(system)) fail. The output generated by ECCE for unsafe(agent(system)) is:

```
unsafe(agent(system)) :- unsafe__1.
unsafe__1 :- \+(trans__7).        unsafe__4 :- \+(trans__5).
unsafe__1 :- unsafe__2.           unsafe__4 :- unsafe__6.
unsafe__2 :- \+(trans__3).        unsafe__6 :- \+(trans__7).
unsafe__2 :- unsafe__4.           unsafe__6 :- unsafe__2.
trans__3.                         trans__5.
trans__7.
```

which the bottom-up postprocessing of ECCE reduces to:

```
unsafe(agent(system)) :-  fail.
```

Note that the goal directed analysis of [17] on its own was unable to deduce failure of unsafe(agent(system)) or similar tasks. In principle, the specialisation method of [20] should be able to handle this example, as it does not require any special treatment of conjunctions. The following example, however, shows a particular verification example where conjunctions play an important role.

Example 4. Take the following simple program, which simulates several problems that can happen during model checking of infinite state process algebras. Here, the predicate trace/2 describes the possible traces of a particular (infinite state) system. In sync_trace/2 we describe the possible traces of two synchronised copies of this system, with different start states.

```
trace(s(X),[dec|T]) :- trace(X,T).
trace(0,[stop]).
trace(s(X),[inc|T]) :- trace(s(s(X)),T).
trace(f(X),[dec|T]) :- trace(X,T).
trace(f(X),[inc|T]) :- trace(f(f(X)),T).
trace(a,[inc,stop]).

sync_trace(T) :- trace(s(0),T), trace(f(a),T).
```

As one can see, the synchronisation of s(0) with f(a) will never produce a complete trace, and hence sync_trace will always fail. Classical partial deduction is unable to infer failure of sync_trace, even when using conjunctions, due to the inherent limitation of the $\mathcal{PD}$-domain to capture the possible states of our system, i.e., the possible first arguments to trace/2. In the RUL domain we can retain much more precise information about the calls to trace/2. E.g., our implementation was able to infer that the first argument to calls to trace/2 descending from trace(f(a),T) will always have the type t940 defined by:

```
t940(a):-true.
t940(f(_460)) :- t940(_460).
```

This is the residual program generated by ECCE.

```
sync_trace([inc,A|B]) :-  p_conj__2(0,A,B,a).
sync_trace__1([inc,A|B]) :-  p_conj__2(0,A,B,a).
p_conj__2(A,dec,[B|C],D) :-  p_conj__3(A,B,C,D).
p_conj__2(A,inc,[B|C],D) :-  p_conj__2(s(A),B,C,f(D)).
p_conj__3(A,dec,[B|C],D) :-   p_conj__4(A,B,C,D).
p_conj__3(A,inc,[B|C],D) :-  p_conj__2(A,B,C,D).
p_conj__4(s(A),dec,[B|C],f(D)) :-  p_conj__4(A,B,C,D).
p_conj__4(s(A),inc,[B|C],f(D)) :-  p_conj__2(A,B,C,D).
```

This program contains no facts and a simple bottom-up post-processing (e.g., the one implemented in ECCE based upon [41]) can infer that sync_trace fails.

Observe that a deterministic regular type analysis on its own (i.e., without conjunctions) cannot infer failure of sync_trace. The reason is that, while the regular types are precise enough to characterise the possible states of our infinite state system, they are not precise enough to characterise the possible traces of the system! For example, the top-down regular type analysis of the SP system produces the following result for the possible answers of sync_trace:

```
sync_trace__ans(X1) :- t230(X1).
t230([X1|X2]) :- t231(X1),t232(X2).
t231(inc) :- true.        t233(inc) :- true.
t231(dec) :- true.        t233(dec) :- true.
t231(stop) :- true.       t233(stop) :- true.
t232([X1|X2]) :- t233(X1),t232(X2).
t232([]) :- true.
```

In other words, the regular type analysis on its own was incapable of detecting the failure. Using our approach, the conjunctive partial deduction component achieves "perfect" precision (by keeping the variable link between the two copies of our system), and it is hence not a problem that the traces cannot be accurately described by regular types.[8] This underlines our belief that adding conjunctions to regular types will be useful for a more precise treatment of synchronisation in infinite state systems. We also believe that it will be particularly useful for refinement checking [48], where a model checker tries to find a trace T that can be performed by one system but not by the other. Such refinement checking can be encoded by the following clause:

---

[8] The non-deterministic regular type analysis of [21] actually is precise enough to capture these traces. However, we strongly believe that there will be more complicated system traces which it cannot precisely describe.

```
not_refinement_of(S1,S2,T) :- trace(S1,T), \+(trace(S2,T)).
```

This clause is very similar to the clause defining `sync_trace` and a non-conjunctive regular type analysis will face the same problems as above.

We have attempted to tackle more verification tasks for infinite state process algebras, which require the conjunctive partial deduction component. Unfortunately, the non-termination of $bottom\_up_P$ was even more of a problem in that setting, and prevented us from performing more involved experiments. So, a priority for future work is to correct $bottom\_up_P$ (e.g., by using some of the widenings described in [42]).

7 Discussion

On the side of partial deduction, the closest work related to ours is (the initially independently developed) [19,20]. We have developed and proven a complete check for $\sqsubseteq$ (the aspect of deciding $\sqsubseteq$ was not covered in [19,20]). There are a few other subtle differences which we have discussed throughout the paper. More importantly, however, in contrast to [19,20]: we can handle conjunctions and can make use of existing control techniques such as characteristic trees as described in [36]. We believe that conjunctive partial deduction is important for specialisation (achieving deforestation, tupling, and solving a dilemma of "classical" partial deduction related to efficiency and precision [32]), but also makes the local control much easier. For example, with conjunctive partial deduction a local control based upon determinacy (and homeomorphic embedding) is often sufficient, while this is not the case with non-conjunctive partial deduction (see, e.g., [25,32]).

On the other hand, [19,20] has a more refined bottom-up answer propagation, while we are still working on a full implementation of the generic combined bottom-up/top-down algorithm of [28,30].

On the side of verification, there are many related works which use logic programming based approaches for model checking [4], [47,8], [11], [14], [43] [13]. All of these works share the view that logic programming is a convenient formalism for expressing specifications and concurrent systems, and that using latest generation Prolog technology (efficient) model checking algorithms can be encoded with relatively little effort. However, to our knowledge, none of these works is capable of handling infinite state process algebras. The work which is most closely related to ours, is probably [4] which uses set-based analysis for model checking. As has recently been formally confirmed in [21], set-based analysis can be reconstructed as an abstract interpretation of the RUL domain. However, we believe, supported by our first experiments (cf., Section 6) that the RUL domain alone is not sufficient to perform any interesting analysis on process algebras. As we have argued in this paper, and shown on some examples, our approach has the potential to handle infinite state process algebras and might be especially useful for refinement checking and for a precise treatment of process synchronisation. Future work will be required to confirm this conjecture.

Acknowledgments. We are very grateful to anonymous referees for their extremely valuable feedback. We would like to thank John Gallagher for his extensive support and feedback, and also for allowing us to re-use parts of his tool. We are also grateful to Fabio Fioravanti, Helko Lehmann, Julio Peralta, German Puebla, and Ulrich Ultes-Nitsche for stimulating discussions and feedback.

References

1. K. R. Apt. Introduction to logic programming. In J. van Leeuwen, editor, *Handbook of Theoretical Computer Science*, chapter 10, pages 495–574. North-Holland Amsterdam, 1990.
2. M. Bruynooghe. A practical framework for the abstract interpretation of logic programs. *The Journal of Logic Programming*, 10:91–124, 1991.
3. M. Bruynooghe, H. Vandecasteele, D. A. de Waal, and M. Denecker. Detecting unsolvable queries for definite logic programs. In C. Palamidessi, H. Glaser, and K. Meinke, editors, *Proceedings of ALP/PLILP'98*, LNCS 1490, pages 118–133. Springer-Verlag, 1998.
4. W. Charatonik and A. Podelski. Set-based analysis of reactive infinite-state systems. In B. Steffen, editor, *Tools and Algorithms for the Construction and Analysis of Systems*, LNCS 1384, pages 358–375. Springer-Verlag, March 1998.
5. E. M. Clarke, O. Grumberg, and D. Peled. *Model Checking*. MIT Press, 1999.
6. C. Consel and S. C. Khoo. Parameterized partial evaluation. *ACM Transactions on Programming Languages and Systems*, 15(3):463–493, 1993.
7. P. Cousot and R. Cousot. Abstract interpretation and application to logic programs. *The Journal of Logic Programming*, 13(2 & 3):103–179, 1992.
8. B. Cui, Y. Dong, X. Du, N. Kumar, C. R. Ramakrishnan, I. V. Ramakrishnan, A. Roychoudhury, S. A. Smolka, and D. S. Warren. Logic programming and model checking. In C. Palamidessi, H. Glaser, and K. Meinke, editors, *Proceedings of ALP/PLILP'98*, LNCS 1490, pages 1–20. Springer-Verlag, 1998.
9. D. De Schreye, R. Glück, J. Jørgensen, M. Leuschel, B. Martens, and M. H. Sørensen. Conjunctive partial deduction: Foundations, control, algorithms and experiments. *The Journal of Logic Programming*, 41(2 & 3):231–277, November 1999.
10. D. A. de Waal and J. Gallagher. The applicability of logic program analysis and transformation to theorem proving. In A. Bundy, editor, *Automated Deduction—CADE-12*, pages 207–221. Springer-Verlag, 1994.
11. G. Delzanno and A. Podelski. Model checking in CLP. In R. Cleaveland, editor, *Proceedings of TACAS'99*, LNCS 1579, pages 223–239. Springer-Verlag, 1999.
12. A. Finkel and P. Schnoebelen. Well-structured transition systems everywhere ! *Theoretical Computer Science*, 256(1–2):63–92, 2001.
13. F. Fioravanti, A. Pettorossi, and M. Proietti. Verifying ctl properties of infinite-state systems by specializing constraint logic programs. In *Proceedings of VCL'2001*, Florence, Italy, September 2001.
14. L. Fribourg. Constraint logic programming applied to model checking. In *Proceedings of LOPSTR'99*, LNCS 1817, pages 30–41. Springer-Verlag, 1999.
15. J. Gallagher. A system for specialising logic programs. Technical Report TR-91-32, University of Bristol, November 1991.
16. J. Gallagher. Tutorial on specialisation of logic programs. In *Proceedings of PEPM'93*, pages 88–98. ACM Press, 1993.

17. J. Gallagher. A bottom-up analysis toolkit. Technical Report CSTR-95-016, University of Bristol, July 1995.
18. J. Gallagher and D. A. de Waal. Fast and precise regular approximations of logic programs. In P. Van Hentenryck, editor, *Proceedings of ICLP'94*, pages 599–613. The MIT Press, 1994.
19. J. P. Gallagher and J. C. Peralta. Using regular approximations for generalisation during partial evaluation. In J. Lawall, editor, *Proceedings of PEPM'00*, pages 44–51. ACM Press, 2000.
20. J. P. Gallagher and J. C. Peralta. Regular tree languages as an abstract domain in program specialisation. *Higher Order and Symbolic Computation*, 14(2–3):143–172, November 2001.
21. J. P. Gallagher and G. Puebla. Abstract interpretation over non-deterministic finite tree automata for set-based analysis of logic programs. In S. Krishnamurthi and C. R. Ramakrishnan, editors, *Proceedings of PADL 2002*, LNCS 2257, pages 243–261. Springer-Verlag, 2002.
22. M. Hermenegildo, R. Warren, and S. K. Debray. Global flow analysis as a practical compilation tool. *The Journal of Logic Programming*, 13(4):349–366, 1992.
23. N. D. Jones. Combining abstract interpretation and partial evaluation. In P. Van Hentenryck, editor, *Static Analysis, Proceedings of SAS'97*, LNCS 1302, pages 396–405, Paris, 1997. Springer-Verlag.
24. N. D. Jones, C. K. Gomard, and P. Sestoft. *Partial Evaluation and Automatic Program Generation*. Prentice Hall, 1993.
25. J. Jørgensen, M. Leuschel, and B. Martens. Conjunctive partial deduction in practice. In J. Gallagher, editor, *Proceedings of LOPSTR'96*, LNCS 1207, pages 59–82, Stockholm, Sweden, August 1996. Springer-Verlag.
26. J.-L. Lassez, M. Maher, and K. Marriott. Unification revisited. In J. Minker, editor, *Foundations of Deductive Databases and Logic Programming*, pages 587–625. Morgan-Kaufmann, 1988.
27. M. Leuschel. The ECCE partial deduction system and the DPPD library of benchmarks. Obtainable via http://www.ecs.soton.ac.uk/~mal, 1996-2000.
28. M. Leuschel. Program specialisation and abstract interpretation reconciled. In J. Jaffar, editor, *Proceedings of JICSLP'98*, pages 220–234, Manchester, UK, June 1998. MIT Press.
29. M. Leuschel. Logic program specialisation. In J. Hatcliff, T. Æ. Mogensen, and P. Thiemann, editors, *Partial Evaluation: Practice and Theory*, LNCS 1706, pages 155–188, Copenhagen, Denmark, 1999. Springer-Verlag.
30. M. Leuschel. Logic program specialisation and top-down abstract interpretation reconciled. Technical Report DSSE-TR-2000-3, Department of Electronics and Computer Science, University of Southampton, May 2000.
31. M. Leuschel, L. Adhianto, M. Butler, C. Ferreira, and L. Mikhailov. Animation and model checking of CSP and B using prolog technology. In *Proceedings of VCL'2001*, pages 97–109, Florence, Italy, September 2001.
32. M. Leuschel and M. Bruynooghe. Logic program specialisation through partial deduction: Control issues. *Theory and Practice of Logic Programming, Special issue on program development*, 2(4 & 5), July 2002. To appear.
33. M. Leuschel and D. De Schreye. Logic program specialisation: How to be more specific. In H. Kuchen and S. Swierstra, editors, *Proceedings of PLILP'96*, LNCS 1140, pages 137–151, Aachen, Germany, September 1996. Springer-Verlag.
34. M. Leuschel and H. Lehmann. Coverability of reset Petri nets and other well-structured transition systems by partial deduction. In J. Lloyd, editor, *Proceedings of CL'2000*, LNAI 1861, pages 101–115, London, UK, 2000. Springer-Verlag.

35. M. Leuschel and H. Lehmann. Solving coverability problems of Petri nets by partial deduction. In M. Gabbrielli and F. Pfenning, editors, *Proceedings of PPDP'2000*, pages 268–279, Montreal, Canada, 2000. ACM Press.

36. M. Leuschel, B. Martens, and D. De Schreye. Controlling generalisation and polyvariance in partial deduction of normal logic programs. *ACM Transactions on Programming Languages and Systems*, 20(1):208–258, January 1998.

37. M. Leuschel and T. Massart. Infinite state model checking by abstract interpretation and program specialisation. In A. Bossi, editor, Logic-Based Program Synthesis and Transformation. *Proceedings of LOPSTR'99*, LNCS 1817, pages 63–82, Venice, Italy, September 1999.

38. M. Leuschel and T. Massart. Logic programming and partial deduction for the verification of reactive systems: An experimental evaluation. In G. Norman, M. Kwiatkowska, and D. Guelev, editors, *Proceedings of AVoCS 2002, Second Workshop on Automated Verification of Critical Systems*, pages 143–149, Brimingham, UK, 2002.

39. J. W. Lloyd. *Foundations of Logic Programming*. Springer-Verlag, 1987.

40. J. W. Lloyd and J. C. Shepherdson. Partial evaluation in logic programming. *The Journal of Logic Programming*, 11(3& 4):217–242, 1991.

41. K. Marriott, L. Naish, and J.-L. Lassez. Most specific logic programs. *Annals of Mathematics and Artificial Intelligence*, 1:303–338, 1990.

42. P. Mildner. *Type Domains for Abstract Interpretation: A Critical Study*. PhD thesis, Dept. of Computing Sc. and Information Techn., PO-Box 331, S-75105 Uppsala, 1999.

43. U. Nilsson and J. Lübcke. Constraint logic programming for local and symbolic model checking. In J. Lloyd, editor, *Proceedings of CL'2000*, LNAI 1861, pages 384–398, London, UK, 2000. Springer-Verlag.

44. G. Puebla, J. Gallagher, and M. Hermenegildo. Towards integrating partial evaluation in a specialization framework based on generic abstract interpretation. In M. Leuschel, editor, *Proceedings of the ILPS'97 Workshop on Specialisation of Declarative Programs and its Application*, K.U. Leuven, Tech. Rep. CW 255, pages 29–38, Port Jefferson, USA, October 1997.

45. G. Puebla and M. Hermenegildo. Abstract Multiple Specialization and its Application to Program Parallelization. *J. of Logic Programming. Special Issue on Synthesis, Transformation and Analysis of Logic Programs*, 41(2&3):279–316, November 1999.

46. G. Puebla, M. Hermenegildo, and J. Gallagher. An Integration of Partial Evaluation in a Generic Abstract Interpretation Framework. In O. Danvy, editor, *Proceedings of PEPM'99*, number NS-99-1 in BRISC Series, pages 75–85. University of Aarhus, Denmark, January 1999.

47. Y. S. Ramakrishna, C. R. Ramakrishnan, I. V. Ramakrishnan, S. A. Smolka, T. Swift, and D. S. Warren. Efficient model checking using tabled resolution. In O. Grumberg, editor, *Proceedings of CAV'97*, LNCS 1254, pages 143–154. Springer-Verlag, 1997.

48. A. W. Roscoe. *The Theory and Practice of Concurrency*. Prentice-Hall, 1999.

49. E. Yardeni and E. Shapiro. A type system for logic programs. *The Journal of Logic Programming*, 10(2):125–154, 1990.

Verification of Sets of Infinite State Processes Using Program Transformation

Fabio Fioravanti[1], Alberto Pettorossi[2], and Maurizio Proietti[1]

[1] IASI-CNR, Viale Manzoni 30, I-00185 Roma, Italy
[2] DISP, University of Roma Tor Vergata, I-00133 Roma, Italy
{fioravanti,adp,proietti}@iasi.rm.cnr.it

Abstract. We present a method for the verification of safety properties of concurrent systems which consist of finite sets of infinite state processes. Systems and properties are specified by using constraint logic programs, and the inference engine for verifying properties is provided by a technique based on unfold/fold program transformations. We deal with properties of finite sets of processes of arbitrary cardinality, and in order to do so, we consider constraint logic programs where the constraint theory is the Weak Monadic Second Order Theory of k Successors. Our verification method consists in transforming the programs that specify the properties of interest into equivalent programs where the truth of these properties can be checked by simple inspection in constant time. We present a strategy for guiding the application of the unfold/fold rules and realizing the transformations in a semiautomatic way.

1 Introduction

Model checking is a well established technique for the verification of temporal properties of concurrent systems consisting of a *fixed* number of *finite state* processes [6]. Recently, there have been various proposals to extend model checking for verifying properties of systems consisting of an *arbitrary* number of *infinite state* processes (see, for instance, [18,21,25]). The verification problem addressed by these new proposals can be formulated as follows: given a system S_N consisting of N infinite state processes and a temporal property φ_N, prove that, for all N, the system S_N verifies property φ_N.

The main difficulty of this verification problem is that most properties of interest, such as *safety* and *liveness* properties, are undecidable for that class of concurrent systems, and thus, there cannot be any complete method for their verification. For this reason, all proposed methods resort to semiautomatic techniques, based on either (i) mathematical induction, or (ii) reduction to finite state model checking by abstraction.

This paper describes a method for verifying safety properties of systems consisting of an arbitrary number of processes whose set of states can be either finite or infinite. For reasons of simplicity, throughout this paper we will refer to these processes as infinite state processes. Our method avoids the use mathematical induction by abstracting away from the number N of processes actually present

A. Pettorossi (Ed.): LOPSTR 2001, LNCS 2372, pp. 111–128, 2002.

in the system. Indeed, this parameter occurs in the encoding of neither the systems nor the safety properties to be verified. These encodings are expressed as *Constraint Logic Programs* [14], CLP for short, whose constraints are formulas of the *Weak Monadic Second-order Theory of k Successors*, denoted WSkS [28]. These programs will be called CLP(WSkS) programs. By using these encodings, the actual cardinality of the set of processes present in the systems is not required in the proofs of the properties of interest.

Our method uses *unfold/fold transformations* [5,20,26] as inference rules for constructing proofs. There are other verification methods proposed in the literature which use program transformation or are based on CLP [7,12,13,17,19, 22,23], but those methods deal either with: (i) finite state systems [19,22], or (ii) infinite state systems where the number N of infinite state processes is fixed in advance [7,12,13,17], or (iii) *parameterized systems*, that is, systems consisting of an arbitrary number of finite state processes [23]. A more detailed discussion of these methods can be found in Section 6.

We assume that in our concurrent systems, every process evolves depending on its local state, called the *process state*, and depending also on the state of the other processes. Correspondingly, the whole system evolves and its global state, called the *system state*, changes. We also assume that each process state consists of a pair $\langle n, s \rangle \in I\!N \times CS$, where $I\!N$ denotes the set of natural numbers and CS is a given finite set. n and s are called the *counter* and the *control state* of the process, respectively. Notice that, during the evolution of the system, each process may reach an infinite number of distinct states.

This notion of process state derives from the specification of the Bakery Protocol (see Section 3 below) where a process is viewed as a finite state automaton which at each instante in time, is in a given control state and holds a natural number in a counter. We think, however, that our notion of process state is general enough to allow the specification of a large class of concurrent systems.

Since two distinct processes in a given system may have the same ⟨counter, control state⟩ pair, a system state is a *multiset* of process states.

As usual in model checking, a concurrent system is specified as a *Kripke structure* $K = \langle S, S_0, R, E \rangle$, where: (i) S is the set of system states, that is, the set of multisets of ⟨control state, counter⟩ pairs, (ii) $S_0 \subseteq S$ is a set of *initial system states*, (iii) $R \subseteq S \times S$ is a *transition relation*, and (iv) $E \subseteq \mathcal{P}(S)$ is a finite set of *elementary properties*.

We also assume that for all $\langle X, Y \rangle \in R$, we have that $Y = (X - \{x\}) \cup \{y\}$ where: (i) x and y are some process states, and (ii) the difference and union operations are to be understood as multiset operations. Thus, a transition from a system state to a new system state consists in replacing a process state by a new process state. This assumption implies that: (i) the number of processes in the concurrent systems does not change over time, and (ii) the concurrent system is asynchronous, that is, the processes of the system do not necessarily synchronize their actions.

We will address the problem of proving safety properties of systems. A safety property is expressed by a formula of the *Computational Tree Logic* [6] (CTL, for short) of the form $\neg EF(unsafe)$, where *unsafe* is an elementary property and *EF* is a temporal operator. The meaning of any such formula is given via the satisfaction relation $\mathcal{K}, X_0 \models \neg EF(unsafe)$ which holds for a Kripke structure $\mathcal{K}$ and a system state X_0 iff there is no sequence of states $X_0, X_1, \ldots, X_n$ such that: (i) for $i = 0, \ldots, n-1$, $\langle X_i, X_{i+1} \rangle \in R$ and (ii) $X_n \in unsafe$.

We may extend our method to prove more complex properties, besides safety properties. In particular, we may consider those properties which can be expressed by using, in addition to $\neg$ and *EF*, other logical connectives and CTL temporal operators. However, for reasons of simplicity, in this paper we deal with safety properties only, and we do not consider nested temporal operators.

Now we outline our method for verifying that, for all initial system states X of a given Kripke structure $\mathcal{K}$, the safety property φ holds. We use the notions of locally stratified program and perfect model and for them we refer to [2].

Verification Method.

Step 1. (*System and Property Specification*) We introduce: (i) a WSkS formula $init(X)$ which characterizes the initial system states, that is, X is an initial system state iff $init(X)$ holds, and (ii) a locally stratified CLP(WSkS) program $P_{\mathcal{K}}$ which defines a binary predicate *sat* such that for each system state X,

$$\mathcal{K}, X \models \varphi \text{ iff } sat(X, \varphi) \in M(P_{\mathcal{K}}) \qquad (\dagger)$$

where $M(P_{\mathcal{K}})$ denotes the perfect model of the program $P_{\mathcal{K}}$.

Step 2. (*Proof Method*) We introduce a new predicate f defined by the following CLP(WSkS) clause F: $f(X) \leftarrow init(X), sat(X, \varphi)$, where X is a variable. We then apply the transformation rules of Section 4, and from program $P_{\mathcal{K}} \cup \{F\}$ we derive a new program P_f.

If the clause $f(X) \leftarrow init(X)$ occurs in P_f then for all initial system states X, we have that $\mathcal{K}, X \models \varphi$ holds.

The choice of the perfect model as the semantics of the program $P_{\mathcal{K}}$ requires a few words of explanation. By definition, $\mathcal{K}, X \models \neg\varphi$ holds iff $\mathcal{K}, X \models \varphi$ does not hold, and by using ($\dagger$), this fact can be expressed by the clause:

C: $sat(X, \neg\varphi) \leftarrow \neg\, sat(X, \varphi)$

where $\neg$ in the head of C is interpreted as a function symbol, while $\neg$ in the body of C is interpreted as negation by (finite or infinite) failure. Now, since clause C is a locally stratified clause and the other clauses for *sat* do not contain negated atoms (see Section 2.2), the semantics of negation by failure is the one captured by the perfect model (recall that for locally stratified programs the perfect model is identical to the stable model and also to the well-founded model [2]).

The paper is structured as follows. In Section 2 we describe Step 1 of our verification method and we introduce CLP(WSkS) programs, that is, constraint logic programs whose constraints are formulas in the WSkS theory. In Section 3 we illustrate our specification method by considering the case of a system of N processes which use the *Bakery Protocol* for ensuring mutual exclusion [16]. In Section 4 we present Step 2 of our verification method and we see how it is realized by applying suitable rules for program transformation. These rules are adaptations to the case of locally stratified CLP(WSkS) programs of the unfold/fold rules for generic CLP programs presented in [9,12]. We also provide a semiautomatic strategy for guiding the application of the transformation rules and proving the properties of interest. In Section 5, we see our strategy in action for the verification of a safety property the N-process Bakery Protocol. Finally, in Section 6 we compare our paper with the literature in the field and we discuss possible enhancements of our method.

2   System and Property Specification Using Constraint Logic Programs over WSkS

In this section we illustrate Step 1 of our verification method and, in particular, we indicate how to specify: (i) a system consisting of a set of infinite state processes, and (ii) a safety property we want to prove. We specify the given system by a Kripke structure $\mathcal{K} = \langle S, S_0, R, E \rangle$ where: (i) S is the set of finite sets of finite strings, which are ground terms of the WSkS theory, and (ii) S_0, R, and E are specified by suitable WSkS formulas. We specify the given safety property by defining a *sat* relation by means of a CLP program $P_{\mathcal{K}}$ whose constraints are WSkS formulas.

2.1   Constraint Logic Programs over WSkS

The Weak Monadic Second Order Theory of k Successors is a decidable theory which can be used for expressing properties of finite sets of finite strings over an alphabet of k symbols [27,28]. The syntax of WSkS is defined as follows. Let us consider a set $\Sigma = \{s_1, \ldots, s_k\}$ of k symbols, called *successors*, and a set *Ivars* of *individual variables*. An *individual term* is either a string σ or a string $x\sigma$, where $x \in$ *Ivars* and $\sigma \in \Sigma^*$, where Σ^* denotes the set of all finite strings of successor symbols. By ε we denote the *empty string*.

Let us also consider the set *Svars* of *set variables* ranged over by $X, Y, \ldots$

WSkS *terms* are either individual terms or set variables.

Atomic formulas of WSkS are either: (i) equalities between individual terms, written $t_1 = t_2$, or (ii) inequalities between individual terms, written $t_1 \leq t_2$, or (iii) membership atomic formulas, written $t \in X$, where t is an individual term and X is a set variable.

The *formulas* of WSkS are constructed from the atomic formulas by means of the usual logical connectives and the quantifiers over individual variables and set variables. Given any two individual terms, t_1 and t_2, we will also write: (i) $t_1 \neq t_2$ as a shorthand for $\neg (t_1 = t_2)$, and (ii) $t_1 < t_2$ as a shorthand for $t_1 \leq t_2 \wedge \neg (t_1 = t_2)$.

The *semantics* of WSkS formulas is defined by considering the interpretation $\mathcal{W}$ with domain Σ^* such that $=$ is interpreted as string equality, $\leq$ is interpreted as the prefix ordering on strings, and $\in$ is interpreted as membership of a string to a *finite* set of strings. We say that a closed WSkS formula φ holds iff the satisfaction relation $\mathcal{W} \models \varphi$ holds. The relation $\mathcal{W} \models \varphi$ is recursive [27].

A CLP(WSkS) program is a set of many-sorted first order formulas [8]. There are three sorts: *string*, *stringset*, and *tree*, interpreted as finite strings, finite sets of strings, and finite trees, respectively. We use many-sorted logic to avoid the formation of meaningless clauses such as $p(X, s_1) \leftarrow X = s_1$, where X is a set variable of sort *stringset* and s_1 is a constant in Σ of sort *string*.

CLP(WSkS) terms are either WSkS terms or *ordinary* terms (that is, terms constructed out of variables, constants, and function symbols which are all distinct from those used for WSkS terms). The WSkS individual terms are assigned the sort *string*, the WSkS set variables are assigned the sort *stringset*, and ordinary terms are assigned the sort *tree*. Each predicate of arity n is assigned the sort $\langle i_1, \ldots, i_n \rangle$, where for $j = 1, \ldots, n$, i_j is the sort of its j-th argument. For instance, the predicate $\in$ is assigned the sort $\langle string, stringset \rangle$. We assume that CLP(WSkS) programs are constructed by complying with the sorts of terms and predicates.

An *atom* is an atomic formula whose predicate symbol is not in $\{\leq, =, \in\}$. As usual, a *literal* is either an atom or a negated atom. A CLP(WSkS) clause is of the form $A \leftarrow c, L_1, \ldots, L_n$, where A is an atom, c is a formula of WSkS, and $L_1, \ldots, L_n$ are literals. We can extend to CLP(WSkS) programs the definitions of *locally stratified* programs and *perfect models*, by adapting the corresponding definitions which are given for logic programs [2].

2.2   The Specification Method

Now we present our method for specifying systems and their safety properties by using CLP(WSkS) programs. Recall that a system is specified as a Kripke structure $\langle S, S_0, R, E \rangle$ and a system state in S is a *multiset* of process states, that is, a multiset of pairs $\langle n, s \rangle$ where $n \in \mathbb{N}$ is a counter and $s \in CS$ is a control state. We assume that CS is a finite set $\{s_1, \ldots, s_h\}$ of symbols.

Now, let us indicate how to specify the four components of the Kripke structure.

(A) The Set S of System States. We consider the following set of successor symbols: $\Sigma = \{1, 2\} \cup CS$. A *process state* is represented as a term of the form $1^n s 2^m$, where: (i) 1^n and 2^m are (possibly empty) strings of 1's and 2's, respectively, and (ii) s is an element of CS. For a process state $1^n s 2^m$ we have that: (i) the string 1^n represents its counter (the empty string ε represents the counter 0), and (ii) the symbol s represents its control state. The string 2^m, with different values of m, is used to allow different terms to represent the same $\langle$counter, control state$\rangle$ pair, so that a *set* of terms each of which is of the form $1^n s 2^m$ can be used to represent a *multiset* of process states. Thus, a *system state* in S, being a multiset of process states, is represented as a *set* of terms, each of which is of the form $1^n s 2^m$.

Now we will show that process states and system states are expressible as formulas in WSkS. First we need the following definitions (for clarifying the reader's ideas, here and in the sequel, we write between parentheses the intended meanings):

- $is\text{-}cn(x) \equiv \exists X \, ((\forall y \; y \in X \rightarrow (y = \varepsilon \lor \exists z \, (y = z \, 1 \land z \in X))) \land x \in X)$
  (x is a term of the form 1^n for some $n \geq 0$, i.e., x is a counter)

- $is\text{-}cs(x) \equiv x = s_1 \lor \ldots \lor x = s_h$
  ($x \in CS$, i.e., x is a control state)

Here are the WSkS formulas which define process states and system states:

- $ps(x) \equiv \exists X \, ((\forall y \; y \in X \rightarrow (\exists n \, \exists s \; y = n \, s \land is\text{-}cn(n) \land is\text{-}cs(s)) \lor$
  $\exists z \, (y = z \, 2 \land z \in X))) \land x \in X)$
  (x is a process state, that is, a term of the form $1^n s 2^m$ for some $n, m \geq 0$ and $s \in CS$)

- $ss(X) \equiv \forall x \, (x \in X \rightarrow ps(x))$ (X is a system state, that is, a set of terms of the form $1^n s 2^m$)

(B) The Set S_0 of Initial System States. The set S_0 of initial system states is specified by a WSkS formula $init(X)$ where the set variable X is the only free variable, that is, $X \in S_0$ iff $\mathcal{W} \models init(X)$.

(C) The Transition Relation R. Now we describe the general form of the WSkS formulas which can be used for defining the transition relation R. We need the following two definitions:

- $cn(x, n) \equiv ps(x) \land is\text{-}cn(n) \land n \leq x \land (\forall y \, (y \leq x \land is\text{-}cn(y)) \rightarrow y \leq n)$
  (n is the counter of process state x)

- $cs(x, s) \equiv ps(x) \land is\text{-}cs(s) \land (\exists y \, \exists z \, (y \leq x \land is\text{-}cn(z) \land y = z \, s)$
  (s is the control state of process state x)

We recall that a transition consists in replacing in a system state an old process state by a new process state. This replacement is defined as follows (here and in the sequel the angle brackets $\langle, \rangle$ are used only to improve readability and they should not be considered as belonging to the syntax of WSkS):

- $replace(\langle n_1, s_1 \rangle, X, \langle n_2, s_2 \rangle, Y) \equiv ss(X) \land ss(Y) \land$
  $\exists x \, (x \in X \land cn(x, n_1) \land cs(x, s_1)) \land$
  $\exists y \, (y \in Y \land cn(y, n_2) \land cs(y, s_2)) \land$
  $\forall z \, ((z \in X \land z \neq x) \leftrightarrow (z \in Y \land z \neq y))$
  ($Y = (X - \{x\}) \cup \{y\}$ for some process states $x \in X$ and $y \in Y$ such that: (i) x has counter n_1 and control state s_1 and (ii) y has counter n_2 and control state s_2)

We assume that any given transition relation R is specified by a finite disjunction of h formulas, that is, $\langle X, Y \rangle \in R$ iff $\mathcal{W} \models r(X, Y)$, where $r(X, Y) \equiv r_1(X, Y) \lor \ldots \lor r_h(X, Y)$ and, for $i = 1, \ldots, h$:

- $r_i(X, Y) \equiv \exists n_1 \, \exists s_1 \, \exists n_2 \, \exists s_2 \, (replace(\langle n_1, s_1 \rangle, X, \langle n_2, s_2 \rangle, Y) \land$
  $event_i(\langle n_1, s_1 \rangle, X, \langle n_2, s_2 \rangle))$

where $event_i(\langle n_1, s_1 \rangle, X, \langle n_2, s_2 \rangle)$ is a WSkS formula. In Section 3 we will present some examples of these formulas.

(D) The Set E of Elementary Properties. Each elementary property $\eta \in E$ of the system states is specified by a formula $e(X)$ where the set variable X is the only free variable, that is, $X \in \eta$ iff $\mathcal{W} \models e(X)$.

To end this section we indicate how to specify a safety property of a system by using a CLP(WSkS) program. Let us consider: (i) a system specified by a Kripke structure $\mathcal{K} = \langle S, S_0, R, E \rangle$ whose elementary properties are $\eta_1, \ldots, \eta_m$ specified by the formulas $e_1(X), \ldots, e_m(X)$, respectively, and whose transition relation is specified by $r_1(X, Y) \lor \ldots \lor r_h(X, Y)$, and (ii) a safety property of the form $\neg EF(\eta)$, where η is an elementary property. We introduce the following CLP(WSkS) program $P_\mathcal{K}$:

$$sat(X, \eta_1) \leftarrow e_1(X)$$
$$\ldots$$
$$sat(X, \eta_m) \leftarrow e_m(X)$$
$$sat(X, \neg\varphi) \leftarrow \neg\, sat(X, \varphi)$$
$$sat(X, EF(\varphi)) \leftarrow sat(X, \varphi)$$
$$sat(X, EF(\varphi)) \leftarrow r_1(X, Y), sat(Y, EF(\varphi))$$
$$\ldots$$
$$sat(X, EF(\varphi)) \leftarrow r_h(X, Y), sat(Y, EF(\varphi))$$

which specifies the safety property $\neg EF(\eta)$ in the sense that, for every system state X in S, the following holds [11]:

$$\mathcal{K}, X \models \neg EF(\eta) \quad \text{iff} \quad sat(X, \neg EF(\eta)) \in M(P_\mathcal{K})$$

Notice that the program $P_\mathcal{K}$ is locally stratified w.r.t. the size of the second argument of sat, and thus, it has a unique perfect model, denoted $M(P_\mathcal{K})$.

3   An Example of the Specification of a System and a Property: The N-Process Bakery Protocol

In this section we illustrate our method for specifying systems and properties in the case of the N-process Bakery Protocol. This protocol ensures mutual exclusion in a system made out of N processes which use a shared resource. Mutual exclusion holds iff the shared resource is used by at most one process at a time.

Let us first give a brief description of the protocol [16]. In this protocol each process state is a $\langle$counter, control state$\rangle$ pair $\langle n, s \rangle$, where the control state s is either $\underline{t}$ or $\underline{w}$ or $\underline{u}$. The constants $\underline{t}$, $\underline{w}$, and $\underline{u}$ stand for *think*, *wait*, and *use*, respectively. Let us denote the set $\{\underline{t}, \underline{w}, \underline{u}\}$ by CS. As in the general case, in this protocol a system state is a multiset of process states.

A system state is initial iff each of its process states is $\langle 0, \underline{t} \rangle$.

The transition relation from a system state X to a new system state Y, is specified as follows (recall that the $-$ and $\cup$ operations refer to multisets):

(T1: from *think* to *wait*) if there exists a process state $\langle n, \underline{t} \rangle$ in X, then $Y = (X - \{\langle n, \underline{t} \rangle\}) \cup \{\langle m{+}1, \underline{w} \rangle\}$, where m is the maximum value of the counters of the processes states in X,

(T2: from *wait* to *use*) if there exists a process state $\langle n, \underline{w} \rangle$ in X such that, for any process state $\langle m, s \rangle$ in $X - \{\langle n, \underline{w} \rangle\}$, either $m = 0$ or $n < m$, then $Y = (X - \{\langle n, \underline{w} \rangle\}) \cup \{\langle n, \underline{u} \rangle\}$, and

(T3: from *use* to *think*) $Y = (X - \{\langle n, \underline{u} \rangle\}) \cup \{\langle 0, \underline{t} \rangle\}$.

The mutual exclusion property is expressed by the CTL formula $\neg EF$ (*unsafe*), where *unsafe* is an elementary property which holds in a system state X iff there are at least two distinct process states in X with control state $\underline{u}$.

In order to give a formal specification of our N-process Bakery Protocol we use the 5 successor symbols: 1, 2, $\underline{t}$, $\underline{w}$, and $\underline{u}$. Thus, we consider the WS5S theory.

(A) The System States. A system state is a set of terms, each of which is of the form $1^n 2^m$, where s is an element of $\{\underline{t}, \underline{w}, \underline{u}\}$.

(B) The Initial System States. A system state X is initial iff $\mathcal{W} \models init(X)$, where:

- $init(X) \equiv \forall x \ (x \in X \rightarrow (cn(x, \varepsilon) \land cs(x, \underline{t})))$
  (all process states in X have counter 0 and control state $\underline{t}$)

(C) The Transition Relation. For specifying the transition relation for the N-process Bakery Protocol we need the following two predicates *max* and *min*:

- $max(X, m) \equiv \exists x \ (x \in X \land cn(x, m)) \land \forall y \ \forall n \ ((y \in X \land cn(y, n)) \rightarrow n \leq m)$
  (m is the maximum counter in the system state X)

- $min(X, m) \equiv \exists x \ (x \in X \land cn(x, m)) \land$
  $\qquad\qquad \forall y \ \forall n \ ((y \in X \land y \neq x \land cn(y, n)) \rightarrow (n = \varepsilon \lor m < n))$
  (In the system state X there exists a process state x with counter m such that the counter of any process state in $X - \{x\}$ is either 0 or greater than m. Recall that the term ε represents the counter 0.)

The transition relation between system states is defined as follows: $\langle X, Y \rangle \in R$ iff $\mathcal{W} \models tw(X, Y) \lor wu(X, Y) \lor ut(X, Y)$, where the predicates *tw*, *wu*, and *ut* correspond to the transition of a process from *think* to *wait*, from *wait* to *use*, and from *use* to *think*, respectively. We have that:

- $tw(X, Y) \equiv \exists n_1 \exists s_1 \exists n_2 \exists s_2 \ replace(\langle n_1, s_1 \rangle, X, \langle n_2, s_2 \rangle, Y) \land$
  $\qquad\qquad s_1 = \underline{t} \land \exists m \ (max(X, m) \land n_2 = m\,1) \land s_2 = \underline{w}$
  ($Y = (X - \{x\}) \cup \{y\}$, where x is a process state in X with control state $\underline{t}$, and y is a process with control state $\underline{w}$ and counter $m{+}1$ such that m is the maximum counter in X. Notice that the term $m\,1$ represents the counter $m{+}1$)

- $wu(X, Y) \equiv \exists n_1 \exists s_1 \exists n_2 \exists s_2 \ replace(\langle n_1, s_1 \rangle, X, \langle n_2, s_2 \rangle, Y) \land$
  $\qquad\qquad s_1 = \underline{w} \land min(X, n_1) \land n_2 = n_1 \land s_2 = \underline{u}$
  ($Y = (X - \{x\}) \cup \{y\}$, where x is a process state in X with counter n_1 and

control state $\underline{w}$ such that the counter of any process state in $X-\{x\}$ is either 0 or greater than n_1, and y is a process state with counter n_1 and control state $\underline{u}$)

- $ut(X, Y) \equiv \exists n_1 \exists s_1 \exists n_2 \exists s_2 \, replace(\langle n_1, s_1 \rangle, X, \langle n_2, s_2 \rangle, Y) \wedge$
$$s_1 = \underline{u} \wedge n_2 = \varepsilon \wedge s_2 = \underline{t}$$
$(Y = (X-\{x\}) \cup \{y\}$, where x is a process state in X with control state $\underline{u}$, and y is a process state with counter 0 and control state $\underline{t}$)

(D) The Elementary Properties. The unsafety property holds in each system state X such that $\mathcal{W} \models unsafe(X)$, where:

- $unsafe(X) \equiv \exists x \exists y \, (x \in X \wedge y \in X \wedge x \neq y \wedge cs(x, \underline{u}) \wedge cs(y, \underline{u}))$
(there exist two distinct process states in X with control state $\underline{u}$)

The following locally stratified CLP(WSkS) program P_{Bakery} defines the predicate sat of Step 1 of our verification method.

$sat(X, unsafe) \leftarrow unsafe(X)$
$sat(X, \neg F) \leftarrow \neg \, sat(X, F)$
$sat(X, EF(\varphi)) \leftarrow sat(X, \varphi)$
$sat(X, EF(\varphi)) \leftarrow tw(X, Y), \, sat(Y, EF(\varphi))$
$sat(X, EF(\varphi)) \leftarrow wu(X, Y), \, sat(Y, EF(\varphi))$
$sat(X, EF(\varphi)) \leftarrow ut(X, Y), \, sat(Y, EF(\varphi))$

Thus, in order to verify the safety of the Bakery Protocol we have to prove that, for all system states X,

if $init(X)$ holds then $sat(X, \neg EF(unsafe)) \in M(P_{Bakery})$.

4   Rules and Strategy for Verification

In this section we show how Step 2 of our verification method is performed by using unfold/fold rules for transforming CLP(WSkS) programs. These rules are presented below. They are similar to those introduced in [9,12]. We also present a semiautomatic strategy for guiding the application of these transformation rules.

For presenting the transformation rules we need the following notation and terminology. By $FV(\varphi)$ we denote the set of free variables occurring in φ. By $v, w, \ldots$ (possibly with subscripts), we denote variables in $Ivars \cup Svars$. We say that the atom A is *failed* in program P iff in P there is no clause whose head is unifiable with A. The set of *useless predicates* of a program P is the maximal set U of predicates occurring in P such that the predicate p is in U iff the body of each clause defining p in P contains a positive literal whose predicate is in U. The set of *useless clauses* of a program P is the set of clauses defining useless predicates in P.

The process of transforming a given CLP(WSkS) program P_0 whereby deriving program P_n, can be formalized as a sequence $P_0, \ldots, P_n$ of programs, called a *transformation sequence*, where for $r = 0, \ldots, n-1$, program P_{r+1} is obtained from program P_r by applying one of the following transformation rules.

R1. Constrained Atomic Definition. Let δ be the clause:

$$newp(v_1, \ldots, v_n) \leftarrow c, A$$

where: (i) $newp$ is a new predicate symbol not occurring in $P_0, \ldots, P_r$, and
(ii) $\{v_1, \ldots, v_n\} = FV(c, A)$. Then $P_{r+1} = P_r \cup \{\delta\}$.
Clause δ is called a *definition clause* and for $i \geq 0$, $Defs_i$ is the set of definition
clauses introduced during the transformation sequence $P_0, \ldots, P_i$. In particular,
$Defs_0 = \emptyset$.

R2. Unfolding. Let $\gamma \in P_r$ be the clause $H \leftarrow c, G_1, L, G_2$.
(R2p) If L is an atom A and $\{A_j \leftarrow c_j, B_j \mid j = 1, \ldots, m\}$ is the set of all renamed
apart clauses in P_r such that the atoms A and A_j are unifiable via a most general
unifier ϑ_j, then $P_{r+1} = (P_r - \{\gamma\}) \cup \{(H \leftarrow c, c_j, G_1, B_j, G_2)\vartheta_j \mid j = 1, \ldots, m\}$.

(R2n) If L is a negated atom $\neg A$ and A is failed in P_r, then $P_{r+1} = (P_r - \{\gamma\}) \cup \{H \leftarrow c, G_1, G_2\}$.

R3. Constrained Atomic Folding. Let γ be the clause $H \leftarrow c, G_1, L, G_2$ in
P_r, where L is either the atom A or the negated atom $\neg A$. Let δ be a definition
clause $newp(v_1, \ldots, v_n) \leftarrow d, A$ in $Defs_r$, such that $\mathcal{W} \models \forall w_1, \ldots, w_m(c \rightarrow d)$,
where $\{w_1, \ldots, w_m\} = FV(c \rightarrow d)$.
(R3p) If L is A then $P_{r+1} = (P_r - \{\gamma\}) \cup \{H \leftarrow c, G_1, newp(v_1, \ldots, v_n), G_2\}$.
(R3n) If L is $\neg A$ then $P_{r+1} = (P_r - \{\gamma\}) \cup \{H \leftarrow c, G_1, \neg newp(v_1, \ldots, v_n), G_2\}$.

R4. Clause Removal. $P_{r+1} = P_r - \{\gamma\}$ if one of the following two cases occurs.
(R4f) γ is the clause $H \leftarrow c, G$ and c is unsatisfiable, that is, $\mathcal{W} \models \forall v_1, \ldots, v_n \neg c$,
where $\{v_1, \ldots, v_n\} = FV(c)$.
(R4u) γ is useless in P_r.

R5. Constraint Replacement. Let γ be the clause $H \leftarrow c_1, G$. If for
some WSkS formula c_2 we have that $\mathcal{W} \models \forall w_1, \ldots, w_n (c_1 \leftrightarrow c_2)$, where
$\{w_1, \ldots, w_n\} = FV(c_1 \leftrightarrow c_2)$, then $P_{r+1} = (P_r - \{\gamma\}) \cup \{H \leftarrow c_2, G\}$.

These rules are different from those introduced in the case of general programs by Seki [24]. In particular, Seki's folding rule can be used for replacing a
clause $\gamma: H \leftarrow c, G_1, \neg A, G_2$ by a new clause $\gamma 1: H \leftarrow c, G_1, newp(\ldots), G_2$, but
not by a new clause $\gamma 2: H \leftarrow c, G_1, \neg newp(\ldots), G_2$. The replacement of clause
γ by clause $\gamma 2$ is possible by using our folding rule R3n.

It can be shown that, under suitable restrictions, the transformation rules
presented above preserve the perfect model semantics [11].

Step 2 of our verification method consists in applying the transformation
rules R1–R5 according to a transformation strategy which we describe below.
We will see this strategy in action for the verification of a safety property of the
N-process Bakery Protocol (see Section 5).

Suppose that we are given a system specified by a Kripke structure $\mathcal{K}$ and a
safety formula φ, and we want to verify that $\mathcal{K}, X \models \varphi$ holds for all initial system
states X. Suppose also that $\mathcal{K}$ and φ are given by a CLP(WSkS) program $P_\mathcal{K}$
as described in Section 2.2. We proceed as follows. First we consider the clause:

F. $f(X) \leftarrow init(X), sat(X, \varphi)$

where: (i) f is a new predicate symbol, and (ii) $\mathcal{W} \models init(X)$ iff X is an initial system state.

Then we apply the following transformation strategy which uses a *generalization function gen*. Given a WSkS formula c and a literal L which is the atom A or the negated atom $\neg A$, the function *gen* returns a definition clause $newp(v_1, \ldots, v_n) \leftarrow d, A$ such that: (i) *newp* is a new predicate symbol, (ii) $\{v_1, \ldots, v_n\} = FV(d, A)$, and (iii) $\mathcal{W} \models \forall w_1, \ldots, w_n (c \rightarrow d)$, where $\{w_1, \ldots, w_n\} = FV(c \rightarrow d)$.

Transformation Strategy

Input: (i) Program $P_\mathcal{K}$, (ii) clause F: $f(X) \leftarrow init(X), sat(X, \varphi)$, and (iii) generalization function *gen*.

Output: A program P_f such that for every system state X, $f(X) \in M(P_\mathcal{K} \cup \{F\})$ iff $f(X) \in M(P_f)$.

Phase A. Defs := $\{F\}$; *NewDefs* := $\{F\}$; $P := P_\mathcal{K}$;
while *NewDefs* $\neq \emptyset$ **do**

1. from $P \cup NewDefs$ derive $P \cup C_{unf}$ by unfolding once each clause in *NewDefs*;
2. from $P \cup C_{unf}$ derive $P \cup C_r$ by removing all clauses with unsatisfiable body;
3. *NewDefs* := $\emptyset$;
   for each clause $\gamma \in C_r$ of the form $H \leftarrow c, G$ and for each literal L in the goal G such that γ cannot be folded w.r.t. L using a clause in *Defs* **do**
   NewDefs := *NewDefs* $\cup \{gen(c, L)\}$;
4. *Defs* := *Defs* $\cup$ *NewDefs*;
5. fold each clause in C_r w.r.t. all literals in its body whereby deriving $P \cup C_{fld}$;
6. $P := P \cup C_{fld}$

end-while

Phase B.

1. from P derive P_u by removing all useless clauses in P;
2. from P_u derive P_f by unfolding the clauses in P_u w.r.t. every failed negative literal occurring in them.

Step 2 of the verification method ends by checking whether or not clause $f(X) \leftarrow init(X)$ occurs in program P_f. If it occurs, then for all initial system states X, we have that $\mathcal{K}, X \models \varphi$.

The correctness of our verification method is a consequence of the following two facts: (i) the transformation rules preserve perfect models, and (ii) perfect models are models of the completion of a program [2].

Theorem 1. [Correctness of the Verification Method] Given a Kripke structure $\mathcal{K}$ and a safety property φ, if $f(X) \leftarrow init(X)$ occurs in P_f then for all initial system states X, we have that $\mathcal{K}, X \models \varphi$.

Proof. Let us assume that $f(X) \leftarrow init(X)$ occurs in P_f and let us consider an initial system state I. Thus, $\mathcal{W} \models init(I)$ and $f(I) \in M(P_f)$. By the correctness of the transformation rules [11], we have that $f(I) \in M(P_{\mathcal{K}} \cup \{F\})$. Since: (i) $M(P_{\mathcal{K}} \cup \{F\})$ is a model of the completion $comp(P_{\mathcal{K}} \cup \{F\})$, (ii) the formula $\forall X (f(X) \leftrightarrow (init(X) \wedge sat(X, \varphi))$ belongs to $comp(P_{\mathcal{K}} \cup \{F\})$, and (iii) $\mathcal{W} \models init(I)$ we have that $sat(I, \varphi) \in M(P_{\mathcal{K}} \cup \{F\})$. Now, since no sat atom in $M(P_{\mathcal{K}} \cup \{F\})$ can be inferred by using clause F, we have that $sat(I, \varphi) \in M(P_{\mathcal{K}})$, that is, $\mathcal{K}, I \models \varphi$. □

The automation of our transformation strategy depends on the availability of a suitable generalization function *gen*. In particular, our strategy terminates whenever the codomain of *gen* is a finite set of definition clauses. Suitable generalization functions with finite codomain can be constructed by following an approach similar to the one described in [12]. More on this issue will be mentioned in Section 6.

Finally, let us notice that our verification method is *incomplete*, in the sense that there exist a Kripke structure $\mathcal{K}$, an initial system state X, and a safety property φ, such that $\mathcal{K}, X \models \varphi$ holds, and yet there is no sequence of applications of the transformation rules which leads from the program $P_{\mathcal{K}} \cup \{f(X) \leftarrow init(X), sat(X, \varphi)\}$ to a program P_f containing the clause $f(X) \leftarrow init(X)$. This incompleteness limitation cannot be overcome, because the problem of verifying properties of finite sets of infinite state processes is undecidable and not semidecidable. This is a consequence of the fact that the uniform verification of parameterized systems consisting of finite state processes is undecidable [3].

5   Verifying the N-Process Bakery Protocol via Program Transformation

In this section we show how Step 2 of our verification method described in Section 4 is performed for verifying the safety of the N-process Bakery Protocol. We apply the unfold/fold transformation rules to the constraint logic program P_{Bakery} (see end of Section 3) according to the transformation strategy of Section 4.

As already remarked at the end of Section 4, the application of our strategy can be fully automatic, provided that we are given a generalization function which introduces new definition clauses needed for the folding steps (see Point 3 of the transformation strategy). In particular, during the application of the transformation strategy for the verification of the N-process Bakery Protocol which we now present, we have that: (i) all formulas to be checked for applying the transformations rules are formulas of WS5S, and thus, they are decidable, and (ii) the generalization function is needed for introducing clauses d3, d9, and d16 (see below).

We start off by introducing the following new definition clause:

    d1. $f(X) \leftarrow init(X), sat(X, \neg EF(unsafe))$

Our goal is to transform the program $P_{Bakery} \cup \{d1\}$ into a program P_f which contains a clause of the form $f(X) \leftarrow init(X)$.

We start Phase A by unfolding clause 1 w.r.t. the sat atom, thereby obtaining:

    2. $f(X) \leftarrow init(X), \neg sat(X, EF(unsafe))$

The constraint $init(X)$ is satisfiable and clause 2 *cannot* be folded using the definition clause d1. Thus, we introduce the new definition clause:

    d3. $newp1(X) \leftarrow init(X), sat(X, EF(unsafe))$

By using clause d3 we fold clause 2, and we obtain:

    4. $f(X) \leftarrow init(X), \neg newp1(X)$

We proceed by applying the unfolding rule to the newly introduced clause d3, thereby obtaining:

    5. $newp1(X) \leftarrow init(X) \wedge unsafe(X)$
    6. $newp1(X) \leftarrow init(X) \wedge tw(X, Y), sat(Y, EF(unsafe))$
    7. $newp1(X) \leftarrow init(X) \wedge wu(X, Y), sat(Y, EF(unsafe))$
    8. $newp1(X) \leftarrow init(X) \wedge ut(X, Y), sat(Y, EF(unsafe))$

Clauses 5, 7 and 8 are removed, because their bodies contain unsatisfiable constraints. Indeed, the following formulas hold: (i) $\forall X \neg(init(X) \wedge unsafe(X))$, (ii) $\forall X \forall Y \neg(init(X) \wedge wu(X, Y))$, and (iii) $\forall X \forall Y \neg(init(X) \wedge ut(X, Y))$.

Clause 6 cannot be folded using either d1 or d3, because $\forall X \forall Y (init(X) \wedge tw(X, Y) \rightarrow init(Y))$ does not hold. Thus, in order to fold clause 6, we introduce the new definition clause:

    d9. $newp2(X) \leftarrow c(X), sat(X, EF(unsafe))$

where $c(X)$ is a new constraint defined by the following WS5S formula:

    $\forall x \ (x \in X \rightarrow ((cn(x, \varepsilon) \wedge cs(x, \underline{t})) \vee (\exists c \ (cn(x, c) \wedge \varepsilon < c) \wedge cs(x, \underline{w}))))$

This formula tells us that every process state in the system state X is either the pair $\langle 0, \underline{t} \rangle$ or the pair $\langle c, \underline{w} \rangle$ for some $c > 0$. We have that $\forall X \forall Y (init(X) \wedge tw(X, Y) \rightarrow c(Y))$ holds and thus, we can fold 6 using d9. We obtain:

    10. $newp1(X) \leftarrow init(X) \wedge tw(X, Y), newp2(Y)$

By unfolding the definition clause d9 we obtain:

    11. $newp2(X) \leftarrow c(X) \wedge unsafe(X)$
    12. $newp2(X) \leftarrow c(X) \wedge tw(X, Y), sat(Y, EF(unsafe))$
    13. $newp2(X) \leftarrow c(X) \wedge wu(X, Y), sat(Y, EF(unsafe))$
    14. $newp2(X) \leftarrow c(X) \wedge ut(X, Y), sat(Y, EF(unsafe))$

Clauses 11 and 14 have unsatisfiable constraints in their bodies and we remove them. Indeed, the following formulas hold: (i) $\forall X \neg(c(X) \wedge unsafe(X))$, and (ii) $\forall X \forall Y \neg(c(X) \wedge ut(X, Y))$.

We fold clause 12 by using the already introduced definition clause d9, because $\forall X \forall Y (c(X) \wedge tw(X, Y) \rightarrow c(Y))$ holds. We obtain:

    15. $newp2(X) \leftarrow c(X) \wedge tw(X, Y), newp2(Y)$

However, clause 13 cannot be folded by using a definition clause introduced so far. Thus, in order to fold clause 13, we introduce the following new definition clause:

d16. $newp3(X) \leftarrow d(X),\ sat(X, EF(unsafe))$

where the constraint $d(X)$ is the WS5S formula:

$$\forall x\ (x \in X \rightarrow ((cn(x, \varepsilon) \wedge cs(x, \underline{t})) \vee$$
$$(\exists c\ (cn(x, c) \wedge \varepsilon < c\ ) \wedge cs(x, \underline{w})) \vee$$
$$(\exists n\ (cn(x, n) \wedge min(X, n) \wedge \varepsilon < n) \wedge cs(x, \underline{u})))$$

This formula tells us that every process state in the system state X is either $\langle 0, \underline{t} \rangle$, or $\langle c, \underline{w} \rangle$ for some $c > 0$, or $\langle n, \underline{u} \rangle$ for some $n > 0$ such that no process state in X has a positive counter smaller than n. We have that $\forall X\, \forall Y\, (c(X) \wedge wu(X, Y) \rightarrow d(Y))$ holds, and thus, we can fold clause 13 using clause d16. We obtain:

17. $newp2(X) \leftarrow c(X) \wedge wu(X, Y),\ newp3(Y)$

We now proceed by applying the unfolding rule to the definition clause d16 and we get:

18. $newp3(X) \leftarrow d(X) \wedge unsafe(X)$
19. $newp3(X) \leftarrow d(X) \wedge tw(X, Y),\ sat(Y, EF(unsafe))$
20. $newp3(X) \leftarrow d(X) \wedge wu(X, Y),\ sat(Y, EF(unsafe))$
21. $newp3(X) \leftarrow d(X) \wedge ut(X, Y),\ sat(Y, EF(unsafe))$

We remove clause 18 because its body contains an unsatisfiable constraint because $\forall X\ \neg(d(X) \wedge unsafe(X))$ holds. Then, we fold clauses 19, 20, and 21 by using the definition clauses d16, d16, and d9, respectively. Indeed, the following three formulas hold:

$$\forall X\, \forall Y\, (d(X) \wedge tw(X, Y) \rightarrow d(Y))$$
$$\forall X\, \forall Y\, (d(X) \wedge wu(X, Y) \rightarrow d(Y))$$
$$\forall X\, \forall Y\, (d(X) \wedge ut(X, Y) \rightarrow c(Y))$$

We get:

22. $newp3(X) \leftarrow d(X) \wedge tw(X, Y),\ newp3(Y)$
23. $newp3(X) \leftarrow d(X) \wedge wu(X, Y),\ newp3(Y)$
24. $newp3(X) \leftarrow d(X) \wedge ut(X, Y),\ newp2(Y)$

Since these last folding steps were performed without introducing new definition clauses, we terminate Phase A of our transformation process. The program derived so far is $P_{Bakery} \cup \{4, 10, 15, 17, 22, 23, 24\}$.

Now we proceed by performing Phase B of our transformation strategy. We remove the useless clauses 10, 15, 17, 22, 23, and 24, which define the predicates $newp1$, $newp2$, and $newp3$. Therefore, we derive the program $P_{Bakery} \cup \{4\}$. Then we apply the unfolding rule to clause 4 w.r.t. the literal $\neg newp1(X)$, where $newp1(X)$ is a failed atom (see Point R2n of the unfolding rule). We obtain:

25. $f(X) \leftarrow init(X)$

Thus, we derive the final program P_f which is $P_{Bakery} \cup \{25\}$. According to Step 2 of our verification method, the presence of clause 25 in P_f proves, as desired, the mutual exclusion property for the N-process Bakery Protocol.

6   Related Work and Conclusions

Several methods have been recently proposed for the verification of *parameterized systems*, that is, systems consisting of an *arbitrary* number of *finite state* processes. Among them the method described in [23] is closely related to ours, in that it uses unfold/fold program transformations for generating induction proofs of safety properties of parameterized systems. However, our paper differs from [23] because we use constraint logic programs with locally stratified negation to specify concurrent systems and their properties, while [23] uses definite logic programs. Correspondingly, we use a different set of transformation rules. Moreover, we consider systems with an arbitrary number of *infinite state* processes and these systems are more general than parameterized systems.

Now we recall the main features of some verification methods based on (constraint) logic programming, which have been recently proposed in the literature. (i) The method described in [17] uses partial deduction and abstract interpretation of logic programs for verifying safety properties of infinite state systems. (ii) The method presented in [13] uses logic programs with linear arithmetic constraints and Presburger arithmetic to verify safety properties of Petri nets. (iii) The method presented in [7] uses constraint logic programs to represent infinite state systems. This method can be applied to verify CTL properties of those systems by computing approximations of least and greatest fixed points via abstract interpretation. (iv) The method proposed in [22] uses tabulation-based logic programming to efficiently verify μ-calculus properties of finite state transitions systems expressed in a CCS-like language. (v) The method described in [19] uses CLP with finite domains, extended with constructive negation and tabled resolution, for finite state local model checking.

With respect to these methods (i)–(v), the distinctive features of our method are that: (1) we deal with systems consisting of an *arbitrary* number of infinite state processes, (2) we use CLP(WSkS) for their description, and (3) we apply unfold/fold program transformations for the verification of their properties.

Verification techniques for systems with an arbitrary number of infinite state processes have been presented also in the following papers.

In [18] the authors introduce a proof technique which is based on induction and model checking. Proofs are carried out by solving a finite number of model checking problems on a finite abstraction of the given system and they are mechanically checked. The technique is illustrated by proving that the N-process Bakery Protocol is starvation free.

In [21] the author presents a proof of the mutual exclusion for the N-process version of the Ticket Protocol [1] which is uniform w.r.t. N and it is based on the Owicki-Gries assertional method. The proof has been mechanically checked by using the Isabelle theorem prover.

In [25] the author presents a proof of the mutual exclusion for the N-process Bakery Protocol. This proof is based on theorem proving, model checking, and abstraction, so to reduce the protocol itself to the case of two processes only.

Similarly to the techniques presented in the above three papers [18,21,25], each step of our verification method can be mechanized, but the construction of the whole proof requires some human guidance. However, in contrast to [18, 21,25] in our approach the parameter N representing the number of processes is *invisible*. Moreover, we do not use induction on N is performed and we do not perform any abstraction on the set of processes.

More recently, in [4] the authors have presented an automated method for the verification of safety properties of parameterized systems with unbounded local data. The method, which is based on multiset rewriting and constraints, is complete for a restricted class of parameterized systems.

The verification method presented in this paper is an enhancement of the *rules + strategies* transformation method proposed in [12] for verifying CTL properties of systems consisting of a fixed number of infinite state processes. In particular, Step 2 of our verification method can be viewed as a strategy for the specialization of program P_K encoding the system and the property of interest w.r.t. the goal $init(X), sat(X, \varphi)$. In [12] we proved the mutual exclusion property for the 2-process Bakery Protocol by using CLP programs with constraints expressed by linear inequations over real numbers. That proof can easily be extended to the case of any fixed number of processes by using CLP programs over the same constraint theory. Here, however, we proved the mutual exclusion property for the N-process Bakery Protocol, *uniformly* for any N, by using CLP programs with constraints over WSkS.

The proof of the mutual exclusion property for the N-process Bakery Protocol presented in Section 5, was done by applying under some human guidance the transformation strategy of Section 4. Notice, however, that our verification method can be made fully automatic by adding to our CLP program transformation system MAP [10]: (i) a solver for checking WSkS formulas, and (ii) suitable generalization functions for introducing new definition clauses. For Point (i) we may use existing solvers, such as MONA [15]. Point (ii) requires further investigation but we believe that one can apply some of the ideas presented in [12] in the case of systems consisting of a fixed number of infinite state processes.

As discussed in the Introduction, the verification method we proposed in this paper, is tailored to the verification of safety properties for *asynchronous* concurrent systems, where each transition is made by one process at a time. This limitation to asynchronous systems is a consequence of our assumption that each transition from a system state X to a new system state Y is of the form $Y = (X - \{x\}) \cup \{y\}$ for some process states x and y. In order to model *synchronous* systems, where transitions may involve more than one process at a time, we may relax this assumption and allow transitions of the form $Y = (X - A) \cup B$ for some multisets of process states A and B. Since these more general transitions whereby the number of processes may change over time, can be defined by WSkS formulas, one might use our method for verifying properties of synchronous systems.

References

1. G. R. Andrews. *Concurrent programming: principles and practice.* Addison-Wesley, 1991.

2. K. R. Apt and R. N. Bol. Logic programming and negation: A survey. *Journal of Logic Programming*, 19, 20:9–71, 1994.
3. K. R. Apt and D. C. Kozen. Limits for automatic verification of finite-state concurrent systems. *Information Processing Letters*, 22(6):307–309, 1986.
4. M. Bozzano and G. Delzanno. Beyond parameterized verification. In *Proceedings of the Eighth International Conference on Tools and Algorithms for the Construction and Analysis of Systems (TACAS'02)"*, Lecture Notes in Computer Science 2280, pages 221–235. Springer, 2002.
5. R. M. Burstall and J. Darlington. A transformation system for developing recursive programs. *Journal of the ACM*, 24(1):44–67, January 1977.
6. E. M. Clarke, O. Grumberg, and D. Peled. *Model Checking*. MIT Press, 2000.
7. G. Delzanno and A. Podelski. Model checking in CLP. In R. Cleaveland, editor, *5th International Conference on Tools and Algorithms for the Construction and Analysis of Systems (TACAS'99)*, Lecture Notes in Computer Science 1579, pages 223–239. Springer-Verlag, 1999.
8. H. Enderton. *A Mathematical Introduction to Logic*. Academic Press, 1972.
9. S. Etalle and M. Gabbrielli. Transformations of CLP modules. *Theoretical Computer Science*, 166:101–146, 1996.
10. F. Fioravanti. MAP: A system for transforming constraint logic programs. available at `http://www.iasi.rm.cnr.it/~fioravan`, 2001.
11. F. Fioravanti. *Transformation of Constraint Logic Programs for Software Specialization and Verification*. PhD thesis, Università di Roma "La Sapienza", Italy, 2002.
12. F. Fioravanti, A. Pettorossi, and M. Proietti. Verifying CTL properties of infinite state systems by specializing constraint logic programs. In *Proceedings of the ACM Sigplan Workshop on Verification and Computational Logic VCL'01, Florence (Italy)*, Technical Report DSSE-TR-2001-3, pages 85–96. University of Southampton, UK, 2001.
13. L. Fribourg and H. Olsén. A decompositional approach for computing least fixed-points of Datalog programs with z-counters. *Constraints*, 2(3/4):305–335, 1997.
14. J. Jaffar and M. Maher. Constraint logic programming: A survey. *Journal of Logic Programming*, 19/20:503–581, 1994.
15. N. Klarlund and A. Møller. *MONA Version 1.4 User Manual*. BRICS Notes Series NS-01-1, Department of Computer Science, University of Aarhus, January 2001.
16. L. Lamport. A new solution of Dijkstra's concurrent programming problem. *Communications of the ACM*, 17(8):453–455, 1974.
17. M. Leuschel and T. Massart. Infinite state model checking by abstract interpretation and program specialization. In A. Bossi, editor, *Proceedings of LOPSTR '99, Venice, Italy*, Lecture Notes in Computer Science 1817, pages 63–82. Springer, 1999.
18. K. L. McMillan, S. Qadeer, and J. B. Saxe. Induction in compositional model checking. In *CAV 2000*, Lecture Notes in Computer Science 1855, pages 312–327. Springer, 2000.
19. U. Nilsson and J. Lübcke. Constraint logic programming for local and symbolic model-checking. In J. W. Lloyd, editor, *CL 2000: Computational Logic*, Lecture Notes in Artificial Intelligence 1861, pages 384–398, 2000.
20. A. Pettorossi and M. Proietti. Transformation of logic programs: Foundations and techniques. *Journal of Logic Programming*, 19,20:261–320, 1994.
21. L. Prensa-Nieto. Completeness of the Owicki-Gries system for parameterized parallel programs. In *Formal Methods for Parallel Programming: Theory and Applications, FMPPTA 2001*. IEEE Computer Society Press, 2001.

22. Y. S. Ramakrishna, C. R. Ramakrishnan, I. V. Ramakrishnan, S. A. Smolka, T. Swift, and D. S. Warren. Efficient model checking using tabled resolution. In *CAV '97*, Lecture Notes in Computer Science 1254, pages 143–154. Springer-Verlag, 1997.
23. A. Roychoudhury and I.V. Ramakrishnan. Automated inductive verification of parameterized protocols. In *CAV 2001*, pages 25–37, 2001.
24. H. Seki. Unfold/fold transformation of stratified programs. *Theoretical Computer Science*, 86:107–139, 1991.
25. N. Shankar. Combining theorem proving and model checking through symbolic analysis. In *CONCUR 2000: Concurrency Theory*, number 1877 in Lecture Notes in Computer Science, pages 1–16, State College, PA, August 2000. Springer-Verlag.
26. H. Tamaki and T. Sato. Unfold/fold transformation of logic programs. In S.-Å. Tärnlund, editor, *Proceedings of the Second International Conference on Logic Programming, Uppsala, Sweden*, pages 127–138. Uppsala University, 1984.
27. J. W. Thatcher and J. B. Wright. Generalized finite automata with an application to a decision problem of second-order logic. *Mathematical System Theory*, 2:57–82, 1968.
28. W. Thomas. Languages, automata, and logic. In G. Rozenberg and A. Salomaa, editors, *Handbook of Formal Languages*, volume 3, pages 389–455. Springer, 1997.

When Size Does Matter
Termination Analysis for Typed Logic Programs

Wim Vanhoof and Maurice Bruynooghe

Department of Computer Science, K.U. Leuven, Belgium
{wimvh,maurice}@cs.kuleuven.ac.be

Abstract. Proofs of termination typically proceed by mapping program states to a well founded domain and showing that successive states of the computation are mapped to elements decreasing in size. Automated termination analysers for logic programs achieve this by measuring and comparing the sizes of successive calls to recursive predicates. The size of the call is measured by a level mapping that in turn is based on a norm on the arguments of the call. A norm maps a term to a natural number. The choice of the norm is crucial for the ability to prove termination. For some programs a fairly complex norm is required. The automated selection of an appropriate norm is a missing link in this research domain and is addressed in this paper. Our proposal is to use the type of a predicate to generate a number of simple norms and to try them in turn for proving the termination of the predicate. Given a term of a certain type, we consider a norm for each of its subtypes, a norm that counts the number of subterms of the term that are of the considered subtype.

1 Introduction and Motivation

Within logic programming, the problem of proving termination of programs has been intensively studied. While termination of logic programs is undecidable in general, in practice it is possible to prove termination automatically for a large class of programs. Since the survey in [22] a lot more work has been done towards automation and several analysers have been build, e.g. [5,17,20]. Nontermination is due to the existence of a derivation containing an infinite sequence of calls to the same predicate, hence termination proofs focus on sequences of calls to recursive predicates. A common approach is to define a level mapping from atoms to the well founded set of natural numbers that measures their size. A sequence of calls to a predicate is finite if the calls are *rigid* i.e. their size does not change under instantiation and there is a decrease in size between any two successive calls. If all sequences of calls to recursive predicates that can occur in a derivation for a query Q of interest are finite, then the derivation must terminate. It follows that two kinds of information are important in automated termination analysis: size information and instantiatedness information.

To explain our contribution, we follow the approach of [7] and restrict our attention to definite programs that are directly recursive, i.e. they do not contain loops other than those induced by clauses having one or more body atoms with

A. Pettorossi (Ed.): LOPSTR 2001, LNCS 2372, pp. 129–147, 2002.

the same predicate symbol as the head. Hence we consider left-to-right termination of such a program with respect to a set of *atomic* queries. To characterise the set of calls that arise during a derivation, one can introduce the concept of a *call set* [7]: given a program P and the set S of atomic queries of interest, the *call set*, denoted $call(P, S)$, is the set of all atoms A such that a variant of A is a selected atom under the left-to-right selection rule in some derivation for (P, Q), for some $Q \in S$. To measure the size of terms and atoms, one usually employs the notions of *norm* and *level mapping*. If $Term_P$ and $Atom_P$ denote the sets of all terms and atoms in the language underlying some program P and $Term_P/ \sim$ and $Atom_P/ \sim$ their quotient sets, a norm is defined as a mapping $\|.\| : Term_P/ \sim \mapsto \mathbb{N}$, a level mapping as $|.| : Atom_P/ \sim \mapsto \mathbb{N}$. Examples of well-known norms are the *listlength* norm, which counts the number of elements in a list, and the *termsize* norm, which counts the number of functors in a term. In [7] it is shown that a directly recursive program P terminates under the left-to-right selection rule for all atomic queries in a set S if and only if a level mapping $|.|$ can be constructed such that for any call $A \in call(P, S)$ that unifies with the head of a clause $H \leftarrow B_1, \ldots, B_n \in P$ under most general unifier θ and B_i a recursive call, it holds that $|A| > |B_i \theta \theta'|$ for any computed answer substitution θ' for $(B_1, \ldots, B_{i-1})\theta$.

In practice, the need to reason over the individual calls in the call set is avoided if only *rigid* level mappings are considered, i.e. level mappings that take into account only arguments that are *instantiated enough* with respect to the particular norm used by the level mapping [5]. A term t is said to be instantiated enough with respect to a norm $\|.\|$ if and only if $\|t\| = \|t\theta\|$ for every substitution θ (this corresponds with the norm being rigid on t). Likewise, the computed answer substitution for the intermediate atoms $B_1, \ldots, B_i$ can be abstracted by the *size relations* of the involved atoms. Given a predicate p/n and a norm $\|.\|$, a size relation for p/n with respect to $\|.\|$ is a relation $R_p \subseteq \mathbb{N}^n$ such that for every $p(t_1, \ldots, t_n) \in Atom_P$: if $P \models p(t_1, \ldots, t_n)$ then $(\|t_1\|, \ldots, \|t_n\|) \in R_p$. The size relation $R_{append} = \{(X, Y, Z) \mid Z = X + Y\}$, for example, may denote that upon success, the size of the third argument in a call to $append/3$ equals the sum of the sizes of its first two arguments. A directly recursive program P can than be shown to terminate under the left-to-right selection rule for all atomic queries in a set S if and only if P is *(rigid) acceptable* with respect to S [10]:

Definition 1. *Let S be a set of atomic queries and P be a definite directly recursive program. Given a norm $\|.\|$, we say that P is acceptable with respect to S if for every predicate p/n there exists a set of argument positions $\{j_1, \ldots, j_m\}$ such that in every call $p(t_1, \ldots, t_n) \in call(P, S)$, each t_{j_k} is instantiated enough w.r.t. $\|.\|$ and*

- *$\forall H \leftarrow B_1, \ldots, B_n \in P$ having p/n as predicate symbol*
- *$\forall B_i$ having p/n as predicate symbol and for every substitution θ such that the arguments of $(B_1, \ldots, B_{i-1})\theta$ all satisfy their associated size relations: $|H\theta| > |B_i\theta|$ where $|p(t_1, \ldots, t_n)| = \sum_{k \in \{j_1, \ldots, j_m\}} \|t_k\|$.*

Whether or not termination can be proven using Definition 1 often depends on the particular norm that is chosen. Some techniques for termination analysis use a specific norm [25], while others provide the user with the possibility of specifying a norm that might be tailored to the program to be analysed [17]. In any case, fixing a particular norm imposes a number of restrictions on the termination analysis, as was noted e.g. in [2,11]. The main problem in this context is that by using a single norm an occurrence of a functor in a term is always measured in the same way, although it might make sense to treat different occurrences of a same functor differently. Consider the following example from [11], in which the predicate flat/2 can convert a list of lists of terms into a list containing all the terms in the lists.

Example 1.

```
flat([],[]).
flat([[]|T], R):- flat(T,R).
flat([[H|T]|T'], [H|R]):- flat([T|T'],R).
```

Here, it might make sense to use a norm that treats the list constructor [.|.] differently depending on which argument of flat/2 it is used in. To measure the size of the second argument of flat/2, the *listlength* norm suffices (taking only outermost occurrences of [.|.] into account) whereas to measure the size of its first argument, it may be worthwhile to consider the innermost occurrences of [.|.] and count, effectively, the sum of the lengths of the elements of the outermost list.

A solution that overcomes these problems has been presented in [11], considering so called *typed norms*. The general idea is to derive for every argument position of each atom in the program an approximation of the set of terms that can occur in that position (expressed through the formalism of rigid types [15]) and to construct a particular norm for each such set. For the above example, [11] would derive that the second argument of flat/2 contains a list of any values, whereas the first argument may contain a list of which the elements are again lists of any values. Accordingly, it would derive exactly the above mentioned norms: $\|.\|_1$ measuring the length of a list and $\|.\|_2$ counting the sum of the lengths of the elements of a list.

$$\|[]\|_1 = 0 \qquad\qquad \|[]\|_2 = 0$$
$$\|[E|Es]\|_1 = 1 + \|Es\|_1 \qquad\qquad \|[E|Es]\|_2 = \|E\|_1 + \|Es\|_2$$

However, while the use of different norms opens up a number of possibilities, it also renders the computation of size relations far from trivial [9], as it involves computing relations that hold between different norms, like e.g. a size relation for flat/2 expressing that $\|t_1\|_2 = \|t_2\|_1$ in any call $flat(t_1, t_2)$.

In this work, we reconsider the use of types in termination analysis. Contrary to earlier type-based approaches, we do *not* construct a particular norm for a term according to its type, but rather characterise the size of the term in several ways, by counting the number of subterms of a particular type it contains. Let us reconsider Example 1. Instead of characterising the size of terms like $[1, 2, 3]$ and $[[1], [2], [3, 4]]$ by the particularly constructed norms ($\|.\|_1$ and $\|.\|_2$ respectively), we characterise their sizes by counting the number of integer values occurring in them, the number of lists of integer values and the number of lists of lists of integer values. The first two of these measurements are applicable to both $[1, 2, 3]$ and $[[1], [2], [3, 4]]$ and enable to compare their sizes. This contrast with the difficulties that are encountered when one has to compare their sizes when measured with different norms $\|.\|_1$ and $\|.\|_2$. Our motivation is twofold:

- First of all, we believe the use of type information to be a powerful tool for termination analysis, as it provides a structured way to automatically derive suited norms. The problems encountered in the derivation of relations between typed norms [9] inspired us to explore a different way of representing these relations. This work complements our earlier work on deriving type based instantiation dependencies [3], which are a necessary ingredient for a type based termination analysis.
- In recent work [27], we have developed a binding-time analysis for logic programs that makes heavy use of termination analysis in order to decide what calls can be safely unfolded during specialisation. For this application, we feel that a lightweight termination analysis that allows to check termination quickly by searching in a structured way through a number of possible norms without requiring the user to assist in the construction of these norms may be more suited than a heavy analysis employing dedicated norms.

In Section 2 we recall the basics of the instantiatedness analysis of [3] and develop a type based size abstraction. In Section 3 we present the actual analysis of size relations in a monomorphic as well as a polymorphic setting. Next, we introduce a type based termination condition in Section 4 and conclude in Section 5 with a discussion and comparison with related work.

2   Characterising Terms

2.1   About Terms and Types

Like terms are constructed from variables and function symbols, types are constructed from type variables and type symbols. We denote by $\mathcal{T} = \mathcal{T}(\Sigma_{\mathcal{T}}, V_{\mathcal{T}})$ the set of types constructed from type variables $V_{\mathcal{T}}$ and type symbols $\Sigma_{\mathcal{T}}$. We assume that the sets of symbols, variables, type symbols and type variables are fixed and do not overlap. We write $t : \tau$ to specify that term t has type τ and f/n to specify that the function or type symbol f has arity n. A type containing variables is said to be *polymorphic*, otherwise it is *monomorphic*.

Example 2. If $int/0$, $list/1$ and $pair/2$ are type symbols and T is a type variable, then some possible types are int, $list(T)$, $list(int)$, $list(list(int))$, $pair(T, int)$, and so on. In this enumeration, $list(T)$ and $pair(T, int)$ are polymorphic, the others are monomorphic.

Besides the usual substitutions which are mappings from variables to terms, we also have type substitutions which are mappings from type variables to types. The application of a type substitution to a polymorphic type gives a new type which is an *instance* of the original type. For each type symbol, a unique type rule associates that symbol with a finite set of function symbols. A finite set of type rules forms a type definition and associates terms with types.

Definition 2. *The type rule for a type symbol $h/n \in \Sigma_T$ is a definition of the form $h(\bar{V}) \longrightarrow f_1(\bar{\tau}_1) ; \dots ; f_k(\bar{\tau}_k)$. where: $\bar{V}$ is an n-tuple of distinct variables from V_T; for $1 \leq i \leq k$, $f_i/m \in \Sigma$ with $\bar{\tau}_i$ an m-tuple from T; and type variables occurring in the right hand side occur in $\bar{V}$. The function symbols $\{f_1, \dots, f_k\}$ are said to be associated with the type symbol h. A finite set of type rules is called a type definition.*

A type rule is monomorphic if it contains no type variables, otherwise it is polymorphic. A polymorphic type rule can be seen as a type rule schema that can be instantiated to other type rules by type substitutions. In addition to types defined by the user, we assume also predefined types which are associated with (possibly infinite) sets of terms. For example, the types int and char may be specified to consists of the integers and characters respectively.

Example 3. A type rule defining the type $list(T)$ is

$$list(T) \longrightarrow [\,]; [T|list(T)].$$

The function symbols $[\,]$ (nil) and $[.|.]$ (cons) are associated with the type symbol *list*.

Note that the type definition defines also the denotation of each type (the set of terms belonging to the type). A term t belongs to the denotation of type $\tau = h(\bar{V})\theta$ if t is a variable or t is of the form $f(t_1, \dots, t_k)$ with $f(\tau_1, \dots, \tau_k)$ occurring on the right-hand side of the type rule associated with the type symbol h and each t_i belongs to the denotation of $\tau_i\theta$. For example 3, terms of polymorphic type $list(T)$ are variables (typed $list(T)$), terms of the form $[\,]$, or terms of the form $[t_1|t_2]$ with t_1 of type T and t_2 of type $list(T)$. As T is a type variable we cannot determine or commit to its structure under instantiation. Hence only a variable (typed T) can belong to the denotation of type T. Applying the type substitution $\{T/int\}$ on $list(T)$ gives the type $list(int)$. Terms of the form $[t_1|t_2]$ are of type $list(int)$ if t_1 is of type int and t_2 is of type $list(int)$.

The next definition specifies the *constituents* of a type τ. These are the possible types for subterms of terms of type τ.

Definition 3. *Let $h(\bar{\tau}) \longrightarrow f_1(\bar{\tau}_1) ; \dots ; f_k(\bar{\tau}_k)$ be an instance of a rule in a type definition ρ and τ an argument of one of the $f_i(\bar{\tau}_i)$. We say that τ is a ρ-constituent of $h(\bar{\tau})$. The constituents relation is the minimal pre-order (reflexive and transitive) $\preceq_\rho: T \times T$ including all pairs $\tau' \preceq_\rho \tau$ such that τ' is a ρ-constituent of τ. The set of ρ-constituents of τ is $Constituents_\rho(\tau) = \{ \tau' \in T \mid \tau' \preceq_\rho \tau \}$. When clear from the context we omit ρ and write $\preceq$ and $Constituents(\tau)$.*

Example 4. With $list/1$ as in Example 3 and the atomic type int, we have:

- $T \preceq list(T)$, $list(T) \preceq list(T)$, $int \preceq list(int)$, $int \preceq int$, $list(T) \preceq list(list(T))$, $T \preceq list(list(T))$, $list(list(T)) \preceq list(list(T))$, $T \preceq T$, ...
- $Constituents(int) = \{int\}$, $Constituents(T) = \{T\}$, $Constituents(list(T)) = \{T, list(T)\}$, $Constituents(list(int)) = \{int, list(int)\}$.

To ensure termination of our analysis, we impose the restriction that each type must have a finite set of constituents. Types with an infinite number of constituents are also problematic for other reasons. Firstly, it is unclear what their denotation is. Secondly, defining a monomorphic instance of such a type by a set of monomorphic type rules requires an infinite set of such type rules. As an example, consider the type rule

$$t(T) \longrightarrow f(t(t(T))).$$

The monomorphic instance $t(int)$ is defined in terms of its constituent type $t(t(int))$, which in turn is defined in terms of its constituent type $t(t(t(int)))$, i.e. defining $t(int)$ requires an infinite set of monomorphic instances and it is unclear what the denotation of $t(int)$ is. Similar conditions are common in other analyses of typed programs, e.g. [23].

We assume that each predicate has a declaration stating the type of its arguments. This allows a compiler to automatically infer a type for each variable. We furthermore assume that programs are type-correct [24], i.e. that for every predicate call, the types of the arguments can be obtained by applying a type substitution on the declared type of the predicate. In a language like Mercury [24], types and type declarations are defined by the user and the compiler checks for type correctness. However, it is also feasible to infer a correct typing based on methods such as [13]. In what follows, we assume that programs are in normal form. A program is in normal form if each atom is of the form $p(X_1, \ldots, X_n)$, $X = Y$ or $X = f(X_1, \ldots, X_n)$ (with $X_1, \ldots, X_n$) different variables). In a type correct program, X and Y have the same type in $X = Y$ and, if X is of type $\tau\theta$ in some unification $X = f(X_1, \ldots, X_n)$ then τ has a type rule including an alternative $f(\tau_1, \ldots, \tau_n)$ and for all i, the type of X_i is $\tau_i\theta$.

2.2 Size Information

In what follows, we measure the "size" of a term with respect to a particular constituent of its type. The τ-size of a term $t : \tau'$ is defined for types $\tau \preceq \tau'$ and is the number of subterms in t having τ as type.

Definition 4. *Let τ and τ' be defined by a type definition ρ. The τ-size of $t : \tau'$ with $\tau \in Constituents(\tau')$ is defined as*

$$\sigma_\tau(t) = \#\{s \mid s : \tau \text{ is a subterm of } t\}.$$

As such, a term can be measured
by a finite number of measures, one
for each of the constituents of its
type. The table denotes the sizes of
several terms s of type $list(list(int))$
when measured by counting, respec-

s	σ_{int}	$\sigma_{list(int)}$	$\sigma_{list(list(int))}$
$[]$	0	0	1
$[[]]$	0	1	2
$[[1]]$	1	2	2
$[[1,2],[3]]$	3	5	3

tively, the subterms of type int, $list(int)$ and $list(list(int))$. Note that a same
functor is measured differently according to which type it belongs to. If the term
$[]$ is considered to be of type $list(list(int))$ (as in the first row of the table, its
$list(int)$-size is 0. If, on the other hand, $[]$ is considered to be of type $list(int)$
(as the innermost $[]$ in the second row of the table, its $list(int)$-size is 1.

When considering a term of type $list(int)$, there is only a minor difference
between counting the number of integer values versus the number of integer lists
in such a term, since both actually end up denoting the length of the list (up to
a constant) and thereby the traditional *listlength* norm. For more involved lists
(or types in general), this is no longer the case. Consider for example the terms
$[[1,2],[3]]$, $[[2],[3]]$ and $[[2],[3|X]]$ of type $list(list(int))$. While in this case, the
$list(list(int))$-size again denotes the length of the outermost lists, the $list(int)$-
size does not. We have that $\sigma_{list(list(int))}([[1,2],[3]]) = \sigma_{list(list(int))}([[2],[3]]) = \sigma_{list(list(int))}([[1,2],[3|X]]) = 3$ while on the other hand $\sigma_{list(int)}([[1,2],[3]]) = 5$,
$\sigma_{list(int)}([[2],[3]]) = 4$ and $\sigma_{list(int)}([[2],[3|X]]) = 3+X$. For the $\mathtt{flat/2}$ predicate
from Example 1, the latter difference implies the difference between the ability
or disability of proving termination for $\mathtt{flat/2}$.

3   Analysing Size Relations

During termination analysis, one is not only interested in the concrete sizes of
terms, but also in the relations that exist between the sizes of the arguments
of a predicate upon success. The latter, expressing a declarative property, are
called *interargument relations*, *size relations* or *size dependencies*. They are hard
to compute when they have to relate sizes measured by different norms as in
e.g. [9] but are straightforward to compute when the applied measurement is the
same, which is the case in our approach since we can compute a size relation
with respect to a particular constituent. Consider a type τ. A τ-*size relation*
for a predicate p/n with type declaration $p(\tau_1,\ldots,\tau_n)$ is a relation $R_p^\tau \subseteq \mathbb{N}$
such that for every $p(t_1 : \tau_1,\ldots,t_n : \tau_n) \in Atom_P$: if $P \models p(t_1,\ldots,t_n)$ then
$(\sigma_\tau(t_1),\ldots,\sigma_\tau(t_n)) \in R_p^\tau$.

Size relations play a crucial role in the formulation of the (abstract) acceptability condition, and hence in the termination analysis. Before giving a
reformulation of the acceptability condition in our typed context (Section 4), we
develop the computation of these size relations. First, we restrict the analysis to
monomorphic programs only, i.e. programs in which none of the types that are
used contains type variables, but we lift this restriction in a second part of this
section.

3.1   The Monomorphic Case

A commonly followed approach (e.g. [5,20]) when computing size relations uses abstract compilation. The program to be analysed is abstracted, using the chosen norm, to a corresponding CLP(Q) program. The latter describes the size dependencies in the original program. Then the least model of the abstract program is approximated; this model expresses the size relations that exist between the arguments of the computed answers of the different predicates. Here we focus on the abstraction process. First, we define the τ-size abstraction of an atom as follows:

Definition 5. *(τ-size abstraction of atoms)*

- *Let τ be a type and X, Y variables of type τ'. If $\tau \in Constituents(\tau')$, then the τ-size abstraction of $X = Y$ is $X = Y$, otherwise it is true.*
- *Let τ be a type, $X, Y_1, \ldots, Y_n$ variables of types $\tau_0, \tau_1, \ldots, \tau_n$ respectively. If $\tau \in Constituents(\tau_0)$, then the τ-size abstraction of $X = f(Y_1, \ldots, Y_n)$ is*

$$X = c + W_1 + \ldots + W_k$$

  where: if $\tau = \tau_0$ then $c = 1$ else $c = 0$ and $\{W_1, \ldots, W_k\} = \{Y_i | 1 \leq i \leq n,\ \tau \preceq \tau_i\}$, otherwise it is true. If $c = 1$, we say that the term $f(Y_1, \ldots, Y_n)$ is counted *in the τ-size abstraction of the atom.*
- *Let τ be a type, $Y_1, \ldots, Y_n$ variables of types $\tau_1, \ldots, \tau_n$ respectively. The τ-size abstraction of $p(Y_1, \ldots, Y_n)$ is $p_\tau(W_1, \ldots, W_k)$ where $\{W_1, \ldots, W_k\} = \{Y_i | 1 \leq i \leq n,\ \tau \preceq \tau_i\}$.*

Note that the τ-size abstraction of a unification $X = Y$ or $X = f(Y_1, \ldots, Y_n)$ is true (the top element of the abstract domain) and carries no information when τ is not a constituent of the type of X. Note also that the term $f(Y_1, \ldots, Y_n)$ is not counted (being of a different type) in the τ-abstraction of the unification if X is of a type other than τ; only its subterms are taken into account. A predicate call is abstracted by a call to a new predicate that reflects the τ-size relation of the called predicate. Since a τ-size relation can only exist between those arguments that can contain a subterm of type τ, only those arguments are taken into account in the abstraction.

Definition 6. *(τ-size abstraction of a clause) The τ-size abstraction of a clause in normal form is obtained by replacing all atoms by their τ-size abstractions.*

If the τ-size abstraction of an atom or clause contains a variable X, then we say that X is *preserved* in the τ-size abstraction of the atom or clause.

Example 5. Consider the definition of the classical `append/3` predicate that we assume to be defined with type declaration $append(list(int), list(int), list(int))$ and both its *int*- and *list(int)*-abstractions.

append/3	$list(int)$-abstraction	int-abstraction

`append(X,Y,Z):-`
`  X = [],`
`  Y = Z.`
	`append_list_int(X,Y,Z):-`
	`  X = 1,`
	`  Y = Z.`
		`append_int(X,Y,Z):-`
		`  X = 0,`
		`  Y = Z.`

`append(X,Y,Z):-`
`  X = [E|Es],`
`  append(Es,Y,Zs),`
`  Z = [E|Zs].`
	`append_list_int(X,Y,Z):-`
	`  X = 1 + Es,`
	`  append_list_int(Es,Y,Zs),`
	`  Z = 1 + Zs.`
		`append_int(X,Y,Z):-`
		`  X = E + Es,`
		`  append_int(Es,Y,Zs),`
		`  Z = E + Zs.`

The int-abstraction of $X = [\,]$ resembles the fact that upon success of the unification, the value of X does not contain an integer value. Likewise, its $list(int)$ abstraction denotes that the value of X contains a single subterm of type $list(int)$. Also, the $list(int)$-abstraction of $X = [E|Es]$ denotes that the value of X contains precisely one more subterm of type $list(int)$ than Es does and the int-abstraction of the unification denotes that the number of integer values in X equals the sum of the number of integer values in E (which is 1) and those in Es. Note that E is preserved in the int-abstraction but not in the $list(int)$-abstraction. The following proposition follows directly from Definitions 5 and 6.

Proposition 1. *A variable $X : \tau'$ is preserved in the τ-abstraction of a clause iff $\tau \in Constituents(\tau')$. A term $f(Y_1, \dots, Y_n)$ is counted in the τ-abstraction iff the term is of type τ.*

To obtain the desired size relations, it suffices to compute a finite approximation of the abstract programs' concrete semantics [5]. Known approaches include polyhedral approximations [1,6] or disjunctions of monotonicity and equality constraints [17].

Example 6. Examples of valid int and $list(int)$ size relations of **append/3** are $\{(X, Y, Z) \mid Z = X + Y\}$ and $\{(X, Y, Z) \mid Z + 1 = X + Y\}$ respectively.

Note that the computation of size relations in a monomorphic setting is a call-independent process: a size relation between the arguments of a predicate does not depend on the particular context in which the predicate was called. Hence, the computation of size relations can be performed bottom-up in the predicate dependency graph of the program [5,12].

3.2 The Polymorphic Case

Type polymorphism is an important abstraction tool: a predicate defined with a type declaration that associates its arguments with a polymorphic type can be called with actual arguments of any type that is an instance of the defined type. For example, the **append/3** predicate from Section 3.1 can be defined with respect to the polymorphic type declaration $append(list(T), list(T), list(T))$ stating that its arguments are lists of some type T. One can abstract the **append/3** program for constituents T and $list(T)$. Note that as T has no other constituents than itself, the T-abstraction corresponds to the int-abstraction of Section 3.1

and the T-size relation is identical to the int-size relation (the $list(T)$-abstraction corresponds to the $list(int)$-abstraction in a similar way).

$list(T)$-abstraction	T-abstraction
`append_list_T(X,Y,Z):-`	`append_T(X,Y,Z):-`
`    X = 1,`	`    X = 0,`
`    Y = Z.`	`    Y = Z.`
`append_list_T(X,Y,Z):-`	`append_T(X,Y,Z):-`
`    X = 1 + Es,`	`    X = E + Es,`
`    append_list_T(Es,Y,Zs),`	`    append_T(Es,Y,Zs),`
`    Z = 1 + Zs.`	`    Z = E + Zs.`

Obviously, having computed the T- and $list(T)$- size abstractions, one can reuse these results for the int- and $list(int)$-size abstractions of a call to `append/3` with actual arguments of type $list(int)$. The question arises whether this is in general the case for all constituents of all instances of the polymorphic type. The ability to reuse is particularly important when analysing large programs distributed over many modules, which is often the case when polymorphism is involved. It is preferable that an analysis does not need the actual code of the predicates it imports (and of the predicates called directly or indirectly by the imported predicates) but only the result of a call independent analysis (e.g. the size relations of the imported predicates for all constituents of the types from their declaration). See [21,4,26] for discussions about module based analysis.

In the remainder of this section we discuss to what extend the size relations that are computed for the constituents of the types in the type *declaration* of a predicate can be reused when computing the size abstraction of a call with respect to a constituent of the *actual* type of some argument, which is an instance of the declared type.

Example 7. Assume that we are interested in computing size abstractions of a call to `append/3` with arguments of type $list(list(int))$. One can easily verify that the $list(list(int))$-size abstraction of the `append/3` predicate is identical to its $list(T)$-size abstraction, and that the $list(int)$- and int-size abstractions correspond with its T-size abstraction. However consider a call to `append/3` with arguments of type $list(nest(V))$ (taken from [23]) with

$$nest(V) \longrightarrow e(V); l(list(nest(V))).$$

For constructing the $list(nest(V))$-size abstraction of `append/3`, one observes that $list(nest(V))$ is not only a constituent of itself but also of $nest(V)$. Hence variables of type $nest(V)$ are preserved and the obtained abstraction (abbreviated to `append_ln_V`) differs from the $list(T)$-size abstraction:

`append_ln_V(X,Y,Z) :- X=1+E+Es, append_ln_V(Es,Y,Zs), Z=1+E+Es.`

In what follows, we formally state sufficient conditions under which the τ-size abstraction of a predicate call (τ being a type constituent of some of the types of the actual arguments of the call) equals the τ'-size relation of the predicate, with τ' being a type constituent of the type declaration of the predicate. In order to do so, we need to be able to compare several size abstractions of the same predicate with respect to different types associated to the variables of the predicate; one in which the types of the variables are derived from the declaration of the predicate and another in which the types of the variables are derived from the types of a particular call. We start with introducing *variable typings*.

Definition 7. *A variable typing ζ is a mapping from program variables to types; $dom(\zeta)$ is the set of variables for which the mapping is defined; $X\zeta$ denotes the type of X under the variable typing ζ. Given variable typings ζ and ζ' over the same domain, ζ' is an instance of ζ if there exists a type substitution α such that $X\zeta' = X\zeta\alpha$ for every $X \in dom(\zeta)$. We denote this by $\zeta' = \zeta\alpha$. To ease notation, we denote the fact that $X \in dom(\zeta)$ and $X\zeta = \tau$ with $X/\tau \in \zeta$.*

The notion of *Constituents* extends in a straightforward way to variable typings. Our goal is to relate the analysis of a clause under a (polymorphic) variable typing ζ_p with its analysis under an instance ζ_i of ζ_p. A first step is to relate constituents of ζ_i with constituents of ζ_p.

Definition 8. *Let ζ_i and ζ_p be variable typings with $\zeta_i = \zeta_p\alpha$ for a substitution α. The type mapping between ζ_i and ζ_p is the minimal relation $R_{\zeta_i}^{\zeta_p} : \mathcal{T} \times \mathcal{T}$ such that:*

- *If $X/\tau_i \in \zeta_i$ and $X/\tau_p \in \zeta_p$ then $(\tau_i, \tau_p) \in R_{\zeta_i}^{\zeta_p}$.*
- *If $(\tau_i, \tau_p) \in R_{\zeta_i}^{\zeta_p}$ and $\tau_p \in V_{\mathcal{T}}$ then $\forall \tau \in Constituents(\tau_i) : (\tau, \tau_p) \in R_{\zeta_i}^{\zeta_p}$.*
- *If $(\tau_i, \tau_p) \in R_{\zeta_i}^{\zeta_p}$ and $\tau_p = h(\overline{V})\alpha'$ and $\tau_i = h(\overline{V})\alpha'\alpha$ and the right-hand side of the type rule for h contains a term $f(\tau_1, \ldots, \tau_k)$, then for each j in $\{1, \ldots, k\}$ $(\tau_j\alpha'\alpha, \tau_j\alpha') \in R_{\zeta_i}^{\zeta_p}$.*

The type function $\phi_{\zeta_i}^{\zeta_p} : \mathcal{T} \mapsto 2^{\mathcal{T}}$ is defined for constituents of the most instantiated variable typing ζ_i: $\phi_{\zeta_i}^{\zeta_p}(\tau_i) = \{\tau_p | (\tau_i, \tau_p) \in R_{\zeta_i}^{\zeta_p}\}$.

When ζ_p and ζ_i are obvious from the context, we will write R and $\phi(\tau)$.

Example 8. The type mapping and type function associated to the variable typings $\zeta_p = \{X/list(T)\}$ and $\zeta_i = \{X/list(list(int))\}$ (i.e. $\alpha = \{T/list(int)\}$) are respectively:

- $R = \{(list(list(int)), list(T)), (list(int), T), (int, T)\}$ and
- $\phi = \{(list(list(int)), \{list(T)\}), (list(int), \{T\}), (int, \{T\})\}$.

With $\zeta_i = \{X/list(nest(V))\}$ (i.e. $\alpha = \{T/nest(V)\}$) we obtain:

- $R = \{(list(nest(V)), list(T)), (nest(V), T), (V, T), (list(nest(V)), T)\}$ and
- $\phi = \{(list(nest(V)), \{list(T), T\}), (nest(V), \{T\}), (V, \{T\})\}$.

In the rest of this section, we show that the τ_i-abstraction of a predicate under variable typing ζ_i is equal to the τ_p-abstraction under variable typing ζ_p when $\phi(\tau_i) = \{\tau_p\}$. One can verify that this is indeed the case for the constituents in Example 8 and that only the $list(nest(V))$-abstraction is different from the abstractions in the polymorphic constituents.

By Definitions 5 and 6, given two constituent types τ_p and τ_i of variable typings ζ_p and ζ_i respectively, the τ_p-size abstraction of a clause under ζ_p equals the τ_i-size abstraction of the clause under ζ_i if both abstractions preserve the same variables, and if every term in the clause of type τ_p under variable typing ζ_p is of type τ_i under variable typing ζ_i (since in that case both abstractions count the same terms). Before we prove under which circumstances this holds, we first stress the relations between the types of a variable in a variable typing ζ_p and an instance variable typing ζ_i.

Proposition 2. *Let ζ_p and ζ_i be two typings over the variables of a clause such that $\zeta_i = \zeta_p \alpha$. If $X : \tau_p \in \zeta_p$ and $X : \tau_i \in \zeta_i$, we have that*

- $\tau_i = \tau_p \alpha$.
- $(\tau_i, \tau_p) \in R$ *or, put differently, $\tau_p \in \phi(\tau_i)$.*
- *if $(\tau_i', \tau_p') \in R$ and $\tau_p' \notin V_{\mathcal{T}}$ then $\tau_i' = \tau_p' \alpha$.*

Theorem 1. *Let ζ_p and ζ_i be two typings over the variables of a clause such that $\zeta_i = \zeta_p \alpha$. Furthermore, let τ_{pp} and τ_{ii} be constituents of ζ_p and ζ_i respectively. If $\phi(\tau_{ii})$ is equal to the singleton set $\{\tau_{pp}\}$ then the τ_{ii}-abstraction of the clause under the typing ζ_i is equal to the τ_{pp}-abstraction of the clause under the typing ζ_p.*

Proof. We first prove that both abstractions preserve the same set of variables and show next that both abstractions count the same terms.

Consider a variable $X : \tau_i$ that is preserved in the τ_{ii}-abstraction under the typing ζ_i. By Proposition 1, $\tau_{ii} \in Constituents(\tau_i)$. Now, $X : \tau_i$ is a variable of ζ_i hence by Proposition 2 there exists a τ_p such that $(\tau_i, \tau_p) \in R$. Moreover, $\tau_{ii} \in Constituents(\tau_i)$ hence, by definition 8, there exists a $\tau_{pp} \in Constituents(\tau_p)$ such that $(\tau_{ii}, \tau_{pp}) \in R$, i.e. $\tau_{pp} \in \phi(\tau_{ii})$ and X is preserved in the τ_{pp}-abstraction under typing ζ_p. Note also that $\tau_i = \tau_p \alpha$, that $\tau_{pp} \alpha \in Constituents(\tau_i)$ and $\tau_{ii} \in Constituents(\tau_{pp} \alpha)$. If $\phi(\tau_{ii})$ is a singleton, then all variables preserved in the τ_{ii}-abstraction are preserved in the same τ_{pp}-abstraction.

We also have to show that the τ_{pp}-abstraction does not contain other variables. Hence consider a variable $X : \tau_p$ that is preserved in the τ_{pp}-abstraction under the typing ζ_p. We have that $\tau_{pp} \in Constituents(\tau_p)$ and hence $\tau_{pp} \alpha \in Constituents(\tau_p \alpha)$. But above, we remarked that $\tau_{ii} \in Constituents(\tau_{pp} \alpha)$, hence by transitivity, $\tau_{ii} \in Constituents(\tau_p \alpha) = Constituents(\tau_i)$ and X is in the τ_{ii}-abstraction under typing ζ_i.

Finally, we have to show that a term $f(Y_1, \ldots, Y_n)$ in an atom of the form $X = f(Y_1, \ldots, Y_n)$ is counted in the τ_{ii}-abstraction iff it is counted in the τ_{pp}-abstraction. It is given that $\phi(\tau_{ii}) = \{\tau_{pp}\}$. Let τ_p and τ_i be the types of X in respectively ζ_p and ζ_i. By Proposition 2, $(\tau_i, \tau_p) \in R$ and $\tau_p \alpha = \tau_i$. As $f(Y_1, \ldots, Y_n)$ has type τ_p, $\tau_p \notin V_{\mathcal{T}}$.

In order to prove that the term is counted in both abstractions, it suffices to show that $\tau_p = \tau_{pp}$ if and only if $\tau_i = \tau_{ii}$. First, let us assume that $\tau_p = \tau_{pp}$.

It is given that $\tau_i = \tau_p\alpha = \tau_{pp}\alpha$. Since $(\tau_{ii}, \tau_{pp}) \in R$ and $\tau_{pp} \notin V_{\mathcal{T}}$, it follows from Proposition 2 that $\tau_{pp}\alpha = \tau_{ii}$ hence $\tau_i = \tau_p\alpha = \tau_{pp}\alpha = \tau_{ii}$. For the other direction, we assume $\tau_i = \tau_{ii}$. Since $(\tau_i, \tau_p) \in R$, we have that $\tau_p \in \phi(\tau_i)$ hence also $\tau_p \in \phi(\tau_{ii}) = \{\tau_{pp}\}$. So, $\tau_p = \tau_{pp}$. $\qquad\square$

Returning to Example 8, it follows from the theorem that the $list(list(int))$-abstraction is equal to the $list(T)$-abstraction and that the $list(int)$-, int-, V-and $nest(V)$-abstractions are equal to the T-abstraction. Only obtaining the $list(nest(V))$-abstraction requires a separate analysis.

Reconsider the situation where τ_{ii} is a constituent of a variable typing ζ_i, instance of ζ_p. When $\phi(\tau_{ii})$ is not a singleton, the obvious thing is to construct the τ_{ii}-abstraction of the clauses defining the predicate under the typing ζ_i. However, to optimise reuse of results, it is preferable to construct a $\phi(\tau_{ii})$-abstraction of the clause under the polymorphic typing ζ_p. In such an abstraction, a variable is preserved (in an atom or an equality) iff its type has a constituent in $\phi(\tau_{ii})$ and a term is counted if its type is one of the types in $\phi(\tau_{ii})$. One can verify that the proof of the above theorem extends to this case and that the τ_{ii}-abstraction under the typing ζ_i is identical to the $\phi(\tau_{ii})$-abstraction under the typing ζ_p. This suggests an implementation where size relations are constructed "on demand": when a size relation of a predicate under a typing ζ_i is needed for a type constituent τ_{ii}, then the size relation resulting from the $\phi(\tau_{ii})$-abstraction under the polymorphic typing ζ_p is used (and first computed if it is not yet available).

The question arises whether there are more cases in which the τ_{ii}-size abstraction can be recovered from the polymorphic abstractions. In [3], an attempt is made for the analog problem of instantiatedness (see also Section 4). In fact, it claims that an analysis with respect to a τ_{ii} constituent can always be approximated by combining several analysis for the individual constituents from $\phi(\tau_{ii})$. However, it is flawed (as pointed out by Peter Stuckey) for a type like $list(nest(V))$, instance of $list(T)$ (see Example 7). Indeed, it can be verified that the $list(nest(V))$-abstraction of a unification $X = [E|Es]$, $x \leftrightarrow e \wedge es$, is not approximated by $((x \leftrightarrow e \wedge es) \wedge (x \leftrightarrow es))$ which is the combination of its T- and $list(T)$-abstractions, $x \leftrightarrow e \wedge es$ and $x \leftrightarrow es$ respectively.

4   Reformulating the Termination Condition

Recall that the basic motivation for computing size relations is to discard the necessity to reason over the computed answer substitutions in the definition of acceptability (Definition 1). In addition to the computed size relations, one needs instantiation information that can be combined with the size relations. Since in our approach we measure the size of a term by counting the number of subterms of a particular type it has, the instantiation information we require is whether further instantiating the term can introduce more subterms of the type of interest. In [3], we introduce precisely such an instantiation property:

Definition 9. *Let ρ define the types τ and τ'. We say that the term $t{:}\tau'$ is τ-instantiated (under ρ) if: (1) τ is a constituent of τ'; and (2) there does not exist an instance $t\sigma{:}\tau'$ containing a variable of type τ.*

The table shows for some terms of type $list(int)$ whether they are $list(int)$-size or int-size instantiated. The term $[1, X]$ is $list(int)$-instantiated because all $list(int)$-subterms of type correct instances of $[1, X]$ are instantiated. On the other hand, $[1|X]$ is not $list(int)$-instantiated because the subterm X of type $list(int)$ is a variable. Also, $[1|X]$ is not int-instantiated as e.g. $[1, Y|Z]$ is an instance with the variable Y of type int.

In [3], we developed an analysis that computes the instantiation dependencies that exist between the arguments of a predicate upon success of the predicate. The dependencies are expressed by positive

t:$list(int)$	$list(int)$-inst.	int-inst.
$[1, 2]$	yes	yes
$[1, X]$	yes	no
$[1\|X]$	no	no
$[\,]$	yes	yes

boolean (POS) formulas at the level of a particular constituent of the types in the definition of the predicate. For the **append/3** predicate from above in which each argument is declared having $list(int)$ as type, it derives for example the int-dependency $z \leftrightarrow x \wedge y$ – denoting that all subterms of Z of type int are instantiated if and only if those of X and Y are. The derived $list(int)$ dependency, on the other hand, is $x \wedge (y \leftrightarrow z)$ – denoting that all subterms of X of type $list(int)$ are instantiated (in other words the backbone of the list is instantiated when **append/3** succeeds) and that those of Y are instantiated if and only if those of Z are.

Given the τ-instantiatedness of a query, one can use the τ-instantiatedness analysis of [3] to compute the τ-instantiatedness of all calls selected when the query is executed under a left-to-right computation rule. (Similar as one can compute the groundness of selected calls based on the results of a bottom-up POS-analysis of the program). Hence, we can reformulate the acceptability condition as follows:

Definition 10. *Let S be a set of atomic queries and P be a definite directly recursive program. P is acceptable with respect to S if for every recursive predicate p/n typed $p(\tau_1^p, \ldots, \tau_n^p)$ such that $call(P, S)$ contains calls to it, the following holds: there exists a type $\tau \in Constituents(\tau_1^p, \ldots, \tau_n^p)$ and a set of argument positions $\{j_1, \ldots, j_m\}$ such that for every call $p(t_1 : \tau_1^i, \ldots, t_n : \tau_n^i) \in call(P, S)$ with $\tau' \in Constituents(\tau_1^i, \ldots, \tau_n^i)$ such that $\tau \in \phi(\tau')$ we have that:*

- *every t_{j_k} is τ'-instantiated*
- *for every $H \leftarrow B_1, \ldots, B_n \in P$ with H having predicate symbol p/n*
- *for every B_i having predicate symbol p/n and for any substitution θ such that the arguments of $(B_1, \ldots, B_{i-1})\theta$ all satisfy their associated τ'-size relations:*

$$|H\theta| > |B_i\theta|$$

where $|p(t_1, \ldots, t_n)| = \sum_{k \in \{j_1, \ldots, j_m\}} c_k \sigma_{\tau'}(t_k)$ and $c_1, \ldots, c_m \in \mathbb{N}$.

Again, the existence of a level mapping that makes the program acceptable implies termination of the program [10]. Flexible level mappings assign different weights to different argument positions [5]. This is reflected in the use of the constants c_i. The above condition only addresses recursive calls having the same type as the polymorphic head. A call with a different type can be considered a call to a different predicate in the monomorphic expansion of the program. There is a caveat, termination is only ensured if the monomorphic expansion of the program is finite. With ζ_p the typing of the polymorphic predicate and $\zeta_p\alpha$ the typing of the recursive call, it means that the sequence $\zeta_p, \zeta_p\alpha, \zeta_p\alpha\alpha, \ldots$ must be finite. A sufficient condition is that α is idempotent.

Example 9. As an example, let us reconsider the `flat/2` predicate from the introduction, now written in normal form:

```
flat(X,Y):- X = [], Y = [].
flat(X,Y):- X = [A|B], A = [], flat(B, Y).
flat(X,Y):- X = [A|B], A = [H|T], N = [T|B], flat(N,R), Y = [H|R].
```

Again, assume that `flat/2` is defined with type $list(list(int))$ for its first argument, and $list(int)$ for its second argument. Assume we want to prove termination for a query $flat([[1,2],[3]], R)$; The analysis of [3] can show that the first argument in every call to `flat/2` is $list(list(int))$-instantiated, $list(int)$-instantiated and int-instantiated. Consequently, the following level mappings are considered (taking only the first argument into account)

$$|flat(t_1,t_2)|_{lli} = \sigma_{lli}(t_1)$$
$$|flat(t_1,t_2)|_{li} = \sigma_{li}(t_1)$$
$$|flat(t_1,t_2)|_i = \sigma_i(t_1)$$

where σ_{lli}, σ_{li} and σ_i are abbreviations for $\sigma_{list(list(int))}$, $\sigma_{list(int)}$ and σ_{int} respectively. First, let us consider the level mapping $|.|_{lli}$. For any substitution θ that satisfies the size relations associated to the second clause of the `flat/2` predicate, we have that $\sigma_{lli}(X\theta) = 1 + \sigma_{lli}(B\theta)$, and consequently

$$|flat(X,Y)\theta|_{lli} > |flat(B,Y)\theta|_{lli}.$$

For the third clause, however, we have that $\sigma_{lli}(X\theta) = 1 + \sigma_{lli}(B\theta)$ and $\sigma_{lli}(N\theta) = 1 + \sigma_{lli}(B\theta)$, and consequently

$$|flat(X,Y)\theta|_{lli} \not> |flat(N,R)\theta|_{lli}.$$

Next, let us consider the level mapping $|.|_{li}$. Again, for any substitution θ that satisfies the size relations associated to the second clause of the `flat/2` predicate, we have that $\sigma_{li}(X\theta) = 1 + \sigma_{li}(B\theta)$, and consequently

$$|flat(X,Y)\theta|_{li} > |flat(B,Y)\theta|_{li}.$$

For the third clause, we have now that $\sigma_{li}(X\theta) = \sigma_{li}(A\theta) + \sigma_{li}(B\theta)$, $\sigma_{li}(A\theta) = 1 + \sigma_{li}(T\theta)$ and $\sigma_{li}(N\theta) = \sigma_{li}(T\theta) + \sigma_{li}(B\theta)$, and consequently also for this clause

$$|flat(X,Y)\theta|_{li} > |flat(N,R)\theta|_{li}.$$

Hence, the `flat/2` predicate is acceptable due to the existence of $|.|_{li}$ and consequently terminating for the given query. One could verify that acceptability is also implied by the existence of $\|.\|_i$. More generally, instead of considering a single size, one could consider a linear combination of sizes. For examples with a size τ_1 such that the first argument remains the same in the first recursive clause and gets smaller in the second, and a size τ_2 where it is the other way around, one could prove acceptability by considering their sum.

Note that the above sketched technique can be used not only to prove termination of a given query, but also to derive a sufficient condition for a query to terminate. Indeed, after computing the size and instantiation relations (a call-independent computation process), one could search for possibly instantiation states of the arguments of a predicate such that the condition of definition 10 is satisfied. Since the domain of possible instantiations is finite for every argument, the search process must terminate.

Example 10. Reconsider the `flat/2` predicate from Example 9. Once more, type information reveals that the first argument has constituents $list(list(int))$, $list(int)$ and int, whereas the second argument has constituents $list(int)$ and int. If we restrict the weights of the arguments that are taken into account by a level mapping to either 0 or 1, we can construct three level mappings that take only the first argument into account, two level mappings that take only the second argument into account and two more that take both arguments into account. Among these, the following can be used to prove acceptability:

$$|flat(t_1, t_2)| = \sigma_{li}(t_1) \qquad\qquad |flat(t_1, t_2)| = \sigma_i(t_1)$$

Consequently, a sufficient condition for `flat/2` to terminate is that its first argument is $list(int)$-instantiated.

5   Discussion & Related Work

In this work, we have defined a sufficient condition for termination of logic programs in the presence of type information. In our approach, no norm needs to be specified beforehand; a number of size-measures are automatically derived from the available type information. The automatic derivation of norms is an important topic in termination analysis, as well as in other analyses in which the size of a term is an important notion. For example in [8], information on the size of the arguments of a predicate is used to determine how many solutions it can produce and to estimate its computational cost. This work is generalised in [18] and applied to control the degree of parallelism in a logic program.

Types have been used before to drive the construction of suitable norms. In [2], norms are defined in terms of type schemata but not derived automatically. Automatic derivation of typed norms is considered in [11], in which typed norms are automatically derived from type graphs. These type graphs are constructed by a separate type graph analysis since the subject programs are untyped. Our work, on the other hand, is similar to the analysis of [19] in that it assumes that type information is present and that norms are derived from the readily available type definitions in the program. Polymorphism is dealt with in [19] by imposing a constraint that states that the size of a polymorphic term must be equal to the size of each of its instances. This contrasts with our work, in which no such constraints are imposed. We do introduce a similar condition, however, in order to distinguish whether the results of a default polymorphic analysis can be reused rather than reanalysing the predicate under a more instantiated variable typing. Neither [11] nor [19] defines a size relation analysis using the defined norms.

While the advantages of using types that are declared by the programmer are well-known, for analysis purposes it might be useful to use a sophisticated analysis like [13] to *derive* the types that are used in a program rather than using (only) the declared types. Consider for example a term of type $pair(T)$, where the latter type is defined as $pair(T) \longrightarrow (list(T) - list(T))$. Both lists have the same type and consequently, both are taken into account when counting the number of "list" subterms in a pair. Under some circumstances, the analysis of [13] is able to derive different types for each of the lists and measurements can be derived that take into account only the subterms of the left-hand side or right-hand-side list of the pair. Also, it seems possible that the type inference of [13] can be adapted to obtain a correct typing for an untyped program, which in turn allows to apply our approach to untyped (Prolog) programs.

Unlike other approaches based on types like [11,19] in which a single size measurement is constructed for each type, we construct a number of different measures for each type. Nevertheless, terms are always compared according to the *same* measure (counting their subterms of a particular type). This reduces the derivation of size-relations – non-trivial in the case of typed norms [9] – to the classical case in which these relations are expressed using a single norm. The drawback is a possible loss of generality because we consider only relations between arguments that have a common constituent. This drawback is eliminated by the authors of [14]. They extend our work by performing a single analysis that simultaneously considers several size-abstractions, following the framework of [16]. The effect is that norms that are determined by different types are mixed, and that dependencies can be maintained between the sizes of terms where each term is measured according to a different measure. Several examples illustrate the extra power and practical relevance of the approach for automated termination analysers. Contrary to our work, the approach of [14] does not consider polymorphic analysis. The definition of a polymorphically typed predicate is re-analysed for every call with arguments whose types are instances of the declared types. We believe that an approach that combines the analysis of [14] with a polymorphic analysis like ours will result in a practical and powerful termination analysis for logic programming.

Acknowledgements. We thank Alberto Pettorossi for providing us with extensive feedback and suggestions that helped to improve the paper substantially. We also thank anonymous referees for their valuable comments and feedback.

References

1. Florence Benoy and Andy King. Inferring argument size relationships with CLP(R). In John P. Gallagher, editor, *Logic Programming Synthesis and Transformation, LOPSTR'96, Proceedings*, volume 1207 of *LNCS*, pages 204–223, 1997.
2. Annalisa Bossi, Nicoletta Cocco, and Massimo Fabris. Typed norms. In Bernd Krieg-Brückner, editor, *ESOP'92, 4th European Symposium on Programming, Proceedings*, volume 582 of *LNCS*, pages 73–92. Springer, 1992.
3. Maurice Bruynooghe, Wim Vanhoof, and Michael Codish. Pos(T): Analyzing dependencies in typed logic programs. In Dines Bjørner, Manfred Broy, and Alexander V. Zamulin, editors, *Perspectives of System Informatics*, PSI 2001, Revised Papers, volume 2244 of *LNCS*, pages 406–420. Springer, 2001.
4. Francisco Bueno, Maria J. García de la Banda, Manuel V. Hermenegildo, Kim Marriott, German Puebla, and Peter J. Stuckey. A model for inter-module analysis and optimizing compilation. In Kung-Kiu Lau, editor, *Logic Based Program Synthesis and Transformation, LOPSTR 2000, Selected Papers*, volume 2042 of *LNCS*, pages 86–102. Springer-Verlag, 2000.
5. Michael Codish and Cohavit Taboch. A semantic basis for the termination analysis of logic programs. *Journal of Logic Programming*, 41(1):103–123, 1999.
6. Patrick Cousot and Nicholas Halbwachs. Automatic discovery of linear restraints among variables of a program. In *Conference Record of the Fifth annual ACM Symposium on Principles of Programming Languages*, pages 84–96. ACM, 1978.
7. Danny De Schreye, Kristof Verschaetse, and Maurice Bruynooghe. A framework for analysing the termination of definite logic programs with respect to call patterns. In ICOT Staff, editor, *Proc. of the Fifth Generation Computer Systems, FGCS92*, pages 481–488. IOS Press, 1992.
8. Saumya K. Debray, Pedro López García, Manuel V. Hermenegildo, and Nai-Wei Lin. Estimating the Computational Cost of Logic Programs. In Baudouin Le Charlier, editor, *Static Analysis, SAS'94, Proceedings*, volume 864 of *LNCS*, pages 255–265. Springer Verlag, 1994. Invited Talk.
9. Stefaan Decorte, Danny De Schreye, and Massimo Fabris. Exploiting the power of typed norms in automatic inference of interargument relations. Report CW 246, Department of Computer Science, K.U. Leuven, Leuven, Belgium, January 1997.
10. Stefaan Decorte, Danny De Schreye, and Henk Vandecasteele. Constraint based automatic termination analysis of Logic Programs. *ACM Transactions on Programming Languages and Systems*, 21(6):1137–1195, November 1999.
11. Stefaan Decorte, Danny de Schreye, and Massimo Fabris. Automatic inference of norms: A missing link in automatic termination analysis. In *Logic Programming – Proceedings of the 1993 International Symposium*, pages 420–436. MIT Press, 1993.
12. N. Dershowitz, N. Lindenstrauss, Yehoshua Sagiv, and Alexander Serebrenik. A general framework for automatic termination analysis of logic programs. *Applicable Algebra in Engineering, Communication and Computing*, 12(1-2):117–156, 2001.
13. John Gallagher and German Puebla. Abstract interpretation over nondeterministic finite tree automata for set-based analysis of logic programs. In Shriram Krishnamurthi and C. R. Ramakrishnan, editors, *Practical Aspects of Declarative Languages, PADL 2002, Proceedings*, volume 2257 of *LNCS*, pages 243–261. Springer Verlag, 2002.

14. Samir Genaim, Michael Codish, John Gallagher, and Vitaly Lagoon. Combining norms to prove termination. In A. Cortesi, editor, *Verification, Model Checking and Abstract Interpretation, Third Int. Workshop, VMCAI 2002, Revised Papers*, volume 2294 of *LNCS*, pages 126–138. Springer-Verlag, 2002.
15. Gerda Janssens and Maurice Bruynooghe. Deriving descriptions of possible values of program variables by means of abstract interpretation. *J. Logic programming*, 13(2&3):205–258, 1992.
16. Vitaly Lagoon and Peter J. Stuckey. A framework for analysis of typed logic programs. In Herbert Kuchen and Kazunori Ueda, editors, *Functional and Logic Programming, FLOPS 2001, Proceedings*, volume 2024 of *LNCS*, pages 296–310. Springer, 2001.
17. Naomi Lindenstrauss and Yehoshua Sagiv. Automatic termination analysis of logic programs. In Lee Naish, editor, *Logic Programming, Proceedings of the Fourteenth International Conference on Logic Programming*, pages 63–77. MIT Press, 1997.
18. P. Lopez, M. Hermenegildo, and S. Debray. A methodology for granularity-based control of parallelism in logic programs. *Journal of Symbolic Computation*, 21(4/5/6):715–734, 1996.
19. Jonathan Martin, Andy King, and Paul Soper. Typed norms for typed logic programs. In John P. Gallagher, editor, *Logic Programming Synthesis and Transformation, LOPSTR'96, Proceedings*, volume 864 of *LNCS*, pages 224– 238. Springer-Verlag, 1996.
20. Frédéric Mesnard and Ulrich Neumerkel. Applying static analysis techniques for inferring termination conditions of logic programs. In Patrick Cousot, editor, *Static Analysis, SAS 2001, Proceedings*, volume 2126 of *LNCS*, pages 93–110. Springer 2001, 2001.
21. G. Puebla and M. Hermenegildo. Some issues in analysis and specialization of modular Ciao-Prolog programs. In M. Leuschel, editor, *Proceedings of the Workshop on Optimization and Implementation of Declarative Languages*, 1999. In Electronic Notes in Theoretical Computer Science, Volume 30 Issue No.2, Elsevier Science.
22. Danny De Schreye and Stefaan Decorte. Termination of logic programs: the never-ending story. *The Journal of Logic Programming*, 19 & 20:199–260, May 1994.
23. Jan-Georg Smaus, Patricia M. Hill, and Andy King. Mode analysis domains for typed logic programs. In Annalisa Bossi, editor, *Logic Programming Synthesis and Transformation, LOPSTR'99, Selected Papers*, volume 1817 of *LNCS*, pages 82–101. Springer-Verlag, 2000.
24. Zoltan Somogyi, Fergus Henderson, and Thomas Conway. The execution algorithm of Mercury, an efficient purely declarative logic programming language. *Journal of Logic Programming*, 29(1–3):17–64, 1996.
25. Jeffrey D. Ullman and Allen Van Gelder. Efficient tests for top-down termination of logical rules. *JACM*, 35(2):345–373, 1988.
26. W. Vanhoof. Binding-time analysis by constraint solving: a modular and higher-order approach for Mercury. In M. Parigot and A. Voronkov, editors, *Logic for Programming and Automated Reasoning, LPAR2000, Proceedings*, volume 1955 of *LNAI*, pages 399–416. Springer, 2000.
27. Wim Vanhoof and Maurice Bruynooghe. Binding-time annotations without binding-time analysis. In Robert Nieuwenhuis and Andrei Voronkov, editors, *Logic for Programming, Artificial Intelligence, and Reasoning, LPAR 2001, Proceedings*, volume 2250 of *LNCS*, pages 707–722. Springer, 2001.

Symbolic Profiling for Multi-paradigm Declarative Languages*

Elvira Albert and Germán Vidal

DSIC, UPV, Camino de Vera s/n, E-46022 Valencia, Spain
{ealbert,gvidal}@dsic.upv.es

Abstract. We present the basis of a source-level profiler for multi-paradigm declarative languages which integrate features from (lazy) functional and logic programming. Our profiling scheme is *symbolic* in the sense that it is independent of the particular language implementation. This is achieved by counting the number of *basic* operations performed during the execution of program calls, e.g., the number of unfolding steps, the number of matching operations, etc. The main contribution of this paper is the formal specification of the attribution of execution costs to *cost centers*, which is particularly difficult in the context of lazy languages. A prototype implementation of the symbolic profiler has been undertaken for the multi-paradigm language Curry. Preliminary results demonstrate the practicality of our approach and its applications in the field of program transformation.

1 Introduction

Profiling tools, in general, are designed for assisting the programmer in the task of generating efficient code (see, e.g., [12]). By analyzing the profiling results, the programmer may find those parts of the program which dominate the execution time. As a consequence of this, the code may be changed, recompiled and profiled again, in hopes of improving efficiency. In the field of program transformation, in particular, we believe that profiling techniques can play an important role:

1. *The most immediate application consists of using the information gathered by the profiler to assess the effectiveness of a program transformation.* This can be done by simply comparing the cost information obtained for the original and the transformed programs. For instance, as we shall see later, we use our profiler to decide whether the optimization of a program function actually provides an improvement over the original function.
2. *In the context of* automatic *program transformation techniques, profiling tools can assist the transformation process in the task of identifying those program calls which are promising candidates to be optimized.* For instance, partial evaluation is an automatic program transformation technique which

* This work has been partially supported by CICYT TIC 2001-2705-C03-01, by Acción Integrada Hispano-Alemana HA2001-0059, by Acción Integrada Hispano-Austriaca HU2001-0019, and by Acción Integrada Hispano-Italiana HI2000-0161.

A. Pettorossi (Ed.): LOPSTR 2001, LNCS 2372, pp. 148–167, 2002.

specializes a given program w.r.t. part of its input data [22]. Some partial evaluators require the user to annotate the program calls to be optimized by partial evaluation (e.g., [4]). In these cases, profiling tools could play an important role in order to automate the process, e.g., they could help in the task of detecting which are the most expensive functions and, thus, promising candidates to be partially evaluated. However, note that the most expensive functions are not the only interesting ones to be partially evaluated. In fact, sometimes the specialization of computationally inexpensive—but often called functions—can lead to dramatic speedups.

3. *A further step along the lines of the previous point would be to integrate the profiler within a program transformation tool.* For instance, the extension of a partial evaluator with the computation of cost information may be useful to determine the improvement achieved by a particular transformation process. A first step towards this direction can be found in [29], where the partial evaluator returns not only the set of residual rules, but also the cost improvement achieved by each rule. The computation of cost information during partial evaluation could also be used to *guide* the specialization process, e.g., to decide when to evaluate and when to residualize an expression depending on the computed costs.

Our work is concerned with the development of a profiling scheme to assist automatic transformation techniques for multi-paradigm declarative languages. Recent proposals for multi-paradigm declarative programming amalgamate principles from functional, logic and concurrent programming [16]. The resulting language includes the most important features of the distinct paradigms, e.g., *lazy* evaluation, higher-order functions, nondeterministic computations, concurrent evaluation of constraints with synchronization on logical variables, and a unified computation model which integrates *narrowing* and *residuation* [16].

Rather surprisingly, there are very few profiling tools for high-level declarative languages. The reason can be found in the difficulty to relate low-level operations with high-level code [27]. This is particularly difficult in the presence of a lazy evaluation mechanism, since the execution of nested calls is interleaved and each part of the execution must be attributed to the right function call.

Two features characterize our profiler: the basic scheme is defined for the *source* language, unlike traditional profilers which work by regularly interrupting the compiled program—hence, the attribution of costs to the user's program constructions is straightforward—and it is *symbolic*, in the sense that it is independent of a particular implementation of the language—thus, we do not return *actual* execution times but a list of symbolic measures: the number of computation steps, the number of allocated cells, the number of nondeterministic branching points, and the number of pattern matching operations.[1] Moreover, the user may annotate the source program with *cost centers* to which execution costs are attributed. We define a formal specification, or *cost semantics*,

---

[1] Nevertheless, the experiments in Section 5 indicate that the speedup predicted using our symbolic cost criteria is a good approximation of the real speedup measured experimentally.

to describe the attribution of costs to cost centers. The specification is given for programs in *flat* form, a sort of intermediate representation used during the compilation of (higher-level) source programs [9,17,25]. Nevertheless, we could say that our profiler is defined at a source-level since the transformation from high-level to flat programs consists mainly in a "desugaring" process. The flat representation was originally designed to provide a common interface for connecting different tools working on functional logic programs. Furthermore, the definition is general enough to cover also other declarative languages, e.g., purely functional or logic languages. This allows people working on programming tools for similar languages (e.g., compiler back-ends, program optimizers) to develop them on the basis of the intermediate representation so that they can exchange or integrate such tools.

This paper establishes a setting in which one can discuss costs attribution, formal properties about costs, or the effects of some program transformations in the context of multi-paradigm declarative languages. Moreover, we provide some preliminary results from the prototype implementation of a profiler for the multi-paradigm declarative language Curry [19]. They show evidence of the practicality of our approach and its applications in the field of program transformation. For instance, a partial evaluator has been recently developed for Curry programs [3,4]. This partial evaluation tool starts out from a program with some annotated function calls and produces (potentially) more efficient, residual definitions for the annotated function calls. Our profiler has been greatly useful to estimate the effectiveness of this partial evaluator, i.e., to determine the efficiency speedups achieved by the partial evaluator for a given annotated program (we refer here to the application stressed in the first item at the beginning of this section). As we will see in Section 5, the idea is to simply perform the profiling of those expressions previously annotated to be partially evaluated (i.e., *cost centers* are introduced on the same expressions to be specialized). Thus, the profiling results allow us to assess whether significant performance improvements have been achieved by the specialization phase. A further step would be to use the profiler for deciding on which expressions the annotations should be introduced (as discussed in the second item at the beginning of this section). This application is a subject of ongoing research.

The rest of the paper is organized as follows. Section 2 informally describes the source language as well as its operational semantics. Section 3 introduces some symbolic cost criteria and outlines the profiling scheme. The specification of our cost semantics for profiling is formally described in Section 4. Section 5 summarizes our experiments with an implementation of the profiler for Curry. Section 6 compares with related work. Finally, Section 7 concludes and points out several directions for further research.

2   The Source Language

We consider modern multi-paradigm languages which integrate the most important features of functional and logic programming (like, e.g., Curry [19] or Toy [24]). In our source language, functions are defined by a sequence of rules:

$$f(c_1, \ldots, c_n) = t$$

where $c_1, \ldots, c_n$ are constructor terms and the right-hand side t is an arbitrary term. *Constructor terms* may contain variables and constructor symbols, i.e., symbols which are not defined by the program rules. Functional logic programs can be seen as term rewriting systems fulfilling several conditions (e.g., inductively sequential systems [8]). Several implementations allow the use of a number of additional features, like higher-order functions, (concurrent) constraints, external (built-in) calls, monadic I/O, nondeterministic functions, etc. We do not describe these features here but refer to [19].

Example 1. Let us consider the following rules defining the well-known function append (where [] denotes the empty list and x:xs a list with first element x and tail xs):[2]

```
append eval flex
append []     ys = ys
append (x:xs) ys = x : append xs ys
```

The evaluation annotation "eval flex" declares append as a *flexible* function which can also be used to *solve* equations over functional expressions (see below). For instance, the equation "append p s =:= [1,2,3]" is solved by instantiating the variables p and s to lists so that their concatenation results in the list [1,2,3].

The basic operational semantics of our source language is based on a combination of needed narrowing and residuation [16]. The *residuation* principle is based on the idea of delaying function calls until they are ready for a deterministic evaluation (by rewriting). Residuation preserves the deterministic nature of functions and naturally supports concurrent computations. On the other hand, the *narrowing* mechanism allows the instantiation of free variables in expressions and, then, applies reduction steps to the instantiated expressions. This instantiation is usually computed by unifying a subterm of the entire expression with the left-hand side of some program rule. To avoid unnecessary computations and to deal with infinite data structures, demand-driven generation of the search space has recently been advocated by a flurry of outside-in, lazy narrowing strategies. Due to some optimality properties, *needed narrowing* [8] is currently the best lazy narrowing strategy for functional logic programs.

The precise mechanism—narrowing or residuation—for each function is specified by *evaluation annotations*. The annotation of a function as *rigid* forces the delayed evaluation by rewriting, while functions annotated as *flexible* can be evaluated in a nondeterministic manner by applying narrowing steps. For instance, in the language Curry [19], only functions of result type "Constraint" are considered flexible (and all other functions rigid). Nevertheless, the user can explicitly provide different evaluation annotations. To provide concurrent computation threads, expressions can be combined by the *concurrent conjunction*

---

[2] Although we consider a first-order representation for programs, we use a curried notation in the examples as it is common practice in functional languages.

operator "&," i.e., the expression e_1 & e_2 can be reduced by evaluating either e_1 or e_2.

3 Symbolic Profiling

Our profiling scheme relies on the introduction of some symbolic costs which are attributed to specific *cost centers*. Our symbolic costs are used to represent the *basic* operations performed during the evaluation of expressions. They are coherent with the cost criteria introduced in [1,10] to measure the cost of functional logic computations. The main novelty lies in the introduction of a particular criterium to measure the creation and manipulation of nondeterministic branching points (which are similar to choice points in logic programming). The costs of a particular functional logic computation are attributed by adding the costs of performing *each step of the computation*. Thus, we only define the symbolic costs associated to the application of a single rule:

- *Number of unfolding steps.* Trivially, the number of steps associated to the application of a program rule is 1.
- *Number of pattern matching operations.* It is defined as the number of constructor symbols in the left-hand side of the applied rule.
- *Number of nondeterministic steps.* This cost abstracts the work needed either to create, update or remove a choice point. It is equal to 0 when the function call matches exactly one program rule, and 1 otherwise. Thus, in principle, we do not accumulate the work performed in previous choices. Nevertheless, in the implementation, we wish to be more flexible and allow the user to indicate (by means of a flag) whether the cost of former nondeterministic branches should also be accrued to the current branch. This is particularly interesting in the presence of failing derivations, as will be shown in Section 5. Unfortunately, the formalization of this approach is not easy: by simply accumulating the cost of all previous derivations to the current one, we probably count the same costs several times since, for instance, two different derivations may share all the steps but the final one. In order to overcome this problem, a new semantics definition which takes into account the *search strategy* is required. This is subject of ongoing work (see [2]).
- *Number of applications.* Following [10], we define the number of applications associated to applying a program rule as the number of non-variable symbols (of arity greater than zero) in the right-hand side of this rule, plus the arities of these symbols. This cost intends to measure the time needed for the storage that must be allocated for executing a computation, i.e., for allocating the expressions in the right-hand sides of the rules.

Profilers attribute execution costs to "parts" of the source program. Traditionally, these "parts" are identified with functions or procedures. Following [27], we take a more flexible approach which allows us to associate a *cost center* with each expression of interest. This provides the programmer with the possibility of choosing an appropriate granularity for profiling, ranging from whole program phases to single subexpressions in a function. Nevertheless, our approach can be easily adapted to work with automatically instrumented cost centers. For instance, if one wants to use the traditional approach in which all functions are profiled, we can automatically annotate each function by introducing a cost center for the entire right-hand side (since, in the flat representation, each function is defined by a single rule). Cost centers are marked with the (built-in) function SCC (for Set Cost Center). For instance, given the program excerpt:

```
length_app x y = length (append x y)
length [] = 0
length (x:xs) = (length xs) + 1
```

which uses the definition of **append** in Example 1, one can introduce the following annotations:

```
length_app x y = SCC cc2 (length (SCC cc1 (append x y)))
```

In this way, the cost of evaluating "**append** x y" is attributed to the cost center cc1, while the cost of evaluating "**length** (**append** x y)" is attributed to the cost center cc2 by excluding the costs already attributed to cc1.

We informally describe the attribution of costs to cost centers as follows. Given an expression "SCC cc e", the costs attributed to cc are the entire costs of evaluating e as far as the enclosing context demands it,

- also *including* the cost of evaluating any function called during the evaluation of the expression e,
- but *excluding* the cost of evaluating any SCC-expressions within e or within any function called from e.

For example, given the initial call "**length_app** (1:2:3:x) (4:5:[])", the first result that we compute is 5, with computed answer $\{x \mapsto []\}$ and associated symbolic costs:

cc1: 4 steps (one for each element of the first input list, plus an additional step to apply the base case, which instantiates x to []), 4 pattern matchings (one for each applied rule, since there is only one constructor symbol in the left-hand sides of the rules defining **append**), 1 nondeterministic branching point (to evaluate the call **append** x (4:5:[])), and 18 applications (6 applications for each element of the first input list).

cc2: 6 steps (one for each element of the concatenated list, plus an additional step to apply the base case), 6 pattern matchings (one for each applied rule, since there is only one constructor symbol in the left-hand sides of the rules defining **length**), 0 nondeterministic branching points (since the computation is fully deterministic), and 25 applications (5 applications for each element of the list).

The next section gives a formal account of the attribution of costs.

4   Formal Specification of the Cost Semantics

This section formalizes a semantics enhanced with cost information for performing symbolic profiling. Our cost-augmented semantics considers programs written in *flat* form. In this representation, all functions are defined by a single rule, whose left-hand side contains only different variables as parameters, and the right-hand side contains case expressions for pattern-matching. Thanks to this representation, we can define a simpler operational semantics, which will become essential to simplify the definition of the associated profiling scheme. The syntax for programs in the flat representation is formalized as follows:

$$
\begin{array}{llll}
\mathcal{R} ::= D_1 \dots D_m & e ::= x & \text{(variable)} \\
D ::= f(x_1, \dots, x_n) = e & \mid\; c(e_1, \dots, e_n) & \text{(constructor)} \\
& \mid\; f(e_1, \dots, e_n) & \text{(function call)} \\
p ::= c(x_1, \dots, x_n) & \mid\; case\ e_0\ of\ \{p_1 \to e_1; \dots; p_n \to e_n\} & \text{(rigid case)} \\
& \mid\; fcase\ e_0\ of\ \{p_1 \to e_1; \dots; p_n \to e_n\} & \text{(flexible case)} \\
& \mid\; SCC(cc, e) & \text{(SCC-construct)}
\end{array}
$$

where $\mathcal{R}$ denotes a program, D a function definition, p a pattern and e an arbitrary expression. We write $\overline{o_n}$ for the *sequence of objects* $o_1, \dots, o_n$. A program $\mathcal{R}$ consists of a sequence of function definitions D such that the left-hand side is linear and has only variable arguments, i.e., pattern matching is compiled into case expressions. The right-hand side of each function definition is an expression e composed by variables, constructors, function calls, case expressions, and *SCC*-constructs. The general form of a case expression is:

$$(f)\,case\ e\ of\ \{c_1(\overline{x_{n_1}}) \to e_1; \dots; c_k(\overline{x_{n_k}}) \to e_k\}$$

where e is an expression, $c_1, \dots, c_k$ are different constructors of the type of e, and $e_1, \dots, e_k$ are arbitrary expressions. The variables $\overline{x_{n_i}}$ are local variables which occur only in the corresponding subexpression e_i. The difference between *case* and *fcase* only shows up when the argument e is a free variable: *case* suspends (which corresponds to residuation) whereas *fcase* nondeterministically binds this variable to the pattern in a branch of the case expression (which corresponds to narrowing).

Example 2. By using case expressions, the rules of Example 1 defining the function **append** can be represented by a single rule as follows:

```
append x y = fcase x of { []       → y ;
                          (z:zs)  → z : append zs y }
```

The standard semantics for flat programs is based on the LNT calculus (Lazy Narrowing with definitional Trees [18]). In Fig. 1, we recall from [5] an extension of the original LNT calculus able to cope with the combination of needed narrowing and residuation (i.e., the operational semantics informally described in Section 2). The calculus is defined by the one-step transition relation $\Rightarrow_\sigma$, which is labeled with the substitution σ computed in the step. The application of the substitution σ to an expression e is denoted by $\sigma(e)$. Let us informally describe the rules of the LNT calculus:

HNF
$$c(e_1, \ldots, e_i, \ldots, e_n) \;\Rightarrow_\sigma\; \sigma(c(e_1, \ldots, e_i', \ldots, e_n))$$
$$\text{if } e_i \text{ is not a constructor term and } e_i \Rightarrow_\sigma e_i'$$

Case Select
$$(f)case\; c(\overline{e_n})\; of\; \{\overline{p_m \to e_m'}\} \;\Rightarrow_{id}\; \sigma(e_i') \quad \text{if } p_i = c(\overline{x_n}) \text{ and } \sigma = \{\overline{x_n \mapsto e_n}\}$$

Case Guess
$$fcase\; x\; of\; \{\overline{p_m \to e_m}\} \;\Rightarrow_\sigma\; \sigma(e_i) \quad \text{if } \sigma = \{x \mapsto p_i\},\; i = 1, \ldots, m$$

Case Eval
$$(f)case\; e\; of\; \{\overline{p_m \to e_m}\} \;\Rightarrow_\sigma\; (f)case\; e'\; of\; \{\overline{p_m \to \sigma(e_m)}\}$$
$$\text{if } e \text{ is neither a variable nor a constructor-rooted}$$
$$\text{term and } e \Rightarrow_\sigma e'$$

Function Eval
$$f(\overline{e_n}) \;\Rightarrow_{id}\; \sigma(e') \quad \text{if } f(\overline{x_n}) = e \in \mathcal{R} \text{ is a rule with fresh}$$
$$\text{variables and } \sigma = \{\overline{x_n \mapsto e_n}\}$$

Fig. 1. LNT calculus

HNF. This rule can be applied to evaluate expressions in head normal form (i.e., rooted by a constructor symbol). It proceeds by recursively evaluating some argument (e.g., the leftmost one) that contains unevaluated function calls. Note that when an expression contains only constructors and variables, there is no rule applicable and the evaluation stops successfully.

Case Select. It simply selects the appropriate branch of a case expression and continues with the evaluation of this branch. The step is labeled with the identity substitution id.

Case Guess. This rule applies when the argument of a *flexible* case expression is a variable. Then, it nondeterministically binds this variable to a pattern in a branch of the case expression. We additionally label the step with the computed binding. Note that there is no rule to evaluate a *rigid* case expression with a variable argument. This situation produces a *suspension* of the evaluation (i.e., an abnormal termination).

Case Eval. This rule can be only applied when the argument of the case construct is a function call or another case construct. Then, it tries to evaluate this expression. If an evaluation step is possible, we return the original expression with the argument updated. The step is labeled with the same substitution computed from the evaluation of the case argument, which is also propagated to the different case branches.

Function Eval. Finally, this rule performs the unfolding of a function call.

This semantics is properly augmented with cost information, as defined by the state-transition rules of Fig. 2. The state consists of a tuple $\langle ccc, k, e \rangle$, where ccc is the current cost center, k is the accumulated cost, and e is the expression to be evaluated. An initial state has the form $\langle CC_0, K_0, e \rangle$, where CC_0 is the *initial cost center*—to which all costs are attributed unless an SCC construct specifies a different cost center—, K_0 is the *empty* cost, and e is the initial expression to be evaluated. Costs are represented by a set of cost variables $\in \{S, C, N, A\}$ indexed by the existing cost centers. Thus, given a cost center cc, S_{cc} records the number of steps attributed to cc, C_{cc} the number of case evaluations (or

rule ccc cost expression	$\Rightarrow$	ccc cost expression

scc_1 cc k $\quad SCC(cc',e)$ $\qquad \Rightarrow_\sigma cc \;\; k' \quad SCC(cc',e')$
  if e is a nonvariable expression which is not rooted by a constructor nor an SCC,
  and $cc' \; k \; e \;\; \Rightarrow_\sigma \;\; cc' \; k' \; e'$

scc_2 cc k $\quad SCC(cc',c(e_1,\ldots,e_n)) \Rightarrow_{id} cc \;\; k \quad c(SCC(cc',e_1),\ldots,SCC(cc',e_n))$

scc_3 cc k $\quad SCC(cc',x)$ $\qquad\qquad \Rightarrow_{id} cc \;\; k \quad x$

scc_4 cc k $\quad SCC(cc',SCC(cc'',e)) \Rightarrow_{id} cc \;\; k \quad SCC(cc'',e)$

hnf $\quad cc \; k \; c(e_1,\ldots,e_i,\ldots,e_n)$ $\qquad \Rightarrow_\sigma cc \; k' \; \sigma(c(e_1,\ldots,e_i',\ldots,e_n))$
  if e_i is not a constructor term and $cc \; k \; e_i \;\; \Rightarrow_\sigma \;\; cc' \; k' \; e_i'$

c_select $\quad cc \; k \; (f)case \; c(\overline{e_n}) \; of \; \{\overline{p_m \to e_m'}\} \Rightarrow_{id} cc \; k' \; \sigma(e_i')$
  if $p_i = c(\overline{x_n})$, $\sigma = \{\overline{x_n \mapsto e_n}\}$, and $k' = k[C_{cc} \leftarrow C_{cc}+1]$

c_guess1 $\quad cc \; k \; fcase \; x \; of \; \{\overline{p_m \to e_m}\} \qquad \Rightarrow_\sigma cc \; k' \; \sigma(e_i)$
  if $\sigma = \{x \mapsto p_i\}$, $m = 1$, and $k' = k[C_{cc} \leftarrow C_{cc}+1]$

c_guess2 $\quad cc \; k \; fcase \; x \; of \; \{\overline{p_m \to e_m}\} \qquad \Rightarrow_\sigma cc \; k' \; \sigma(e_i)$
  if $\sigma = \{x \mapsto p_i\}$, $m > 1$, and $k' = k[C_{cc} \leftarrow C_{cc}+1, \; N_{cc} \leftarrow N_{cc}+1]$

c_eval $\quad cc \; k \; (f)case \; e \; of \; \{\overline{p_m \to e_m}\} \qquad \Rightarrow_\sigma cc \; k' \; (f)case \; e' \; of \; \{\overline{p_m \to \sigma(e_m)}\}$
  if e is neither a variable nor an operation-rooted term
  and $cc \; k \; e \;\; \Rightarrow_\sigma \;\; cc' \; k' \; e'$

fun_eval $\quad cc \; k \; f(\overline{e_n}) \qquad\qquad\qquad\qquad \Rightarrow_{id} cc \; k' \; \sigma(e)$
  if $f(\overline{x_n}) = e \in \mathcal{R}$ is a rule with fresh variables, $\sigma = \{\overline{x_n \mapsto e_n}\}$, and
  $k' = k[S_{cc} \leftarrow S_{cc}+1, A_{cc} \leftarrow A_{cc}+size(e)]$

Fig. 2. Cost-augmented LNT calculus

basic pattern matching operations) attributed to cc, N_{cc} the number of nondeterministic branching points attributed to cc, and A_{cc} the number of applications attributed to cc.

Let us briefly describe the cost variations due to the application of each state-transition rule of Fig. 2:

SCC rules. These rules are used to evaluate expressions rooted by an SCC symbol. The first rule, scc_1, applies to expressions of the form $SCC(cc',e)$, where e is a nonvariable expression which is not rooted by a constructor nor by an SCC symbol. Basically, it performs an evaluation step on e and, then, it returns the current cost center cc' unchanged. Rules scc_2 and scc_3 propagate SCC symbols to the arguments of a constructor-rooted expression, or remove them when the enclosed expression is a variable or a constructor constant. Note that rule scc_2 does not increment the current cost with a "constructor application". This happens because the considered language is first-order and, thus, the cost of constructor (or function) applications is only considered when performing a function unfolding (in rule *fun_eval*) in order to allocate the symbols in the right-hand sides of the rules. Finally, scc_4 is used to remove an SCC construct when the argument is another SCC construct. These rules could be greatly simplified under an eager evaluation semantics. In particular, we would only need the rule:

$$\langle cc, k, SCC(cc',e)\rangle \;\; \Rightarrow_\sigma \;\; \langle cc, k', b\rangle \quad \text{if} \quad \langle cc', k, e\rangle \;\; \Rightarrow_\sigma^* \;\; \langle cc', k', b\rangle$$

where b is a value, i.e., a constructor term containing no unevaluated functions. Thus, the main difference is that, within an eager calculus, inner subexpressions could be fully evaluated and the SCC constructs could be just dropped; meanwhile, in our lazy calculus, we must carefully keep and appropriately propagate the SCC construct since the evaluation of an inner subexpression could be demanded afterwards.

HNF. The *hnf* rule tries to evaluate some argument (of the constructor-rooted term) which contains unevaluated function calls. If an evaluation step is possible, we return the original expression with the argument and the associated cost updated.

Case select. Rule *c_select* updates the current cost by adding one to C_{cc}, where cc is the current cost center.

Case guess. In this case, the current cost is always updated by adding one to C_{cc}, where cc is the current cost center, since a variable has been instantiated with a constructor term. Moreover, when there is nondeterminism involved, we should also increment cost variable N. In particular, we distinguish two cases:

  c_guess1 : This rule corresponds to a case expression with a single branch. For instance, a function with a constructor argument defined by a single rule, like "f 0 = 0", will be represented in the flat representation as follows: f x = fcase x of {0 → 0}. Trivially, the application of this rule is fully deterministic, even if variable x gets instantiated and, thus, cost variable N is not modified.

  c_guess2 : This rule corresponds to a case expression with several branches. In order to account for the nondeterministic step performed, we add 1 to N_{cc} where cc is the current cost center.

Case eval. The *c_eval* rule can be applied when the argument of the case construct is a function call, an SCC expression or another case construct. Then, it tries to evaluate this expression. If an evaluation step is possible, we return the original expression with the argument and the associated cost updated.

Function eval. The *fun_eval* rule updates the current cost k by adding one to S_{cc} and by adding $size(e)$ to A_{cc}, where cc is the current cost center and e is the right-hand side of the applied rule. Function $size$ counts the number of applications in an expression and it is useful to quantify memory usage. Following [10], given an expression e, a call to $size(e)$ returns the total number of occurrences of n-ary symbols, with $n > 0$, in e, plus their arities; of course, SCC symbols are not taken into account.

Arbitrary *derivations* are denoted by $\langle CC_0, K_0, e \rangle \Rightarrow^*_\sigma \langle cc, k, e' \rangle$, which is a shorthand for the sequence of steps $\langle CC_0, K_0, e \rangle \Rightarrow_{\sigma_1} \ldots \Rightarrow_{\sigma_n} \langle cc, k, e' \rangle$ with $\sigma = \sigma_n \circ \cdots \circ \sigma_1$ (if $n = 0$ then $\sigma = id$). We say that a derivation $\langle CC_0, K_0, e \rangle \Rightarrow^*_\sigma \langle cc, k, e' \rangle$ is *successful* when e' contains no function calls (i.e., it is a constructor term). Then, we say that e evaluates to e' with computed answer σ and associated cost k. Regarding non-successful derivations (i.e., suspended or failing derivations), we simply return the suspended (or failing) expression together with the cost associated to the performed steps. This information may be useful when considering nondeterministic computations, as we will see in Section 5.

We note that, in order to be sound with current implementations of functional logic languages, one should consider the effect of *sharing*. By using a sharing-based implementation of the language, the system avoids repeated computations when the same expression is demanded several times. The definition of a sharing-based semantics for functional logic programs in flat form is subject of ongoing work [2].

length_app $(1 : x)$ []	
$\Rightarrow^{fun\_eval}$	$[S_0 = 1 \quad C_0 = 0 \quad A_0 = 5 \quad N_0 = 0]$ SCC 2 (len (SCC 1 (app $(1 : x)$ [])))
$\Rightarrow^{fun\_eval}$	$[S_2 = 1 \quad C_2 = 0 \quad A_2 = 5 \quad N_2 = 0]$ SCC 2 (case (SCC 1 (app $(1 : x)$ [])) of $\{[] \to 0; (x' : x'_s) \to (\text{len } x'_s) + 1\}$)
$\Rightarrow^{fun\_eval}$	$[S_1 = 1 \quad C_1 = 0 \quad A_1 = 5 \quad N_1 = 0]$ SCC 2 (case (SCC 1 (case $(1 : x)$ of$\{[] \to []; (z : z_s) \to z : \text{app } z_s \, []\}$)) of $\{[] \to 0; (x' : x'_s) \to (\text{len } x'_s) + 1\}$)
$\Rightarrow^{case\_select}$	$[S_1 = 1 \quad C_1 = 1 \quad A_1 = 5 \quad N_1 = 0]$ SCC 2 (case (SCC 1 $(1 : \text{app } x \, [])$) of $\{[] \to 0; (x' : x'_s) \to (\text{len } x'_s) + 1\}$)
$\Rightarrow^{scc_2}$	[] SCC 2 (case ((SCC 1 1) : SCC 1 (app x [])) of $\{[] \to 0; (x' : x'_s) \to (\text{len } x'_s) + 1\}$)
$\Rightarrow^{case\_select}$	$[S_2 = 1 \quad C_2 = 1 \quad A_2 = 5 \quad N_2 = 0]$ SCC 2 (len (SCC 1 (app x []))) + 1
$\Rightarrow^{scc_2}$	[] (SCC 2 (len (SCC 1 (app x [])))) + 1
$\Rightarrow^{fun\_eval}$	$[S_2 = 2 \quad C_2 = 1 \quad A_2 = 10 \quad N_2 = 0]$ (SCC 2 (case (SCC 1 (app x [])) of $\{[] \to 0; (x'' : x''_s) \to (\text{len } x''_s) + 1\}$)) + 1
$\Rightarrow^{fun\_eval}$	$[S_1 = 2 \quad C_1 = 1 \quad A_1 = 10 \quad N_1 = 0]$ (SCC 2 (case (SCC 1 (case x of$\{[] \to []; (z' : z'_s) \to z' : \text{app } z'_s \, []\}$)) of $\{[] \to 0; (x'' : x''_s) \to (\text{len } x''_s) + 1\}$)) + 1
$\Rightarrow^{case\_guess}_{\{x \mapsto []\}}$	$[S_1 = 2 \quad C_1 = 2 \quad A_1 = 10 \quad N_1 = 1]$ (SCC 2 (case (SCC 1 []) of $\{[] \to 0; (x'' : x''_s) \to (\text{len } x''_s) + 1\}$)) + 1
$\Rightarrow^{scc_3}$	[] (SCC 2 (case [] of $\{[] \to 0; (x'' : x''_s) \to (\text{len } x''_s) + 1\}$)) + 1
$\Rightarrow^{case\_select}$	$[S_2 = 2 \quad C_2 = 2 \quad A_2 = 10 \quad N_2 = 0]$ (SCC 2 0) + 1
$\Rightarrow^{scc_2}$	[] 1

Fig. 3. Example of LNT derivation for "length_app $(1{:}x)$ []"

Let us illustrate our cost-augmented LNT calculus by means of an example. In Fig. 3, we detail a successful derivation for the expression:

length_app $(1 : x)$ []

using the following definitions for length_app and len in flat form:

```
length_app x y = len (app x y)
len x  = fcase x of { []      → 0 ;
                      (y:ys) → (len ys) + 1 }
```

Here, we use `len` and `app` as shorthands for `length` and `append`, respectively. We annotate each transition in the derivation with the name of the applied rule. Also, the values of the current cost center appear over the derived expression. In some steps, we write [] to denote that there is no modification of the current costs. We notice that the symbol "+" is considered as a built-in operator of the language and, thus, we treat it similarly to constructor symbols. This explains the fact that, in some steps, the symbol SCC is propagated to its arguments.

There is a precise equivalence between the cost semantics of Fig. 2 and the attribution of costs as explained in Section 3. To be precise, the number of steps, pattern matching operations and nondeterministic branching points coincide in both cases. There exists, however, a significant difference regarding the number of applications. Consider, for instance, function `append`. From the evaluation of "append [] []" in the source language we compute 0 applications, since the first rule of `append` contains no symbol of arity greater than zero. However, the same evaluation in the flat language produces 6 applications, since the right-hand side of the rule depicted in Example 2 comprises the right-hand sides of the two source rules. For the development of a profiling tool, both alternatives are possible.

5   Experimental Evaluation

The practicality of the ideas presented in this work is demonstrated by the implementation of a symbolic profiler for the multi-paradigm language Curry [19].[3] Firstly, in order to have a useful profiling tool, one has to extend the basic scheme to cover all the high-level features of the language (concurrent constraints, higher-order functions, calls to external functions, I/O, etc). This extension has not been especially difficult starting out from the basic scheme of Section 4. An interesting aspect of our profiling tool is that it is completely written in Curry, which simplifies further extensions as well as its integration into existing program transformation tools. Source programs are automatically translated into the flat syntax by using the facilities provided by the module `Flat` of PAKCS [17] for meta-programming in Curry.

Our prototype implementation is basically a meta-interpreter for the language Curry enhanced with cost information as described throughout the paper. Thus, given its interpretive nature, it cannot be directly used to profile "real" applications. Nevertheless, in its present form, it may serve to check alternative design choices for the formal specification of Fig. 2 that, otherwise, would be impossible to understand and explain clearly. Moreover, it has been of great help to assess the effectiveness of a partial evaluator for Curry programs [3,4]. Below we show several experiments which illustrate the usefulness of our profiling tool.

---

[3] Available at: http://www.dsic.upv.es/users/elp/profiler.

Table 1. Profiling results

	benchmark	cost center	steps	pat_mat	apps	runtime
naive	foo1	cc1	130	119	1466	1660 ms.
		cc2	25	25	245	
	foo2	cc3	5	5	45	340 ms.
		cc4	15	15	155	
optimized	foo1	cc1	130	119	1466	1640 ms.
		cc2	6	5	49	
	foo2	cc3	5	5	45	20 ms.
		cc4	6	5	49	

Our first example shows a traditional use of the developed tool to assist the programmer in the task of deciding whether the optimization of a program function will actually improve program performance. The source program is as follows:

```
append []      ys = ys
append (x:xs) ys = x : append xs ys
filter p []        = []
filter p (x:xs)    = if p x then x : filter p xs else filter p xs
qsort []      = []
qsort (x:l)   = append (qsort (filter (<x) l))
                       (x : qsort (filter (>=x) l))
rev [] = []
rev (x:xs) = append (rev xs) [x]
foo1 x = SCC cc1 (qsort (SCC cc2 (rev x)))
foo2 x = SCC cc3 (append (SCC cc4 (rev x)) [])
```

In this program, we have considered two possible uses of function rev in the body of foo1 and foo2. Profiling has been applied to the initial calls:

```
foo1 [0,1,2,3]
foo2 [0,1,2,3]
```

The profiling results for these calls are shown in the first four rows of Table 1 (*naive*). For each benchmark, the columns show the cost center, the symbolic costs for this cost center (steps, pattern matchings and applications,[4] respectively), and the actual runtime (by using larger input lists to obtain significant runtimes). Note that this does not mean that our symbolic costs are not directly related to runtimes, but simply that, given the interpretive nature of the profiler, it cannot handle the large inputs needed to obtain a measurable runtime. Times are expressed in milliseconds and are the average of 10 executions on a 800 MHz Linux-PC (Pentium III with 256 KB cache). All programs (including the profiler) were executed with the Curry→Prolog compiler [9] of PAKCS.

---

[4] Nondeterministic branching points are ignored in this example since computations are fully deterministic.

Clearly, the information depicted in Table 1 is helpful to assist the user in finding out which program function may benefit from being optimized. For instance, if one intends to use `rev` as an argument of `qsort` (like in `foo1`), there is no urgent need to optimize `rev`, since it takes only a small percentage of the total costs. On the other hand, if the intended use is as an argument of `append`, then the optimization of `rev` may be relevant. In order to demonstrate this, we have replaced `rev` with a version of reverse with an accumulating parameter (which can be obtained by program transformation). The new profiling results are shown in the last four rows of Table 1 (*optimized*). By observing `foo1`, we notice that there is no significant runtime improvement (compare the first and fifth rows). However, the runtime of `foo2` is highly improved (compare the third and seventh rows).

Our second example illustrates the interest in computing failing derivations when nondeterministic computations arise. The source program is a simplified version of the classical map coloring program which assigns a color to each of three countries such that countries with a common border have different colors:

```
isColor Red    = success
isColor Yellow = success
isColor Green  = success
coloring x y z = isColor x & isColor y & isColor z
correct x y z = diff x y & diff x z & diff y z
gen_test x y z = SCC cc1 (coloring x y z & correct x y z)
test_gen x y z = SCC cc2 (correct x y z & coloring x y z)
```

Here, "&" is the concurrent conjunction, "success" is a predefined constraint which is always solvable, and the predefined function "`diff`" is the only rigid function (it makes use of the strict equality predicate in order to check whether its arguments are different, but no instantiation is allowed). We have included two functions `gen_test` and `test_gen` which implement the "generate & test" and the (much more efficient) "test & generate" solutions, respectively. Rather surprisingly, the profiling results for any of the six possible solutions coincide for both functions: 8 steps, 3 matching operations, 3 nondeterministic steps, and 69 applications. These counterintuitive results are explained as follows. The actual improvement is not related to the *successful* derivations, which are almost identical in both cases, but to the number (and associated costs) of *failing* derivations. Thus, our current implementation considers two possibilities:

1. the computation of the costs for each derivation is independent of previous branches in the search tree (i.e., the calculus of Fig. 2);
2. the computation of the costs for each derivation also includes the costs of all previous branches in the search tree.

By using the second alternative, we can sum up the costs of the whole search space for each of the previous functions (including failing derivations):

`gen_test`: 192 steps, 81 pattern matchings, 81 nondeterministic branching points, and 1695 applications (for 27 derivations);

Table 2. Improvements by partial evaluation

Benchmark	Original			Residual			Speedup
	steps	pat_mat	apps	steps	pat_mat	apps	
all_ones	22	22	198	11	11	110	1.29
app_last	22	33	209	11	11	77	2.83
double_app	27	27	243	16	17	254	1.17
double_flip	18	18	234	9	9	117	1.25
kmp	101	160	1279	11	60	402	12.94
length_app	23	23	195	12	13	184	1.39

`test_gen`: 165 steps, 60 pattern matchings, 60 nondeterministic branching points, and 1428 applications (for 21 derivations).

From these figures, the greater efficiency of `test_gen` can be easily explained.

Finally, we have applied our profiling tool to check the improvements achieved by a partial evaluator of Curry programs [3,4] over several well-known benchmarks. In particular, we have performed the profiling of those expressions previously annotated to be partially evaluated (i.e., *cost centers* are introduced on the same expressions to be specialized). Table 2 shows our profiling results for several well-known benchmarks of partial evaluation. Some of them are typical from deforestation (the case of `all_ones`, `app_last`, `double_app`, `double_flip`, `length_app`) and `kmp` is the well-known "KMP test".[5] For each benchmark, we show the number of steps, pattern matching operations and applications for the original and residual programs, respectively; we do not include information about the amount of nondeterminism since it is not changed by the partial evaluator. The last column of Table 2 shows the actual speedup (i.e., the ratio *original/residual*, where *original* refers to the runtime in the original program and *residual* is the runtime in the partially evaluated program). Runtime input goals were chosen to give a reasonably long overall time.

From the figures in Table 2, we observe that the cost information collected by the profiler allows us to quantify the potential improvement which has been achieved by the residual program. For instance, the more significant improvements on the symbolic costs are produced for the KMP benchmark which, indeed, shows an actual speedup of 12.94 for sufficiently large input goals. Fewer improvements have been obtained for the remaining benchmarks, which is also sensible with the minor speedups tested experimentally. To be more precise, one should determine the appropriate weight of each symbolic cost for a specific language environment. Nevertheless, our experiments show the potential usefulness of our profiler to check whether a sufficient reduction (w.r.t. the symbolic costs) has been achieved by partial evaluation and, thus, the residual program can be safely returned. A further step is the "smart" use of the profiling information to guide the partial evaluation process, which is subject of ongoing work.

---

[5] The complete code of these benchmarks can be found, e.g., in [7].

6   Related Work

One of the most-often cited profilers in the literature is gprof—a call graph execution profiler developed by Graham et al. [15]. Apart from collecting information about call counts and execution time as most traditional profilers, gprof is able to account to each routine the time spent by the routines that it invokes. This accounting is achieved by assembling a call graph made up by nodes that are routines of the program and directed arcs that represent calls from call sites to routines. By post-processing these data, times are propagated along the edges of the graph to attribute time for routines to the routines they call. Although these ideas have been of great influence, their approach has not been directly transferred to profiling declarative programs (which heavily depend on recursion) mainly because programs that exhibit a large degree of recursion are not easily analyzed by gprof.

To the best of our knowledge, there is no previous work about profiling within the field of (narrowing-based) functional logic programming. The remaining of this section is devoted to briefly review some related research on profiling for the logic and functional programming paradigms separately.

As for logic programming, the profiler for Prolog developed by Debray [14] shows that traditional profiling techniques are inadequate for logic programming languages. In particular, this profiler is especially designed to gather information related to the control flow in logic programming languages, including backtracking and is able to deal with primitives like assert and retract. Our profiler shares with this approach some ideas for collecting information about nondeterministic branching points. A more recent reference is the work by Jahier and Ducassé [20,21], which proposes a program execution monitor to gather data about Mercury executions. For this purpose, they define a high-level primitive built on top of the execution tracer for Mercury, which delivers information extracted from the current state at a particular point (e.g., execution depth, port, live arguments, etc). Our approach is more related with the design of the tracer, in the sense that our profiler relies on an operational semantics which may also show the state transitions performed along the process, apart from collecting cost information. Regarding parallel logic programs, Tick [28] developed a performance analysis for estimating the parallelism exploited using "kaleidescope visualization". This technique consists in summarizing the execution of a program in a single image or signature. According to [28], there are two inputs to the algorithm: a trace file and a source program. The trace file input contains information about events logged in the trace. This information could be targeted by profiling techniques in the style of the one described in this paper. The implementation of profiling tools has been carried out for some logic programming languages. For instance, the ECLiPSe logic programming system contains a timing profiler which interrupts the program execution every 0.01s to measure the time spent in every predicate of a program. For the Mercury language, there exist two profiling tools: the mprof Mercury profiler—which is a conventional call-graph profiler in the style of the above gprof profiler—and the Mercury deep profiler mdprof [13]—which is a new profiler that associates with every profiling measurement a very detailed context about the ancestor functions or predicates and their call sites. This approach shares some ideas with cost center "stack" profiling [26], which we discuss below.

Modern functional profilers have been heavily influenced by the notion of *cost center*, which basically permits to attribute costs to program expressions rather than profiling every program function [26,27]. Nevertheless, similar ideas (i.e., the concept of "current function") already appeared in the profiler for the SML of New Jersey [11]. Recent profilers for the non-strict lazy functional language Haskell have been developed relying on the notion of cost center. Along these lines, the profiling technique developed by Sansom and Peyton-Jones [27] is the closest to our work. A similarity with them is that we also present a formal specification of the attribution of execution costs to cost centers by means of an appropriate cost-augmented semantics. A significant difference, though, is that our flat representation for programs is first-order, contains logical features (like nondeterminism), and has an operational semantics which combines narrowing and residuation. A further extension of the cost center profiling is cost center "stack" profiling [26], which allows full inheritance of the cost of functions. The basic idea is to attribute the cost of executing a profiled function to the function *and* to the stack of functions responsible for the call. Our approach could also be extended towards this direction in order to develop a more flexible profiling tool.

It is worth mentioning the *monitor semantics* presented in [23]. This is a non-standard model of program execution that captures "monitoring activity" as found in debuggers, profilers, tracers, etc. Their framework is general enough in the sense that the monitoring semantics can be automatically obtained from any denotational semantics. It could be interesting to investigate whether this framework can also be applied in our context.

In the field of functional logic programming, there is a recent line of research which investigates techniques to estimate the effectiveness achieved by partial evaluation. The work in [1] formally defines several abstract cost criteria to measure the effects of program transformations (the similarities with our symbolic costs are discussed throughout the paper). Their goal is more restrictive than the one behind profiling techniques. In particular, the purpose of [1] is to estimate the effectiveness achieved by a concrete residual program by means of some cost recurrence equations obtained along the partial evaluation process. A further step in the line of generating residual programs with cost information has been taken in [29]. This work introduces the scheme of a narrowing-driven partial evaluator enhanced with the computation of symbolic costs. Thus, for each residual rule, the new scheme provides the cost variation due to the partial evaluation process.

Finally, Watterson and Debray [30] propose an approach to reduce the cost of "value" profiling (i.e., a profiling technique which provides information about the runtime distribution of the values taken by a variable). Their approach avoids wasting resources where the profile can be guaranteed to not be useful for optimizations. We believe that such performance optimizations could also be tried in our framework.

7 Conclusions and Further Work

This paper investigates the definition of a source-level, symbolic profiling scheme for a multi-paradigm functional logic language. Our scheme is based on several symbolic costs (comprehensive with those of [1,10] to measure the cost of functional logic computations) and uses the idea of cost centers to attribute costs to program expressions. The formalization of our scheme is carried out by a cost-augmented semantics, carefully designed for the flat representation of multi-paradigm declarative programs. An implementation of the profiling tool (extended to cover all the features of the language Curry) is presented. Preliminary results are encouraging and give evidence of the practicality of our approach and the benefits of using profiling information in the field of program transformation.

Future work includes two different lines of research. Currently, our main concern is to investigate the combination of the symbolic profiler with existing partial evaluation techniques for functional logic languages [6,7] in order to "guide" the specialization process. We are also working on the definition of a new semantics characterization able to cope with all the features of modern multi-paradigm language implementations: sharing of common variables, nondeterminism, search strategies, concurrency, etc. A preliminary definition of such a semantics can be found in [2]. A cost extension of this enhanced semantics may be useful to collect cost information in the context of these realistic languages.

Acknowledgments. We gratefully acknowledge the anonymous referees for many useful suggestions and the participants of LOPSTR 2001 for fruitful feedback.

Part of this research was done while the authors were visiting the University of Kiel supported by the "Acción Integrada Hispano-Alemana HA2001-0059" project. We wish to thank Michael Hanus and Frank Huch for many helpful comments on the topics of this paper.

References

1. E. Albert, S. Antoy, and G. Vidal. Measuring the Effectiveness of Partial Evaluation in Functional Logic Languages. In *Proc. of LOPSTR 2000*, pages 103–124. Springer LNCS 2042, 2001.
2. E. Albert, M. Hanus, F. Huch, J. Oliver, and G. Vidal. An Operational Semantics for Declarative Multi-Paradigm Languages. Available from URL: http://www.dsic.upv.es/users/elp/papers.html, 2002.
3. E. Albert, M. Hanus, and G. Vidal. Using an Abstract Representation to Specialize Functional Logic Programs. In *Proc. of LPAR 2000*, pages 381–398. Springer LNAI 1955, 2000.

4. E. Albert, M. Hanus, and G. Vidal. A Practical Partial Evaluator for a Multi-Paradigm Declarative Language. In *Proc. of FLOPS'01*, pages 326–342. Springer LNCS 2024, 2001.
5. E. Albert, M. Hanus, and G. Vidal. A Residualizing Semantics for the Partial Evaluation of Functional Logic Programs, 2002. Submitted for publication. Available at http://www.dsic.upv.es/users/elp/papers.html.
6. E. Albert and G. Vidal. The Narrowing-Driven Approach to Functional Logic Program Specialization. *New Generation Computing*, 20(1):3–26, 2002.
7. M. Alpuente, M. Falaschi, and G. Vidal. Partial Evaluation of Functional Logic Programs. *ACM Transactions on Programming Languages and Systems*, 20(4):768–844, 1998.
8. S. Antoy, R. Echahed, and M. Hanus. A Needed Narrowing Strategy. *Journal of the ACM*, 47(4):776–822, 2000.
9. S. Antoy and M. Hanus. Compiling Multi-Paradigm Declarative Programs into Prolog. In *Proc. of FroCoS'2000*, pages 171–185. Springer LNCS 1794, 2000.
10. S. Antoy, B. Massey, and P. Julián. Improving the Efficiency of Non-Deterministic Computations. In *Proc. of WFLP'01*, Kiel, Germany, 2001.
11. A.W. Appel, B.F. Duba, and D.B. MacQueen. Profiling in the Presence of Optimization and Garbage Collection. Technical Report CS-TR-197-88, Princeton University, 1988.
12. J.L. Bentley. *Writing Efficient Programs*. Prentice-Hall, Englewood Cliffs, N.J., 1982.
13. T. C. Conway and Z. Somogyi. Deep profiling: engineering a profiler for a declarative programming language. Technical Report Technical Report 2001/24, Department of Computer Science, University of Melbourne (Australia), 2001.
14. S.K. Debray. Profiling Prolog Programs. *Software, Practice and Experience*, 18(9):821–840, 1988.
15. S.L. Graham, P.B. Kessler, and M.K. McKusick. gprof: a Call Graph Execution Profiler. In *Proc. of CC'82*, pages 120–126, Boston, MA, 1982.
16. M. Hanus. A unified computation model for functional and logic programming. In *Proc. of POPL'97*, pages 80–93. ACM, New York, 1997.
17. M. Hanus, S. Antoy, J. Koj, R. Sadre, and F. Steiner. PAKCS 1.2: The Portland Aachen Kiel Curry System User Manual. Technical report, University of Kiel, Germany, 2000.
18. M. Hanus and C. Prehofer. Higher-Order Narrowing with Definitional Trees. *Journal of Functional Programming*, 9(1):33–75, 1999.
19. M. Hanus (ed.). Curry: An Integrated Functional Logic Language. Available at: http://www.informatik.uni-kiel.de/~mh/curry/.
20. E. Jahier and M. Ducasse. A Generic Approach to Monitor Program Executions. In *Proc. of ICLP'99*, pages 139–153. MIT Press, 1999.
21. E. Jahier and M. Ducasse. Generic Program Monitoring by Trace Analysis. *Theory and Practice of Logic Programming*, 2(4,5), 2002.
22. N.D. Jones, C.K. Gomard, and P. Sestoft. *Partial Evaluation and Automatic Program Generation*. Prentice-Hall, Englewood Cliffs, NJ, 1993.
23. A. Kishon, P. Hudak, and C. Consel. Monitoring Semantics: A Formal Framework for Specifying, Implementing, and Reasoning about Execution Monitors. *ACM Sigplan Notices*, 26(6):338–352, 1991.
24. F. López-Fraguas and J. Sánchez-Hernández. TOY: A Multiparadigm Declarative System. In *Proc. of RTA'99*, pages 244–247. Springer LNCS 1631, 1999.
25. W. Lux and H. Kuchen. An Efficient Abstract Machine for Curry. In *Proc. of WFLP'99*, pages 171–181, 1999.

26. R.G. Morgan and S.A. Jarvis. Profiling large-scale lazy functional programs. *Journal of Functional Programming*, 8(3), 1998.
27. P.M. Sansom and S.L. Peyton-Jones. Formally Based Profiling for Higher-Order Functional Languages. *ACM Transactions on Programming Languages and Systems*, 19(2):334–385, 1997.
28. E. Tick. Visualizing Parallel Logic Programs with VISTA. In *Proc. of the Int'l Conf. on Fifth Generation Computer Systems*, pages 934–942. ICOT, 1992.
29. G. Vidal. Cost-Augmented Narrowing-Driven Specialization. In *Proc. of PEPM'02*, pages 52–62. ACM Press, 2002.
30. S. Watterson and S. Debray. Goal-Directed Value Profiling. In *Proc. of CC'01*, pages 319–334. Springer LNCS 2027, 2001.

Correct Object-Oriented Systems in Computational Logic

Kung-Kiu Lau[1] and Mario Ornaghi[2]

[1] Department of Computer Science, University of Manchester
Manchester M13 9PL, United Kingdom
kung-kiu@cs.man.ac.uk
[2] Dipartimento di Scienze dell'Informazione, Universita' degli studi di Milano
Via Comelico 39/41, 20135 Milano, Italy
ornaghi@dsi.unimi.it

Abstract. In our previous work in program development, we have defined *steadfastness*, a notion of correctness that captures at once modularity, correctness and reusability. This paper extends it to Object-Oriented Systems, namely systems of cooperating objects, and is a first step towards the introduction of correctness in Object-Oriented Design Frameworks. Such frameworks are increasingly recognised as more reusable than single objects, and promise to be useful components in next-generation Component-based Software Development.

1 Introduction

It is increasingly recognised that classes are not the best focus for design. Typical design artefacts are rarely just about one object, but about groups of objects and the way they interact. Object-Oriented Design (OOD) Frameworks, or just *frameworks* for short, are such groups of interacting objects. They have widely been accepted as more useful components than single objects, and are the focus of much attention in the evolution of current OO technology into Component-based Software Development (CBD). The goal of CBD is to provide the engineering science and tools for constructing software products by plugging components together, and frameworks would be suitable as such components.

To support CBD, a framework should have a good component *interface* providing all the information we need for its *correct reuse*. Conditions for correct reuse can be detailed as follows:

- We need to know what each component does (correctly): framework operations should have *declarative specifications* and composition of frameworks should yield the specification of the operations of the composite.
- We need an *assembly guide* to correctly reusing frameworks: the interface should provide *context dependencies*, i.e. conditions to be met in order to preserve correctness of framework operations (with respect to their specifications).

A. Pettorossi (Ed.): LOPSTR 2001, LNCS 2372, pp. 168–190, 2002.
© Springer-Verlag Berlin Heidelberg 2002

– We need to know what framework composition yields: the specifications of a composite framework should indicate when and how we can *correctly compose* the operations inherited from its components.

These conditions imply that a semantics for frameworks and their interfaces should incorporate a notion of *a priori correctness*, namely *pre*-proved correctness of any given component operation with respect to its own specifications, as well as *pre*-stated conditions (context dependencies) that will guarantee that component and operation compositions will preserve correctness.

Moreover, reusability requires open frameworks (to be composed with open, i.e. non-fixed, external parts) and open programs (programs using open operations of the open external parts); thus *a priori* correctness should consider *open programs* in *open contexts*.

In current OO technology, it is supposed to be possible to model frameworks [7,5] in UML [13] (see e.g. [4]). However, it is not yet clear how frameworks are defined in UML, and a formal semantics is currently lacking. Such a semantics is necessary for a universally accepted and well understood definition of frameworks and interfaces, and a deeper understanding of correct reuse.

We have studied correct reuse and *a priori* correctness in the context of non-OO frameworks which we called *specification frameworks* [8]. We believe that they are a good starting point for formalising correct reuse in OOD frameworks. This paper represents a first step in this direction. In Section 2, before considering OOD frameworks, we briefly recall specification frameworks and *steadfastness*, namely our a priori correctness for logic programs [10]. Then we introduce our formalisation of OO Systems. It is based on a three-level architecture, containing an object level, a system level and a global level. Section 3 introduces the basic definitions and the syntax of the system level, while Section 4 contains the three-level formalisation and the main results. Correct OO Systems represent our first step towards a formalisation of correct reuse in OOD frameworks. In the conclusions we briefly discuss the perspectives of our future work, and we briefly comment on related approaches.

2   Specification Frameworks: Non-OO Frameworks

Specification frameworks are based on a three-tier formalism, as shown in the example of Fig. 1.

At the bottom level, we have *programs*, for computing (specified) relations. Programs are standard or constraint logic programs and may be *open*. An open program contains at least one *open program predicate*, that is, a predicate that occurs in the body of some clause but in none of the heads. For example, the program $P_{sort}(split, merge)$ in Fig. 1 is open in the predicates *split* and *merge*.

In the middle, we have *specifications*. A specification S_p declaratively defines the meaning of a program predicate p, in terms of the problem context formalised at the top level. We may have *strict* and *non-strict* specifications. For every interpretation of the problem context, a strict specification S_p defines

```
┌────────────────────────────────────────────────────────────────────────┐
│  Specification Framework 𝓛𝓘𝓢𝓣(X, ◁; split, merge)                       │
├────────────────────────────────────────────────────────────────────────┤
│  Context 𝓛𝓘𝓢𝓣(X, ◁ : [X, X]);                                           │
│    EXTENDS:          𝓝𝓐𝓣;                                               │
│    DECLS:            X, ListX : sort;                                    │
│                        nil : [ ] → ListX;                               │
│                         . : [X, ListX] → ListX;                         │
│                        @ : [X, Nat, ListX];                             │
│                       nocc : [X, ListX] → Nat;                          │
│    CONSTRS:          TotalOrder(◁);                                      │
│    AXIOMS:           . . .                                               │
├────────────────────────────────────────────────────────────────────────┤
│  Specifications:                                                         │
│    S_sort  :  sort(X, Y) ↔ perm(X, Y) ∧ ord(Y);                         │
│    S_merge :  ord(X) ∧ ord(Y) → (merge(X, Y, Z) ↔ ord(Z) ∧ perm(X|Y, Z));│
│    S_split :  l(X) > 1 ∧ split(X, Y, Z) → perm(X, Y|Z) ∧ l(Y) < l(X) ∧ l(Z) < l(X);│
│               l(X) > 1 → ∃Y, Z . split(X, Y, Z);                        │
├────────────────────────────────────────────────────────────────────────┤
│  Programs:                                                               │
│    P_sort(split, merge) :      sort(nil, nil) ←                         │
│                               sort([X], [X]) ←                          │
│                         sort([X, Y|A], W) ← split([X, Y|A], I, J), sort(I, U),│
│                                             sort(J, V), merge(U, V, W)  │
└────────────────────────────────────────────────────────────────────────┘
```

Fig. 1. The open specification framework $\mathcal{LIST}$.

one interpretation of p; for example, S_{sort} is strict. A non-strict specification allows a family of interpretations of p, i.e., it allows different correct implementations; for example, S_{merge} and S_{split} are non-strict. Non-strict specifications are fundamental to improving reusability.

At the top, we have the *meta-level* or *context*, that embodies the relevant knowledge of the problem domain. The purpose of the context is to give a precise meaning to specifications and to support reasoning about program correctness. We formalise a context as a first-order theory axiomatising the necessary data types and the problem domain. We distinguish between *closed* and *open* contexts.

A context is *closed* iff it has a *reachable isoinitial model*; isoinitial semantics is similar to initial semantics of algebraic ADT's, from which our contexts are inspired (see [2] for algebraic ADT's; see [9] for a discussion of initial and isoinitial theories). For example, $\mathcal{LIST}$ includes the closed context $\mathcal{NAT}$; $\mathcal{NAT}$ contains the usual first-order axioms for arithmetic, and has the standard structure of natural numbers as a reachable isoinitial model.

We have introduced $\mathcal{NAT}$ and the symbols @ and $nocc$ in a formalisation of lists for specification purposes. The intended meaning of $x@(i, l)$ is that x occurs at position i in the list l, while $nocc(x, l)$ denotes the number of occurrences of x in l. In this way, we can define, for example, ordered lists by

$ord(L) \leftrightarrow \forall x, y : X; i : Nat.\ x@(i, L) \wedge y@(s(i), L) \rightarrow x \triangleleft y$, where s is the successor function. The context for lists is open.

An open context contains a set Π of *open symbols*. By suitable *closure* operations, it can be closed, i.e. made into a closed context, in many different ways, giving rise to many different *closed instances*. For example, in Fig. 1 the open context symbols are X and $\triangleleft$, and a closure is shown in Fig. 2. Closures must satisfy the *constraints* CONSTR (see [8]), to guarantee that programs are inherited while preserving *a priori* correctness.

Specification Framework $\mathcal{NL}$ extends $\mathcal{LIST}(X, \triangleleft; split, merge)$

CLOSE: $X = Nat$;
$\qquad\qquad x \triangleleft y \leftrightarrow x \leq y$;
CONSTRSAT: $Theorem : TotalOrder(\triangleleft)$;

Specifications:
$\qquad S'_{merge} : ord(x) \rightarrow (merge([x], y, z) \leftrightarrow ord(z) \wedge perm([x]\|y, z))$
$\qquad S'_{split}\ : split([x, y|z], [x], [y|z])$

Programs ... (correct programs for merge and split)

Fig. 2. A closure of $\mathcal{LIST}$.

In a framework $\mathcal{F}$, we distinguish between an *import interface* and an *export interface*: the former indicates which information is to be provided for reusing $\mathcal{F}$, and the latter indicates what can be obtained by reusing $\mathcal{F}$. The import interface has *context dependencies*, namely conditions to be satisfied in order to guarantee *correct reuse*. The import interface corresponds to the *open context symbols* and the *open program predicates*.

At the context level, importing is implemented by *union* and *closure* operations. Union allows us to amalgamate different contexts, and can be formalised by pushouts, as in algebraic ADT's [2]. Closure allows us to fix the open symbols, and is independent from union. For example, in Fig. 2 union is not needed because natural numbers are already included and closure can be performed within the framework itself.

Constraints codify the *context dependencies* for the closures of context symbols. *Explicit closures* of open relations and functions will be needed in the next section. They look like explicit definitions, where the defined symbol σ is not a new one, but is the open symbol to be closed. If σ has constraints, they must become theorems after the closure. In Fig. 2, $x \triangleleft y$ is closed by the explicit closure

$$x \triangleleft y \leftrightarrow x \leq y$$

and the CONSTRSAT (constraint satisfaction) section proves $TotalOrder(\lhd)$ as a theorem.

The closure of an open program predicate p with specification S_p has to provide a program for p, which is to be correct with respect to S_p. That is, S_p is the *context dependency* for p. Specifications work as *polymorphic* context dependencies through the operation of *specification reduction*. We have different kinds of specifications, with different reducibility conditions to guarantee that, if a specification S' reduces to a specification S, then correctness with respect to S' entails correctness with respect to S (we say that S' correctly overrides S). For example, S_{merge} is a conditional specification (CS) and, by CS reduction, S'_{merge} *correctly overrides* it. Similarly, S'_{split} correctly overrides S_{split}. A correct implementation of S'_{merge} and S'_{split} gives rise to the insertion sort algorithm. Different overridings of S_{merge} and S_{split} allow us to specify and implement different correct algorithms, like merge sort or quick sort.

The export interface contains the non-open context symbols and the corresponding theorems, as well as the correct programs and their specifications. The exported context can be reused for reasoning and specification purposes, e.g., for specification reduction. By *a priori correctness*, the exported programs can be correctly reused according to their specifications. For example, S_{sort} and $P_{sort}(split, merge)$ are exported. Thus $P_{sort}(split, merge)$ *correctly composes* with the local P_{merge} and P_{split} programs, and can be *correctly composed* with any program P' open in a predicate *sort* with a specification S'_{sort} such that S_{sort} reduces to S'_{sort}.

In OO terminology, we could consider $\mathcal{LIST}$ as an *abstract class* with parameter X, *attribute* $\lhd$, *implemented method* P_{sort} (with specification S_{sort}) and *abstract methods* specified by S_{merge} and S_{split}. We can give different non-abstract subclasses, with different implementations of the abstract methods, correct with respect to different specifications S_{merge} and S_{split} that correctly override those of the superclass.

After closing X over Nat (or over other sorts included by union) we can use the non-abstract subclasses to create instances by closing $\lhd$ in different ways. Like objects in OO terminology, different instances have different signatures, which may be obtained by prefixing the instance identifiers. For example, we may have an instance a with closure $x\ a.\lhd y \leftrightarrow x \leq y$, and an instance d with closure $x\ d.\lhd y \leftrightarrow y \leq x$. Both a and d will *correctly reuse* the same P_{sort} program of $\mathcal{LIST}$, together with the S_{sort} specification, that is, $a.P_{sort}$, $a.S_{sort}$ and $d.P_{sort}$, $d.S_{sort}$ are the same. The difference is in the local closure of $\lhd$ and in the corresponding implementation of the ordering predicate: $a.P_{sort}$ will sort lists in ascending order, and $d.P_{sort}$ in descending order. Moreover, if a and d are created by different subclasses, they polymorphically (but correctly, by specification reduction) implement the operations specified by S_{merge} and S_{split} in the superclass $\mathcal{LIST}$.

This discussion shows that typical OO features can be modelled by adapting specification frameworks, and we already used them to model OOD frameworks

[8]. However, in our previous work *a priori* correctness was disregarded. We now consider it in the next section .

3   OO Systems: Towards OOD Frameworks

A formalisation of OOD frameworks should consider at least the following features:

(a) An OOD framework should have good component *interface*, providing all the information we need for the *correct reuse* of it; moreover, for correct method reuse (a kind of) *a priori* correctness is needed.
(b) An OOD framework defines a collection of *instances*, where each instance is a possibly distributed system of cooperating objects.
(c) The instances of an OOD framework have states and methods that can update states.

Concerning (a), open specification frameworks containing steadfast programs meet this requirement. So, specification frameworks will provide the basis for our treatment. With respect to (b), we could adapt specification frameworks in a direct way, but this would give rise to a formalisation hiding the distributed nature of systems of cooperating objects. Instead, here we give a three-level architecture, which allows us to introduce more expressive specifications, and to deal with *a priori* correctness for methods that do not change the states of the instances of an OOD framework. We call such static OOD frameworks *OO systems*.

We introduce some preliminary notions in Section 3.1. Then, in Section 3.2, we discuss some problems related to the constraint and specification language, and we introduce OO systems. In Section 4, we consider our three-level architecture.

3.1   Classes, Objects, and Systems

An OO system S is a set of related classes, where each class contains *attributes*, *constraints*, *specifications* and *methods*. Like in many OO approaches, we distinguish between *data* and *objects*, and we specify data and operations (programs) on them by a specification framework D (see Section 2), called the *data* (framework). D also codifies the problem domain, so that it can give meaning to specifications.

For simplicity, we will assume that D is closed, and we will indicate by i_D its isoinitial model, and call it the *data model*.

We introduce OO systems gradually, starting from classes and objects.

Objects and Classes. We start from the following features of objects (see e.g. [1]): (a) objects have identities; (b) each object o has one implementation class C, which fixes its attributes and methods. Moreover, in class-based approaches, we have inheritance and overriding polymorphism, related to subclassing and subtyping. We will not consider these aspects here, since our main concern is the characterisation of frameworks as systems of cooperating objects.

Concerning (a), we introduce a special sort Obj together with a denumerable set of constants $o_1, o_2, \ldots : [\ ] \to Obj$, used to name objects, and we give the *unique name axioms* $\neg o_i = o_j$ (for $i \neq j$). Constants of sort Obj will be called *object identities*. We will assume that the above axiomatisation of Obj always belongs to the data $\mathcal{D}$.

Concerning (b), we introduce (implementation) classes as follows: a *class* C implicitly includes the data $\mathcal{D}$, and introduces a set of *attributes*, declared as new open dotted constant, function or relation symbols. C also introduces *constraints, specifications and methods*, but we delay their treatment to Section 3.2.

Through the dot notation, a class C works as a template for generating *objects of class* C. If o is (the identifier of) an object of class C, $o.a$ is an *attribute of* o. The *object signature* of o contains the attributes of o and the signature of the data $\mathcal{D}$.

For example, the class *Town* in Fig. 3 specifies *towns* as objects with roads, where each road is of sort Obj, i.e., it is in turn an object. The signature of the object $\underline{mi}$ of class *Town* contains the data signature and the object attribute $\underline{mi}.road : [Obj].$[1]

Class *Town*;
ATTRS:
.*road* : $[Obj]$;

CONSTRS: ...; SPECS: ...; PROGS: ...;

Object $\underline{mi}$: *Town*;
STATE: $\underline{mi}.road(x) \leftrightarrow x = \underline{l1} \lor x = \underline{l2}$

Fig. 3. An object of class *Town*

Object attributes are *open*; they can be closed by explicit closures (see Section 2), that we call *state axioms*.

By the properties of explicit closures, state axioms fix a unique expansion of the data model i_D, i.e., a unique intended interpretation of the attributes, representing the *current state* of the object. Different state axioms represent different states, and state transitions can be codified as updates of the state axioms.

For example, the state axiom of the object $\underline{mi}$ in Fig 3 is

$$\underline{mi}.road(x) \leftrightarrow x = \underline{l1} \lor x = \underline{l2}$$

---

[1] Object identifiers are underlined, in accordance with UML.

that is, $\underline{mi}$ has two roads, $\underline{l1}$ and $\underline{l2}$. If a new road $\underline{l3}$ is built, then the state axiom is updated into

$$\underline{mi}.road(x) \leftrightarrow x = \underline{l1} \vee x = \underline{l2} \vee x = \underline{l3}.$$

Systems. An OO system with classes $C_1, \ldots, C_n$ and data $\mathcal{D}$ is indicated by $\mathcal{S}[\mathcal{D}, C_1, \ldots, C_n]$. It is a blueprint for systems of cooperating objects, that we call *system instances*.

Each instance has a *population* O of objects. We introduce the *class predicates* $C_1, \ldots, C_n : [Obj]$, with the following intended meaning: $C_i(o)$ means that o is an object of the current population, with class C_i. We do not consider subclassing here, so each object of the population has one class;[2] this is stated by the *population constraints*

$$\neg \exists x : Obj. \ C_i(x) \wedge C_j(x) \quad (\text{for } i \neq j).$$

Class predicates are *open*. A *closure* of a class predicate C_i of the form

$$C_i(x) \leftrightarrow x = o_1 \vee \cdots \vee x = o_n$$

is called a *class axiom*, and a finite population O can be represented by a set of class axioms $CAx(O)$, one for each class, such that:

- $CAx(O)$ is consistent with the population constraints;
- o belongs to O with class C_i iff $CAx(O) \vdash C_i(o)$.

That is, the class axioms $CAx(O)$ fix the current population O and the classes of objects of O. O underlies a population signature $\Sigma(O)$, according to the class axioms:

Definition 1 (Population Signature). *Let $\mathcal{S}[\mathcal{D}, C_1, \ldots, C_n]$ be an OO system, and O be a population represented by a set of class axioms $CAx(O)$. The corresponding* population signature $\Sigma(O)$ *contains the data signature of $\mathcal{D}$, the class predicates $C_1, \ldots, C_n$ and all the object attributes $o.a$ such that $CAx(O) \vdash C_j(o)$ (i.e., o belongs to O with class C_j) and $.a$ is an attribute of C_j.*

For example, the OO system in Fig. 4 has data $\mathcal{LIST}(Obj)$ and two classes *Road* and *Town*. The figure also shows an instance, whose O population is fixed by the class axioms. The corresponding signature $\Sigma(O)$ contains the object attributes $\underline{l1}.source : [\ ] \rightarrow Obj$, $\underline{l1}.target : [\ ] \rightarrow Obj$, $\underline{l2}.source : [\ ] \rightarrow Obj$, $\underline{l2}.target : [\ ] \rightarrow Obj$ for the objects of class *Road*, and $\underline{mi}.road : [Obj]$, $\underline{mn}.road : [Obj]$, for those of class *Town*.

Once we have fixed a population $O = \{o_1, \ldots, o_n\}$ and its signature $\Sigma(O)$ by $CAx(O)$, we have to fix the states of the objects of O, by suitable state axioms. A set of state axioms $SAx(o_1)$, $\ldots$, $SAx(o_n)$ fixing the states of all the objects

---

[2] Subclassing and subtyping could be treated as well, but with more complex constraints.

System *Roads and Towns*;

DATA: $\mathcal{LIST}(Obj)$

Class *Road*;

ATTRS: *.source, .target* : $[\,] \rightarrow Obj$;

CONSTRS: ...; SPECS: ...; PROGS: ...;

Class *Town*;

ATTRS: *.road* : $[Obj]$;

CONSTRS: ...; SPECS: ...; PROGS: ...;

Instance Of *Roads and Towns*;

CLASS AX: $Town(x) \leftrightarrow x = \underline{mi} \lor x = \underline{mn}$; $Road(x) \leftrightarrow x = \underline{l1} \lor x = \underline{l2}$;

Object $\underline{l1}$;

STATE: $\underline{l1}.source = \underline{mi}$; $\underline{l1}.target = \underline{mn}$;

Object $\underline{l2}$;

STATE: $\underline{l2}.source = \underline{mn}$; $\underline{l2}.target = \underline{mi}$;

Object $\underline{mi}$;

STATE: $\underline{mi}.road(x) \leftrightarrow x = \underline{l1}$;

Object $\underline{mn}$;

STATE: $\underline{mn}.road(x) \leftrightarrow x = \underline{l2}$.

Fig. 4. The Roads and Towns System and an instance of it.

of O will be called a set of *system state axioms for the population* O and will be indicated, collectively, by $SAx(O)$.

Each triple $\langle O, CAx(O), SAx(O)\rangle$ defined as before is an *instance definition*. For example, Fig. 4 shows an instance definition with population $O = \{\underline{l1}, \underline{l2}, \underline{mi}, \underline{mn}\}$, $CAx(O)$ as declared in the CLASS AX (class axioms) section, and $SAx(O)$ as given in the STATE sections of the objects $\underline{l1}, \underline{l2}, \underline{mi}, \underline{mn}$.

The model-theoretic semantics of instance definitions is given by the following proposition:

Proposition 1 (System States). *Let* $\langle O, CAx(O), SAx(O)\rangle$ *be an instance definition for an OO system* $\mathcal{S}[\mathcal{D}, C_1, \ldots, C_n]$. *There is one* $\Sigma(O)$-*expansion* i_O *of the data model* i_D *such that* $i_O \models CAx(O) \cup SAx(O)$.

That is, each instance definition fixes a *system state*:

Definition 2 (System States). *A system state of a system* $\mathcal{S}[\mathcal{D}, C_1, \ldots, C_n]$ *is a* $\Sigma(O)$-*interpretation* i_O *such that* $i_O \models CAx(O) \cup SAx(O)$, *for some instance definition* $\langle O, CAx(O), SAx(O)\rangle$.

3.2   Class Constraints, Specifications, and Programs

To fully model UML class diagrams by our OO systems, we need to introduce constraints. For example, the class diagram in Fig. 5, corresponding to our OO system of Fig. 4, contains *multiplicity constraints*, that is, every *road* object has one target and one source *town*, and each *town* has a set of 0 or more roads of class *Road*. Multiplicity constraints are just an example. Constraints are an

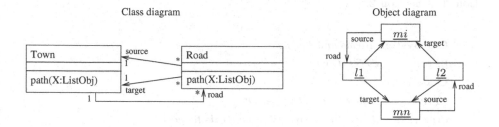

Fig. 5. UML diagrams for *Roads and Towns*.

essential modelling feature of UML class diagrams, and OCL (Object Constraint Language, see e.g. [14]) has been introduced for expressing them. We need a similar constraint language, using first-order logic. For example, the multiplicity constraint 1 on the *Town* side of *road* can be expressed in the class *Road* by a constraint like:

$$\exists! t. \ t.road(this)$$

We can consider it as an abbreviation of a first-order formula like $\forall x. \ Road(x) \to \exists! t. \ road(x, t)$, by considering $.road$ as a binary relation symbol and the expression $x.road(y)$ as a syntactic variant of $road(x, y)$. This solution corresponds to the *global level* that will be introduced in Section 4 and will allow us to directly employ our theory of steadfastness to prove *a priori* correctness.

However the global level hides the distributed nature of OO systems, where each object o has its own attribute signature and state, and computations are performed in a distributed way, through a collaboration among objects. To model systems of cooperating objects, we need to also consider this distributed view, and show that reasoning at the global level allows us to prove properties of the distributed *object level*.

In Section 4, we will consider a three-level formalisation, with a global level, an object level, and a system modelling level, that we will call the OO system level. The latter level, considered here, is the bridge between the object and the global levels, through a global and an object semantics.

In this section we introduce the OO system syntax for constraints, specifications and programs. It completes the syntax introduced in Section 3.1.

Firstly we introduce the $C(x)$-*quantifiers* (or *class quantifiers*) $[\forall x : C(x)].$ and $[\exists x : C(x)].$, where C is a class predicate.

Now, let $\mathcal{S} = [\mathcal{D}, C_1, \ldots, C_n]$ be an OO system. Each class C_j of $\mathcal{S}$ has its own constraint language, where C_j-*constraints* are built from the usual logical symbols and the class quantifiers, starting from atomic formulas which may contain all the function and relation symbols of $\mathcal{D}$, and function and relation symbols of the form $this.a_j$, where $.a_j$ is an attribute of the class C_j, or $x.a_i$, where $.a_i$ is an attribute of class C_i and x is bounded by a $C_i(x)$-quantifier.

C_j-*specifications* have the same general syntax of C_j-constraints, with the restriction that they must be program-predicate specifications of the kind mentioned in Section 2.

OO System *Roads and Towns*

DATA: $\mathcal{LIST}(Obj)$

Class *Road*;

ATTRS: $.source, .target : [\ ] \rightarrow Obj$;

CONSTRS: $Town(this.source) \wedge Town(this.target)$;
$[\exists!t : Town(t)]\boldsymbol{.}\ t.road(this)$;

SPECS: $this.path(L) \leftrightarrow this@(0, L) \wedge (\forall o : Obj\boldsymbol{.}\ o \in L \rightarrow Road(o)) \wedge$
$([\forall a : Road(a), b : Road(b)]\boldsymbol{.}\ \forall i : Nat\boldsymbol{.}$
$a@(i, L) \wedge b@(s(i), L) \rightarrow a.target = b.source)$;

PROGS: $this.path([this|L]) \leftarrow Town(T), T = this.target, T.path(L)$;

Class *Town*;

ATTRIBUTES: $.road : [Obj]$;

CONSTRS: $[\forall o : Road(o)]\boldsymbol{.}\ (this.road(o) \leftrightarrow o.source = this)$;
SPECS: $this.path(l) \leftrightarrow l = [\ ] \vee [\exists x : Road(x)]\boldsymbol{.}\ this.road(x) \wedge x.path(l)$;
PROGS: $this.path([\ ])\ \ \ \leftarrow$
$this.path([X|L]) \leftarrow this.road(X), Road(X), X.path(L)$;

Fig. 6. The complete *Roads and Towns* OO system

Concerning (logic) programs, we assume that $\mathcal{D}$ contains Clark's equality axioms for the signature to be used in program terms. Thus unification works as usual. We say that *a program predicate .p is defined in a class* C_j if C_j contains a program $P_{this.p}$ that has clauses with head predicate $this.p$, and bodies of the form L, K, B, where L, K, B are possibly empty lists of atoms such that:

- L contains *local constraints* of the form $X = this.c$, where $.c : [\ ] \rightarrow Obj$ is an attribute of C_j; or of the form $this.a(\tau_1, \ldots, \tau_n)$, where $.a$ is an attribute of C_j and $\tau_1, \ldots, \tau_n$ are terms;
- K contains *class constraints* of the form $C_i(X)$ where C_i is a class predicate;
- B contains predicates of the form $this.q$, where $.q$ (possibly coinciding with $.p$ in the case of recursion) is defined in C_j; or of the form $X.r$, where K contains a class constraint $C_i(X)$ and $.r$ is defined in the class C_i (with $i \neq j$).

Using the above syntax, the *Roads and Towns* system can be completed as in Fig. 6.

4   A Three-Level Formalisation of OO Systems

Our formalisation of OO systems is based on a three-level architecture, containing an *object level*, a *system level* and a *global level*. The object level takes into account the distributed nature of systems of collaborating objects, and corresponds to the *object level* of UML. The system level corresponds to the class-based view of class diagrams, and corresponds to the *model level* of UML. Finally, the global level is similar to the *meta-model level* of UML, and considers the system $\mathcal{S}$ as a whole; it allows us to reason about properties that cannot be confined to single classes, and to formally treat *a priori* correctness of the (static) methods of $\mathcal{S}$.

In Sections 4.1 and 4.2 we will define the object and global levels, and state precise links between them and the system level by syntactic maps, which we call *projections*: ↓ projections will map the system level into the "lower" object level, and the ↑ projections will map it into the "upper" global level.

The ↓ projections define the *object-level semantics* of class constraints, specifications and programs. This semantics can be seen as a formal counterpart of the *object level* semantics of UML class diagrams.

The ↑ projections define a *global semantics*, where the OO system is considered as a whole; the organisation in classes disappears and we get a single non-OO open specification framework of the kind considered in Section 2. Thus *a priori* correctness in the context of specification frameworks works at the global level in OO systems.

The global level works as a meta-level for the object one. This is shown in Section 4.3, where we introduce syntactic and semantic maps between the global and the object level, discuss the links between the two levels and prove that global-level correctness entails object-level correctness. A general picture will be given (in Fig. 11) in Section 4.3.

4.1   The Object Level

Here we define the *object-level semantics* of OO system constraints, specifications and programs.

At this level, we are interested in populations of cooperating objects. Each population O has its own signature $\Sigma(O)$, and system states with population O are represented by Σ_O-interpretations (see Definition 2). Thus, object-level semantics has to interpret constraints and specifications of an OO system $\mathcal{S}[\mathcal{D}, C_1, \ldots, C_n]$ in terms of $\Sigma(O)$-interpretations. To this end, for every class C_j and every object $o \in O$ with class C_j, we define a map of C_j-constraints and C_j-specifications into $\Sigma(O)$-formulas, which we call *o-constraints and o-specifications*. The interpretation of o-constraints and o-specifications is the usual one of first-order $\Sigma(O)$-formulas, and can be taken as the *intended* object-level semantics of C_j-constraints and C_j-specifications. We get a distributed semantics, where each object $o \in O$ has its own o-constraints and o-specifications.

For a class C_j and an object $o \in O$ of class C_j, the map of C_j-constraints and C_j-specifications into the corresponding o-constraints and o-specifications is defined by the following $\downarrow_o O$ projection:

Definition 3 ($\downarrow_o O$ **Projections**). *Let O be a population for an OO system S with class axioms $CAx(O)$, K be a C_j constraint, and o be an object of class C_j. The $\downarrow_o O$ projection for o is the recursive translation:*

- *For an atomic formula $\sigma(t_1, \ldots, t_n)$, the projection is:*

$$\sigma(t_1, \ldots, t_n) \downarrow_o O = \sigma^*(t_1 \downarrow_o O, \ldots, t_n \downarrow_o O)$$

where, if σ is of the form this.a, then σ^* is o.a; otherwise σ and σ^* coincide.
- *For a class C with class axiom $C(x) \leftrightarrow x = o_1 \vee \cdots \vee x = o_k$, $C(x)$-quantifiers are translated as follows:*

$$([\forall x : C(x)] \centerdot F) \downarrow_o O = F[x/o_1] \downarrow_o O \wedge \ldots \wedge F[x/o_k] \downarrow_o O$$
$$([\exists x : C(x)] \centerdot F) \downarrow_o O = F[x/o_1] \downarrow_o O \vee \ldots \vee F[x/o_k] \downarrow_o O$$

where the replacements $[x/\ldots]$ are applied to all the variable and prefix occurrences of x in F.
If the class axiom is $C(x) \leftrightarrow false$, i.e. no object of class C exists, then

$$([\forall x : C(x)] \centerdot F) \downarrow_o O = true$$
$$([\exists x : C(x)] \centerdot F) \downarrow_o O = false.$$

- *For the usual logical symbols, we have:*

$$(\forall x : s \centerdot F) \downarrow_o O = \forall x : s \centerdot F \downarrow_o O$$
$$(\exists x : s \centerdot F) \downarrow_o O = \exists x : s \centerdot F \downarrow_o O$$
$$(\neg F) \downarrow_o O = \neg F \downarrow_o O$$
$$(A \wedge B) \downarrow_o O = A \downarrow_o O \wedge B \downarrow_o O$$
$$(A \vee B) \downarrow_o O = A \downarrow_o O \vee B \downarrow_o O$$
$$(A \rightarrow B) \downarrow_o O = A \downarrow_o O \rightarrow B \downarrow_o O.$$

As an example, Fig. 7 shows the $\underline{mi}$-constraints and the $\underline{mi}$-specifications of the object $\underline{mi}$ belonging to the population considered in Fig. 4. Fig. 7 also shows the $\underline{mi}$-program.

Concerning programs, the purpose of $\downarrow_o O$-projections is to give their *object-level semantics*. We now define $\downarrow_o O$-projection and then discuss it.

Program clause projection replaces *this* by o, and then eliminates the possible class constraints as follows:

$$(o.P(\tau) \leftarrow L, C(X), K, B) \downarrow_o O = \{(o.P(\tau) \leftarrow N, K, B)[X/o_i] | 1 \le i \le k\}$$

where the class axiom for C is $C(x) \leftrightarrow x = o_1 \vee \cdots \vee x = o_k$. If the class axiom is $C(x) \leftrightarrow false$, then the clause is deleted. Such class constraint elimination is iterated, until the set K of class constraints becomes empty.

Population O: $Town(x) \leftrightarrow x = \underline{mi} \vee x = \underline{mn}$; $Road(x) \leftrightarrow x = \underline{l1} \vee x = \underline{l2}$;

Object $\underline{mi}$: $Town$;

CONSTRS: $(\underline{mi}.road(\underline{l1}) \leftrightarrow \underline{l1}.source = \underline{mi}) \wedge (\underline{mi}.road(\underline{l2}) \leftrightarrow \underline{l2}.source = \underline{mi})$;

SPECS: $\underline{mi}.path(l) \leftrightarrow l = [\,] \vee (\underline{mi}.road(\underline{l1}) \wedge \underline{l1}.path(l)) \vee (\underline{mi}.road(\underline{l2}) \wedge \underline{l2}.path(l))$;

PROGS: $\underline{mi}.path([\,]) \quad \leftarrow$

$\underline{mi}.path([\underline{l1}|L]) \leftarrow \underline{mi}.road(\underline{l1}), \underline{l1}.path(L)$;

$\underline{mi}.path([\underline{l2}|L]) \leftarrow \underline{mi}.road(\underline{l2}), \underline{l2}.path(L)$;

Fig. 7. $\underline{mi}$-constraints, specifications, and program.

For a C_j-program P and an object $o \in O$ with class C_j, the projection $P \downarrow_o O$ is obtained by translating all the clauses of P in the above way. $P \downarrow_o O$ will be called the *o-program* corresponding to P.

Fig. 7 shows the $\underline{mi}$-program corresponding to the *path* program of the class *Town* of Fig. 6.

The purpose of the $\downarrow_o$ O-projection is not to model the distributed computations of a population of cooperating objects, but to give an *object-level semantics* for such computations, while abstracting away from implementation details. With regard to the computation model, we follow the general OO approach, where programs of an object o are just *o-copies* of class programs. An o-copy simply replaces *this* by o, as shown in Fig. 8.

Object $\underline{mi}$: $Town$;

STATE: $\underline{mi}.road(\underline{l1}) \leftarrow$;

PROGS: $\underline{mi}.path([\,]) \quad \leftarrow$

$\underline{mi}.path([X|L]) \leftarrow \underline{mi}.road(X), Road(X), X.path(L)$;

Fig. 8. The object $\underline{mi}$ and its method.

To model the OO view of computations, we have to model them as collaborations, where each object uses its current state axioms to solve local constraints and (possibly) evaluate (local or remote) addresses of other objects, in order to send them messages. We will consider the simpler case, where state axioms can be represented as sets of Prolog facts, or more precisely, the Clark's completion of these facts. In Fig. 8, the state axiom is represented by the fact $\underline{mi}.road(\underline{l1})$, which implicitly stands for its completion $\forall x : Obj.$ $\underline{mi}.road(x) \leftrightarrow x = \underline{l1}$. The $\underline{mi}.path([X|L])$-call locally solves $\underline{mi}.road(X)$ and gets the address $X = \underline{l1}$; by the call $Road(\underline{l1})$, the object $\underline{l1}$ is asked for its class; if $\underline{l1}$ answers $Road$, then $Road(\underline{l1})$ succeeds and the message $path(L)$ is sent to it; otherwise $Road(\underline{l1})$ fails. As we can see, this behaviour is equivalent to that of the $\downarrow_o$ O-projection of Fig. 7, when the population is the one considered there, independently of the current state of the objects. The object-level semantics of the collaboration is given collectively by the o-programs of all the objects o of the population, shown in Fig. 9.

$$mi.path([\,]) \quad \leftarrow$$
$$mi.path([\underline{l1}|L]) \leftarrow \underline{mi}.road(\underline{l1}), \underline{l1}.path(L);$$
$$mi.path([\underline{l2}|L]) \leftarrow \underline{mi}.road(\underline{l2}), \underline{l2}.path(L);$$
$$mn.path([\,]) \quad \leftarrow$$
$$mn.path([\underline{l1}|L]) \leftarrow \underline{mn}.road(\underline{l1}), \underline{l1}.path(L);$$
$$mn.path([\underline{l2}|L]) \leftarrow \underline{mn}.road(\underline{l2}), \underline{l2}.path(L);$$
$$l1.path([\underline{l1}|L]) \leftarrow \underline{mi} = \underline{l1}.target, \underline{mi}.path(L);$$
$$l1.path([\underline{l1}|L]) \leftarrow \underline{mn} = \underline{l1}.target, \underline{mn}.path(L);$$
$$l2.path([\underline{l2}|L]) \leftarrow \underline{mi} = \underline{l2}.target, \underline{mi}.path(L);$$
$$l2.path([\underline{l2}|L]) \leftarrow \underline{mn} = \underline{l2}.target, \underline{mn}.path(L);$$

Fig. 9. The object-level semantics of the collaboration $\{\underline{mi}, \underline{mn}, \underline{l1}, \underline{l2}\}$.

This example explains our choice of considering $\downarrow_o$ O-projections as the intended object-level semantics of programs and justifies Definition 4 below.

Definition 4 (Collaboration Program). *Let* $\mathcal{S}[\mathcal{D}, C_1, \ldots, C_n]$ *be an OO system and O be a population for it. The collaboration program of O is the union of the o-programs, for the objects o of the population.*

To conclude, we show how the $\downarrow_o$ O-projections allow us to precisely define a model-theoretic semantics for OO systems and their correctness.

Let $\mathcal{S}[\mathcal{D}, C_1, \ldots, C_n]$ be an OO system, and O be a population for it with class axioms $CAx(O)$ and population signature Σ_O.

We do not bother to represent states by state axioms, but instead we define system states in a more abstract, purely model-theoretic way:[3]

Definition 5 ((Model-theoretic) System States). *A $\Sigma(O)$-interpretation i_O is a system state with population O iff $i_O \models CAx(O)$.*

We define constraint satisfaction as follows:

Definition 6 (Constraint Satisfaction). *A C_j-constraint K is satisfied by a system state i_O with population O if, for every object $o \in O$ with class C_j, $i_O \models K \downarrow_o O$.*

We define the object models as the system states that satisfy the constraints:

Definition 7 (Object Models). *i_O is an object model of $\mathcal{S}[\mathcal{D}, C_1, \ldots, C_n]$ with population O iff it satisfies all the class constraints of $\mathcal{S}$.*

With respect to UML, OO systems formalise class diagrams, and their object models formalise the object diagrams that are instances of the class diagrams which satisfy the constraints.

---

[3] System states defined by state axioms become particular cases.

Now we can define program correctness. The specifications of the collaboration program of O are the o-specifications of the various classes of the system. They are standard first-order $\Sigma(O)$-formulas, and we can use the definition of correctness in a class of interpretations, as given in [10].

Definition 8 (Program Correctness). *The programs of $S[\mathcal{D}, C_1, \ldots, C_n]$ are correct in a population O if the collaboration program of O is correct with respect to its specifications in the class of object models of S with population O.*

We remark that correctness is a collective property of the population O, i.e., it is a property of the collaboration among the objects of O.

We define correct OO systems as follows:

Definition 9 (Correct OO systems). *An OO system $S[\mathcal{D}, C_1, \ldots, C_n]$ is correct if its programs are correct in every population for it.*

4.2   The Global Level

The proof methods for program correctness given in [10] apply directly, if we consider a fixed population. However, we cannot reason thus in general, for *any* population, because different populations generate different signatures and projections. Thus we cannot reason about the correctness of OO systems and about other properties like specification reduction. The global level allows us to overcome this difficulty. It is defined as follows.

We associate with an OO system $S[\mathcal{D}, C_1, \ldots, C_n]$ a global signature Σ_G, where the dot notation is replaced by an extra argument of sort Obj, namely:

(a) for every class C_i and every relation declaration $.r : a$ of C_i, Σ_G contains the declaration $r : [Obj|a]$;
(b) for every class C_i and every function declaration $.f : a \to s$ of C_i, Σ_G contains the declaration $f : [Obj|a] \to s$.

We assume that the *same* attribute or program predicate does *not* occur in two different classes. Since in our example of *Roads and Towns*, the program predicate *path* occurs in both *Town* and in *Road*, we assume the following class renaming: *path* is implicitly renamed into $path_{Town}$, in class *Town*, and into $path_{Road}$, in class *Road*. We remark that class renaming is not needed at the object level, because dot renaming suffices there.

Under the above assumption, the global signature is the union of all the class signatures, transformed by (a) and (b) above.

The same transformation maps the program signature of the various classes into the global program signature: a program predicate declaration $.p : [a]$ is mapped into $p : [Obj|a]$.

In global formulas, class bound quantifiers are interpreted as the following abbreviations:

$$[\forall x : C(x)].\ F(x) \quad \text{abbreviates} \quad \forall x : Obj.\ C(x) \to F(x)$$
$$[\exists x : C(x)].\ F(x) \quad \text{abbreviates} \quad \exists x : Obj.\ C(x) \wedge F(x)$$

Now we can translate constraints, specifications and programs at the system level into global formulas. This translation will be called the *global projection*, and will be indicated by ↑.

For a class C_j and a constraint K of C_j, the projection $F\uparrow$ is defined by the following steps.

(i) If K contains *this*, then K is replaced by $[\forall x : C_j(x)]$. $F[this/x]$, where x is a new variable of sort *Obj*.
(ii) In the formula resulting from (i), the dot notation $\tau.a(\tau_1,\ldots,\tau_n)$ is treated as a syntactic variant of the standard notation $a(\tau,\tau_1,\ldots,\tau_n)$. It should be clear how to recursively translate from the dot notation into the standard one, so we omit the details.

In this way, the projection $K\uparrow$ is a Σ_G-formula. The same ↑-projection also works for specifications.

Definition 10 (Global Constraints and Specifications). *Let* $S[\mathcal{D}, C_1, \ldots, C_n]$ *be an OO system.*

The global constraints *for* S *are all the* Σ_G*-formulas obtained as* ↑*-projections of the* C_j*-constraints, for* $1 \le j \le n$.

The global specifications *for* S *are all the specifications obtained as* ↑*-projections of the* C_j*-specifications, for* $1 \le j \le n$.

At the global level, the organisation in classes disappears, but classes survive in class axioms and in class bounded quantifiers. This situation is shown in Fig. 10, which shows the global constraints and the global specifications obtained by the ↑-projection from those of the *Roads and Towns* OO system. Fig. 10 also contains one global program. For global programs, we proceed as follows.

Global (*Roads and Towns*) ↑;

DATA: $\mathcal{LIST}(Obj)$;

DECLS: $Road, Town : [Obj]$;
$source, target : [Obj] \to Obj$;
$link : [Obj, Obj]$;

CONSTRS: $[\forall x : Road(x)]$. $Town(source(x)) \wedge Town(target(x)$;
$[\forall x : Road(x)]$. $[\exists!t : Town(t)]$. $link(t,x)$;
$[\forall x : Town(x)]$. $[\forall r : Road(r)]$. $link(x,r) \leftrightarrow source(r) = x$;

SPECS: $[\forall x : Road(x)]$. $path_{Road}(x, L) \leftrightarrow x@(0, L) \wedge (\forall o : Obj$. $o \in L \to Link(o)) \wedge$
$([\forall a : Road(a), b : Road(b)]$. $\forall i : Nat$.
$a@(i, L) \wedge b@(s(i), L) \to target(a) = source(b))$
$[\forall t : Town(t)]$. $path_{Town}(t, l) \leftrightarrow l = [\,] \vee [\exists x : Road(x)]$. $link(t,x) \wedge path(x, l)$;

PROGS: $path_{Town}(X, [\,])$ $\leftarrow Town(X)$
$path_{Town}(X, [X|L]) \leftarrow T = target(X), Road(X), path_{Road}(T, L)$
$path_{Road}(T, [X|L])$ $\leftarrow link(T, X), Town(T), Road(X), path_{Town}(X, L))$

Fig. 10. The global *Roads and Town* system.

A program clause of a class C_j of the form $this.p(\tau) \leftarrow L, K, B$ is translated into $p(X, \tau) \leftarrow L', C_j(X), K', B'$, where L', K', B' are obtained by replacing $this$ by a new variable X, and by passing from the dot to the standard notation. By this $\uparrow$-projection we build the global program:

Definition 11 (The Global Program). *Let $\mathcal{S}[\mathcal{D}, C_1, \ldots, C_n]$ be an OO system. The global program for $\mathcal{S}$ is the set of all clauses obtained as $\uparrow$-projections of the C_j-programs, for $1 \leq j \leq n$.*

Now we can define global models and global correctness. Let Σ_G be the global signature of an OO system $\mathcal{S}[\mathcal{D}, C_1, \ldots, C_n]$. We say that a Σ_G-interpretation i_G has population O if, for every class predicate C_j and object identifier o, $i_G \models C_j(o)$ iff $o \in O$ with class C_j. Global models are assumed to have finite populations.

Definition 12 (Global Models). *Let $\mathcal{S}[\mathcal{D}, C_1, \ldots, C_n]$ be an OO system, and Σ_G be the corresponding global signature. A Σ_G-interpretation i_G is a global model of $\mathcal{S}$ if i_G has a finite population O, is an expansion of the data model i_D and satisfies the population constraints and the global constraints.*

Definition 13 (Global Correctness). *Let $\mathcal{S}[\mathcal{D}, C_1, \ldots, C_n]$ be an OO system, and P_G be its global program. $\mathcal{S}$ is globally correct if P_G is correct with respect to its global specifications in the class of global models.*

To conclude, we define the global framework as follows. It is just a non-OO specification framework of the kind considered in Section 2. Thus, we can apply the proof methods of [10] and we can reason about specification reduction. In the next section we will show that reasoning at the global level correctly reflects onto the object level.

Definition 14 (Global Framework). *The global framework associated with an OO system $\mathcal{S}$ is the specification framework which has the global signature of $\mathcal{S}$, and contains the data, class constraints, global constraints, global specifications and the global program of $\mathcal{S}$.*

4.3 Main Results

Now we introduce a semantic map $\Downarrow$ from global models to the object level models. With this map, we show that we can reason on the object level using the global level as a meta-level. The general picture is shown in Fig. 11.

The projections $\uparrow$ and $\downarrow_o O$ have already been explained. The map $\Downarrow$ is a semantic map from Σ_G- interpretations with population O into $\Sigma(O)$-interpretations. As the picture shows, $\Downarrow$ is not injective.

For an OO system $\mathcal{S}[\mathcal{D}, C_1, \ldots, C_n]$, a global interpretation i_G with population O, and a C_j-constraint F, the following reflection property can be proved:

$$i_G \models F \uparrow \quad \text{iff} \quad i_G \Downarrow \models (F \downarrow_{o_1} O \wedge \cdots \wedge F \downarrow_{o_k} O)$$

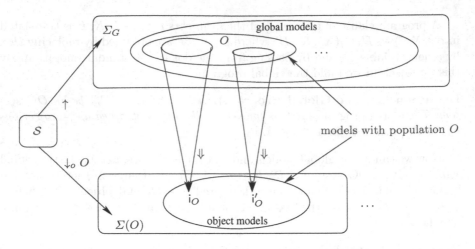

Fig. 11. The links among the three levels.

where $o_1, \ldots, o_k$ are the objects of O with class C_j. That is, constraints that hold at the global level reflect onto constraints that hold at the object level. Similar reflection properties hold for the specifications and the intended models of programs. In particular, this allows us to show that we can prove correctness at the global level, so as to guarantee it at the object level.

Now we define $\Downarrow$. We will adopt the following notation:

- $i, j, \ldots$ will denote interpretations;
- $\sigma^i, \sigma^j, \ldots$, will indicate the interpretations of σ in $i, j, \ldots$;
- $\mathcal{S}[\mathcal{D}, C_1, \ldots, C_n]$ will be an OO system with global signature Σ_G, and O a population for it with class axioms $CAx(O)$ and signature $\Sigma(O)$.

Definition 15 (The $\Downarrow$ map). *Let i_G be a Σ_G-interpretation such that $i_G \models CAx(O)$. Then $i_G \Downarrow$ is the $\Sigma(O)$ interpretation such that, for every object $o \in O$:*

- *for every relation attribute $o.a$ of o, $\langle \alpha_1, \ldots, \alpha_n \rangle \in o.a^{i_G \Downarrow}$ iff $\langle o, \alpha_1, \ldots, \alpha_n \rangle \in a^{i_G}$, and*
- *for every function attribute $o.f$ of o, $o.f^{i_G \Downarrow}(\alpha_1, \ldots, \alpha_n) = f^{i_G}(o, \alpha_1, \ldots, \alpha_n)$.*

Theorem 1 (Constraint Reflection). *Let F be a C_j-constraint of $\mathcal{S}$, i_G be a Σ_G-interpretation such that $i_G \models CAx(O)$, and $C_j(x) \leftrightarrow x = o_1 \vee \cdots \vee x = o_k$ be the class axiom for C_j. Then*

$$i_G \models F \uparrow \quad iff \quad i_G \Downarrow \models (F \downarrow_{o_1} O \wedge \cdots \wedge F \downarrow_{o_k} O).$$

Proof. (Sketch) $F \uparrow$ is $[\forall x : C_j(x)]. \ F[this/x]$. Since $i_G \models C_j(x) \leftrightarrow x = o_1 \vee \ldots \vee x = o_k$, $i_G \models F \uparrow$ iff $i_G \models F[this/o_1] \uparrow \wedge \cdots \wedge F[this/o_k] \uparrow$ (we will say that we have O-*eliminated* the class bounded quantifier). Thus it suffices to prove that $i_G \models F[this/o_i] \uparrow$ iff $i_G\Downarrow \models F \downarrow_{o_i} O$, where $1 \leq i \leq k$. To prove this, we O-eliminate the class bounded quantifiers of $F[this/o_i] \uparrow$. We get a formula that is structurally equivalent to $F \downarrow_{o_i} O$, and the the proof can be concluded by an induction on the structure of formulas. The base case follows from the definition of $\Downarrow$.

A reflection result also holds for interpretations involving program predicates and specifications. The definition of the $\Downarrow$-map readily extends to the interpretations of program predicates and the proof of Theorem 1 readily extends to a proof of the following one.

Theorem 2 (Specification Reflection). *Let* $S_{this.p}$ *be a* C_j-*specification,* j_G *be a* $(\Sigma_G + p)$-*interpretation such that* $j_G \models CAx(O)$, *and* $C_j(x) \leftrightarrow x = o_1 \vee \cdots \vee x = o_k$ *be the class axiom for* C_j. *Then* $j_G\Downarrow$ *is a* $(\Sigma(O) + \{o_1.p, \ldots, o_k.p\})$-*interpretation and*

$$j_G \models S_{this.p} \uparrow \quad iff \quad j_G\Downarrow \models (S_{this.p} \downarrow_{o_1} O \wedge \cdots \wedge S_{this.p} \downarrow_{o_k} O).$$

We can express system properties using the syntax introduced in Section 3.2. Since each class C_j has its syntax, we will call C_j-formulas the constraint and specification formulas that can be expressed in C_j. The following theorem follows from Theorems 1 and 2.

Theorem 3 (Reasoning Reflection). *Let* F *be a* C_j-*formula of* S. *If* $F \uparrow$ *is a theorem of the global framework, then, for every population* O, *every system model* i_O *with population* O, *and every* $o \in O$ *with class* C_j, *we have that* $i_O \models F \downarrow_o O$.

This theorem allows us, in particular, to reason about constraints, specifications and specification reduction, when subclassing is considered.

Concerning the reflection properties of programs, we show that the models of the global program are mapped into those of the collaboration program.

We use the j-models semantics given in [10], which we briefly recall here, but taking constraints into account in order to deal with local and class constraints.

We say that an open program P has type $\delta \Leftarrow (\gamma)(\pi)$ if δ are the predicates defined by P, γ the constraints occurring in it, and π its open predicates. Constraints γ are assumed to be computed by a constraint solver, while open predicates π have specifications, but no programs; π allow reuse through specification reduction, as explained in Section 2. By $P : \delta \Leftarrow (\gamma)(\pi)$ we indicate that P has type $\delta \Leftarrow (\gamma)(\pi)$.

Let Γ be a signature that contains the signature of $P : \delta \Leftarrow (\gamma)(\pi)$, except the defined predicates δ. We call a Γ-interpretation a *pre-interpretation* for $P :$ $\delta \Leftarrow (\gamma)(\pi)$.[4] For a pre-interpretation j, we define the *j-models* as the $(\Gamma + \delta)$-expansions of j that are models of P.

---

[4] This definition of pre-interpretation extends that in [11].

We can show (see [10]) that there is the *minimum j-model of P*, indicated by $=j^P$. Intuitively, j^P corresponds to the success set of P when computations are performed in accordance with j. We can consider j as an interpretation of the constraints according to a specific constraint solver, and of the open predicates according to a specific reuse. Thus, j-models can be assumed as the semantics of open programs with constraints.

Now, let S be an OO system with global signature Σ_G, and O be a population for it. The global and the collaboration programs have the following features.

The global program GP has type:

$$GP : \delta_G \Leftarrow (\lambda_G, \gamma), (\pi_G)$$

where the defined predicates δ_G coincide with the (global-level) predicates that are defined in at least one class, the open predicates π_G are the (global-level) program predicates that are not defined by any class, λ_G are the the local constraint symbols and γ the class constraint symbols used in GP.

We say that the set $\{o_1.a, \ldots, o_k.a\}$ is the O-expansion of the C_j-attribute .a declared in C_j, if $o_1, \ldots, o_k$ are the objects of O with class C_j. The collaboration program CP_O of the population O has type:

$$CP_O : \delta_O \Leftarrow (\lambda_O), (\pi_O)$$

where the defined predicates δ_O coincide with the (union of) the O-expansions of the predicates defined in at least one class C_j, the local constraint symbols λ_O are the O-expansions of the local constraint symbols used in at least one class program, and the open predicates π_O coincide with the O-expansions of the program predicates not defined by the classes of S. There are no class constraints in CP, because they are eliminated by the $\downarrow_o O$ projections.

As an example, the global program of the *Road and Towns* system has type

$$GP : path_{Road}, path_{Town} \Leftarrow (target, link, Road, Town)();$$

it has no open predicates. The collaboration program with population $\underline{mi}$, $\underline{mn}$, $\underline{l1}$, $\underline{l2}$ has type

$$CP : \underline{l1}.path, \underline{l2}.path, \underline{mi}.path, \underline{mn}.path \Leftarrow (\underline{l1}.target, \underline{l2}.target, \underline{mi}.link, \underline{mn}.link)().$$

We can see that the $\Downarrow$-map, extended to program predicates, maps $(\Sigma_G + \pi_G)$-interpretations into $(\Sigma(O) + \pi_O)$-interpretations and $(\Sigma_G + \pi_G + \delta_G)$-interpretations into $(\Sigma(O) + \pi_O + \delta_O)$-interpretations.

The following program reflection theorem holds:

Theorem 4 (Program Models Reflection). . *Let $GP : \delta_G \Leftarrow (\lambda_G, \gamma), (\pi_G)$ be the global program of an OO system S, and $CP_O : \delta_O \Leftarrow (\lambda_O), (\pi_O)$ be the collaboration program with population O. Let j be a $(\Sigma + \pi_G)$-interpretation such that $j \models CAx(O)$. Then*

$$(j^{GP})\Downarrow = (j\Downarrow)^{CP_O}.$$

Proof. A detailed proof would require much material from [10]. Here we say only that the ideas behind the proof are very similar to those used in partial evaluation. Indeed, by the definitions of the $\uparrow$ and $\downarrow_o O$ projections, CP_O can be obtained from GP by a kind of partial evaluation of the class constraints of GP using the class axioms $CAx(O)$.

The following theorem can be proved as a consequence of Theorems 2 and 4. It allows us to reason about correctness.

Theorem 5 (Correctness Reflection). *S is correct iff it is globally correct.*

5 Conclusion

We have defined system correctness for OO systems, namely for (possibly) distributed sets of cooperating objects. We have introduced global frameworks as a meta-level to deal with properties of OO systems, in particular to deal with their *a priori correctness*, namely pre-proved correctness that holds in all the system states. We have also shown how we can give a semantics for UML object and class diagrams with constraints.

This is a sound basis for introducing correctly reusable OO modules. They can be formalised as open OO systems, namely OO systems where the collaboration and global programs are open, because the collaboration is assumed to be with generic classes, that we call templates. A template T, like a class, has constraints, and specifies program predicates π by non-strict specifications S_π, but it does not contain programs for them. T works as a placeholder for classes which contain the programs for π. A class C correctly instantiates T if the signature of C contains (modulo renaming) that of T, the constraints of C allow us to prove (at the global level, see Theorem 3) those of T, and the specifications S'_π of C correctly override S_π (also at the global level). Different correct instantiations correspond to different correct reuses.

We can deal with open OO systems without any modification of our formalisation, because we can deal with open programs. As the global framework is an open specification framework, we have correct reusability with interfaces and context dependencies, as discussed in Section 2. Thus, an open OO system represents a reusable unit like an OOD framework.

Open OO systems allow us to formalise OOD frameworks, such as *Catalysis* frameworks [5], with one proviso: we have considered only static programs, namely programs that do not change the current state of an OO system. That is we can only deal with correctness of query methods, in any given state of the system. Methods (programs) that change the current state are allowed, but we do not yet have a formalisation of their *a priori correctness*. Our next step will be to introduce timed objects, and to deal with the correctness of dynamic programs.

Our approach is model-theoretic, so it is different from proof-theoretic or type theoretic approaches [1,12]. It is closer to other model-theoretic approaches, like the algebraic ones [2]. In particular our treatment is similar to that of [6,3].

However, our work extends the algebraic methods since, by the architecture of specification frameworks, it allows us to introduce pre-proved correctness, even at the level of distributed systems of objects.

References

1. M. Abadi and L. Cardelli. *A Theory of Objects*. MIT Press, 1985.
2. E. Astesiano, H.-J. Kreowski, and B. Krieg-Brückner, editors. *Algebraic Foundations of Systems Specifications*. Springer, 1999.
3. R.H. Bourdeau and B. H.C. Cheng. A formal semantics for object model diagrams. *IEEE Trans. Soft. Eng.*, 21(10):799–821, 1995.
4. J. Cheesman and J. Daniels. *UML Components: A Simple Process for Specifying Component-based Software*. Addison-Wesley, 2001.
5. D.F. D'Souza and A.C. Wills. *Objects, Components, and Frameworks with UML: The Catalysis Approach*. Addison-Wesley, 1999.
6. H. Ehrig and B. Mahr. *Fundamentals of Algebraic Specification 2*. Springer-Verlag, 1989.
7. G. Larsen. Designing component-based frameworks using patterns in the UML. *Comms. ACM*, 42(10):38–45, October 1999.
8. K.-K. Lau and M. Ornaghi. OOD frameworks in component-based software development in computational logic. In P. Flener, editor, *Proc. LOPSTR 98, Lecture Notes in Computer Science 1559*, pages 101–123. Springer-Verlag, 1999.
9. K.-K. Lau and M. Ornaghi. Isoinitial semantics for logic programs. In J.W. Lloyd et al, editor, *Proceedings of the First Int. Conf. on Computational Logic, Lecture Notes in Artificial Intelligence 1861*, pages 223–238. Springer-Verlag, 2000.
10. K.-K. Lau, M. Ornaghi, and S.-Å. Tärnlund. Steadfast logic programs. *J. Logic Programming*, 38(3):259–294, March 1999.
11. J.W. Lloyd. *Foundations of Logic Programming*. Springer-Verlag, second edition, 1987.
12. D. Miller. Forum: A multiple-conclusion specification logic. *TCS*, 165(1):201–231, 1996.
13. J. Rumbaugh, I. Jacobson, and G. Booch. *The Unified Modeling Language Reference Manual*. Addison-Wesley, 1999.
14. J. Warmer and A. Kleppe. *The Object Constraint Language*. Addison-Wesley, 1999.

A Framework for Developing Embeddable Customized Logics

Sébastien Ferré* and Olivier Ridoux

IRISA, Campus Universitaire de Beaulieu, 35042 RENNES cedex,
{ferre,ridoux}@irisa.fr

Abstract. Logic-based applications often use *customized logics* which are composed of several logics. These customized logics are also often *embedded* as a black-box in an application. Their implementation requires the specification of a well-defined interface with common operations such as a parser, a printer, and a theorem prover. In order to be able to compose these logics, one must also define composition laws, and prove their properties. We present the principles of *logic functors* and their compositions for constructing customized logics. An important issue is how the operations of different sublogics inter-operate. We propose a formalization of the logic functors, their semantics, implementations, and their composition.

1 Introduction

We present a framework for building embeddable automatic theorem provers for *customized logics.* The framework defines *logic functors* as logic components; for instance, one component may be the propositional logic, another component may be the interval logic, also called intervals. Logic functors can be composed to form new logics, for instance, propositional logic on intervals.

Each logic functor has its own proof-theory, which can be implemented as a theorem prover. We desire that the proof-theory and the theorem prover of the composition of logic functors should result from the composition of the proof-theories and the theorem provers of the component logic functors.

All logic functors and their compositions implement a common *interface.* This makes it possible to construct generic applications that can be instantiated with a logic component. Conversely, customized logics built using the logic functors can be *embedded* in an application that comply with this interface.

Logic functors specify off-the-shelf software components, the validation of the composition of which reduces to a form of type-cheking, and their composition automatically results in an automatic theorem prover. Logic functors can be assembled by laymen, and used routinely in system-level programming, such as compilers, operating systems, file-systems, and information systems.

This article is organized as follows. Section 2 presents our motivations, and Section 3 introduces the notions of logics and logic functors, and several logic

---

* This author is supported by a scholarship from CNRS and Région Bretagne

A. Pettorossi (Ed.): LOPSTR 2001, LNCS 2372, pp. 191–215, 2002.
© Springer-Verlag Berlin Heidelberg 2002

functor properties like *completeness* and *correctness*. Section 4 introduces a simple nullary logic functor as an example, and a more sophisticated unary logic functor that raises important questions on the properties of logics that result from a composition of logic functors. Section 5 answers these questions by introducing a new property, called *reducedness*. In Section 6, we compare this work with the literature. Appendix A presents some nullary logic functors, and Appendix B presents some n-ary logic functors.

2   Motivations

2.1   Logic-Based Information Processing Systems

In [FR00b,FR01], we have proposed a Logical Information System that is built upon a variant of Formal Concept Analysis [GW99,FR00a]. The framework is generic in the sense that any logic whose deduction relation forms a lattice can be plugged-in. However, if one leaves the logic totally undefined, then one puts too much responsibility on the end-users or on a knowledge-base administrator. It is unlikely they can design such a logical component themselves. By using the framework developed in this article, one can design a toolbox of logical components, and the user has only the responsibility of composing those components. The design of this Logical Information System is the main motivation for this research.

However, we believe the application scope of this research goes beyond our Logical Information System. Several information processing domains have logic-based components in which logic plays a crucial role: e.g., logic-based information retrieval [SM83,vRCL98], logic-based diagnosis [Poo88], logic-based programming [Llo87,MS98], logic-based program analysis [SFRW98,AMSS98, CSS99]. These components model an information processing domain in logic, and also they bring to the front solutions in which logic is the main engine. This can be illustrated by the difference between using a logic of programs and programming in logic.

The logic in use in these system is often not defined by a single pure deduction system, but rather it combines several logics together. The designer of an application has to make an *ad hoc* proof of consistency and an *ad hoc* implementation (i.e., a theorem prover) every time he designs a new *ad hoc* logic. Since these logics are often variants of a more standard logic we call them *customized logics*.

In order to favour separation of concerns, it is important that the application that is based on a logic engine, and the logic engine itself, be designed separately. This implies that the interface of the logic engine should not depend on the logic itself. This is what we call *embeddability* of the logical component.

If we need to separately design the application and its logical components, then who should develop the embedded logic components?

2.2   The Actors of the Development of an Information Processing System

In this section, we present our views on the Actors of the development on an information processing system. Note that Actors are not necessarily incarnated in one person; each Actor may gather several persons possibly not living at the same time. In short, Actors are roles, rather than persons. Sometimes, Actors may even be incarnated in computer programs.

The first Actor is the Theorist; he invents an abstract framework, like, for instance, relational algebra, lattice theory, or logic.

If the abstract framework has applications, then a second Actor, the System Programmer, implements (part of) the theory in a *generic* system for these applications. This results in systems like data-bases, static analysers, or logic programming systems.

Then the third Actor, the Application Designer, applies the abstract framework to a concrete objective by *instantiating* a generic system. This can be done by composing a data-base schema, or a program property, or a logic program.

Finally, the User, the fourth Actor, maintains and uses an application. He queries a data-base, he analyses programs, or he runs logic programs.

It is the relation between the System Programmer and the Application Designer that interests us.

2.3   Genericity and Instantiation

Genericity is often achieved by designing a language: e.g., a data-base schema language, a lattice operation language, and a programming language. Correspondingly, instantiation is done by programming and composing: e.g., drawing a data-base schema, composing an abstract domain for static analysis, or composing a logic program.

We propose to do the same for logic-based tools. Indeed, on one hand the System Programmer is competent for building a logic subsystem, but he does not know the application; he only knows the range of applications. On the other hand the Application Designer knows the application, but is generally not competent for building a logic subsystem. In this article, we will act as System Programmers by providing elementary components for safely building a logic subsystem, and also as Theorists by giving formal results on the composition laws of these components.

We explore how to systematically build logics using basic components that we call *logic functors*. By "construction of a logic" we mean the definition of its syntax, its semantics, and its abstract implementation as a deduction system. All logic functors we describe in this article have also a concrete implementation as an actual program. We have also implemented a *logic composer* that takes the description of a customized logic and builds a concrete logic component.

2.4 Customized Logics

The range of logic functors can be very large. In this article we consider only sums of logics, propositions (on arbitrary formulas), intervals, valued attributes (abstracted w.r.t. values), strings (e.g., "begin with", "contains"), and $\mathcal{ONL}$ (a modal epistemic logic functor [Lev90]).

The whole framework is geared towards manipulating logics as lattices, as in abstract interpretation. Deduction is considered as a relation between formulas, and we study the conditions under which this relation is a partial order. This excludes non-monotonic logics, but they can be used as nullary logic functors. Note that non-monotonicity is seldom a goal in itself, and that notoriously non-monotonic features have a monotonic rendering; e.g., Closed World Assumption can be reflected in the monotonic modal logic $\mathcal{ONL}$. Note also that in our framework not all logics are lattices (nor their deduction relation is a partial order), but the most interesting ones can always be completed in a lattice.

We will consider as a motivating example an application for dealing with bibliographic entries. Each entry has a description made of its author name(s), title, type of cover, publisher, and date. The User navigates through a set of entries by comparing descriptions with queries that are written in the same language. For instance, let us assume the following entry set:

- descr(entry$_1$) =
  [author:"Kipling"/ title:"The Jungle Book"/ paper-back/
  publisher:"Penguin"/ year: 1985],
- descr(entry$_2$) =
  [author:"Kipling"/ title:"The Jungle Book"/ hard-cover/
  publisher:"Century Co."/ year: 1908],
- descr(entry$_3$) =
  [author:"Kipling"/ title:"Just So Stories"/ hard-cover/
  publisher:""/ year: 1902].

An answer to the query:
    title: contains "Jungle"
    is:

| hard-cover | publisher:"Century Co." | year: 1900..1950 |
| paper-back | publisher:"Penguin" | year: 1950..2000 |

because several entries (entry$_1$ and entry$_2$) have a description that entails the query (i.e., they are possible answers), and the application asks the user to make his query more specific by suggesting some relevant refinements. Note that author:"Kipling" is not a relevant refinement because it is true of all matching entries. For every possible answer entry we have descr(entry)$\models$query, and for every relevant refinement x the following holds

1. there exists a possible answer e$_1$ such that descr(e$_1$)$\models$x, and
2. there exists a possible answer e$_2$ such that descr(e$_2$)$\not\models$x.

We will not go any further in the description of this application (see [FR00b, FR01]). We simply note that:

1. descriptions, queries, and answers belong to the same logical language, which combines logical symbols and expressions such as strings, numbers, or intervals, and
2. one can design a similar application with a different logic, e.g., for manipulating software components. Thus, it is important that all different logics share a common interface for being able to separately write programs for the navigation system and for the logic subsystem it uses.

2.5 Summary

We define tools for building *automatic* theorem provers for *customized logics* for allowing Users who are not sophisticated logic actors. Note also that the User may be a program itself: e.g., a mobile agent running on a host system [IB96]. This rules out interactive theorem provers.

Validating a theorem prover built by using our tools must be as simple as possible. We want this because the Application designer, though it may be more sophisticated than the User, is not a logic actor.

Finally, the resulting theorem provers must have a common interface so that they can be *embedded* in generic applications. Deduction is decidable in all the logic components that we define. Thus, the logic components can be safely embedded in applications as black-boxes.

3 Logics and Logic Functors

If an Application Designer has to define a customized logic by the means of composing primitive components, these components should be of a 'high-level', so that the resulting logic subsystem can be proven to be correct. Indeed, if the primitive components are too low-level, proving the correctness of the result is similar to proving the correctness of a program. Thus, we decided to define logical components that are very close to be logics themselves.

Our idea is to consider that a logic interprets its formulas as functions of their atoms. By abstracting atomic formulas from the language of a logic we obtain what we call a *logic functor*. A logic functor can be applied to a logic to generate a new logic. For instance, if propositional logic is abstracted over its atomic formulas, we obtain a logic functor called *prop*, which we can apply to, say, a logic on intervals, called *interv*, to form propositional logic on intervals, *prop(interv)*.

3.1 Logics

We formally define the class of logics as structures, whose axioms are merely type axioms. Section 4 and Appendix A present examples of logics. All proofs are omitted. They are given in the companion research-report [FR02] .

Definition 1 (Syntax) *A syntax AS is a denumerable set of (abstract syntax tree of) formulas.*

A *semantics* associates to each formula a subset of an *interpretation domain* where the formula is true of all elements. This way of treating formulas as unary predicate is akin to description logics [DLNS96].

Definition 2 (Semantics) *Given a syntax AS, a semantics S based on AS is a pair* $(I, \models)$, *where*

- *I is the* interpretation domain,
- $\models \ \in \mathcal{P}(I \times AS)$, *(where $\mathcal{P}(X)$ denotes the power-set of set X), is a satisfaction relation between interpretations and formulas.*

$i \models f$ *reads "i is a* model *of f". For every formula* $f \in AS$, $M(f) = \{i \in I \mid i \models f\}$ *denotes the set of all models of formula f. For every formulas* $f, g \in AS$, *an entailment relation is defined as "f entails g" iff* $M(f) \subseteq M(g)$.

The entailment relation is never used formally in this paper, but we believe it provides a good intuition for the frequent usage in proofs of the inclusion of sets of models.

The formulas define the language of the logic, the semantics defines its interpretation, and an *implementation* defines how the logic implements an *interface* that is common to all logics. This common interface includes a deduction relation, a conjunction, a disjunction, a tautology, and a contradiction.

Definition 3 (Implementation) *Given a syntax AS and a symbol* $'undef' \notin AS$, *an implementation P based on AS is a 5-tuple* $(\sqsubseteq, \sqcap, \sqcup, \top, \bot)$, *where*

- $\sqsubseteq \ \in \mathcal{P}(AS \times AS)$ *is the* deduction relation,
- $\sqcap, \sqcup \in AS \times AS \to AS \cup \{undef\}$ *are the* conjunction *and the* disjunction,
- $\top, \bot \in AS \cup \{undef\}$ *are the* tautology *and the* contradiction.

Operations $\sqsubseteq$, $\sqcap$, $\sqcup$, $\top$, $\bot$ are all defined on the syntax of some logic, though they are not necessarily connectives of the logic, simply because the connectives of a logic may be different from these operations. Similarly, the syntax and the semantics may define quantifiers, though they are absent from the interface.

Note that this common interface can be implemented partially (by using *undef*) if it is convenient. Because the interface is the same for every logic, generic logic-based systems can be designed easily.

Definition 4 (Logic) *A logic L is a triple* (AS_L, S_L, P_L), *where AS_L is (the abstract syntax of) a set of formulas, S_L is a semantics based on AS_L, and P_L is an implementation based on AS_L.*

When necessary, the satisfaction relation $\models$ of a logic L will be written $\models_L$, the interpretation domain I will be written I_L, the models $M(f)$ will be written $M_L(f)$, and each operation op will be written op_L.

In object oriented terms, this forms a class $\mathbb{L}$, which comprises a slot for the type of an internal representation, and several methods for a deduction relation, a conjunction, a disjunction, a tautology, and a contradiction. A logic L is simply an instance of this class.

Definition 3 shows that operations $\sqcap$, $\sqcup$ can be partially defined, and that operations $\top$, $\bot$ can be undefined.

Definition 5 (Total/partial, bounded/unbounded) *A logic is* partial *if either operations $\sqcap$ or $\sqcup$ or both are partially defined. It is* unbounded *if either operations $\top$ or $\bot$ or both is undefined.*

In the opposite case, a logic is respectively called total *and* bounded.

When necessary, we make it precise for which operation a logic is total/partial.

Total logics are usually preferred, because they make applications simpler. Indeed, they do not have to test for *undef*. Section 4.2 shows that the propositional logic functor applied to a partial logic always constructs a total logic.

There is no constraint, except for their types, on what $\sqsubseteq$, $\sqcap$, $\sqcup$, $\top$, $\bot$ can be. So, we define a notion of *consistency* and *completeness* that relates the semantics and the implementation of a logic. These notions are defined respectively for each operation of an implementation, and only for the defined part of them.

Definition 6 (Completeness/consistency) *Let L be a logic. An implementation P_L is* consistent *(resp.* complete*) in operation $op \in \{\sqsubseteq, \top, \bot, \sqcap, \sqcup\}$ w.r.t. a semantics S_L iff for all $f, g \in AS_L$*

- $(op = \sqsubseteq)$ $f \sqsubseteq g \Longrightarrow M_L(f) \subseteq M_L(g)$ *(resp. $M_L(f) \subseteq M_L(g) \Longrightarrow f \sqsubseteq g$),*
- $(op = \top)$ $\top$ *is defined $\Longrightarrow$ always consistent (resp. $M_L(\top) = I$),*
- $(op = \bot)$ $\bot$ *is defined $\Longrightarrow M_L(\bot) = \emptyset$ (resp. always complete),*
- $(op = \sqcap)$ $f \sqcap g$ *is defined $\Longrightarrow M_L(f \sqcap g) \subseteq M_L(f) \cap M_L(g)$*
  (resp. $f \sqcap g$ is defined $\Longrightarrow M_L(f \sqcap g) \supseteq M_L(f) \cap M_L(g)$),
- $(op = \sqcup)$ $f \sqcup g$ *is defined $\Longrightarrow M_L(f \sqcup g) \subseteq M_L(f) \cup M_L(g)$*
  (resp. $f \sqcup g$ is defined $\Longrightarrow M_L(f \sqcup g) \supseteq M_L(f) \cup M_L(g)$).

We say that an implementation is consistent *(resp.* complete*) iff it is consistent (resp. complete) in the five operations. We abbreviate "P_L is complete/consistent in op w.r.t. S_L" in "op_L is complete/consistent".*

Note that it is easy to make an implementation consistent and complete for the last four operations $\sqcap$, $\sqcup$, $\top$, $\bot$, by keeping them undefined, but then the implementation is of little use. Note also that a consistent $\sqsubseteq$ can always be extended into a partial order because it is contained in $\subseteq$.

In general, consistent and complete logics are preferred to ensure matching between the expected answers, specified by the semantics, and actual answers, specified by the implementation. Thus, in these preferred logics deduction can be extended into a partial order. However, some logics defined on concrete domains are not complete. An important issue is how to build complete logics with components that are not complete.

We must add to the five operations of an implementation, a parser and a printer for handling the concrete syntax of formulas. Indeed, an application should input and output formulas in a readable format. However, we do not consider them further, because they do not determine any logical problem. On the contrary, the five logical operations (deduction, conjunction, disjunction, tautology, and contradiction) are at the core of the logics we consider.

3.2   Logic Functors

Logic functors also have a syntax, a semantics, and an implementation, but they are all abstracted over one or more logics that are considered as formal parameters. We formally define the class of logic functors as structures. Section 4 and Appendix B presents examples of logic functors.

Given $\mathbb{L}$ the class of logics, logic functors are functions of type $\mathbb{L}^n \to \mathbb{L}$. In object oriented terms, this defines a *template* $\mathbb{F}$. For reasons of uniformity, logics are considered as logic functors with arity 0 (a.k.a. atomic functors, or nullary logic functors).

Let $\mathbb{AS}$ be the class of all syntaxes, $\mathbb{S}$ be the class of all semantics, and $\mathbb{P}$ be the class of all implementations. The syntax of a logic functor is simply a function from the syntaxes of the logics which are its arguments, to the syntax of the resulting logic.

Definition 7 (Logic functor) *A logic functor F is a triple (AS_F, S_F, P_F) where*

- *the abstract syntax AS_F is a function of type $\mathbb{AS}^n \to \mathbb{AS}$, such that $AS_{F(L_1,..,L_n)} = AS_F(AS_{L_1}, .., AS_{L_n})$;*
- *the semantics S_F is a function of type $\mathbb{S}^n \to \mathbb{S}$, such that $S_{F(L_1,..,L_n)} = S_F(S_{L_1}, .., S_{L_n})$;*
- *the implementation P_F is a function of type $\mathbb{P}^n \to \mathbb{P}$, such that $P_{F(L_1,..,L_n)} = P_F(P_{L_1}, .., P_{L_n})$.*

A logic functor in itself is neither partial or total, unbounded or bounded, complete or uncomplete, nor consistent or inconsistent. It is the logics that are built with a logic functor that can be qualified this way. However, it is possible to state that if a logic L has some property, then $F(L)$ has some other property. In the following, the definition of every new logic functor is accompanied with theorems stating under which conditions the resulting logic is total, consistent, or complete.

These theorems have all the form *hypothesis on L $\Rightarrow$ conclusion on $F(L)$*. We consider them as type assignments, F : *hypothesis $\to$ conclusion*. Similarly, totality/consistency/completeness properties on logics are considered as type assignments, L : *properties*, so that proving that $F(L)$ has some property regarding totality, consistency, or completeness, is simply to type-check it.

4   Composition of Logic Functors

We define a nullary logic functor and a propositional unary logic functor, and we observe that completeness may not propagate well when we compose them. We introduce a new property, called *reducedness*, that helps completeness propagate via composition of logic functors. From now on, the definitions are definitions of instances of $\mathbb{L}$ or $\mathbb{F}$.

4.1   Atoms

One of the most simple logic we can imagine is the logic of unrelated atoms *atom*. These atoms usually play the role of atomic formulas in most of known logics: propositional, first-order, description, etc.

Definition 8 (Syntax) AS_{atom} *is a set of atom names.*

Definition 9 (Semantics) S_{atom} *is* $(I, \models)$ *where* $I = \mathcal{P}(AS_{atom})$ *and* $i \models a$ *iff* $a \in i$.

The implementation reflects the fact that the atoms being unrelated they form an anti-chain for the deduction relation (a set where no pair of elements can be ordered).

Definition 10 (Implementation) P_{atom} *is* $(\sqsubseteq, \sqcap, \sqcup, \top, \bot)$ *where for every* $a, b \in AS_{atom}$
- $a \sqsubseteq b$ *iff* $a = b$
- $a \sqcap b = a \sqcup b = \begin{cases} a & \text{if } a = b \\ \text{undef} & \text{otherwise} \end{cases}$
- $\top$ *and* $\bot$ *are undefined.*

Theorem 11 (Completeness/consistency) P_{atom} *is consistent and complete in* $\sqsubseteq$, $\top$, $\bot$, $\sqcap$, $\sqcup$ *w.r.t.* S_{atom}.

In summary, P_{atom} is not bounded and is partial in both conjunction and disjunction, but it is consistent and complete w.r.t. S_{atom}.

4.2   Propositional Logic Abstracted over Atoms

Let us assume that we use a logic as a description/querying language. Since it is almost always the case that we want to express conjunction, disjunction, and negation, the choice of propositional logic is natural. For instance, the / used to separate description fields in the bibliographical application (see Section 2) can be interpreted as conjunction. Similarly, disjunction and negation could be used, especially to express information like "published in 1908 or 1985". Propositional logic, *Prop*, is defined by taking a set of *atoms A*, and by forming a set of propositional formulas *Prop(A)* by the closure of *A* for the three boolean connectives, $\wedge$, $\vee$, and $\neg$: the *boolean closure*.

Prop is usually considered as a free boolean algebra, since there is no relation between atoms, i.e., they are all pairwise incomparable for the deduction order. However in applications, atoms are often comparable. For instance, boolean queries based on string matching use atoms whose meaning is *contains s, is s, begins with s,* and *ends with s* where *s* is a character string. In this example, the atom *is* `"The Jungle Book"` implies *ends with* `"Jungle Book"`, which implies *contains* `"Jungle"`.

This leads to considering the boolean closure as a logic functor *prop*. So doing, the atoms can come from another logic where they have been endowed with a deduction order.

Definition 12 (Syntax) *The syntax AS_{prop} of the logic functor prop maps the syntax AS_A of a logic of atoms A to its syntactic closure by the operators $\land$, $\lor$, and the operator $\neg$.*

The interpretation of these operators is that of the connectives with the same names. It is defined by induction on the structure of the formulas. For atomic formulas of $AS_{prop(A)}$ (i.e., AS_A) the semantics is the same as in the logic A.

Definition 13 (Semantics) S_{prop} *is* $(I_A, \models_A) \mapsto (I_A, \models)$ *such that*

$$i \models f \ \textit{iff} \ \begin{cases} i \models_A f & \textit{if } f \in AS_A \\ i \not\models f_1 & \textit{if } f = \neg f_1 \\ i \models f_1 \ \textit{and } i \models f_2 & \textit{if } f = f_1 \land f_2 \\ i \models f_1 \ \textit{or } i \models f_2 & \textit{if } f = f_1 \lor f_2. \end{cases}$$

Definition 14 (Implementation) P_{prop} *is* $(\sqsubseteq_A, \sqcap_A, \sqcup_A, \top_A, \bot_A) \mapsto (\sqsubseteq, \sqcap, \sqcup, \top, \bot)$ *such that*

- $f \sqsubseteq g$ *is true iff there exists a proof of the sequent $\vdash \neg f \lor g$ in the sequent calculus of Table 1 (inspired from leanTAP [BP95,Fit98]).*
  In the rules, Δ is always a set of literals (i.e., atomic formulas or negations of atomic formulas), Γ is a sequence of propositions, L is a literal, X is a proposition, β is the disjunction of β_1 and β_2, α is the conjunction of α_1 and α_2, and $\overline{L}$ denotes the negation of L ($\overline{a} := \neg a$ and $\overline{\neg a} := a$).
- $f \sqcap g = f \land g$,
- $f \sqcup g = f \lor g$,
- $\top = a \lor \neg a$, *for any* $a \in AS_A$,
- $\bot = a \land \neg a$, *for any* $a \in AS_A$.

Rules $\top$-Axiom, $\bot$-Axiom, $\sqsubseteq$-Axiom, $\sqcap$-Rule, and $\sqcup$-Rule play the role of the ordinary axiom rule. The first two axioms are variants of the third one when either a or b is missing. Rules $\sqcap$-Rule, and $\sqcup$-Rule interpret the propositional connectives in the logic of atoms.

Note that the logic has a connective $\neg$, but its implementation has no corresponding operation. However, the deduction relation takes care of it. This is

Table 1. Sequent calculus for deduction in propositional logic.

$\top$-Axiom: $\qquad \neg b, \Delta \vdash \Gamma \qquad$ if $\top_A$ is defined and $\top_A \sqsubseteq_A b$

$\bot$-Axiom: $\qquad a, \Delta \vdash \Gamma \qquad$ if $\bot_A$ is defined and $a \sqsubseteq_A \bot_A$

$\sqsubseteq$-Axiom: $\qquad a, \neg b, \Delta \vdash \Gamma \qquad$ if $a \sqsubseteq_A b$

$\sqcap$-Rule: $\qquad \dfrac{a \sqcap_A b, \Delta \vdash \Gamma}{a, b, \Delta \vdash \Gamma} \qquad$ if $a \sqcap_A b$ is defined

$\sqcup$-Rule: $\qquad \dfrac{\neg(a \sqcup_A b), \Delta \vdash \Gamma}{\neg a, \neg b, \Delta \vdash \Gamma} \qquad$ if $a \sqcup_A b$ is defined

$\neg\neg$-Rule: $\qquad \dfrac{\Delta \vdash X, \Gamma}{\Delta \vdash \neg\neg X, \Gamma} \qquad\qquad$ literal-Rule: $\dfrac{\overline{L}, \Delta \vdash \Gamma}{\Delta \vdash L, \Gamma}$

β-Rule: $\qquad \dfrac{\Delta \vdash \beta_1, \beta_2, \Gamma}{\Delta \vdash \beta, \Gamma} \qquad\qquad$ α-Rule: $\dfrac{\Delta \vdash \alpha_1, \Gamma \qquad \Delta \vdash \alpha_2, \Gamma}{\Delta \vdash \alpha, \Gamma}$

an example of how more connectives or quantifiers can be defined in a logic or a logic functor, though the interface does not refer to them. A logic functor for the predicate calculus could be defined in the same way, but since this theory is not decidable, the resulting logic functor would be of little use to form embeddable logic components. Instead of the full predicate calculus, it would be better to define a logic functor for a decidable fragment of it, like the fragments in the family of description logics [DLNS96].

Definition 15 (Validity) *A sequent $\Delta \vdash \Gamma$ is called* valid *in $S_{prop(A)}$ iff it is* true *for every interpretation. It is* true *for an interpretation $i \in I$ iff there is an element in Δ that is false for i, or there is an element in Γ that is true for i.*

Lemma 16 *A sequent $\Delta \vdash \Gamma$ is valid in $S_{prop(A)}$ iff $\bigcap_{\delta \in \Delta} M(\delta) \subseteq \bigcup_{\gamma \in I} M(\gamma)$.*

4.3 Properties of *prop(A)*

We present the properties of $prop(A)$ w.r.t. the properties of A.

Theorem 17 (Consistency) $P_{prop(A)}$ *is consistent in $\sqsubseteq, \top, \bot, \sqcap, \sqcup$ w.r.t. $S_{prop(A)}$ if P_A is consistent in $\sqsubseteq, \bot, \sqcup$ and complete in $\top, \sqcap$ w.r.t. S_A.*

There is no such lemma for completeness. In fact, the logic of atoms is not necessarily total, and thus not all sequent $a_1, a_2, \Delta \vdash \Gamma$ can be interpreted as $a_1 \sqcap_A a_2, \Delta \vdash \Gamma$. So, there is a risk of incompleteness.

For instance, imagine 3 atoms a_1, a_2, b such that $M(a_1) \cap M(a_2) \subseteq M(b)$, and $M(a_i) \neq \emptyset$, $M(b) \neq I$, and $M(a_i) \not\subseteq M(b)$. If the implementation is complete, then the sequent $a_1, a_2, \neg b \vdash$ should be provable. However, if the logic of atoms is only partial, the conjunction $a_1 \sqcap_A a_2$ may not be defined, and rule $\sqcap$-Rule does not apply. In this case, the sequent would not be provable. One can build a similar example for disjunction.

5 Reducedness

5.1 Formal Presentation

We define a property of an atomic logic A, which is distinct from completeness, is relative to the definedness of the logic operations, and helps in ensuring the completeness of $prop(A)$.

Definition 18 (Openness) *A sequent $\Delta \vdash \Gamma$ is called* open *in $P_{prop(A)}$ iff it is the conclusion of no deduction rule, and it is not an axiom. Otherwise, it is called* closed.

An open sequent is a node of a proof tree that cannot be developed further, but is not an axiom. In short, it is a failure in a branch of a proof search.

Lemma 19 *A sequent $\Delta \vdash \Gamma$ is open according to implementation P_A iff*

- Γ *is empty*,
- $\forall a \in \Delta : a \not\sqsubseteq_A \perp_A$ *(when $\perp_A$ is defined)*,
- $\forall \neg b \in \Delta : \top_A \not\sqsubseteq_A b$ *(when $\top_A$ is defined)*,
- $\forall a, \neg b \in \Delta : a \not\sqsubseteq_A b$,
- $\forall a \neq b \in \Delta : a \sqcap_A b$ *is undefined*,
- $\forall \neg a \neq \neg b \in \Delta : a \sqcup_A b$ *is undefined*.

So, an open sequent $\Delta \vdash \Gamma$ can be characterized by a pair (A, B), where $A \subseteq AS_A$ is the set of positive literals of Δ, and $B \subseteq AS_A$ is the set of negative literals of Δ (let us recall that Γ is empty). The advantage of noting open sequents by such a pair is that they are then properly expressed in terms of the logic of atoms.

Incompleteness arises when an open sequent is valid; the proof cannot be developed further though the semantics tells the sequent is true.

Lemma 20 *An open sequent (A, B) is valid in the atom semantics S_A iff $\bigcap_{a \in A} M_A(a) \subseteq \bigcup_{b \in B} M_A(b)$.*

Definition 21 (Validity) *A family of open sequents $((A_i, B_i))_{i \in I}$ is valid in atom semantics S_A iff every open sequent (A_i, B_i) is valid in S_A.*

Definition 22 (Reducedness) *An implementation P_A is reduced on a set F of open sequent families, w.r.t. a semantics S_A, iff every non-empty family of F is not valid.*

Theorem 23 (Completeness) *$P_{prop(A)}$ is complete in $\sqsubseteq$ on a subset of pairs of formulas $\Pi \subseteq AS_{prop(A)} \times AS_{prop(A)}$, w.r.t. $S_{prop(A)}$, if $\sqcap_A$ is consistent and $\sqcup_A$ is complete, and P_A is reduced on open sequent families of all $f \vee \neg g$ formula proof trees (where $(f, g) \in \Pi$) w.r.t. S_A. It is also complete in $\top, \perp, \sqcap, \sqcup$ w.r.t. $S_{prop(A)}$.*

Theorem 23 is somewhat complicated to allow the proof of completeness on a subset of $prop(A)$. In some logics, it is possible to show that every open sequent is not valid. Then every non empty open sequent family is not valid, and so, atom implementation P_A is reduced on every set of open sequent families. In such a case, we merely say that P_A is *reduced* w.r.t. S_A.

5.2   Application to *prop(atom)*

The following lemma shows that the nullary logic functor *atom* is reduced. So, the implementation of logic *prop(atom)* is complete.

Lemma 24 (Reducedness) P_{atom} *is reduced w.r.t.* S_{atom}.

Corollary 25 $P_{prop(atom)}$ *is totally defined, and complete and consistent w.r.t.* $S_{prop(atom)}$.

5.3   Discussion

All this leads to the following methodology. Nullary logic functors are defined for tackling concrete domains like intervals and strings. They must be designed carefully, so that they are consistent and complete, and reduced. More sophisticated logics can also be built using non-nullary logic functors (e.g., see Appendix B). Then, they can be composed with logic functor *prop* in order to form a total, consistent and complete logic. The resulting logic is also reduced because any total, consistent and complete logic is trivially reduced. Furthermore, its implementation forms a lattice because totality, consistency and completeness make the operations of the implementation isomorphic to set operations on the models.

Reducedness formalizes the informal notion of an implementation being defined enough. Thus, it seems that it is useful to define it as a coherence relation between the semantics and the implementation, *via* a notion of maximaly defined implementation.

Definition 26 (Maximal definedness) *An implementation* $(\sqsubseteq, \sqcap, \sqcup, \top, \bot)$ *is maximally defined w.r.t. a semantics* $(I, \models)$ *iff*

- $\forall f, g : \forall h : M(h) = M(f) \cap M(g) \Rightarrow f \sqcap g = h$
- $\forall f, g : \forall h : M(h) = M(f) \cup M(g) \Rightarrow f \sqcup g = h$
- $\forall h : M(h) \supseteq I \Rightarrow h \sqsupseteq \top$
- $\forall h : M(h) \subseteq \emptyset \Rightarrow h \sqsubseteq \bot$
- $\forall h : M(h) \subseteq M(g) \Rightarrow h \sqsubseteq g$

An implementation obeying this definition would be consistent, and complete, and it seems it would be reduced.

However, it is more subtle than that. Reducedness is more fundamentaly a property of the semantics itself. One can build atomic logic functors whose semantics is such that no definition of its implementation makes it reduced. In fact, the problem comes when intersection of models can be empty and no formula has an empty model. Note that in logic *atom* no intersection of models can be empty.

We will describe more nullary reduced logic functors in Appendix A, and more n-ary logic functors Appendix B.

6   Conclusion

We propose *logic functors* to construct logics that are used very concretely in logic-based applications. This makes the development of logic-based systems safer and more efficient because the constructed logic can be *compiled* to produce a fully automatic theorem prover. We have listed a number of logic functors, but many others can be built.

6.1   Related Works

Our use of the word *functor* is similar to ML's one for designating *parameterized modules* [Mac88]. However, our logic functors are very specialized contrary to functors in ML which are general purpose (in short, we have fixed the signature), and they carry a semantic component. Both the specialization and the semantic component allow us to express composition conditions that are out of the scope of ML functors. We could have implemented logic functors in a programming language that offers ML-like functors, but we did not so, mainly for the sake of compatibility with the rest of our application that was already written in λProlog.

The theory of *institutions* [GB92] shares our concern for *customized logics*, and also uses the word *functor*. However, the focus and theoretical ground are different. Institutions focus on the relation between notations and semantics, whereas we focus on the relation between semantics and implementations. In fact, the implementation class $\mathbb{P}$ is necessary for us to enforce *embeddability*. We consider the notation problem in the printing and parsing operations of an implementation. The theory of institutions is developed using category theory and in that theory there are functors from signatures to formulas, from signatures to models, and from institutions to institutions. Our logic functors correspond to parameterized institutions.

An important work which shares our motivations is LeanTAP [BP95,BP96]. The authors of LeanTAP have also recognized the need for embedding customized logics in applications, and the need for offering the Application Designer some means to design a correct logic subsystem. To this end, they propose a very concise style of theorem proving, which they call *lean theorem proving*, and they claim that a theorem prover written in this style is so concise that it is very easy to modify it in order to accomodate a different logic. And indeed, they have proposed a theorem prover for first-order logic, and several variants of it for modal logic, etc. Note that the first-order theorem prover is less than 20 clauses of Prolog. We think that their claim does not take into account the fact that the System Programmer and the Application Designer are really different Actors. There is no doubt that modifying their first-order theorem prover was easy for these authors, but we also think it could have been undertaken by few others. A hint for this is that it takes a full journal article to revisit and justify the first-order lean theorem prover [Fit98]. So, we think lean theorem proving is an interesting technology, and we have used it to define logic functor *prop*, but it does not actually permit the Application Designer to build a customized logic.

Our main concern is to make sure that logic functors can be composed in a way that preserves their logical properties. This led us to define technical properties that simply tell us how logic functors behave: total/partial, consistent/complete, and reduced/unreduced. This concern is complementary to the concern of actually implementing customized logics, e.g., in logical frameworks like Isabelle [Pau94], Edinburgh LF [HHP93], or Open Mechanized Reasoning Systems [GPT96], or even using a programming language. These frameworks allow users to implement a customized logic, but do not help users in proving the completeness and consistency of the resulting theorem prover. Note that one must not be left with the impression that these frameworks do not help at all. For instance, axiomatic types classes have been introduced in Isabelle [Wen97] in order to permit automatic admissibility check. Another observation is that these frameworks mostly offer environments for interactive theorem proving, which is incompatible with the objective of building fully automatic embeddable logic components. Note finally that our implementation is written in λProlog, which is sometimes considered as a logical framework.

In essence, our work is more similar to works on static program analysis toolbox (e.g., PAG [AM95]) where authors assemble known results of lattice theory to combine domain operators like product, sets of, and lists in order to build abstract domains and derive automatically a fixed-point solver for these domains. The fact that in the most favourable cases (e.g., $prop(A)$), our deduction relations form (partial) lattices is another connection with these works. However, our framework is more flexible because it permits to build lattices from domains that are not lattices. In particular, logic functor $prop$ acts as a lattice completion operator on every other reduced logic. Moreover, we believe that non-lattice logics like $interv$ (see Appendix A.1) can be of interest for program analysis.

Figure 1 summaries our analysis of these related works. The dark shade of System Programmer task is essentially to implement a Turing-complete programming language (recall that Actors are roles not single persons). The light shade of System Programmer task is to implement a very specific programming language for one Application Designer task. In this respect, we should have mentionned the studies on Domain Specific Languages (DSL) as related works, but we know no example of a DSL with similar aims. Note also that what remains of the task of the Application Designer is more rightly called *gluing* than *programming* when the System Programmer has gone far enough in the Application Designer's direction.

6.2   Summary of Results and Further Works

Our logic functors specify logical "components off-the-shelf" (COTS). As such, the way they behave w.r.t. composition is defined for every logic functor.

The principle of composing logic functors has been implemented in a prototype. It includes a logic composer that reads logic specifications such as $sum(prop(atom), prop(interv))$ (sums of propositions on atoms and propositions on intervals) and automatically produces a printer, a parser, and a theorem

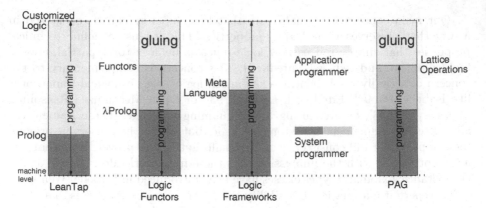

Fig. 1. Several related works and the respective tasks of the System Programmer and the Application Designer

prover. The theorem prover is built by instantiating the theorem prover associated to each logic functor at every occurrence where it is used. The logic composer, each logic functor implementation, and the resulting implementations are written in λProlog.

Our paper suggests a software architecture for logic-based systems, in which the system is generic in the logic, and the logic component can be separately defined, and plugged in when needed. We have realized a prototype Logical Information System along these lines [FR00b].

Coming back to the bibliography example of the introduction, we construct a dedicated logic with logic functors defined in this article:

$$prop(aik(prop(sum(atom, valattr(sum(interv, string)))))).$$

According to results of this article, the composition of these logic functors is such that the generated implementation is total, bounded, and consistent and complete in all five operations of the implementation. It allows to build descriptions and queries such as

```
descr(entry₁) =
   [author: is "Kipling" ∧ title: is "The Jungle Book" ∧
   paper-back ∧  publisher: is "Penguin" ∧ year: 1985],
query =
   title: contains "Jungle" ∧ year: 1950.. ∧
   (paper-back ∨ hard-cover).
```

Note that $entry_1$ is a possible answer to the query because

$$descr(entry_1) \sqsubseteq_{prop(aik(prop(sum(atom,valattr(sum(interv,string))))))} query,$$

which is automatically proved using the generated implementation.

We plan to validate the use of logic functors within the Logical Information System. This application will also motivate the study of other logic functors like, e.g., modalities or taxonomies, because they are useful for making queries and answers more compact.

Another possible extension of this work is to vary the type of logic functors and their composition. In the present situation, all logic functors have type $\mathbb{L}^n \to \mathbb{L}$. It means that the only possibility is to choose the atomic formulas of a logic. However, one may wish to act on the interpretation domain, or on the quantification domain. So, one may want to have a class $\mathbb{D}$ of domains, and logic functors that take a domain as argument, e.g., $\mathbb{D} \to \mathbb{L}$. At a similar level, one may wish to act on the interface, either to pass new operations through it, e.g., negation or quantification, or to pass new structures, e.g., specific sets of models. The extension to higher-order logic functors, e.g., $(\mathbb{L} \to \mathbb{L}) \to \mathbb{L}$, would make it possible to define a fixed-point logic functor, μ, with which we could construct a logic as $L = \mu F$ where F is a unary logic functor.

Finally, we plan to develop new logic functors for the purpose of program analysis. For instance, in [RBM99,RB01] we have proposed to combine the domain of boolean values with the domain of types to form a logic of positive functions that extends the well-known domain *Pos* [CSS99]. We called this *typed analysis*. The neat result is to compute at the same time the properties of groundness and of properness [O'K90]. Our project is to define logic functors for every type constructors, and to combine them according to the types inferred/checked in the programs (e.g., *list(list(bool))*, where *bool* is simply $\{true, false\}$). This will make it possible to redo what we have done on typed analysis, but also to explore new static analysis domains by combining the logic functors for types with other nullary logic functors than *bool*.

Acknowledgements. We are pleased to acknowledge the careful reading of this article by Alberto Pettorossi. Remaining mistakes are ours.

References

[AM95]   M. Alt and F. Martin. Generation of efficient interprocedural analyzers with PAG. In *Static Analysis Symp.*, LNCS 983, pages 33–50, 1995.

[AMSS98] T. Armstrong, K. Marriott, P. Schachte, and H. Søndergaard. Two classes of boolean functions for dependency analysis. *Science of Computer Programming*, 31:3–45, 1998.

[BP95]   B. Beckert and J. Posegga. leanT^AP: Lean, tableau-based deduction. *J. Automated Reasoning*, 11(1):43–81, 1995.

[BP96]   B. Beckert and J. Posegga. Logic programming as a basis for lean automated deduction. *J. Logic Programming*, 28(3):231–236, 1996.

[CSS99]   M. Codish, H. Søndergaard, and P.J. Stuckey. Sharing and groundness dependencies in logic programs. *ACM TOPLAS*, 21(5):948–976, 1999.

[DLNS96] F. Donini, M. Lenzerini, D. Nardi, and A. Schaerf. Reasoning in description logics. In G. Brewka, editor, *Principles of Knowledge Representation and Reasoning*, Studies in Logic, Language and Information, pages 193–238. CLSI Publications, 1996.

[Fit98]   M. Fitting. leanTAP revisited. *Journal of Logic and Computation*, 8(1):33–47, February 1998.

[FR00a]   S. Ferré and O. Ridoux. A file system based on concept analysis. In Y. Sagiv, editor, *Int. Conf. Rules and Objects in Databases*, LNCS 1861, pages 1033–1047. Springer, 2000.

[FR00b]   S. Ferré and O. Ridoux. A logical generalization of formal concept analysis. In G. Mineau and B. Ganter, editors, *Int. Conf. Conceptual Structures*, LNCS 1867, pages 371–384. Springer, 2000.

[FR01]   S. Ferré and O. Ridoux. Searching for objects and properties with logical concept analysis. In H. S. Delugach and G. Stumme, editors, *Int. Conf. Conceptual Structures*, LNCS 2120, pages 187–201. Springer, 2001.

[FR02]   S. Ferré and O. Ridoux. Logic functors: a framework for developing embeddable customized logics. Rapport de recherche 4457, INRIA, 2002.

[GB92]   J.A. Goguen and R.M. Burstall. Institutions: Abstract model theory for specification and programming. *J. ACM*, 39(1):95–146, 1992.

[GPT96]   F. Giunchiglia, P. Pecchiari, and C. Talcott. Reasoning theories - towards an architecture for open mechanized reasoning systems. In F. Baader and K. U. Schulz, editors, *1st Int. Workshop: Frontiers of Combining Systems*, pages 157–174. Kluwer Academic Publishers, March 1996.

[GW99]   B. Ganter and R. Wille. *Formal Concept Analysis — Mathematical Foundations*. Springer, 1999.

[HHP93]   R. Harper, F. Honsell, and G. Plotkin. A framework for defining logics. *JACM*, 40(1):143–184, January 1993.

[IB96]   V. Issarny and Ch. Bidan. Aster: A framework for sound customization of distributed runtime systems. In *16th Int. Conf. Distributed Computing Systems*, 1996.

[Lev90]   H. Levesque. All I know: a study in autoepistemic logic. *Artificial Intelligence*, 42(2), March 1990.

[Llo87]   J.W. Lloyd. *Foundations of Logic Programming*. Symbolic computation — Artificial Intelligence. Springer, Berlin, 1987.

[Mac88]   D.B. MacQueen. An implementation of Standard ML modules. In *LISP and Functional Programming*, pages 212–223, 1988.

[MS98]   K. Marriott and P.J. Stuckey. *Programming with Constraints: An Introduction*. The MIT Press, 1998.

[O'K90]   R.A. O'Keefe. *The Craft of Prolog*. MIT Press, 1990.

[Pau94]   L. C. Paulson. *Isabelle: a generic theorem prover*. LNCS 828. Springer, New York, NY, USA, 1994.

[Poo88]   D. Poole. Representing knowledge for logic-based diagnosis. In *Int. Conf. Fifth Generation Computer Systems*, pages 1282–1290. Springer, 1988.

[RB01]   O. Ridoux and P. Boizumault. Typed static analysis: Application to the groundness analysis of typed prolog. *Journal of Functional and Logic Programming*, 2001(4), 2001.

[RBM99]   O. Ridoux, P. Boizumault, and F. Malésieux. Typed static analysis: Application to groundness analysis of Prolog and λProlog. In *Fuji Int. Symp. Functional and Logic Programming*, pages 267–283, 1999.

[SFRW98]   M. Sagiv, N. Francez, M. Rodeh, and R. Wilhelm. A logic-based approach to program flow analysis. *Acta Informatica*, 35(6):457–504, June 1998.

[SM83]   G. Salton and M. J. McGill. *Introduction to Modern Information Retrieval*. McGraw-Hill, 1983.

[vRCL98] C.J. van Rijsbergen, F. Crestani, and M. Lalmas, editors. *Information Retrieval: Uncertainty and Logics. Advanced models for the representation and retrieval of information.* Kluwer Academic Publishing, Dordrecht, NL, 1998.

[Wen97] M. Wenzel. Type classes and overloading in higher-order logic. In E.L. Gunter and A. Felty, editors, *Theorem proving in higher-order logics, LNCS 1275*, pages 307–322. Springer-Verlag, 1997.

A More Nullary Reduced Logic Functors

Ad-hoc logics are often designed for representing concrete observations on a domain. They serve as a language to write atomic formulas. In the bibliographical application atomic formulas could be *between* 1900 *and* 1910 or *contains* "Kipling". In order to serve as arguments to the logic functor *prop* (or other similar boolean logic functors if available), they must be equipped with a "natural" conjunction and "natural" disjunction, i.e., they must be consistent and complete (cf. Definition 6). However, these operations can usually be only partially defined. For instance, the "natural" disjunction of two intervals is only defined if the intervals overlap.

By definition, applying the logic functor *prop* to such an atomic logic produces a logic that is always total and bounded (Definition 14). It also provides a consistent and complete implementation if the atom logic also has a consistent, complete, and reduced implementation (Lemmas 17 and 23).

So, for every nullary logic functor presented in this section, we prove that its implementation is consistent, complete, and reduced w.r.t. its semantics.

A.1 Intervals

Intervals are often used to express incomplete knowledge either in the database or in the queries. For instance, in the bibliographical application, `year: 1900..1910` may express an interval of dates between 1900 and 1910. We can also express open intervals such that `year: ..1910`, which means "before 1910".

Definition 27 (Syntax) $AS_{interv} = \{[x,y] \mid x,y \in \mathbb{R} \uplus \{-,+\}\}$.

The symbol $-$ denotes the negative infinity (smaller than any real number), and the symbol $+$ denotes the positive infinity (greater than any real number). So, $\mathbb{R} \uplus \{-,+\}$ is a totally ordered set bounded by $-$ and $+$.

Definition 28 (Semantics) S_{interv} is $(I, \models)$ where $I = \mathbb{R}$ and $i \models [x,y] \iff x \leq i \leq y$.

For simplifying further proofs it should be noted that models of interval formulas are intervals of the real numbers. In particular, $M_{interv}([+,-]) = \emptyset$.

Property 29 $M_{interv}(f) = $ interval f (recall that formulas are only syntax, so "interval f" is the interval ordinarily written f).

Definition 30 (Implementation) P_{interv} is $(\sqsubseteq, \sqcap, \sqcup, \top, \bot)$ where for every $[x_1, y_1], [x_2, y_2] \in AS_{interv}$

- $[x_1, y_1] \sqsubseteq [x_2, y_2]$ iff $x_2 \leq x_1$ and $y_1 \leq y_2$,
- $[x_1, y_1] \sqcap [x_2, y_2] = [\max(x_1, x_2), \min(y_1, y_2)]$,
- $[x_1, y_1] \sqcup [x_2, y_2] = \begin{cases} [\min(x_1, x_2), \max(y_1, y_2)] & \text{if } x_2 \leq y_1 \text{ and } x_1 \leq y_2 \\ undef & otherwise \end{cases}$,
- $\top = [-, +]$,
- $\bot = [+, -]$.

Note that conjunction is defined for every pair of intervals, but disjunction is only defined for pairs of overlapping intervals.

Theorem 31 (Completeness/consistency) P_{interv} is consistent and complete in $\sqsubseteq, \top, \bot, \sqcap, \sqcup$ w.r.t. S_{interv}.

P_{interv} is partial in disjunction, but it is consistent and complete. Furthermore, the following lemma shows that it is reduced, and so, it can serve as argument of the logic functor *prop*.

Lemma 32 (Reducedness) P_{interv} is reduced w.r.t. S_{interv}.

A.2 Strings

Often, descriptions and queries contain string specifications, like *is*, *start with* and *contains*. Moreover, these specification can be ordered by an entailment relation. For instance, the atom *is* "The Jungle Book" entails *ends with* "Jungle Book", which entails *contains* "Jungle".

Definition 33 (Syntax) $AS_{string} = {}^{\wedge 0|1} \Sigma^* \$^{0|1} \uplus \{\#\}$, where Σ is some (infinite) signature such that $\{\wedge, \$, \#\} \cap \Sigma = \emptyset$.

The optional symbol $\wedge$ denotes the beginning of a string; it is the left bound of a string. The optional symbol $\$$ denotes the end of a string; it is the right bound of a string. So, "*contains s*" is written s, "*starts with s*" is written $\hat{}s$, and *is s* is written $\hat{}s\$$. The symbol $\#$ denotes the empty language (matched by no string).

Definition 34 (Semantics) S_{string} is $(I, \models)$ where $I = {}^{\wedge}\Sigma^*\$$ and $i \models f \iff i = \alpha f \beta$.

So, models are made of complete strings. More precisely,

Property 35 $M_{string}(f)$ is ${}^{\wedge}\Sigma^* f \Sigma^*\$$ if f is not bounded, $f\Sigma^*\$$ if f is only left-bounded, ${}^{\wedge}\Sigma^* f$ if f is only right-bounded, and f if f is bounded.

Note also that only formula $\#$ has an empty model.

Definition 36 (Implementation) P_{string} *is* $(\sqsubseteq, \sqcap, \sqcup, \top, \bot)$ *where for every* $f, g \in AS_{string}$

- $f \sqsubseteq g$ *iff* $f = \alpha g \beta$,

- $f \sqcap g = \begin{cases} f & \text{if } f \sqsubseteq g \\ g & \text{if } g \sqsubseteq f \\ \# & \text{if } f \not\sqsubseteq g \text{ and } g \not\sqsubseteq f \text{ and both } f \text{ and } g \text{ are} \\ & \text{either left-bounded or right-bounded, or one of them is bounded} \\ undef & \text{otherwise} \end{cases}$

- $\sqcup$ *is undefined,*
- $\top = \epsilon$,
- $\bot = \#$.

Theorem 37 (Completeness/consistency) P_{string} *is consistent and complete in* $\sqsubseteq$, $\top$, $\bot$, $\sqcap$, *and* $\sqcup$ *w.r.t.* S_{string}.

P_{string} is partial, but it is consistent and complete. Furthermore, the following lemma shows that it is reduced, and so, the composition $prop(string)$ is also consistent and complete.

Lemma 38 (Reducedness) P_{string} *is reduced w.r.t.* S_{string}.

B   More n-ary Logic Functors

We present in this appendix some more n-ary logic functors. Some of them produce reduced logics that are not necessarily total. In this case, partiality is not a problem, since it is enough to wrap them in logic functor *prop*. A few other functors produce logics that are not reduced, but that are total (if the logics to which they are applied are also total). They are useful, but only as the outermost logic functor of a composition. Using them in, say, the logic functor *prop*, would produce an incomplete logic, which is seldom desired.

In each case, we present the syntax, the semantics, the implementation and results about consistency and completeness, and reducedness.

B.1   Complete Knowledge

The logic "All I Know" [Lev90] represents knowledge judgements in a modal way, instead of by an extra-logical rule as with closed world assumption. Note also that it is a monotonous logic.

Definition 39 (Syntax) AS_{aik} *is the optional wrapping of the syntax of some logic by the All I Know modality. We will use square brackets [and] as a concrete syntax.*

The syntax of *aik* operates on *descriptions* expressed as logical formulas. For any description f_d, $[f_d]$ represents its closure in a complete description (f_d is all that is true), f_d represents a positive fact, and if *aik* is composed with *prop*, $\neg f_d$ represents a negative fact.

Definition 40 (Semantics) S_{aik} is $(I_d, \models_d) \mapsto (I, \models)$ such that

$$I = \mathcal{P}(I_d) \setminus \{\emptyset\} \ and \ \begin{cases} i \models f_d & iff \ i \subseteq M_d(f_d) \\ i \models [f_d] & iff \ i = M_d(f_d) \end{cases}$$

Definition 41 (Implementation) P_{aik} is
$(\sqsubseteq_d, \sqcap_d, \sqcup_d, \top_d, \bot_d) \mapsto (\sqsubseteq, \sqcap, \sqcup, \top, \bot)$ such that

- the deduction $\sqsubseteq$ is defined according to Table 2

- $f \sqcap g = \begin{cases} f_d \sqcap_d g_d & if \ f = f_d \ and \ g = g_d \\ f & if \ f \sqsubseteq g \\ g & if \ g \sqsubseteq f \\ \bot & if \ f = [f_d] \not\sqsubseteq g \\ \bot & if \ g = [g_d] \not\sqsubseteq f \end{cases}$

- $f \sqcup g = undef$
- $\top = \top_d$
- $\bot = \bot_d$.

Table 2. Definition of logical deduction in logic functor aik.

$\sqsubseteq$	g_d	$[g_d]$
f_d	$f_d \sqsubseteq_d g_d$	$f_d \sqsubseteq_d \bot_d$
$[f_d]$	$f_d \sqsubseteq_d g_d$	$f_d \equiv_d g_d$ or $f_d \sqsubseteq_d \bot_d$

Theorem 42 (Completeness/consistency) P_{aik} has the following completeness and consistence properties:

The tautology, $\top$, is defined (resp. complete) if the description tautology, $\top_d$, is defined (resp. complete). The case of the contradiction, $\bot$, is similar w.r.t. to consistency.

Conjunction $\sqcap$ is consistent and complete if the description conjunction $\sqcap_d$ is consistent and complete. Disjunction $\sqcup$ is always consistent and complete because it is undefined.

The deduction $\sqsubseteq$ is consistent and complete if the description deduction $\sqsubseteq_d$ is consistent and complete, and no formula in AS_{L_d} has only 1 model (which is usually the case).

Lemma 43 (Reducedness) $P_{aik(L_d)}$ is reduced for open sequent families included in $S = \{(A, B) \mid A \subseteq AS_{aik(L_d)}, B \subseteq L_d\}$, if $\sqsubseteq_d$ is consistent and complete, $\top_d$ is defined and complete, $\bot_d$ is defined and consistent, and $\sqcap_d$ is totally defined.

To summarize, logic functor *prop* can be applied to a logic $aik(L_d)$ if $\top_d$ is defined and complete, $\bot_d$ is defined and consistent, $\sqsubseteq_d$ and $\sqcap_d$ are consistent, complete, and total for $\sqcap_d$. In this case, $\sqsubseteq_{prop(aik(L_d))}$ is consistent and complete when the right argument has no closed formula $[g_d]$ among its atoms. This is satisfying when used in a logical information system, because closed formulas appear only in object descriptions, and so as left argument of deduction $\sqsubseteq$.

B.2   Valued Attributes

Valued attributes are useful for attaching several properties to objects. For instance, a bibliographical reference has several attributes, like `author`, `year`, or `title`, each of which has a value. We want to express some conditions on these values, and for this, we consider a logic L_V, whose semantics is in fact the domain of values for the attributes. Attributes themselves are taken in an infinite set $Attr$ of distinct symbols. Thus, a logic of valued attributes is built with the logic functor $valattr$, whose argument is the logic of values, and that is defined as follows:

Definition 44 (Syntax) *Given a set $Attr$ of attribute name, $AS_{valattr}$ is the product of $Attr$ with the syntax of some logic:*
$$AS_{valattr(L)} = \{a : f \mid f \in L \wedge a \in Attr\}$$

Definition 45 (Semantics) $S_{valattr}$ *is* $(I_V, \models_V) \;\mapsto\; (I, \models)$ *such that* $I = A \to I_V \uplus \{undef\}$ *and* $i \models a : v$ *iff* $i(a) \neq undef$ *and* $i(a) \models_V v$.

Definition 46 (Implementation) $P_{valattr}$ *is*
$(\sqsubseteq_V, \sqcap_V, \sqcup_V, \top_V, \perp_V) \mapsto (\sqsubseteq, \sqcap, \sqcup, \top, \perp)$ *such that*
$-\ a : v \sqsubseteq b : w$ *iff* $v \sqsubseteq_V w$ *and* $(a = b$ *or* $v \sqsubseteq_V \perp_V)$,

$$- \ a : v \sqcap b : w = \begin{cases} a : (v \sqcap_V w) & \text{if } a = b \\ a : \perp_V & \text{if } v \sqsubseteq_V \perp_V \text{ or } w \sqsubseteq_V \perp_V, \\ undef & \text{otherwise} \end{cases}$$

$$- \ a : v \sqcup b : w = \begin{cases} a : (v \sqcup_V w) & \text{if } a = b \\ a : v & \text{if } w \sqsubseteq_V \perp_V \\ b : w & \text{if } v \sqsubseteq_V \perp_V, \\ undef & \text{otherwise} \end{cases}$$

$-\ \top$ *and* $\perp$ *are undefined.*

Theorem 47 (Completeness/consistency) $P_{valattr(V)}$ *is consistent and complete in* $\sqsubseteq$, $\top$, $\perp$, $\sqcap$, $\sqcup$ *w.r.t.* $S_{valattr(V)}$ *if* P_V *is consistent and complete w.r.t.* S_V.

$P_{valattr}$ is partially defined in both conjunction and disjunction, but it is consistent and complete provided that its implementation argument is. Furthermore, the following lemma shows that $P_{valattr(V)}$ is reduced provided that its argument is. So, the logic functor $prop$ can be applied to logic functor $valattr$ to form a complete and consistent logic.

Lemma 48 (Reducedness) $P_{valattr(V)}$ *is reduced w.r.t.* $S_{valattr(V)}$ *if* P_V *is reduced w.r.t.* S_V.

B.3   Sums of Logics

The sum of two logics allows one to form descriptions/queries about objects that belong to different domains. Objects from one domain are described by formulas of a logic L_1, while other objects use logic L_2. A special element '?' represents the absence of information, and the element '#' represents a contradiction. For instance, the bibliographical application may be part of a larger knowledge base whose other parts are described by completely different formulas. Even inside the bibliographical part, journal articles use facets that are not relevant to conference article (and vice-versa).

We write *sum* the logic functor used for constructing the sum of 2 logics. Note that *sum* could easily be generalized to arbitrary arities.

Definition 49 (Syntax) AS_{sum} *forms the disjoint union of two logics plus formulas ? and #.*

Definition 50 (Semantics) S_{sum} *is* $(I_{L_1}, \models_{L_1}), (I_{L_2}, \models_{L_2}) \mapsto (I, \models)$ *such that*

$$
I = I_{L_1} \uplus I_{L_2} \text{ and } i \models f = \begin{cases} i \models_{L_1} f & \text{if } i \in I_{L_1}, f \in AS_{L_1} \\ i \models_{L_2} f & \text{if } i \in I_{L_2}, f \in AS_{L_2} \\ true & \text{if } f =? \\ false & \text{otherwise} \end{cases}
$$

We will prove that $P_{sum(L_1,L_2)}$ is reduced w.r.t. $S_{sum(L_1,L_2)}$ if P_{L_1} and P_{L_2} are reduced w.r.t. S_{L_1} and S_{L_2}, making the logic functor *sum* usable inside the logic functor *prop*. The development of this logic functor is rather complex but we could not find simpler but reduced definitions for *sum*.

Definition 51 (Implementation) P_{sum} *is*
$(\sqsubseteq_{L_1}, \sqcap_{L_1}, \sqcup_{L_1}, \top_{L_1}, \bot_{L_1}), (\sqsubseteq_{L_2}, \sqcap_{L_2}, \sqcup_{L_2}, \top_{L_2}, \bot_{L_2}) \mapsto (\sqsubseteq, \sqcap, \sqcup, \top, \bot)$ *such that*

$$
- \ f \sqsubseteq g = \begin{cases} f \sqsubseteq_{L_1} g & \text{if } f,g \in AS_{L_1} \\ f \sqsubseteq_{L_2} g & \text{if } f,g \in AS_{L_2} \\ true & \text{if } f \sqsubseteq_{L_1} \bot_{L_1} \text{ or } f \sqsubseteq_{L_2} \bot_{L_2} \text{ or } f = \# \text{ or } g =? \\ false & \text{otherwise} \end{cases}
$$

$$
- \ f \sqcap g = \begin{cases} f \sqcap_{L_1} g & \text{if } f,g \in AS_{L_1} \\ f \sqcap_{L_2} g & \text{if } f,g \in AS_{L_2} \\ f & \text{if } g =? \\ g & \text{if } f =? \\ \# & \text{otherwise} \end{cases}
$$

$$
- \ f \sqcup g = \begin{cases} f \sqcup_{L_1} g & \text{if } f,g \in AS_{L_1} \\ f \sqcup_{L_2} g & \text{if } f,g \in AS_{L_2} \\ g & \text{if } f = \# \text{ or } f \sqsubseteq_{L_1} \bot_{L_1} \text{ or } f \sqsubseteq_{L_2} \bot_{L_2} \\ f & \text{if } g = \# \text{ or } g \sqsubseteq_{L_1} \bot_{L_1} \text{ or } g \sqsubseteq_{L_2} \bot_{L_2} \\ ? & \text{if } f =? \text{ or } g =? \\ ? & \text{if } f \in AS_{L_1}, g \in AS_{L_2} \text{ and } \top_{L_1} \sqsubseteq_{L_1} f \text{ and } \top_{L_2} \sqsubseteq_{L_2} g \\ ? & \text{if } f \in AS_{L_2}, g \in AS_{L_1} \text{ and } \top_{L_1} \sqsubseteq_{L_1} g \text{ and } \top_{L_2} \sqsubseteq_{L_2} f \\ undef & \text{otherwise} \end{cases}
$$

$$
- \ \top =? \qquad \bot = \#
$$

Theorem 52 (Completeness/consistency) $P_{sum(L_1,L_2)}$ *is consistent and complete in* $\sqsubseteq$, $\top$, $\bot$, $\sqcap$, $\sqcup$ *w.r.t.* $S_{sum(L_1,L_2)}$ *if* P_{L_1} *and* P_{L_2} *are consistent and complete w.r.t.* S_{L_1} *and* S_{L_2}.

Lemma 53 (Reducedness) $P_{sum(L_1,L_2)}$ *is reduced w.r.t.* $S_{sum(L_1,L_2)}$ *if* P_{L_1} *and* P_{L_2} *are reduced and consistent in* $\top$, $\bot$ *w.r.t.* S_{L_1} *and* S_{L_2}.

5

B.4   Sets of Models

The logic functor *set* is useful to describe for instance sets of authors or keywords. Each item is specified by a formula of the logic argument of *set*. Models of sets of subformulas are sets of models of subformulas.

Definition 54 (Syntax) AS_{set} *is the set of finite subsets of formulas of a logic.*

Definition 55 (Semantics) S_{set} *is* $(I_e, \models_e) \mapsto (I, \models)$ *such that*

$$I = \mathcal{P}(I_e) \text{ and } i \models f \iff \forall f_e \in f : i \cap M_e(f_e) \neq \emptyset.$$

Definition 56 (Implementation) P_{set} *is*
$(\sqsubseteq_e, \sqcap_e, \sqcup_e, \top_e, \bot_e) \rightarrow (\sqsubseteq, \sqcap, \sqcup, \top, \bot)$ *such that for all* $f, g \in AS_{set(e)}$

- $f \sqsubseteq g \iff \forall g_e \in g : \exists f_e \in f : f_e \sqsubseteq_e g_e$
- $f \sqcap g = (f \cup g)$
- $f \sqcup g = \{f_e \sqcup_e g_e \mid f_e \in f, g_e \in g, f_e \sqcup_e g_e \text{ defined}\}$
- $\top = \emptyset$
- $\bot = \{\bot_e\}$, *if* $\bot_e$ *is defined*

Theorem 57 (Completeness/consistency) *The deduction* $\sqsubseteq$ *is consistent (resp. complete) if deduction on elements* $\sqsubseteq_e$ *is also consistent (resp. complete). The tautology* $\top$ *is always defined and complete. The contradiction* $\bot$ *is defined (resp. consistent) if the element contradiction* $\bot_e$ *is also defined (resp. consistent). The conjunction* $\sqcap$ *is always totally defined, consistent and complete. The disjuction* $\sqcup$ *is totally defined, complete if the element disjunction* $\sqcup_e$ *is also complete, but not consistent in general.*

The logic functor *set* is not reduced but it is still useful as the outermost functor of a composition.

Computing Environment-Aware Agent Behaviours with Logic Program Updates

José J. Alferes[1], Antonio Brogi[2], João A. Leite[1], and Luís M. Pereira[1]

[1] Centro de Inteligência Artificial, Universidade Nova de Lisboa, Portugal,
{jja | jleite | lmp}@di.fct.unl.pt
[2] Dipartimento di Informatica, Università di Pisa, Italy,
brogi@di.unipi.it

Abstract. The ability of reacting to changes in the external environment is of crucial importance within the context of software agents. Such feature must however be suitably reconciled with a more deliberative rational behaviour. In this paper we show how different behaviours of environment-aware agents can be naturally specified and computed in terms of logic program updates. Logic program updates are specified, in our setting, by the language of updates LUPS. We show how such language can be used to model the more reactive behaviours, while keeping the more deliberative features provided by its underlying Dynamic Logic Programming paradigm. The obtained declarative semantics sets a firm basis for the development, implementation, and analysis of environment-aware agents.

1 Introduction

The paradigm shift from stand-alone isolated computing to environment-aware computing clearly indicates that the ability of reacting to changes occurring in the external environment is a crucial capability of software agents. Reactivity must however be suitably reconciled with rationality. Indeed the ability of an agent to reason on available information is as important as its ability to promptly react to sudden changes occurring in the external environment.

The way in which an agent combines rationality and reactivity determines the quality of the services offered by the agent. Consider for instance a software agent whose task is to recommend investments based on the analysis of trends in the stock market [7]. A scarcely reactive behaviour may generate well-evaluated recommendations based on outdated information, while a scarcely rational behaviour may quickly generate recommendations based only on the most recently acquired information.

While developing environment-aware agents, the environment in which the agents will operate is at least partially unknown. Typically, even if the set of possible observable behaviours of the environment is known, the precise dynamic behaviour of the environment is not predictable at software development time.

A. Pettorossi (Ed.): LOPSTR 2001, LNCS 2372, pp. 216–232, 2002.

On the other hand, the availability of a well-founded description of the possible behaviours of environment-aware programs is crucial for performing tasks such as verification and analysis before putting the program at work with the external environment.

In this paper we provide a formal characterization of the behaviours of environment-aware agents. Our approach can be summarized as follows:

- We consider an agent to be *environment-aware* if it is capable of reacting to changes occurring in the external environment. As the environment may dynamically change while the agent is performing its computations, such changes may influence the agent behaviour.
- Agents have a partial representation of the external environment, represented by their *perceptions* of the environment. The type of such perceptions of course depends on the sensing capabilities owned by the agent. We will focus on the way in which the behaviour of an agent may be influenced by its perceptions, rather than on the way in which the agent will get such perceptions. For instance, we will abstract from the way in which a software agent accesses some piece of information available in the external environment (e.g., by receiving a message, by downloading a file, or by getting data from physical sensors). Formally, if we denote by $percs(P)$ the set of possible perceptions of an agent P, the set $\mathcal{E}$ of all possible environment configurations can be defined as $\mathcal{E} \subseteq \mathcal{P}(percs(P))$, that is, as the set of all possible sets of perceptions of the environment that P may (simultaneously) get.
- We choose *logic programming* as the specification language of environment-aware agents. We show that the computation of a program P that reacts to a sequence of environment configurations $\langle E_1, E_2, \ldots E_n \rangle$ can be naturally modelled by means of a *Dynamic Logic Program* (DLP)[1], that is, by a sequence $Q_0 \oplus Q_1 \oplus Q_2 \oplus \ldots \oplus Q_n$ of (generalized) logic programs [1] whose semantics defines the effects of first updating Q_0 with Q_1, then updating the result with Q_2, and so on.
- From a programming perspective, we show that the environment-aware behaviours of a program reacting to sequences of environment configurations can be specified by a set of LUPS [3] rules that program the way in which the knowledge of the program will be updated by a sequence of environment configurations. More precisely, the behaviour of a program P that reacts to the sequence of environment configurations $\langle E_1, E_2, \ldots E_n \rangle$ is described by the sequence of LUPS updates: $P \otimes E_1 \otimes E_2 \otimes \ldots \otimes E_n$ where each E_i is a set of (temporary) updates representing an environment configuration.
- The formal semantics of LUPS (with the modification of [22]) is defined in terms of a program transformation, by first transforming a sequence of LUPS updates into a DLP, and this DLP into a generalized logic program:

$$P \otimes E_1 \otimes \cdots \otimes E_n \longrightarrow_\Upsilon Q_0 \oplus \cdots \oplus Q_n \longrightarrow_\tau G \longrightarrow SM$$

where Υ is the mapping from LUPS to DLP, τ is the mapping from DLP to generalized logic programs, and where SM denotes the set of stable models [12] of a generalized logic program.

It is important to observe that the LUPS language features the possibility of programming different types of updates. We will show how this very feature can be actually exploited to specify different environment-aware behaviours of programs such as those explored in [7]. We will also show how the declarative semantics of LUPS programs provides a formal characterization of environment-aware behaviours, which can be exploited for resource-bounded analyses of the possible behaviours of a program w.r.t. a set $\mathcal{E}$ of possible environment configurations.

Since LUPS has been shown to embed both Logic Programs under the Stable Models Semantics [12] and Revision Programs [24], and has been successfully used to model dynamic environments where the governing rules change with time, by showing that LUPS is also capable of encoding environment-aware behaviours such as those explored in [7] we believe to take a step further in the direction of showing that LUPS is indeed an appropriate language to design executable specifications of *real* agents, i.e. agents that exhibit both reactive and rational (deliberative) behaviours.

The remainder of this paper is structured as follows: in Section 2 we recap the framework of Dynamic Logic Programming and the language of updates LUPS (the formal definitions can be found in Appendix); in Section 3 we show how several environment-aware agent behaviours can be formally encoded in LUPS, and we provide a simple illustrative example; in Section 4 we draw some considerations on reasoning about such behaviours; in Section 5 we elaborate on related work, to conclude in Section 6.

2   LUPS: A Language for Dynamic Updates

In this section we briefly present Dynamic Logic Programming (DLP) [1], and the update command language LUPS [3]. The complete formal definitions can be found in [1,3], and the most relevant ones in Appendix. Both papers, together with the implementations of DLP and LUPS, and the Lift Controller example below, are available from:

$$\text{http://centria.di.fct.unl.pt/\~jja/updates/}$$

The idea of Dynamic Logic Programming is simple and quite fundamental. Suppose that we are given a sequence of generalized logic program (i.e., programs possibly with default negation in rule heads) modules $P_1 \oplus \cdots \oplus P_n$. Each program P_s $(1 \leq s \leq n)$ contains knowledge that is given as valid at state s. Different states may represent different time instants or different sets of knowledge priority or perhaps even different viewpoints. Consequently, the individual program modules may contain mutually contradictory as well as overlapping information. The role of DLP is to use the mutual relationships existing between different sequentialized states to precisely determine, at any given state s, the *declarative* as well as the *procedural* semantics of the combined program, composed of all modules. The declarative semantics at some state is determined by the stable models of the program that consists of all those rules that are "valid" in that state. Intuitively a rule is "valid" in a state if either it belongs to the state or belongs to some previous state in the sequence and is not rejected (i.e., it is inherited by a form of non-monotonic inertia). A rule r from a prior state is rejected if there is another conflicting rule (i.e., a rule with a true body whose head is the complement of the head of r) in a subsequent state. A transformational semantics into generalized program, that directly provides a means for DLP implementation, has also been defined.

LUPS [3] is a logic programming command language for specifying logic program updates. It can be viewed as a language that declaratively specifies how to construct a Dynamic Logic Program. A sentence U in LUPS is a set of simultaneous update commands that, given a pre-existing sequence of logic programs, whose semantics corresponds to our knowledge at a given state, produces a new DLP with one more program, corresponding to the knowledge that results from the previous sequence after performing all the simultaneous update commands.

A program in LUPS is a sequence of such sentences, and its semantics is defined by means of a dynamic logic program generated by the sequence of commands. In [3], a translation of a LUPS program into a generalized logic program is also presented, where stable models exactly correspond to the semantics of the original LUPS program.

LUPS update commands specify assertions or retractions to the current program. In LUPS a simple assertion is represented by the command:

$$\textbf{assert } L \leftarrow L_1, \ldots, L_k \textbf{ when } L_{k+1}, \ldots, L_m \tag{1}$$

meaning that if $L_{k+1}, \ldots, L_m$ is true in the current program, then the rule $L \leftarrow L_1, \ldots, L_k$ is added to the new program (and persists by inertia, until possibly retracted or overridden by some future update command, by the addition of a rule with complementary head and true body). To represent rules and facts that do not persist by inertia, i.e. that are one-state only persistent, LUPS includes the modified form of assertion:

$$\textbf{assert event } L \leftarrow L_1, \ldots, L_k \textbf{ when } L_{k+1}, \ldots, L_m \tag{2}$$

The retraction of rules is performed with the two update commands:

$$\textbf{retract } L \leftarrow L_1, \ldots, L_k \textbf{ when } L_{k+1}, \ldots, L_m \tag{3}$$

$$\textbf{retract event } L \leftarrow L_1, \ldots, L_k \textbf{ when } L_{k+1}, \ldots, L_m \tag{4}$$

meaning that, subject to precondition $L_{k+1}, \ldots, L_m$ (verified at the current program) rule $L \leftarrow L_1, \ldots, L_k$ is either retracted from its successor state onwards, or just temporarily retracted in the successor state (if governed by **event**).

Normally assertions represent newly incoming information. Although its effects may persist by inertia (until contravened or retracted), the assert command itself does not persist. However, some update commands may desirably persist in the successive consecutive updates. This is the case of, e.g., laws which subject to preconditions are always valid, rules describing the effects of an action, or, as we shall see, rules describing behaviours of environment-aware programs.

For example, in the description of the effects of actions, the specification of the effects must be added to all sets of updates, to guarantee that, whenever the action takes place, its effects are enforced. To specify such persistent update commands, LUPS introduces the commands:

$$\textbf{always } L \leftarrow L_1, \ldots, L_k \textbf{ when } L_{k+1}, \ldots, L_m \tag{5}$$

$$\textbf{always event } L \leftarrow L_1, \ldots, L_k \textbf{ when } L_{k+1}, \ldots, L_m \tag{6}$$

$$\textbf{cancel } L \leftarrow L_1, \ldots, L_k \textbf{ when } L_{k+1}, \ldots, L_m \tag{7}$$

The first two commands state that, in addition to any new set of arriving update commands, the persistent update command keeps executing along with them too. The first case without, and the second case with, the **event** keyword. The third statement cancels the execution of this persistent update, once the conditions for cancellation are met.

3   Programming Environment-Aware Behaviours

We will now show how different environment-aware behaviours can be programmed in LUPS. We will start by considering the environment-aware behaviours that have been analysed in [7]. Therein different environment-aware behaviours are formally defined and compared to one another. Agents are specified by definite logic programs, and perceptions are (positive) atoms. Namely an environment configuration is simply a set of (positive) atoms. Environment-aware behaviours are defined by extending the standard bottom-up semantics of definite logic programs, defined in terms of the immediate consequence operator $T(P)$ [10]. The idea is to model the environment-aware behaviour of a definite program P by means of an operator $\varphi(P)(I, E)$ which given a Herbrand interpretation I (representing the partial conclusions of the program so far) and a Herbrand interpretation E (representing one set of environment perceptions) returns the new set of conclusions that the program P is able to draw. Different possible definitions of $\varphi(P)$ are analysed and compared to one another in [7]:

$$\tau_i(P)(I, E) = I \cup T(P)(I \cup E) \qquad \text{(uncontrolled) inflationary}$$

$$\tau_{\omega i}(P)(I, E) = \tau_i^\omega(P)(I, E) \qquad \text{controlled inflationary}$$

$$\tau_n(P)(I, E) = T(P)(I \cup E) \qquad \text{(uncontrolled) non-inflationary}$$

$$\tau_{\omega n}(P)(I, E) = \tau_n^\omega(P)(I, E) \qquad \text{controlled non-inflationary}$$

where τ_X^ω, for $X \in \{i, n\}$, is defined by:

$$\tau_X^0(P)(I, E) = I$$

$$\tau_X^{k+1}(P)(I, E) = \tau_X(P)\left(\tau_X^k(P)(I, E), E\right)$$

$$\tau_X^\omega(P)(I, E) = \bigcup_{k < \omega} \tau_X^k(P)(I, E)$$

The behaviour expressed by $\tau_i(P)$ is called *inflationary* as the $\tau_i(P)$ operator is inflationary on its first argument I. Intuitively speaking, every previously reached conclusion is credulously maintained by $\tau_i(P)$. The operator $\tau_{\omega i}(P)$ expresses a *controlled* behaviour as the program P reacts to the changes occurred in the external environment only after terminating the internal computation triggered by the previous perceptions. The operators $\tau_n(P)$ and $\tau_{\omega n}(P)$ model the corresponding behaviours for the non-inflationary case. These different definitions of $\varphi(P)$ model environment-aware behaviours which differ from one another in the way they combine rationality and reactivity aspects. More precisely, as shown in [7], they differ from one another in their degree of credulousness (or skepticism) w.r.t. the validity of the information perceived from the environment and in the conclusions derived thereafter.

In this paper, we show how persistent LUPS updates can be used to naturally program different forms of environment-aware behaviours. In this setting, environment evolution is described by updates asserting new events that state that perceptions (non-persistently) become true or false:

$$\text{assert event } E_i$$

where E_i is a literal. Roughly speaking, the four environment-aware behaviours considered in [7] can be programmed by the following LUPS updates:

$$
\begin{aligned}
(\tau_i) \quad & \textbf{always } L \textbf{ when } \overline{L}_P, \overline{L}_E \\
(\tau_{\omega i}) \quad & \textbf{always } L \leftarrow \overline{L}_P \textbf{ when } \overline{L}_E \\
(\tau_n) \quad & \textbf{always event } L \textbf{ when } \overline{L}_P, \overline{L}_E \\
(\tau_{\omega n}) \quad & \textbf{always event } L \leftarrow \overline{L}_P \textbf{ when } \overline{L}_E
\end{aligned}
$$

where $\overline{L}_E$ denotes a conjunction of environment perceptions, and $\overline{L}_P$ denotes a (possibly empty) conjunctions of program-defined literals.

The rule for (τ_i) states that, whenever the events $\overline{L}_E$ occur, if the literals in $\overline{L}_P$ were already true then L is added as a fact and remains true by inertia until overridden, thus modelling an inflationary behaviour. By having the **event** keyword, in rule (τ_n) L is added only in the following state, and then removed. Consequently, the behaviour modelled by this rule is non-inflationary as the truth of L does not remain by inertia. In $(\tau_{\omega i})$ rather than testing for the truth of $\overline{L}_P$ in the previous state and adding L, the logic program rule $L \leftarrow \overline{L}_P$ is asserted. This allows the conclusion L, and any other conclusion depending on L via other rules with the same behaviour, to be reached in the same single state after the occurrence of $\overline{L}_E$. This way all the conclusions are obtained before any other change in the external environment is analysed, as desired in the controlled behaviour. The behaviour modelled by $(\tau_{\omega n})$ is similar, but the rule is only added in the following state and then removed, so as to model a non-inflationary behaviour. Also note that all these behaviours are modelled via persistent update commands. Indeed, e.g. in (τ_i), we want L to be added whenever the pre-conditions are met, and not only tested once, as it would happen if an **assert** command would be introduced instead.

In this paper, rather than providing a deeper analysis of each of the behaviours specified by the rules above, including the proof on the equivalence to the behaviours specified in [7], we will present a single detailed example where all these behaviours occur. The example also illustrates a (limited) use of default negation, in that a single stable model exists for each state.

3.1   Example: A Lift Controller

Consider an agent that is in charge of controlling a lift. The available perceptions are sets made up from the predicates $push(N)$ and $floor$. Intuitively, $floor$ means that the agent receives a signal from the lift indicating that a new floor has been reached. $push(N)$ signifies that a lift button to go to floor N was just pushed, whether the one inside the lift or the one at the floor.

Upon receipt of a $push(N)$ signal, the lift records that a request for going to floor N is pending. This can easily be modelled by an inflationary (uncontrolled) rule. It is inflationary because the request remains registered in subsequent states (until served). It is uncontrolled because, in our example, the request is not handled immediately. In the LUPS language (where all rules with variables simply stand for their ground instances, and operations (sums and subtractions) restrict those instances):

$$\textbf{always } request(F) \textbf{ when } push(F) \qquad (8)$$

Based on the pending requests at each moment, the agent must prefer where it is going:

$$\textbf{always } going(F) \leftarrow preferredReq(F) \qquad (9)$$

$$\textbf{always } preferredReq(F) \leftarrow request(F), not\ unpreferred(F) \qquad (10)$$

$$\textbf{always } unpreferred(F) \leftarrow request(F2), better(F2, F) \qquad (11)$$

Note that these rules reflect a controlled inflationary behaviour. This is so because the decision of where to go must be made immediately, i.e., before other perceptions take place. The predicate $better$ can be programmed with rules with a controlled inflationary behaviour, according to some preference criterion. For example, if one wants to say that the preferred request is the one for going to the closest floor, one may write:

$$\textbf{always } better(F1, F2) \leftarrow at(F),\ |\ F1 - F\ |\ <\ |\ F2 - F\ | \qquad (12)$$

The internal predicate at stores, at each moment, the number of the floor where the lift is. Thus, if a $floor$ signal is received, depending on where the lift is going, the $at(F)$ must be incremented/decremented.

$$\textbf{always event } at(F + 1) \textbf{ when } floor, at(F), going(G),\ G > F \qquad (13)$$

$$\textbf{always event } at(F - 1) \textbf{ when } floor, at(F), going(G),\ G < F \qquad (14)$$

For compactness, and because it would not bring out new features, we do not give here the full specification of the program, where lift movements are limited within a top and a ground floor. This can however be done by suitably constraining the rules defining at by means of a $topFloor(T)$ and a $groundFloor(G)$ predicates.

Since the floor in which the lift is at changes whenever new $floor$ signals come in, these rules are modelled with a non-inflationary behaviour. To guarantee that the floor in which the lift is at does not change unless a floor signal is received, the following non-inflationary rule is needed:

$$\textbf{always event}\ at(F)\ \textbf{when}\ not\ floor, at(F) \tag{15}$$

When the lift reaches the floor to which it was going, it must open the door (with a non-inflationary behaviour, to avoid tragedies). After opening the door, it must remove the pending request for going to that floor:

$$\textbf{always event}\ opendoor(F)\ \textbf{when}\ going(F), at(F) \tag{16}$$

$$\textbf{always}\ not\ request(F)\ \textbf{when}\ going(F), at(F) \tag{17}$$

To illustrate the behaviour of this program, consider now that initially the lift is at the 5th floor, and that the agent receives a sequence of perceptions, starting with $\{push(10), push(2)\}$, and followed by $\{floor\}$, $\{push(3)\}$, $\{floor\}$. This is modelled by the LUPS program

$$(P \cup E_0) \otimes E_1 \otimes E_2 \otimes E_3 \otimes E_4$$

where P is the set of commands (8)-(17), E_0 comprises the single command **assert event** $at(5)$ (for the initial situation), and each other E_i contains an assert-event command for each of the elements in the corresponding perception, i.e.:

$$E_0 = \{\textbf{assert event}\ at(5)\}$$
$$E_1 = \{\textbf{assert event}\ push(10);\quad \textbf{assert event}\ push(2)\}$$
$$E_2 = \{\textbf{assert event}\ floor\}$$
$$E_3 = \{\textbf{assert event}\ push(3)\}$$
$$E_4 = \{\textbf{assert event}\ floor\}$$

According to LUPS semantics, at E_1 both $push(10)$ and $push(2)$ are true. So at the moment of E_2 both requests (for 2 and 10) become true, and immediately (i.e., before receiving any further perception) $going(2)$ is determined (by rules (9)-(12)). Note the importance of these rules having a controlled behaviour for guaranteeing that $going(2)$ is determined before another external perception is accepted. At the moment of E_3, $at(4)$ becomes true by rule (14), since $floor$ was true at E_2, and, given that the rules for the at predicate are all non-inflationary, the previous $at(5)$ is no longer true. Both request facts remain true, as they where introduced by the inflationary rule (8). Since $push(3)$ is true at E_3, another request (for 3) is next also true. Accordingly, by rules (9)-(12), $going(3)$ becomes then true (while $going(2)$ is no longer true). Moreover, by rule (14), $at(3)$ is next true. It is easy to check that given the $floor$ signal at E_4, in the subsequent state $request(3)$ becomes false (by rule (17)), and $opendoor(3)$ becomes true and in any next state becomes false again (since rule (16) is non-inflationary). Note that the falsity of $request(3)$ causes $going(2)$ to be true again, so that the lift will continue its run.

Finally, note that the behaviour of the lift controller agent can be extended so as to take into account emergency situations. For instance, the update rule:

$$\textbf{always event } opendoor(F) \leftarrow at(F) \textbf{ when } firealarm \qquad (18)$$

tells the agent to open the door when there is a fire alarm (perception) independently of whether the current floor was the planned destination. Note that this rule reflects a controlled non-inflationary behaviour and refines the agent behaviour defined by rule (16) only in the case of an emergency.

4   Reasoning about Environment-Aware Behaviours

The declarative semantics of LUPS provides a formal characterization of environment-aware behaviours, which can be exploited for resource-bounded analyses of the possible behaviours of a program w.r.t. a set $\mathcal{E}$ of possible environment configurations. For instance the states that a program P may reach after reacting to a sequence of n environment configurations are formally characterized by:

$$\Phi(P, \mathcal{E}, n) = \bigcup_{E_{i_k} \in \mathcal{E}} Sem(P \otimes E_{i_1} \otimes E_{i_2} \otimes \ldots \otimes E_{i_n})$$

Namely, $\Phi(P, \mathcal{E}, n)$ is a set of stable models that denotes all the possible states that P can reach after reacting n times to the external environment.

We define the notion of *beliefs* of an environment-aware program as the largest set of (positive and negative) conclusions that the program will be certainly able to draw after n steps of computation, for whatever sequence of environment configurations:

$$\mathcal{B}(P, \mathcal{E}, n) = \left(\bigcap_{M \in \Phi(P, \mathcal{E}, n)} M^+ \right) \cup \left(\bigcap_{M \in \Phi(P, \mathcal{E}, n)} M^- \right)$$

where M^+ and M^- denote, respectively, the positive part and the negative part of a (possibly partial) interpretation M. Formally: $M^+ = M \cap HB$ and $M^- = \{not\ A \mid A \in M\}$.

Notice that in general $\mathcal{B}(P, \mathcal{E}, n)$ is a partial interpretation.

We now introduce the notion of *invariant* for environment-aware programs. The invariant of a conventional program defines the properties that hold at each stage of the program computation. Analogously, the invariant of an environment-aware program defines the largest set of conclusions that the program will be able to draw at any time in any environment. A resource-bounded characterization of the invariant of an environment-aware program after n steps of computation can be formalized as follows, where in general $\mathcal{I}(P, \mathcal{E}, n)$ is again partial:

$$\mathcal{I}(P, \mathcal{E}, n) = \left(\bigcap_{M \in \mathcal{B}(P, \mathcal{E}, i), i \in [1, n]} M^+ \right) \cup \left(\bigcap_{M \in \mathcal{B}(P, \mathcal{E}, i), i \in [1, n]} M^- \right)$$

5   Related Work

The use of computational logic for modelling single and multi-agent systems has been widely investigated (e.g., see [26] for a quite recent roadmap). The agent-based architecture described in [21] aims at reconciling rationality and reactivity. Agents are logic programs which continuously perform an "observe-think-act" cycle, and their behaviour is defined via a proof procedure which exploits iff-definitions and integrity constraints. One difference between such approach and ours is that in [21] the semantics is a proof-theoretic operational one, while our approach provides a declarative, model-theoretic characterization of environment-aware agents. The semantical differences between exploiting iff-definitions and logic programs under the stable models semantics have been extensively studied and are naturally inherited when comparing both systems. But most important, the theory update performed by the observation part of the cycle in [21] amounts to a simple monotonic addition of facts and integrity constraints which, unlike in our proposal, does not allow for the full fledged rule updates supported by LUPS.

Different action languages [13,15] have been proposed to describe and reason on the effects of actions (c.f. [14] for a survey). Intuitively, while action languages and LUPS are both concerned with modelling changes, action languages focus on the notions of causality and fluents, while LUPS focusses its features on declarative updates for general knowledge bases . As shown in [2], it is possible, in some cases, to establish a correspondence between actions languages such as the languages $\mathcal{A}$ of [13] and $\mathcal{C}$ of [15], and update languages such as LUPS. Since update languages were specifically designed to allow assertions and retraction of rules to allow for a knowledge base to evolve, action languages by only allowing the effects of actions to be fluents restrict themselves to purely extensional updates. From this purely syntactical point of view LUPS is more expressive. Action languages such as $\mathcal{C}$, on the other hand, was designed to express the notion of causality which is semantically different from the underlying notion of inertia found in the DLP semantics. It is thus natural to observe differences in the semantics between action languages and update languages (see [2,3] for a more detailed discussion of the relation between the two approaches)

AgentSpeak(L) [25] is a logical language for programming Belief-Desire-Intention (BDI) agents, originally designed by abstracting the main features of the PRS and dMARS systems [19]. Our approach shares with AgentSpeak(L) the objective of using a simple logical specification language to model the execution of an agent, rather than employing modal operators. On the other hand, while

AgentSpeak(L) programs are described by means of a proof-theoretic operational semantics, our approach provides a declarative, model-theoretic characterization of environment-aware agents. The relation of our approach with the agent language 3APL [17] (which has been shown to embed AgentSpeak(L)) is similar inasmuch as 3APL is provided only with an operational characterization.

MetateM (and Concurrent MetateM) [4,11] is a programming language based on the notion of direct execution of temporal formulae, primarily used to specify reactive behaviours of agents. It shares similarities with the LUPS language inasmuch as both use rules to represent a relation between the past and the future, i.e. each rule in MetateM and in LUPS consists of conditions about the past (present) and a conclusion about the future. While the use of temporal logics in MetateM allows for the specification of rather elaborate temporal conditions, something for which LUPS was not designed, the underlying DLP semantics of LUPS allows the specification of agents capable of being deployed in dynamic environments where the governing laws change over time. While, for example, the temporal connectives $\Box$ and $\bigcirc$ of MetateM can be used to model the inflationary and non-inflationary behaviours, respectively, obtained when only considering definite logic programs, if we move to the more general class of logic programs with non-monotonic default negation both in the premises and conclusions of clauses, LUPS and DLP directly provide an update semantics needed to resolve the contradictions naturally arising from conflicting rules acquired at different time instants, something apparently not possible in MetateM. This partially amounts to the difference between updating theories represented in classical logic and those represented by non-monotonic logic programs (cf. [1,9]).

Related to the problem of environment-aware agents are also (real-time) reactive systems [16], that constantly interact with a given physical environment (e.g. automatic control and monitoring systems). In these real-time systems safety is often a critical issue, and so the existence of programming languages that allow programs to be easily designed and validated is crucial. With this purpose, Synchronous Declarative Languages have been designed (e.g. LUSTRE [8] and SIGNAL [5]). Such languages provide idealized primitives allowing users to think of their programs as reacting instantaneously to external events, and variables are functions of multiform time each having an associated clock defining the sequence of instants where the variable takes its values. Our approach shares with these the declarative nature and the ability to deal with changing environments. However, their very underlying assumption that a program is always able to react to an event before any other event occurs, goes against the situations we want to model. As stated in the introduction, we are interested in modelling situations where rationality and reactivity are combined, where one cannot assume that the results are obtained before other events occur. On the contrary, with our approach (e.g., in a (uncontrolled) inflationary behaviour) external events may occur before all the conclusions reachable from previous events have been determined. Being based on LUPS, our approach also allows for modelling environments where the governing laws change over time, and where it is possible to reason with incomplete information (via nonmonotonic default negation). Both these aspects are out of the scope of the synchronous declarative languages. On the other hand, the ability of these languages to deal with various clocks, and the synchronization primitives, cannot be handled by our approach. The usefulness of these features to the problems we want to model, as well as the possibility of incorporating them in our approach, are subjects of current work.

Our representation of the possible environment-aware behaviours somehow resembles the possible world semantics of modal logics [18]. More precisely, the beliefs and the invariant of an environment-aware program (introduced in Sect. 4) are resource-bounded approximations of the set of formulae that are *possibly* true (i.e., true in a possible world) and *necessarily* true (i.e., true in every possible word). While the scope of our logic programming based characterization is narrower than a full-fledged modal logic, the former is simpler than the latter and it accounts for an effective prototyping of environment-aware agents.

It is important to observe that the use of LUPS to model environment-aware behaviours extends the approach of [7] in several ways: (1) different behaviours can be associated with different rules, while in [7] all the rules in a program must have the same behaviour; (2) LUPS allows for negative literals both in clause bodies and in clause heads of programs, while in [7] only definite programs are considered; (3) environment perceptions can be both positive and negative literals (rather than just positive literals).

6   Concluding Remarks

We have shown how different environment-aware behaviours of agents can be naturally expressed in LUPS. The LUPS specification provides a formal declarative characterization of such behaviours, that can be exploited for performing resource-bounded analyses and verifications as illustrated in Sect. 4. Moreover, the available LUPS implementation can be exploited for experimenting and prototyping different specifications of environment-aware agents.

In Section 3 we have shown how the four main environment-aware behaviours analysed in [7] can be expressed in LUPS.

Future work will be devoted to investigate further the greater expressive power featured by LUPS updates. For instance, we can model environment evolution by general LUPS updates and hence represent the environment itself as a dynamically evolving program (rather just as a sequence of perceptions). Another interesting direction for future work is to extend the stable semantics of LUPS programs in order to support an incremental, state-based characterization of environment-aware behaviours of programs in the style of [7]. A further interesting extension is to introduce quantitative aspects in the analysis of environment-aware behaviours, by associating probability distributions to the possible environment configurations along the lines of [6].

Acknowledgements. This work was partially supported by the bilateral Italian-Portuguese project "Rational and Reactive Agents", funded jointly by ICCTI and CNR, and by POCTI project FLUX. João Alexandre Leite is partially supported by PRAXIS XXI scholarship no. BD/13514/97. Thanks are due to the anonymous referees for their remarks which helped us in improving the paper.

References

1. J. J. Alferes, J. A. Leite, L. M. Pereira, H. Przymusinska, and T. C. Przymusinski. Dynamic updates of non-monotonic knowledge bases. *The Journal of Logic Programming*, 45(1–3):43–70, September/October 2000.
2. J. J. Alferes, J. A. Leite, L. M. Pereira, and P. Quaresma. Planning as abductive updating. In D. Kitchin, editor, *Proceedings of the AISB'00 Symposium on AI Planning and Intelligent Agents*, pages 1–8. AISB, 2000.
3. J. J. Alferes, L. M. Pereira, H. Przymusinska, and T. Przymusinski. LUPS: A language for updating logic programs. *Artificial Intelligence*, 2002. To appear. A shorter version appeared in M. Gelfond, N. Leone and G. Pfeifer (eds), LPNMR'99, LNAI 1730, Springer-Verlag.
4. H. Barringer, M. Fisher, D. Gabbay, G. Gough, and R. Owens. METATEM: A framework for programming in temporal logic. In *REX Workshop on Stepwise Refinement of Distributed Systems: Models, Formalisms, Correctness (LNCS Volume 430)*, pages 94–129. Springer-Verlag: Heidelberg, Germany, June 1989.
5. A. Benveniste, P Le Guernic, and C. Jacquemot. Synchronous programming with events and relations: the signal language and its semantics. *Science of Computer Programming*, 16:103–149, 1991.
6. A. Brogi. Probabilistic behaviours of reactive agents. *Electronic Notes in Theoretical Computer Science*, 48, 2001.
7. A. Brogi, S. Contiero, and F. Turini. On the interplay between reactivity and computation. In F. Sadri and K. Satoh, editors, *Proceedings of the CL-2000 Workshop on Computational Logic in Multi-Agent Systems (CLIMA'00)*, pages 66–73, 2000.
8. P. Caspi, D. Pilaud, N. Halbwachs, and J. A. Plaice. LUSTRE: A declarative language for programming synchronous systems. In *Conference Record of the Fourteenth Annual ACM Symposium on Principles of Programming Languages*, pages 178–188. ACM SIGACT-SIGPLAN, ACM Press, January 21–23, 1987.
9. T. Eiter, M. Fink, G. Sabbatini, and H. Tompits. On properties of update sequences based on causal rejection. *Theory and Practice of Logic Programming*, 2002. To appear.
10. M. Van Emden and R. Kowalski. The semantics of predicate logic as a programming language. *Journal of ACM*, 4(23):733–742, 1976.
11. M. Fisher. A survey of concurrent METATEM: The language and its applications. In D. Gabbay and H. J. Ohlbach, editors, *Proceedings of the First International Conference on Temporal Logic (ICTL'94)*, volume 827 of *LNAI*, pages 480–505. Springer, 1994.
12. M. Gelfond and V. Lifschitz. The stable model semantics for logic programming. In R. Kowalski and K. A. Bowen, editors, *5th International Conference on Logic Programming*, pages 1070–1080. MIT Press, 1988.
13. M. Gelfond and V. Lifschitz. Representing actions and change by logic programs. *Journal of Logic Programming*, 17:301–322, 1993.
14. M. Gelfond and V. Lifschitz. Action languages. *Linkoping Electronic Articles in Computer and Information Science*, 3(16), 1998.

15. E. Giunchiglia and V. Lifschitz. An action language based on causal explanation: Preliminary report. In *AAAI'98*, pages 623–630, 1998.
16. David Harel and A. Pnueli. On the development of reactive systems. In K. R. Apt, editor, *Logics and Models of Concurrent Systems*, volume 13 of *NATO, ASI Series*, pages 447–498. Springer-Verlag, New York, 1985.
17. Koen V. Hindriks, Frank S. de Boer, Wiebe van der Hoek, and John-Jules Ch. Meyer. A formal embedding of AgentSpeak(L) in 3APL. In G. Antoniou and J. Slaney, editors, *Advanced Topics in Artificial Intelligence (LNAI 1502)*, pages 155–166. Springer-Verlag: Heidelberg, Germany, 1998.
18. G. Hughes and M. J. Cresswell. *A new introduction to modal logic*. RoutLedge, 1996.
19. F. F. Ingrand, M. P. Georgeff, and A. S. Rao. An architecture for real-time reasoning and system control. *IEEE Expert*, 7(6), 1992.
20. K. Inoue and C. Sakama. Negation as failure in the head. *Journal of Logic Programming*, 35:39–78, 1998.
21. R. Kowalski and F. Sadri. Towards a unified agent architecture that combines rationality with reactivity. In D. Pedreschi and C Zaniolo, editors, *Proceedings of LID-96*, volume 1154 of *LNAI*, pages 137–149, 1996.
22. J. A. Leite. A modified semantics for LUPS. In P. Brazdil and A. Jorge, editors, *Progress in Artificial Intelligence, Proceedings of the 10th Portuguese International Conference on Artificial Intelligence (EPIA01)*, volume 2258 of *LNAI*, pages 261–275. Springer, 2001.
23. V. Lifschitz and T. Woo. Answer sets in general non-monotonic reasoning (preliminary report). In B. Nebel, C. Rich, and W. Swartout, editors, *Proceedings of the 3th International Conference on Principles of Knowledge Representation and Reasoning (KR-92)*. Morgan-Kaufmann, 1992.
24. V. Marek and M. Truszcczyński. Revision programming. *Theoretical Computer Science*, 190(2):241–277, 1998.
25. A. S. Rao. AgentSpeak(L): BDI agents speak out in a logical computable language. In W. van der Velde and J. W. Perram, editors, *Agents Breaking Away (LNAI 1038)*, pages 42–55. Springer-Verlag: Heidelberg, Germany, 1996.
26. F. Sadri and F. Toni. Computational logic and multiagent systems: a roadmap. Technical report, Department of Computing, Imperial College of Science, Technology and Medicine, 1999.

A   Background

In this Appendix we provide some background on Generalized Logic Programs, Dynamic Logic Programming and *LUPS*.

A.1   Generalized Logic Programs

Here we recapitulate the syntax and stable semantics of generalized logic programs[1] [1].

---

[1] The class of GLPs (i.e. logic programs that allow default negation in the premises and heads of rules) can be viewed as a special case of yet broader classes of programs, introduced earlier in [20] and in [23], and, for the special case of normal programs, their semantics coincides with the stable models semantics [12].

By a *generalized logic program* P in a language $\mathcal{L}$ we mean a finite or infinite set of propositional clauses of the form $L_0 \leftarrow L_1, \ldots, L_n$ where each L_i is a literal (i.e. an atom A or the default negation of an atom $not\ A$). If r is a clause (or rule), by $H(r)$ we mean L_0, and by $B(r)$ we mean $L_1, \ldots, L_n$. If $H(r) = A$ (resp. $H(r) = not\ A$) then $not\ H(r) = not\ A$ (resp. $not\ H(r) = A$). By a (2-valued) *interpretation* M of $\mathcal{L}$ we mean any set of literals from $\mathcal{L}$ that satisfies the condition that for any A, *precisely one* of the literals A or $not\ A$ belongs to M. Given an interpretation M we define $M^+ = \{A : A$ is an atom, $A \in M\}$ and $M^- = \{not\ A : A$ is an atom, $not\ A \in M\}$. Wherever convenient we omit the default (negative) atoms when describing interpretations and models. Also, rules with variables stand for the set of their ground instances. We say that a (2-valued) interpretation M of $\mathcal{L}$ is a stable model of a generalized logic program P if $\xi(M) = least\,(\xi(P) \cup \xi(M^-))$, where $\xi(.)$ univocally renames every default literal $not\ A$ in a program or model into new atoms, say not_A. In the remaining, we refer to a GLP simply as a logic program (or LP).

A.2   Dynamic Logic Programming

Hext we recall the semantics of *dynamic logic programming* [1]. A dynamic logic program $\mathcal{P} = \{P_s : s \in S\} = P_0 \oplus \ldots \oplus P_n \oplus \ldots$, is a finite or infinite sequence of LPs, indexed by the finite or infinite set $S = \{1, 2, \ldots, n, \ldots\}$. Such sequence may be viewed as the outcome of updating P_0 with P_1, ..., updating it with $P_n, \ldots$ The role of dynamic logic programming is to ensure that these newly added rules are in force, and that previous rules are still valid (by inertia) for as long as they do not conflict with more recent ones. The notion of dynamic logic program at state s, denoted by $\bigoplus_s \mathcal{P} = P_0 \oplus \ldots \oplus P_s$, characterizes the meaning of the dynamic logic program when queried at state s, by means of its stable models, defined as follows:

Definition 1 (Stable Models of DLP). *Let* $\mathcal{P} = \{P_s : s \in S\}$ *be a dynamic logic program, let* $s \in S$. *An interpretation* M *is a* stable model of $\mathcal{P}$ at state s *iff*

$$M = least\,([\rho\,(\mathcal{P})_s - Rej(\mathcal{P}, s, M)] \cup Def\,(\rho\,(\mathcal{P})_s, M))$$

where

$$\rho\,(\mathcal{P})_s = \bigcup_{i \leq s} P_i$$

$$Rej(\mathcal{P}, s, M) = \{r \in P_i : \exists r' \in P_j, i < j \leq s, H(r) = not\ H(r') \wedge M \vDash B(r')\}$$

$$Def(\rho\,(\mathcal{P})_s, M) = \{not\ A \mid \nexists r \in \rho\,(\mathcal{P})_s : (H(r) = A) \wedge M \vDash B(r)\}$$

If some literal or conjunction of literals ϕ *holds in all stable models of* $\mathcal{P}$ *at state* s, *we write* $\bigoplus_s \mathcal{P} \vDash \phi$. *If* s *is the largest element of* S *we simply write* $\bigoplus \mathcal{P} \vDash \phi$.

A.3 LUPS

Here we recall the semantics of the language of updates $LUPS$ closely following its original formulation in [3], with the semantical modification of [22]. The object language of $LUPS$ is that of generalized logic programs. A sentence U in $LUPS$ is a set of simultaneous update commands (described in Section 2), that, given a pre-existing sequence of logic programs $P_0 \oplus \cdots \oplus P_n$ (i.e. a dynamic logic program), whose semantics corresponds to our knowledge at a given state, produces a sequence with one more program, $P_0 \oplus \cdots \oplus P_n \oplus P_{n+1}$, corresponding to the knowledge that results from the previous sequence after performing all the simultaneous commands. A program in $LUPS$ is a sequence of such sentences.

Knowledge can be queried at any state $t \leq n$, where n is the index of the current knowledge state. A query will be denoted by:

$$\textbf{holds } L_1, \ldots, L_k \textbf{ at } t?$$

and is true iff the conjunction of its literals holds at the state obtained after the tth update. If $t = n$, the state reference "at t" is skipped.

Definition 2 (LUPS). *An update program in LUPS is a finite sequence of updates, where an update is a set of commands of the form (1) to (7).*

The semantics of $LUPS$ is defined by incrementally translating update programs into sequences of generalized logic programs and by considering the semantics of the DLP formed by them.

Let $\mathcal{U} = U_1 \otimes \ldots \otimes U_n$ be a $LUPS$ programs. At every state t the corresponding DLP, $\Upsilon_t(\mathcal{U}) = \mathcal{P}_t$, is determined.

The translation of a $LUPS$ program into a dynamic program is made by induction, starting from the empty program P_0, and for each update U_t, given the already built dynamic program $P_0 \oplus \cdots \oplus P_{t-1}$, determining the resulting program $P_0 \oplus \cdots \oplus P_{t-1} \oplus P_t$. To cope with persistent update commands, associated with every dynamic program in the inductive construction, a set containing all currently active persistent commands is considered, i.e. all those commands that were not cancelled until that point in the construction, from the time they were introduced. To be able to retract rules, a unique identification of each such rule is needed. This is achieved by augmenting the language of the resulting dynamic program with a new propositional variable "$N(R)$" for every rule R appearing in the original $LUPS$ program. To properly handle non-inertial commands, we also need to uniquely associate those rules appearing in non-inertial commands with the states they belong to. To this end, the language of the resulting dynamic logic program must also be extended with a new propositional variable "$Ev(R, S)$" for every rule R appearing in a non-inertial command in the original $LUPS$ program, and every state S.

Definition 3 (Translation into dynamic logic programs). *Let $\mathcal{U} = U_1 \otimes \cdots \otimes U_n$ be an update program. The corresponding dynamic logic program $\Upsilon(\mathcal{U}) = \mathcal{P} = P_0 \oplus \cdots \oplus P_n$ is obtained by the following inductive construction, using at each step t an auxiliary set of persistent commands PC_t:*

Base step: $P_0 = \{\}$ with $PC_0 = \{\}$.

Inductive step: Let $\Upsilon_{t-1}(\mathcal{U}) = \mathcal{P}_{t-1} = P_0 \oplus \cdots \oplus P_{t-1}$ with the set of persistent commands PC_{t-1} be the translation of $\mathcal{U}_{t-1} = U_1 \otimes \cdots \otimes U_{t-1}$. The translation of $\mathcal{U}_t = U_1 \otimes \cdots \otimes U_t$ is $\Upsilon_t(\mathcal{U}) = \mathcal{P}_t = P_0 \oplus \cdots \oplus P_{t-1} \oplus P_t$ with the set of persistent commands PC_t, where:

$PC_t = PC_{t-1} \cup \{\textbf{assert } R \textbf{ when } \phi : \textbf{always } R \textbf{ when } \phi \in U_t\} \cup$
$\cup \{\textbf{assert event } R \textbf{ when } \phi : \textbf{always event } R \textbf{ when } \phi \in U_t\} \cup$
$- \{\textbf{assert [event] } R \textbf{ when } \phi : \textbf{cancel } R \textbf{ when } \psi \in U_t \wedge \bigoplus \mathcal{P}_{t-1} \vDash \psi\}$
$- \{\textbf{assert [event] } R \textbf{ when } \phi : \textbf{retract } R \textbf{ when } \psi \in U_t \wedge \bigoplus \mathcal{P}_{t-1} \vDash \psi\}$

$NU_t = U_t \cup PC_t$

$P_t = \{not\ N(R) \leftarrow: \textbf{retract } R \textbf{ when } \phi \in NU_t \wedge \bigoplus \mathcal{P}_{t-1} \vDash \phi\} \cup$
$\cup \{N(R) \leftarrow; H(R) \leftarrow B(R), N(R) : \textbf{assert } R \textbf{ when } \phi \in NU_t \wedge \bigoplus \mathcal{P}_{t-1} \vDash \phi\} \cup$
$\cup \{H(R) \leftarrow B(R), Ev(R, t) : \textbf{assert event } R \textbf{ when } \phi \in NU_t \wedge \bigoplus \mathcal{P}_{t-1} \vDash \phi\} \cup$
$\cup \{not\ N(R) \leftarrow Ev(R, t) : \textbf{retract event } R \textbf{ when } \phi \in NU_t \wedge \bigoplus \mathcal{P}_{t-1} \vDash \phi\} \cup$
$\cup \{not\ Ev(R, t-1) \leftarrow; Ev(R, t) \leftarrow\}$

Definition 4 (LUPS Semantics). *Let* $\mathcal{U}$ *be an update program. A query*

$$\text{holds } L_1, \ldots, L_n \text{ at } t$$

is true in $\mathcal{U}$ *iff* $\bigoplus_t \Upsilon(\mathcal{U}) \vDash L_1, \ldots, L_n$.

Further details, properties, and examples about the language of updates LUPS and its semantics can be found in [3,22].

Extracting General Recursive Program Schemes in Nuprl's Type Theory

James L. Caldwell[*]

Department of Computer Science, University of Wyoming, Laramie Wyoming
jlc@cs.uwyo.edu

Abstract. Nuprl supports program synthesis by extracting programs from proofs. In this paper we describe the extraction of "efficient" recursion schemes from proofs of well-founded induction principles. This is part of a larger methodology; when these well-founded induction principles are used in proofs, the structure of the program extracted from the proof is determined by the recursion scheme inhabiting the induction principle. Our development is based on Paulson's paper *Constructing recursion operators in intuitionistic type theory*, but we specifically address two possibilities raised in the conclusion of his paper: the elimination of non-computational content from the recursion schemes themselves and, the use of the Y combinator to allow the recursion schemes to be extracted directly from the proofs of well-founded relations.

1 Introduction

In this paper we describe the formal derivation, in Nuprl[11,2], of a number of abstract induction principles. Since Nuprl's type theory is constructive, these proofs implicitly contain computational content; programs may be extracted from proofs. The relationship between induction and recursion is well known; in the case of the induction principles proved here, the programs extracted from these proofs are efficient *general recursive* program schemes. In further proof development, when one of these induction theorems is instantiated as a lemma, the program extracted from that proof will include the recursion scheme extracted from the proofs described here. Thus, careful proofs of the induction principles presented here result in efficient and readable extracted code in program developments that use these induction principles. This effort supports the larger Nuprl project goals of developing practical proof-based programming methodologies.

In a widely cited paper [21], Paulson derived recursion schemes in a theory of well-founded relations. In the final section of that paper, Paulson suggests some alternative approaches which would improve his results by achieving the following goals.

i.) Paulson's recursion schemes include non-computational content, *i.e.* there are arguments to the recursion schemes that do not actually contribute to

---

[*] This research was supported by NSF CCR-9985239

A. Pettorossi (Ed.): LOPSTR 2001, LNCS 2372, pp. 233–244, 2002.

the computations, they are artifacts of proofs that have found their way into the resulting program. Non-computational junk included in the recursion scheme will appear in every program derived using the corresponding induction scheme. In the development described here, we eliminate all non-computational junk from the recursion schemes.

ii.) The second improvement Paulson suggests, is to use the fixed point combinator Y as the extract of the proofs of the induction principles. He introduces a new operator (**wfrec**) which is characterized by adding new proof rules to the system and by extending the evaluator. We use the standard Nuprl methodology for defining general recursive functions via the fixed point combinator Y and avoid the introduction of the **wfrec** operator.

To accomplish (i.) we refine the specification of well-founded relations using Nuprl's set and intersection types, replacing the $\exists (\Sigma)$ and $\forall (\Pi)$ types where appropriate. Using Allen's [1] terminology, the set and intersection types are *non-propositional types*, *i.e.* their inhabitants do not contain all the computational content required for proofs of their own well-formedness. Because the inhabitants of these types do not carry complete information, their use in specifications may result in a technically more complicated proof. However, the missing information is precisely the non-computational junk we hope to eliminate from extracted programs.

Addressing point (ii.). Nuprl admits definitions of general recursive functions via the fixed point combinator Y. Nuprl's underlying computation system is an untyped λ-calculus so Y is easily defined, if not typed itself[1]. The possibility of using Y to define recursive functions within the Nuprl type system was first noted by Allen in 1984 who realized that *applications* of Y (if they indeed terminate) could be assigned a type. Nuprl's so-called direct-computation rules stipulate that computation anywhere in a term preserves typing; *i.e.* the form of the computation rules explicitly guarantees that the system has the subject reduction property. Now, if a term containing Y terminates, it must do so by a finite number of computation steps, including unfolding of the Y combinator. This fact combined with that fact that computation preserves typing means that there is never a requirement to actually assign a type to the Y combinator itself; in any terminating computation, it simply disappears after some finite number of steps. Based on Allen's proof, Howe [15,16] developed the current methodology for defining and using general recursive functions in Nuprl. Jackson [17,18] incorporated Howe's methodology into his tactics for Nuprl 4.

In this paper we give a new definition of well-founded relations use his methodology to extract recursion schemes corresponding to a number of induction principles given in Paulson's paper.

We will only present details of Nuprl's type theory here as necessary but we briefly reiterate the most elementary ideas of the propositions-as-types interpretation which encodes logic via type-theory. Under this interpretation, the

---

[1] In [2], Allen has recently argued that a minor reinterpretation of the function rules would allow Y itself to be typed.

implication $\phi \Rightarrow \psi$ is just encoded as the function type $\phi \to \psi$. The implication is true if there is some term $\lambda x.M$ inhabiting the type $\phi \to \psi$. The conjunction $\phi \wedge \psi$ is encoded as the Cartesian product $\phi \times \psi$. The conjunction is true if there is an pair $\langle a, b \rangle$ inhabiting $\phi \times \psi$. Disjunction $\phi \vee \psi$ is encoded as a disjoint union type $\phi + \psi$. The disjunction is true if it is inhabited by a term of the form $inl(a)$ for some $a \in \phi$ or by a term of the form $inr(b)$ for some $b \in \psi$. False is encoded as the type Void which has no inhabitants. True is encoded by a type having a single inhabitant.

A detailed hyper-text account of Nuprl's type theory is available online [2] and the reader is urged to examine this document. Most of the notation used here will be familiar. With only very minor differences, the definitions and theorems presented in this paper appear as they do on the screen in the Nuprl system. It should be noted that the display form of any construct in the Nuprl system is under user control and so may differ from user to user as notational tastes often do.

2 Efficient Induction Schemes

Nuprl provides support (in the form of proof rules) for inducting over built-in types of numbers and lists. The extracts of these induction rules are primitive recursion schemes. User specified inductive types are defined via the rec constructor, its uses are also supported by proof rules. Elimination of rec types, corresponding to induction on the structure of the type, results in program extracts containing the recind operator. In Nuprl practice, explicit definition of recursive functions by recind has been superseded by definitions using Y.

The available forms of induction in the system are not fixed, new forms can be added by proving the new induction principle as a theorem. The extract of the proof is a recursion scheme. Of course, any proof will have as its extract a correspondingly correct recursion scheme, but we have gone to some lengths to insure our recursion schemes are free of non-computational content. This approach differs somewhat from Paulson's where a rule for well-founded induction is added to the proof system. Here, we *prove* a relation satisfies the definition of well-foundedness and extract the recursion scheme from the proof. However, there are limits on the approach which will be discussed in the final section of this paper.

2.1 Well-Founded Relations and Recursion Schemes

A type of well-founded binary relations R over a type A is defined in the Nuprl standard library as follows.

$$\text{WellFnd}\{i\}(A;x,y.R[x;y]) \overset{\text{def}}{=}$$
$$\forall P:A \to \mathbb{P}\{i\}. (\forall j:A. (\forall k:A.R[k;j] \Rightarrow P[k]) \Rightarrow P[j]) \Rightarrow \forall n:A.P[n]$$

Before describing this definition we introduce Nuprl term structure. Nuprl terms are of the form <opid>{<parms>}(<bterms>) where <opid> is the name of the operator, `<parms>` is a possibly empty, comma separated list of parameters, and `<bterms>` is a, possibly empty, semi-colon separated list of bound terms. A bound term is of the form `<bvars>.<term>` where `<bvars>` is a, possibly empty, comma separated list of variable names and `<term>` is a term. The variable names in the list `<bvars>` are bound in `<term>`. In this term language, $\lambda x.M$ is a display form for the Nuprl term `lambda{}(x.M)` and $\forall x:T.M$ is a display for the term `all{}(T;x.M)`.

The display form `WellFnd{i}(A;x,y.R[x; y])` indicates that the definition is parameterized by the polymorphic universe level i and that it takes two arguments, the first is a type and the second is the term `x,y.R[x;y]` where x and y are bound in the application `R[x;y]`. The definition specifies that a relation R over a type A is well-founded if, for every property P of A satisfying the induction hypothesis $\forall j:A.(\forall k:A.\ R[k;j]) \Rightarrow P[k]) \Rightarrow P[j]$, we can show `P[n]` is true of every element $n \in A$.

The following lemma establishes that the natural numbers are well-founded over the ordinary less than relation. The extract of the proof is a program scheme for recursion on the natural numbers [2]

$\vdash$ `WellFnd{i}(`$\mathbb{N}$`;x,y.x < y)`
Extraction: λ`P,g.(letrec f(i) = g(i)(`λ`j,p.f(j)))`

To better understand the type of the extract, consider the goal after unfolding the definition of well-founded.

$\vdash \forall P:\mathbb{N}{\to}\mathbb{P}\{i\}.(\forall i:\mathbb{N}.(\forall j:\mathbb{N}.j < i \Rightarrow P[j]) \Rightarrow P[i]) \Rightarrow \forall i:\mathbb{N}.P[i]$

In the extracted term λ`P,g.(letrec f(i) = g(i)(`λ`j,p.f(j)))`, the subterm g corresponds to the computational content of the antecedent of the outermost implication. Thus, g is a function of two arguments, the first being the principal argument on which the recursion is formed, the second argument being a function inhabiting the proposition $(\forall j:\mathbb{N}.\ j < i \Rightarrow P[j])$ *i.e.* a function which accepts some element j of type $\mathbb{N}$ along with evidence for the proposition j < i and which produces evidence for `P[j]`. In this scheme, the evidence for j < i is contained in the argument p, the innermost λ-binding. The variable p occurs nowhere else in the term and so, clearly, does not contribute to the actual computation of `P[j]`; instead it is a vestige of the typing for well-founded relations. The argument p is not part of what one would ordinarily consider part of the computation, certainly no programmer would clutter his programs with an unused argument.

Before we introduce an alternative typing of well-founded relations we briefly introduce Nuprl's comprehension subtypes (set types) and intersection types and discuss decidability, stability and squash stability.

---

[2] For readability, we display the application Y(λ`f,x.M`) as `letrec f(x) = M`.

2.2   Comprehension Subtypes and Intersection Types in Nuprl

Methods of generating efficient and readable extracts by the use of comprehension subtypes (as opposed to the existential) were presented in [8]. We reiterate the main points here.

x:T×P[x] is the *dependent product type* (or sigma-type Σx:T.P[x]) consisting
    of pairs <a,b> where a∈T and b∈P[a]. Two pairs <a,b> and <a',b'> are
    equal in x:T×P[x] when a=a'∈T and b=b'∈P[a]. Under the propositions
    as types interpretation, this is existential quantification and so is sometimes
    displayed as ∃x:T.P[x].
{y:T|P[y]} denotes a *comprehension subtype* (or set type) when T is a type and
    P[y] is a proposition possibly containing free occurrences of the variable y.
    Elements a of this type are elements of T such that P[a] is true. Equality
    for set types is just the equality of the type T restricted to those elements
    satisfying P.

In the case of an existential, <a,p>∈∃x:T.P[x], the second element of the
pair is the evidence for P[a]. In the context of a program extracted from a ∀∃
theorem, p is the computational content of the proof that P[a] in fact holds. This
verification often has no computational significance. Notice that the inhabitants
of {x:T|P[x]} are simply the projections of the first elements of the inhabitants
of ∃x:T.P[x], *i.e.* they do not include the part that often turns out to be non-
computational junk.

y:T→P[y] is the *dependent function type* (or pi-type Πx:T.P) containing func-
    tions with domain of type T and where P[y] is a term and y is a variable
    possibly occurring free in P. Functions are denoted by λ-terms, thus we write
    (λx.M[x]) ∈ y:T→P[y] whenever a∈T, P[a] is a type, and M[a]∈P[a].
    These are the functions whose range may depend on the element of the do-
    main applied to. Function equality is extensional. Under the propositions
    as types interpretation this is universal quantification and so is sometimes
    displayed as ∀x:T.P[x].
∩x:T.P[x] denotes the *intersection* type. An element a is a member of ∩x:T.P
    [x] if for every z∈T, a∈P[z] (hence the name intersection type.) Informally,
    one may think of it as a function type where the domain has been discarded.

Thus, for our purposes, intersection types can be used to type polymorphic
functions *e.g.* for list functions such as append that do not depend on the type
of elements in the list, append∈∩T:U{i}.(T List) →(T List) →(T List)
. Note that the possibility of defining such implicitly polymorphic functions is
possible because the computation system is untyped.

2.3   Decidability, the Squash Type, and Squash Stability

Decidability for an arbitrary proposition P is not constructively valid. However,
for many P it is decidable (*i.e.* there is an algorithm to decide) which of P or
$\neg P$ holds. We write Dec(P) to denote the term (P ∨¬P).

If a proposition P[x] is decidable, given an element a∈{x:T | P[x]}, we can (re)construct the evidence for P[a]. Recall that this is the information that is not carried by inhabitants of the set type. To reconstruct it, simply run the decision procedure on P[a]. Since a does indeed inhabit the set type we know P[a] is true. The decision procedure will return a term of the form inl(t) such that t∈P[a]. Thus, if ∀x:T.Dec(P[x]), from knowing a∈{x:T|P[x]} we can reconstruct a term t such that ⟨a,t⟩∈∃x:T.P[x]. So, if the proposition P[x] is decidable, the set type and the existential form are equivalent, both logically and in terms of the information content of their inhabitants. It turns out that there are weaker conditions that establish this equivalence.

The notion of *stability* is related to decidability and is important in intuitionistic mathematics. A proposition P is stable if $(\neg\neg P \Rightarrow P)$, in this case we write Stable(P). Classically, the propositions Stable(P) and Dec(P) are tautologies and therefore are equivalent; intuitionistically, neither is valid, however, they are related. For any proposition P, Dec(P)⇒Stable(P) holds intuitionistically, but the converse does not. Stability is a weaker notion than decidability, but it is strong enough to establish the equivalence between set types and the existential.

A notion that is weaker still is *squash stability*. Informally, a proposition is squash stable if knowing it is inhabited at all is enough to reconstruct an inhabitant. First we describe the squash operator. We write ↓(P) to be the *squashed type*, {True | P}. Inhabitants of this type are all the inhabitants of True (there is only one) given the fact that P holds. Thus, if P is inhabited at all, ↓(P) contains the single inhabitant of True and is empty otherwise. Squash eliminates all interesting computational content and ↓(P) is inhabited only if P was. We give the following definition, SqStable{P} $\stackrel{\text{def}}{=}$ ↓(P) ⇒ P. Thus, if we can reconstruct an inhabitant of P simply from knowing ↓(P) is inhabited we write SqStable(P). Squash stability is weaker even that stability, for every proposition P, Stable(P) ⇒SqStable(P) holds, but not the converse. This is the weakest notion that effectively allows set types to be identified with existentials.

Many propositions are squash stable. Any stable or decidable proposition is squash stable. Equality on integers and the order relations on the integers are decidable and thus are also squash stable. Type membership is squash stable as is type equality.

2.4   Squash Stable Well-Founded Relations and Recursion Operators

As an alternative to the first definition of well-founded relations, which contained unwanted non-computational content in the extract, we have defined a notion of well-foundedness that hides the ordering in a set type.

$$WF_0\{i\}(A;x,y.R[x;\ y]) \stackrel{\text{def}}{=}$$
$$\forall P:A{\rightarrow}\mathbb{P}\{i\}.(\forall j:A.(\forall k:\{k:A|\ R[k;j]\}.P[k]) \Rightarrow P[j]) \Rightarrow \forall n:A.P[n]$$

This type can only usefully be applied in proofs when R is squash stable, thus we call it *squash stable well-foundedness*. However, it should also be noted that for program development, the constraint that R be squash stable seems not to matter. Indeed, it is hard to imagine an ordering relation, useful in computation, that is not squash stable.

Since the ordering relation is hidden in the right side of a set type it does not contribute to the computational content. The following lemma that the natural numbers are squash stable well-founded has the expected extract term.

$\vdash$ WF$_0$\{i\}(ℕ;x,y.x < y)
Extraction: λP,g.(letrec f(i) = (g(i)(λj.f j)))

By our own criteria for naturalness (if an argument does not appear in the body of the extracted term it should not be an argument), P should not appear in the extract. We further modify the type of squash stable well-foundedness to eliminate it using Nuprl's intersection type.

WF\{i\}(A;x,y.R[x; y]) $\overset{\text{def}}{=}$
∩P:A→ℙ\{i\}.(∀j:A.(∀k:\{k:A| R[k;j]\}.P[k]) ⇒ P[j]) ⇒ ∀n:A.P[n]

Now the well-foundedness of the natural numbers appears as follows.

$\vdash$ WF\{i\}(ℕ;x,y.x < y)
Extraction: λg.(letrec f(i) = (g(i)(λj.f j)))

The following two theorems characterize the relationship between the definition of well-foundedness and our definition of squash stable well-foundedness. The first says that squash stable well-foundedness implies well-foundedness.

$\vdash$ ∀T:𝕌. ∀R:T → T → ℙ.
WF\{i\}(T;x,y.R[x;y]) ⇒ WellFnd\{i\}(T;x,y.R[x;y])

The second says that if the relation is squash stable, well-foundedness implies squash stable well-foundedness.

$\vdash$ ∀T:𝕌. ∀R:T → T → ℙ.
(∀x,y:T. SqStable(R[x;y])) ⇒
WellFnd\{i\}(T;x,y.R[x;y]) ⇒ WF\{i\}(T;x,y.R[x;y])

2.5   Measure Induction and Lexicographic Induction Schemes

Using squash stable well-foundedness we prove a measure induction principle.

$\vdash$ ∩T:𝕌.∩ρ:T → ℕ.WF\{i\}(T;x,y.ρ(x) < ρ(y))
Extraction: λg.(letrec f(i) = (g(i)(λj.f(j))))

Thus, once a measure function ρ: T →ℕ is shown to exist we can apply well-founded induction on the type T. Note that the measure function ρ does not occur in the body of the extract. It is used to provide evidence for termination, but of course, termination measures are not typically included as arguments to functions.

Using a squash stable well-founded relation we are able to define an induction scheme for the lexicographic ordering of inverse images onto natural numbers.

⊢ ∩T:U.∩T':U.∩ρ:T → N.∩ρ':T' → N.
WF{i}(T × T'; x,y.ρ(x.1) < ρ(y.1)
∨ (ρ(x.1) = ρ(y.1) ∧ ρ'(x.2) < ρ'(y.2)))
Extraction: λg.(letrec f(i) = (g(i)(λj.f(j))))

2.6 Applications

The author and his students have used these induction principles to extract readable efficient programs. For each induction principle, a tactic is defined that instantiates the corresponding theorem and cleans up trivial subgoals.

The measure induction principle described here was used to derive a decision procedure for a sequent presentation of classical propositional logic [9]. The computational core of the decision procedure is the normalization lemma, stated as follows:

⊢ ∀G:Sequent
{L:Sequent List|
↓((∀s∈L. ρ(s) = 0)
∧ ((∀s∈L. |= s) ⇒ |= G)
∧ (∀a:Assignment. (∃s∈L. a |≠ s) ⇒ a |≠ G))}

Here the type **Sequent** is modeled as a pair of lists of propositional formulas, |= S indicates the sequent S is valid, a |≠ S means assignment a falsifies sequent S. The measure ρ : **Sequent** →N is the number of propositional connectives occurring in the formulas in the sequent.

The proof is by measure induction on the sequent G. The measure induction tactic is invoked with **sequent_rank** as the measure. Decomposing G into its component formula lists, **hyp** and **concl**, results in the following subgoal.

1. hyp: Formula List
2. concl: Formula List
3. IH: ∀k:{k:Sequent| ρ(k) < ρ(<hyp, concl>)}
{L:Sequent List|
↓((∀s∈L. ρ(s) = 0)
∧ ((∀s∈L. |= s) ⇒ |= k)
∧ (∀a:Assignment. (∃s∈L. a |≠ s) ⇒ a |≠ k))}
⊢ {L:Sequent List|
↓((∀s∈L. ρ(s) = 0)
∧ ((∀s∈L. |= s) ⇒ |= <hyp, concl>)
∧ (∀a:Assignment. (∃s∈L. a |≠ s) ⇒ a |≠ <hyp, concl>))}

The proof proceeds by inductively decomposing non-zero rank elements of the sequent <hyp,concl> if there are any; if not we directly argue the theorem holds. Thus, to proceed with the proof we case split on whether the list **hyp** contains any non-zero rank formula. In the case where all formulas in **hyp** are atomic we do a case split on whether **concl** is atomic or not.

The program extracted from this proof is shown below in Fig. 1, it normalizes classical propositional sequents by eliminating propositional operators. The program in Fig. 1 is the raw extract term after one step of rewriting which unfolds the extract of the measure induction theorem and contracts β-redexes. Note that the term ext{list_exists_decomposition} is a call to the extract of a proof of a list decomposition theorem. In the context of this extract, it is being applied to four arguments.

```
letrec normalize(S) =
  let <hyp,concl> = S in
    case ∃f∈hyp.(ρ(f) > 0)
    of inl(%2) =>
        let M,f@0,N = (ext{list_exists_decomposition}
                         (Formula)(λf.ρ(f) > 0)(hyp)(%2)) in
          case f@0:
            ⌜x⌝ → [];
            ⌜∼⌝x → (normalize(<M @ N, x::concl>));
            x1⌜∧⌝x2 → (normalize(<x1::x2::(M @ N), concl>));
            x1⌜∨⌝x2 → (normalize(<x1::(M @ N), concl>)
                              @ normalize(<x2::(M @ N), concl>));
            y1⌜⇒⌝y2 → (normalize(<y2::(M @ N), concl>)
                              @ normalize(<M @ N, y1::concl>));
      | inr(_) =>
          case ∃f∈concl.(ρ(f) > 0)
          of inl(%5) =>
              let M,f@0,N = (ext{list_exists_decomposition}
                               (Formula)(λf.ρ(f) > 0)(concl)(%5)) in
                case f@0:
                  ⌜x⌝ → [];
                  ⌜∼⌝x → (normalize(<x::hyp, M @ N>));
                  x1⌜∧⌝x2 → (normalize(<hyp, x1::(M @ N)>)
                                  @ normalize(<hyp, x2::(M @ N)>));
                  x1⌜∨⌝x2 → (normalize(<hyp, x1::x2::(M @ N)>));
                  y1⌜⇒⌝y2 → (normalize(<y1::hyp, y2::(M @ N)>));
        | inr(_) => <hyp, concl>::[]
```

Fig. 1. Extract of the Classical Normalization Lemma

Lexicographic measure induction was the induction scheme used in [10] to extract a decision procedure for intuitionistic propositional decidability.

3   Related Work

The most closely related work is, of course, Paulson [21], which we have discussed throughout the paper.

The definition of general recursive functions in Nuprl using the Y combinator is not new [15,16,18]. Howe was also the first to prove induction principles in Nuprl that had general recursive program schemes as their extracts, but he did not apply non-propositional types to rid the extracted schemes of non-computational junk as we have here. The value is in developing the practice and methodology.

Extracting general recursive functions from formal constructive proofs has been given theoretical consideration in other systems[13,20]. Only more recently have researchers using the other major implemented constructive systems, Coq [5] and Alf [3], considered mechanisms to extend their systems to allow definitions of general recursive functions [14,4,6,7].

4   Final Remarks

4.1   Remarks on the Proofs and the Limitations of the Method

The proofs having the efficient recursion schemes as their extracts would perhaps more correctly be called verifications. The extract terms are explicitly provided using the UseWitness tactic. After this step, the remaining proof is to show that the extract does indeed inhabit type. These proofs are surprisingly intricate. Also, proofs of well-foundedness of the lexicographic measure induction are widely published [12,19], but they rely on the least element principle which is non-constructive. The proof used here is by nested inductions on the natural numbers.

The method of applying well-founded induction principles in proofs has a limitation; lemmas can not be used in proving well-formedness goals. This is because the instantiation of the property being proved (P in the definition squash stable well-foundedness) will generate a well-formedness subgoal which is equivalent to the original goal; *i.e.* to show well-formedness, one is required to show well-formedness. In practice, this limitation has not been a burden since well-formedness goals are typically proved by following the structure of the type. A mechanism for incorporating derived rules into Nuprl has been designed. Once implemented, this feature will eliminate this restriction on the use of these principles.

We have only formalized a few of Paulson's well-founded induction schemes, however, we have applied them extensively. Some of the more complex schemes that we have not formalized (but will in future work) have been used elsewhere, notably the application of lexicographic exponentiation in the certification of Buchberger's algorithm [22].

Acknowledgments. The author thanks the anonymous reviewers for their detailed and thoughtful comments.

References

1. Stuart Allen. *A Non-Type-Theoretic Semantics for Type-Theoretic Language.* PhD thesis, Cornell University, Ithaca, NY, 1987. TR 87-866.
2. Stuart Allen. *NuprlPrimitives - Explanations of Nuprl Primitives and Conventions.* Computer Science Department, Cornell University, Ithaca, NY. www.cs.cornell.edu/Info/People/sfa/Nuprl/NuprlPrimitives/Welcome.html, 2001.
3. T. Altenkirch, V. Gaspes, B. Nordström, and B. von Sydow. *A user's guide to ALF.* Computer Science Department, Chalmers University of Technology, Göteborg, Sweden. Manuscript available at www.cs.chalmers.se/ComputingScience/Research/Logic/alf/guide.html, 1994.
4. Antonia Balaa and Yves Bertot. Fix-point equations for well-founded recursion in type theory. In *Theorem Proving in Higher Order Logics*, volume 1869 of *Lecture Notes in Computer Science*, pages 1–16. Springer, 2000.
5. Bruno Barras, Samuel Boutin, Cristina Cornes, Judicael Courant, Jean-Christophe Filliatre, Eduardo Gimenez, Hugo Herbelin, Gerard Huet, Cesar Munoz, Chetan Murthy, Catherine Parent, Christine Paulin-Mohring, Amokrane Saibi, and Benjamin Werner. *The Coq Proof Assistant Reference Manual : Version 6.1.* Technical Report RT-0203, INRIA, Rocquencourt, France, 1997.
6. Ana Bove. Simple general recursion in type theory. *Nordic Journal of Computing*, 8(1):22–42, 2001.
7. Ana Bove and Venanzio Capretta. Nested general recursion and partiality in type theory. In *Theorem Proving in Higher Order Logics*, volume 2152 of *Lecture Notes in Computer Science*, pages 121–135, 2001.
8. James Caldwell. Moving proofs-as-programs into practice. In *Proceedings, 12th IEEE International Conference Automated Software Engineering*, pages 10–17. IEEE Computer Society, 1997.
9. James Caldwell. Formal methods technology transfer: A view from NASA. *Formal Methods in System Design*, 12(2):125–137, 1998.
10. James Caldwell. Intuitionistic tableau extracted. In *Automated Reasoning with Analytic Tableaux and Related Methods*, Lecture Notes in Artifical Intelligence, Saratoga Springs, NY, June 1999. Springer.
11. Robert L. Constable and et al. *Implementing Mathematics with the Nuprl Development System.* Prentice-Hall, N.J., 1986.
12. J. H. Gallier. *Logic for Computer Science: Founations of Automatic Theorem Proving.* Harper and Row, 1986.
13. Didier Galmiche. Program development in constructive type theory. *Theoretical Computer Science*, 94:237–259, 1992.
14. Herman Geuvers, Erik Poll, and Jan Zwanenburg. Safe proof checking in type theory with y. In F. Flum and M. Rodriguez-Artalejo, editors, *Computer Science Logic (CSL'99)*, pages 439–452, September 1999.
15. D. Howe. *Automating Reasoning in an Implementation of Constructive Type Theory.* PhD thesis, Cornell University, Ithaca, NY, April 1988.
16. Douglas J. Howe. Reasoning about functional programs in Nuprl. In *Functional Programming, Concurrency, Simulation and Automated Reasoning*, volume 693 of *Lecture Notes in Computer Science*, Berlin, 1993. Springer Verlag.

17. Paul Jackson. The Nuprl proof developemnt system, version 4.2 reference manual and user's guide. Computer Science Department, Cornell University, Ithaca, N.Y. Manuscript available at
    http://www.cs.cornell.edu/Info/Projects/NuPrl/manual/it.html, July 1995.
18. Paul B. Jackson. *Enhancing the Nuprl proof development system and applying it to computational abstract algebra*. PhD thesis, Cornell University, 1995.
19. Zohar Manna and Richard Waldinger. *The Logical Basis for Computer Programming: Volume II: Deductive Systems*. Addison Wesley, 1990.
20. Michel Parigot. Recursive programming with proofs. *Theoretical Computer Science*, 94:335–356, 1992.
21. L. C. Paulson. Constructing recursion operators in intuitionistic type theory. *Journal of Symbolic Computation*, 2(4):325–355, 1986.
22. Laurent Théry. A Certified Version of Buchberger's Algorithm. In H. Kirchner and C. Kirchner, editors, *15th International Conference on Automated Deduction*, LNAI 1421, pages 349–364, Lindau, Germany, July 5–July 10, 1998. Springer-Verlag.

Extracting Exact Time Bounds from Logical Proofs

Mauro Ferrari, Camillo Fiorentini, and Mario Ornaghi

Dipartimento di Scienze dell'Informazione
Università degli Studi di Milano
{ferram,fiorenti,ornaghi}@dsi.unimi.it

Abstract. Accurate evaluation of delays of combinatorial circuits is crucial in circuit verification and design. In this paper we present a logical approach to timing analysis which allows us to compute exact stabilization bounds while proving the correctness of the boolean behavior.

1 Introduction

Accurate evaluation of delay times of combinatorial logic components is crucial in circuit verification and design [4,8]. For example, it is fundamental in determining the clock rate. Thus, various *timing analysis* methods have been developed in the literature for detecting different kinds of delays, as worst case or minimum delays, as well as for evaluating exact data-dependent delays (see [4, 8] for a discussion). In traditional approaches, timing analysis does not take into account data dependencies. In this way *false paths*, i.e., paths that cannot be activated by any input, may be detected and false path elimination is necessary to ensure accurate timing analysis. Moreover, many approaches model worst case and minimum gate delays as constants, while such delays may depend on the rising and falling times of the input signals and more accurate *gate models* are needed [4].

Among the timing analysis methods that have been developed in the literature, here we consider the logically based ones, see, e.g., [1,2,5,7,8]. Their logical nature automatically excludes false paths, since they are based on sound logical semantics. A semantics represents an abstraction from the physical details, and takes into account only aspects that are relevant for a given kind of analysis. For example, if we are only interested in the functional analysis of a combinatorial logic network, models based on Classical Logic are sufficient, while three valued logic allows us to take into account unstable or unknown signals [2]. Models based on Intuitionistic Logic and on Lax Logic have been proposed in [7,8]; they support in a uniform way both functionality analysis and input-dependent timing analysis with accurate gate models for combinatorial circuits.

In this paper we consider a modification of the approaches based on Intuitionistic and Lax logic. The main differences are in the adopted propositional language and in the formalization of time bounds. We consider optimal (exact) time bound evaluation for any kind of formulas, while the aforementioned approaches consider optimal bounds for restricted classes of formulas. Moreover,

A. Pettorossi (Ed.): LOPSTR 2001, LNCS 2372, pp. 245–265, 2002.

for suitable restrictions on waveforms, we have a completeness result for the logic $\mathbf{F}_{\mathrm{Cl}}$, which is a maximal axiomatizable and decidable intermediate logic [10].

In Section 2 we introduce and briefly discuss waveforms, and we define our propositional language and its waveform interpretation. In Section 3 we introduce time bounds and a constructive semantics based on time bounds. A calculus $\mathcal{ND}$ that is valid with respect to such a semantics is presented in Section 4. In Subsection 4.1 we prove the main result to extract a function calculating exact delays from proofs of $\mathcal{ND}$ and in Subsection 4.2 we apply it to an example; we also show that proofs of Classical Logics are inadequate to accomplish such an analysis. Finally, in Section 5 we briefly discuss the logical aspects of the proposed semantics.

2 Waveforms and Circuits

In the logical approach to circuit analysis a semantics represents an abstraction from the physical details and takes into account aspects that are relevant for a given kind of analysis, disregarding other aspects. To give an example, let us consider the gates INV and NAND of Figure 1; their behavior is specified by the following formulas of Classical Logic

$$\mathrm{INV}(x,y) \equiv (x \rightarrow \neg y) \wedge (\neg x \rightarrow y) \tag{1}$$

$$\mathrm{NAND}(x,y,z) \equiv (x \wedge y \rightarrow \neg z) \wedge (\neg x \vee \neg y \rightarrow z) \tag{2}$$

Indeed, the truth table of $\mathrm{INV}(x,y)$ represents the input/output behavior of the INV gate assuming x as input and y as output. Analogously, $\mathrm{NAND}(x,y,z)$ represents the NAND gate, where x and y are the inputs and z is the output. Similarly, the classical behavior of the XOR circuit is specified by the formula

$$\mathrm{XOR}(x,y,z) \equiv ((x \wedge \neg y) \vee (\neg x \wedge y) \rightarrow z) \wedge ((x \wedge y) \vee (\neg x \wedge \neg y) \rightarrow \neg z) \tag{3}$$

where x and y represent the inputs and z the output.

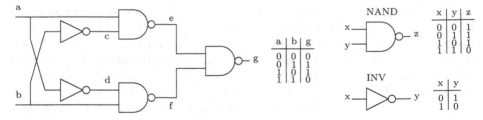

Fig. 1. The XOR circuit and its components

Classical semantics allows us to study the input/output behavior of combinatorial circuits, but does not allow us to represent temporal information about the stabilization properties of the circuits. Indeed, a more realistic description of the XOR circuit of Figure 1 should consider the instant at which the signals become stable and the delays in the propagation of signals; e.g., an "informal" characterization of the behavior of the above circuit should be as follows:

$$\begin{array}{|c|}\hline (a \text{ stable to } 1 \text{ at } t_1) \text{ and } (b \text{ stable to } 0 \text{ at } t_2) \\ \textbf{or} \\ (a \text{ stable to } 0 \text{ at } t_1) \text{ and } (b \text{ stable to } 1 \text{ at } t_2) \\ \hline \end{array} \Rightarrow (g \text{ stable to } 1 \text{ at } F(t_1, t_2))$$

$$\begin{array}{|c|}\hline (a \text{ stable to } 1 \text{ at } t_1) \text{ and } (b \text{ stable to } 1 \text{ at } t_2) \\ \textbf{or} \\ (a \text{ stable to } 0 \text{ at } t_1) \text{ and } (b \text{ stable to } 0 \text{ at } t_2) \\ \hline \end{array} \Rightarrow (g \text{ stable to } 0 \text{ at } G(t_1, t_2))$$

where F and G are functions from $\mathbf{N}^2$ in $\mathbf{N}$ and $\mathbf{N}$ represents discrete time.

To formalize this, we need to introduce some notions. As in [8,9], a *signal* is a discrete timed boolean function $\sigma \in \mathbf{N} \to \mathbf{B}$. A *circuit* is characterized by a set $\mathbf{S}$ of *observables* (the atomic formulas of our language) and a *waveform* is a map $V \in \mathbf{S} \to (\mathbf{N} \to \mathbf{B})$ associating with every observable a signal. A waveform represents an observable property of a circuit C, and an observable *behavior* of C is described by a set of waveforms.

As an example, to represent the XOR circuit of Figure 1, we need the set of observables $\{a, b, c, d, e, f, g\}$ representing the connections between the gates of the circuit. A waveform represents a possible behavior of the circuit. For example Figure 2 describes a waveform for the NAND circuit. It puts in evidence that the output z rises to 1 at time t_2 with a certain delay δ_1 with respect to the time t_1 where the input x falls to 0. On the other hand, the output z falls to 0, and stabilizes to 0, at time t_6, with a certain delay δ_2 with respect to the time t_5 where both the inputs are stable to 1. We remark that $\delta_1 \neq \delta_2$; indeed, in a realistic description the delays are input dependent.

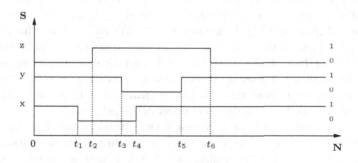

Fig. 2. A waveform for NAND

Since we are interested in studying stabilization properties of a circuit, we consider only waveforms that stabilize at some time. In particular, we introduce the following notions of stabilization for a waveform:

1. V is *stable* iff, for every $a \in \mathbf{S}$ and for every $t \in \mathbf{N}$, $V(a)(t) = V(a)(0)$;
2. V is *eventually stable* iff, for every $a \in \mathbf{S}$, there exists $t \in \mathbf{N}$ such that, for every $k \geq t$, $V(a)(k) = V(a)(t)$.

We denote with STABLE the set of all the stable waveforms and with ESTABLE the set of all the eventually stable waveforms.

To express *stabilization properties* of waveforms and behaviors, we use a propositional language $\mathcal{L}_\mathbf{S}$ based on a denumerable set of *observables* $\mathbf{S} = \{a, b, c_1, c_2, \dots\}$. Formulas of $\mathcal{L}_\mathbf{S}$ are inductively defined as follows: for every $a \in \mathbf{S}$, a is an *atomic* formula of $\mathcal{L}_\mathbf{S}$; if $A, B \in \mathcal{L}_\mathbf{S}$, then $A \wedge B$, $A \vee B$, $A \to B$, $\neg A$ and $\Box A$ belong to $\mathcal{L}_\mathbf{S}$.

We say that a waveform V *validates a stabilization property A at time t*, written $t, V \Vdash A$, if one of the following conditions holds:

$t, V \Vdash a$, where $a \in \mathbf{S}$, iff $V(a)(k) = 1$ for all $k \geq t$;
$t, V \Vdash \Box B$ iff $k, V \Vdash B$ for some $k \geq t$;
$t, V \Vdash B \wedge C$ iff $t, V \Vdash B$ and $t, V \Vdash C$;
$t, V \Vdash B \vee C$ iff either $t, V \Vdash B$ or $t, V \Vdash C$;
$t, V \Vdash B \to C$ iff, for every $k \in \mathbf{N}$, $k, V \Vdash B$ implies $l, V \Vdash C$ for some $l \geq k$;
$t, V \Vdash \neg a$, where $a \in \mathbf{S}$, iff $V(a)(k) = 0$ for all $k \geq t$;
$t, V \Vdash \neg\Box B$ iff $k, V \Vdash \neg B$ for some $k \geq t$;
$t, V \Vdash \neg(B \wedge C)$ iff either $t, V \Vdash \neg B$ or $t, V \Vdash \neg C$;
$t, V \Vdash \neg(B \vee C)$ iff $t, V \Vdash \neg B$ and $t, V \Vdash \neg C$;
$t, V \Vdash \neg(B \to C)$ iff $t, V \Vdash B$ and $t, V \Vdash \neg C$;
$t, V \Vdash \neg\neg B$ iff $t, V \Vdash B$.

It is easy to check that $t, V \Vdash A$ implies $h, V \Vdash A$, for all $h \geq t$. For a atomic, a and $\neg a$ denote the stability of the observable signal $V(a)$ (at time t, with value 1 and 0 respectively). Indeed $t, V \Vdash a$ ($t, V \Vdash \neg a$) iff the signal $V(a)$ is stable to 1 (to 0 respectively) from t on.

Implication underlies a propagation delay, i.e., $t, V \Vdash A \to B$ means that, whenever, at some t', A "stabilizes" ($t', V \Vdash A$) then, after a certain amount of time s, B will "stabilize" ($t' + s, V \Vdash B$). E.g., if V is the waveform of Figure 2, we have $0, V \Vdash (x \wedge y) \to \neg z$; indeed $t, V \Vdash x \wedge y$ iff $t \geq t_5$ and $t \Vdash \neg z$ for all $t \geq t_6$, hence the stabilization delay is at most $t_6 - t_5$. We also remark that, differently from the other connectives, the validity of an implication is independent of t, indeed, $t, V \Vdash (B \to C)$ iff $0, V \Vdash (B \to C)$. Intuitively this corresponds to the fact that an implication does not represent a *property observable at a given time*, but a *global property* expressing a behavior invariant with respect to time shift. This is what has to be expected to express delay properties.

The unary modal operator $\Box$ means future stabilization; e.g., for the waveform of Figure 2, $0, V \Vdash \Box x$ since there is a moment in the future where x stabilizes to 1, but $0, V \not\Vdash x$. Validation of $\wedge, \vee$ is defined as expected. As for the negation, the above semantics defines it as a constructive negation and the validity of $\neg A$ is defined recursively on the structure of A (for a discussion on this negation see [11,13]). We remark that such a constructive understanding of the negation is essential in our approach where $\neg a$ states the *positive* information "a stabilizes to 0" and is different from the usual intuitionistic understanding of negation as "a implies falsehood".

A logical characterization of stable and eventually stable waveforms is the following:

$$V \in \textsc{Stable} \quad \text{iff} \quad 0, V \Vdash A \vee \neg A \text{ for every } A \in \mathcal{L}_\mathbf{S}$$

$$V \in \textsc{EStable} \quad \text{iff} \quad 0, V \Vdash \Box A \vee \neg\Box A \text{ for every } A \in \mathcal{L}_\mathbf{S}$$

Now, to represent the classical input/output behavior of a boolean function in our semantics, we associate with an eventually stable waveform V the classical interpretation V^{CL} done as follows: for every $a \in \mathbf{S}$,

$$V^{\mathrm{CL}}(a) = \begin{cases} 0 & \text{if } 0, V \Vdash \neg \Box a \\ 1 & \text{if } 0, V \Vdash \Box a \end{cases}$$

Definition 1. *Given a boolean function $f : \mathbf{B}^n \to \mathbf{B}$, a formula $F(a_1, \dots, a_n, b)$ of $\mathcal{L}_{\mathbf{S}}$ represents f iff, for every $V \in$ ESTABLE,*

$$0, V \Vdash \Box F(a_1, \dots, a_n, b) \quad \textit{iff} \quad f(V^{\mathrm{CL}}(a_1), \dots, V^{\mathrm{CL}}(a_n)) = V^{\mathrm{CL}}(b)$$

We remark that the above definition does not work if $0, V \Vdash \Box A \vee \neg \Box A$ does not hold, that is if V is not eventually stable. Indeed, in our approach we do not treat the case of oscillating signals; to treat such signals a different semantics (e.g., a multi-valued semantics) should be considered.

The *formal verification task* of the circuit of Figure 1 consists in exhibiting a formal proof (in the adequate logic) of the formula

$$\mathrm{INV}(b, c) \wedge \mathrm{INV}(a, d) \wedge \mathrm{NAND}(a, c, e) \wedge \mathrm{NAND}(b, d, f) \wedge \mathrm{NAND}(e, f, g) \to \mathrm{XOR}(a, b, g)$$

If our aim is only to prove the correctness of the above circuit Classical Logic is sufficient. But if we aim to extract information about the stabilization delays of the circuit from the correctness proof, we need to introduce an intensional semantics of formulas that takes into account temporal information.

3   Stabilization Bounds

The validation $\Vdash$ provides an interpretation of formulas as stabilization properties, but the information about stabilization delays is not explicit. To extract stabilization delays we need an analysis of all the waveforms of a behavior. To deal with delays in our logic, we use the notion of *stabilization bound* introduced in [7] and inspired by the *evaluation forms* of [11]. Evaluation forms correspond to structural truth evaluations of formulas; stabilization bounds combine both truth and timing analysis.

In [8] the information about delays is linked to the operator $\Box$ (indicated by $\bigcirc$ in [8]). In contrast, we interpret $\Box$ as a "don't care" operator and we do not associate any time information with it (the only possible delay is 0), but we associate a stabilization information with atomic formulas and with every logical connective not in the scope of the $\Box$ operator. A stabilization bound for a and $\neg a$, with $a \in \mathbf{S}$, fixes an upper bound for the stabilization of the signal $V(a)$. The stabilization bounds for $\wedge, \to, \vee$ are defined as in [8], while the interpretation of $\neg$ and $\Box$ is peculiar of our approach.

Formally, we assign to every formula A of $\mathcal{L}_{\mathbf{S}}$ a set of *stabilization bounds* $\lceil A \rceil$ and an equivalence relation $\sim_A$ between elements of $\lceil A \rceil$, inductively on the structure of A:

- If $A = a$ or $A = \neg a$, with $a \in \mathbf{S}$, then $\lceil A \rceil = \mathbf{N}$, and $t \sim_A t'$ for every $t, t' \in \lceil A \rceil$.
- If $A = \Box B$ or $A = \neg \Box B$ then $\lceil A \rceil = \{0\}$, and $0 \sim_A 0$.
- $\lceil B \wedge C \rceil = \lceil B \rceil \times \lceil C \rceil$ and $(\beta, \gamma) \sim_{B \wedge C} (\beta', \gamma')$ iff $\beta \sim_B \beta'$ and $\gamma \sim_C \gamma'$.
- $\lceil A_1 \vee A_2 \rceil = \lceil A_1 \rceil \oplus \lceil A_2 \rceil$ (where $\oplus$ denotes the disjoint sum, that is the set of pairs $(1, \alpha)$ or $(2, \alpha')$ with $\alpha \in \lceil A_1 \rceil$ and $\alpha' \in \lceil A_2 \rceil$) and $(i, \alpha) \sim_{A_1 \vee A_2} (j, \alpha')$ iff $i = j$ and $\alpha \sim_{A_i} \alpha'$.
- $\lceil B \to C \rceil = \{f \mid f : \lceil B \rceil \to \lceil C \rceil \text{ s.t. } \beta \sim_B \beta' \text{ implies } f(\beta) \sim_C f(\beta')\}$, and $f \sim_{B \to C} f'$ iff $f(\beta) \sim_C f'(\beta)$ for every $\beta \in \lceil B \rceil$.
- $\lceil \neg (A_1 \wedge A_2) \rceil = \lceil \neg A_1 \rceil \oplus \lceil \neg A_2 \rceil$ and $(i, \alpha) \sim_{\neg(A_1 \wedge A_2)} (j, \alpha')$ iff $i = j$ and $\alpha \sim_{\neg A_i} \alpha'$.
- $\lceil \neg (B \vee C) \rceil = \lceil \neg B \rceil \times \lceil \neg C \rceil$ and $(\beta, \gamma) \sim_{\neg(B \vee C)} (\beta', \gamma')$ iff $\beta \sim_{\neg B} \beta'$ and $\gamma \sim_{\neg C} \gamma'$.
- $\lceil \neg (B \to C) \rceil = \lceil B \rceil \times \lceil \neg C \rceil$ and $(\beta, \gamma) \sim_{\neg(B \to C)} (\beta', \gamma')$ iff $\beta \sim_B \beta'$ and $\gamma \sim_{\neg C} \gamma'$.
- $\lceil \neg \neg B \rceil = \lceil B \rceil$ and $\beta \sim_{\neg \neg B} \beta'$ iff $\beta \sim_B \beta'$.

The equivalence relation $\sim_A$ is needed to cut undesired functions in the definition of $\lceil B \to C \rceil$. Intuitively, a stabilization bound $\alpha \in \lceil A \rceil$ intensionally represents a set of waveforms V that validate A for the "same reasons" and with the "same delay bounds". Formally, let us denote with V^t the waveform obtained by shifting V of t, i.e.,

$$V^t(a)(k) = V(a)(t + k) \text{ for all } a \in \mathbf{S}, k \in \mathbf{N}$$

A waveform V *validates A with stabilization bound* α, and we write $\alpha, V \models A$, if one of the following conditions holds.

- $t, V \models a$, with $a \in \mathbf{S}$, iff $t, V \Vdash a$;
- $t, V \models \neg a$, with $a \in \mathbf{S}$, iff $t, V \Vdash \neg a$;
- $0, V \models \Box B$ iff $t, V \Vdash B$ for some $t \in \mathbf{N}$;
- $(\beta, \gamma), V \models B \wedge C$ iff $\beta, V \models B$ and $\gamma, V \models C$;
- $(i, \alpha), V \models A_1 \vee A_2$ iff $\alpha, V \models A_i$, where $i \in \{1, 2\}$;
- $f, V \models B \to C$ iff, for every $t \in \mathbf{N}$ and $\beta \in \lceil B \rceil$, $\beta, V^t \models B$ implies $f(\beta), V^t \models C$;
- $0, V \models \neg \Box B$ iff $t, V \Vdash \neg B$ for some $t \in \mathbf{N}$;
- $(i, \alpha), V \models \neg(A_1 \wedge A_2)$ iff $\alpha, V \models \neg A_i$, where $i \in \{1, 2\}$;
- $(\beta, \gamma), V \models \neg(B \vee C)$ iff $\beta, V \models \neg B$ and $\gamma, V \models \neg C$;
- $(\beta, \gamma), V \models \neg(B \to C)$ iff $\beta, V \models B$ and $\gamma, V \models \neg C$;
- $\beta, V \models \neg \neg B$ iff $\beta, V \models B$.

To give an example, the INV and NAND gates of the previous section have the following sets of stabilization bounds:

$$\lceil \text{INV}(x, y) \rceil = (\mathbf{N} \to \mathbf{N}) \times (\mathbf{N} \to \mathbf{N})$$
$$\lceil \text{NAND}(x, y, z) \rceil = (\mathbf{N} \times \mathbf{N} \to \mathbf{N}) \times (\mathbf{N} \oplus \mathbf{N} \to \mathbf{N})$$

A stabilization bound for $\text{INV}(x, y)$ is, for example, the pair of identical functions $(f_{\text{INV}}, f_{\text{INV}})$ where

$$f_{\text{INV}}(t) = t + \delta_I \tag{4}$$

$(f_{\text{INV}}, f_{\text{INV}})$ provides an example of a data-independent stabilization bound for the INV gate. It represents the set of valuations V such that $V(y)$ stabilizes at time $t + \delta_I$ if $V(x)$ stabilizes at time t with constant delay δ_I. Indeed

$$(f_{\text{INV}}, f_{\text{INV}}), V \Vdash \text{INV}(x, y) \text{ iff } \begin{cases} x \text{ stable to } 1 \text{ at } t \implies y \text{ stable to } 0 \text{ at } t + \delta_I \\ x \text{ stable to } 0 \text{ at } t \implies y \text{ stable to } 1 \text{ at } t + \delta_I \end{cases}$$

Analogously, the pair $(f_{\text{NAND}}^-, f_{\text{NAND}}^+) \in \lceil \text{NAND}(x, y, z) \rceil$, with

$$f_{\text{NAND}}^-((t_1, t_2)) = \max\{t_1, t_2\} + \delta_N \quad \text{and} \quad f_{\text{NAND}}^+((i, t)) = t + \delta_N \qquad (5)$$

provides an example of a data-independent stabilization bound for the NAND gate. Indeed in f_{NAND}^-, δ_N is independent of t_1 (the time at which x stabilizes to 1) and of t_2 (the time at which y stabilizes to 1); in f_{NAND}^+, δ_N is independent of the pair (i, t).

We point out that, in the general case, stabilization bounds represent data-dependent information; e.g., a stabilization bound for $\text{NAND}(x, y, z)$ may consist of a pair of functions (η^-, η^+), where η^- calculates the stabilization bound for output stable to 0 and η^+ for output stable to 1.

It is easy to prove that validity is preserved by time shifting, i.e., $\alpha, V \models A$ implies $\alpha, V^t \models A$ for every $t \in \mathbf{N}$.

Moreover, it is easy to check the following result:

Proposition 1. *Let T be the following time evaluation function:*

- $T(t) = t$, *for $t \in \mathbf{N}$;*
- $T((\alpha, \beta)) = \max\{T(\alpha), T(\beta)\}$;
- $T((i, \alpha)) = T(\alpha)$, *for $i = 1, 2$;*
- $T(f) = 0$, *with f any function.*

Let V be a waveform and let A be a formula. For every $t \in \mathbf{N}$, $t, V \Vdash A$ if and only if there is $\alpha \in \lceil A \rceil$ such that $T(\alpha) \leq t$ and $\alpha, V \models A$.

Proposition 1 links the intensional semantics based on stabilization bounds and the extensional semantics of Section 2. Stabilization bounds convey a detailed temporal information allowing us to model exact temporal bounds of the kind considered in [8]. In our setting exact bounds are formalized as follows. Let A be a formula, let $\alpha \in \lceil A \rceil$ and let V be a waveform; α is *exact for V and A* if $\alpha, V \models A$ and one of the following conditions holds:

- $A = \square B$ or $A = \neg \square B$;
- $A = a$ or $A = \neg a$, with $a \in \mathbf{S}$, and, for all $t \in \mathbf{N}$, $t, V \models A$ implies $\alpha \leq t$;
- $A = B \wedge C$, $\alpha = (\beta, \gamma)$, β is exact for B and V, and γ is exact for C and V;
- $A = B_1 \vee B_2$, $\alpha = (k, \beta_k)$, with $k \in \{1, 2\}$, and β_k is exact for V and B_k;
- $A = B \rightarrow C$ and, for all $\beta \in \lceil B \rceil$, if β is exact for V and B, then $\alpha(\beta)$ is exact for V and C;
- $A = \neg\neg B$ and α is exact for V and B;
- $A = \neg(B_1 \wedge B_2)$, $\alpha = (k, \beta_k)$, with $k \in \{1, 2\}$, and β_k is exact for V and $\neg B_k$;
- $A = \neg(B \vee C)$, $\alpha = (\beta, \gamma)$, β is exact for V and $\neg B$, γ is exact for V and $\neg C$;

- $A = \neg(B \to C)$, $\alpha = (\beta, \gamma)$, β is exact for V and B, γ is exact for V and $\neg C$.

For instance, let A be the formula $(x \wedge y \to \neg z) \wedge (\neg x \vee y \to z)$ describing the NAND gate, and let V be the waveform of Figure 2. Let $\beta = (\beta^-, \beta^+)$ where $\beta^- : \mathbf{N}^2 \to \mathbf{N}$ and $\beta^+ : \mathbf{N} \oplus \mathbf{N} \to \mathbf{N}$; $\beta, V \models A$ iff $\beta^-((t_4, t_5)) = t$ with $t \geq t_6$. An exact stabilization bound for V and A is given by $t = t_6$, which is the "exact instant" where z stabilizes to 0. We remark that such a detailed analysis cannot be accomplished using the approach of [8,9].

4   Timing Analysis of a Circuit

Let us consider the problem to compute the stabilization delays of the XOR circuit of Figure 1. Firstly we have to provide a complete description of the components of the circuit. This means that, for every component of the circuit, we have to provide a formula A representing the component and a time bound $\alpha \in \lceil A \rceil$ which is exact for the set V of observed behaviors (the set of waveforms resulting from an experimental analysis of the component).

In our example the description is given by the formulas:

- INV(b, c) and INV(a, d) obtained by instantiating the formula INV(x, y) of (1);
- NAND(a, c, e), NAND(b, d, f) and NAND(e, f, g) obtained by instantiating the formula NAND(x, y, z) of (2).

We remark that such formulas uniquely characterize the structure of the circuit of Figure 1. Indeed, NAND(e, f, g) describes the NAND gate occurring in the XOR circuit, having as inputs e and f and as output g; in turn, e is the output of the NAND gate having as input a and c, described by the formula NAND(a, c, e), and f is the output of the NAND gate having as input b and d, described by the formula NAND(b, d, f) and so on. Hence

$$\mathcal{C}_{\text{XOR}} = \{\text{INV}(a, d), \text{INV}(b, c), \text{NAND}(a, c, e), \text{NAND}(b, d, f), \text{NAND}(e, f, g)\} \quad (6)$$

is the description of the circuit of Figure 1.

As for the stabilization bounds, in our example we assume that:

- All the instances of the INV gate occurring in the circuit have the same stabilization bound $(f_{\text{INV}}, f_{\text{INV}})$ described in (4);
- All the instances of the NAND gate occurring in the circuit have the same stabilization bound $(f_{\text{NAND}}^-, f_{\text{NAND}}^+)$ described in (5).

Starting from this information we would like to compute an exact stabilization bound for the whole circuit. In this section we prove that such a stabilization bound can be extracted from a formal correctness proof of the circuit in a constructive calculus. Here, we use the natural deduction calculus $\mathcal{ND}$ described in Table 1. $\mathcal{ND}$ is obtained by adding to the natural calculus for Intuitionistic Logic (see [12]) the rules for constructive negation $\neg$, the rules for the modal operator $\Box$ and the rule KP$_\Box$. In Table 1 we put between square brackets the assumptions

Table 1. The calculus $\mathcal{ND}$

$$A \quad \text{IAx} \qquad \frac{A \quad B}{A \wedge B} \ \text{I}\wedge \qquad \frac{A_1 \wedge A_2}{A_i} \ \text{E}\wedge_i \ \ i\in\{1,2\}$$

$$\frac{A_i}{A_1 \vee A_2} \ \text{I}\vee_i \ \ i\in\{1,2\} \qquad \frac{A \vee B \quad \begin{matrix}[A]\\ \vdots\ \pi_1\\ C\end{matrix} \quad \begin{matrix}[B]\\ \vdots\ \pi_2\\ C\end{matrix}}{C} \ \text{E}\vee$$

$$\frac{\begin{matrix}[A]\\ \vdots\ \pi\\ B\end{matrix}}{A \to B} \ \text{I}{\to} \qquad \frac{A \quad A \to B}{B} \ \text{E}{\to} \qquad \frac{A \quad \neg A}{B} \ \text{Contr} \quad \begin{matrix}\text{where} \ B \ = \ p \ \text{or}\\ B = \neg p \ \text{with} \ p \in \mathbf{S}\end{matrix}$$

$$\frac{\neg A_i}{\neg(A_1 \wedge A_2)} \ \text{I}\neg\wedge_i \ \ i\in\{1,2\} \qquad \frac{\neg(A \wedge B) \quad \begin{matrix}[\neg A]\\ \vdots\ \pi_1\\ C\end{matrix} \quad \begin{matrix}[\neg B]\\ \vdots\ \pi_2\\ C\end{matrix}}{C} \ \text{E}\neg\wedge$$

$$\frac{A}{\neg\neg A} \ \text{I}\neg\neg \qquad \frac{\neg\neg A}{A} \ \text{E}\neg\neg \qquad \frac{\neg A \quad \neg B}{\neg(A \vee B)} \ \text{I}\neg\vee \qquad \frac{\neg(A_1 \vee A_2)}{\neg A_i} \ \text{E}\neg\vee_i \ \ i\in\{1,2\}$$

$$\frac{A \quad \neg B}{\neg(A \to B)} \ \text{I}\neg{\to} \qquad \frac{\neg(A \to B)}{A} \ \text{E}\neg{\to}_1 \qquad \frac{\neg(A \to B)}{\neg B} \ \text{E}\neg{\to}_2$$

$$\frac{\begin{matrix}[\neg A]\\ \vdots\ \pi_1\\ B \wedge \neg B\end{matrix}}{\Box A} \ \text{I}\Box \qquad \frac{\begin{matrix}[A]\\ \vdots\ \pi_1\\ B \wedge \neg B\end{matrix}}{\neg\Box A} \ \text{I}\neg\Box \qquad \frac{\begin{matrix}[\Box A]\\ \vdots\ \pi_1\\ B \vee C\end{matrix}}{(\Box A \to B) \vee (\Box A \to C)} \ \text{KP}\Box$$

of the proof *discharged* by the application of the rule; $\pi : \{A_1,\ldots,A_n\} \vdash B$ denotes the fact that π is a proof with *undischarged* assumptions $A_1,\ldots,A_n$ and consequence B (for a detailed presentation of such notions see [12]).

It is easy to check that the calculus $\mathcal{ND}$ formalizes a fragment of Classical Logic according to the following translation. Let $\widetilde{H}$ be the formula obtained by deleting from $H \in \mathcal{L}_{\mathbf{S}}$ all the occurrences of $\Box$. If $\{A_1,\ldots,A_n\} \vdash B$ is provable in $\mathcal{ND}$, then $\{\widetilde{A}_1,\ldots,\widetilde{A}_n\} \vdash \widetilde{B}$ is provable in the natural deduction calculus $\mathcal{ND}_{\mathbf{Cl}}$ for Classical Logic.

Coming back to our example, if there exists a proof

$$\Pi \ : \ \mathcal{C}_{\mathrm{XOR}} \vdash \mathrm{XOR}(a,b,g)$$

in $\mathcal{ND}$, then, since $\mathrm{INV}(x, y)$, $\mathrm{NAND}(x, y, z)$ and $\mathrm{XOR}(x, y, z)$ represent the corresponding boolean functions inv, $nand$ and xor according to Definition 1, the input/output behavior of the XOR circuit of Figure 1 is proved to be correct. Obviously, this holds also if Π is a proof of Classical Logic. But, how we are going to show, from proofs of $\mathcal{ND}$ we can also extract information about the stabilization delays. In the following subsection we present the main result about the extraction of stabilization bounds form proofs of $\mathcal{ND}$, and in Subsection 4.2 we apply such a result to compute the propagation delays of the XOR circuit; finally, we also show that proofs of Classical Logics are inadequate to accomplish such an analysis.

4.1   Computing Stabilization Delays

Here we describe how to associate with every proof $\pi : \{A_1, \ldots, A_n\} \vdash B$ of $\mathcal{ND}$ a function $F_\pi : \lceil A_1 \rceil \times \cdots \times \lceil A_n \rceil \to \lceil B \rceil$. Here we denote with $\underline{\alpha}$ an element of $\lceil A_1 \rceil \times \cdots \times \lceil A_n \rceil$. The function is defined by induction on the structure of π as follows.

Assumption Introduction:

$$\pi \equiv A$$

F_π is the identity function

(7)

Conjunction Introduction: in this case π is the proof

$$
\frac{
\begin{array}{cc}
\begin{array}{c} A_1, \ldots, A_k \\ \vdots\ \pi_1 \\ B \end{array}
&
\begin{array}{c} A_{k+1}, \ldots, A_n \\ \vdots\ \pi_2 \\ C \end{array}
\end{array}
}{B \wedge C}\ \mathrm{I}\wedge
$$

(8)

$$F_\pi(\underline{\alpha}) = (F_{\pi_1}(\alpha_1, \ldots, \alpha_k), F_{\pi_2}(\alpha_{k+1}, \ldots, \alpha_n))$$

The function F_π is defined similarly for the cases corresponding to the rules $\mathrm{I}\neg\vee$, $\mathrm{I}\neg\to$.

Conjunction Elimination: in this case π is the proof

$$
\frac{
\begin{array}{c} A_1, \ldots, A_n \\ \vdots\ \pi_1 \\ B_1 \wedge B_2 \end{array}
}{B_i}\ \mathrm{E}\wedge_i
$$

(9)

$$F_\pi(\underline{\alpha}) = (F_{\pi_1}(\underline{\alpha}))_i$$

The function F_π is defined similarly for the cases corresponding to the rules $\mathrm{E}\neg\vee$, $\mathrm{E}\neg\to$.

Disjunction Introduction: in this case π is the proof

$$
\begin{array}{c}
A_1, \ldots, A_n \\
\vdots\ \pi_1 \\
\dfrac{B_i}{B_1 \vee B_2}\ \mathrm{IV}_i
\end{array}
\tag{10}
$$

$$
F_\pi(\underline{\alpha}) = (i, F_{\pi_1}(\underline{\alpha}))
$$

The function F_π is defined similarly for the case corresponding to the rule $I\neg\wedge$.

Disjunction Elimination: in this case π is the proof

$$
\dfrac{
\begin{array}{ccc}
\begin{array}{c} A_1, \ldots, A_k \\ \vdots\ \pi_1 \\ B \vee C \end{array} &
\begin{array}{c} A_{k+1}, \ldots, A_l, [B] \\ \vdots\ \pi_2 \\ D \end{array} &
\begin{array}{c} A_{l+1}, \ldots, A_n, [C] \\ \vdots\ \pi_3 \\ D \end{array}
\end{array}
}{D}\ \vee\mathrm{E}
\tag{11}
$$

$$
F_\pi(\underline{\alpha}) =
\begin{cases}
F_{\pi_2}(\alpha_{k+1}, \ldots, \alpha_l, \beta) & \text{if } F_{\pi_1}(\alpha_1, \ldots, \alpha_k) = (1, \beta) \\
F_{\pi_3}(\alpha_{l+1}, \ldots, \alpha_n, \gamma) & \text{if } F_{\pi_1}(\alpha_1, \ldots, \alpha_k) = (2, \gamma)
\end{cases}
$$

The function F_π is defined similarly for the case corresponding to the rule $E\neg\wedge$.

Implication Introduction: in this case π is the proof

$$
\begin{array}{c}
A_1, \ldots, A_n, [B] \\
\vdots\ \pi_1 \\
\dfrac{C}{B \rightarrow C}\ \rightarrow\mathrm{I}
\end{array}
\tag{12}
$$

$F_\pi(\underline{\alpha})$ is the function $f : \lceil B \rceil \rightarrow \lceil C \rceil$ such that $f(\beta) = F_{\pi_1}(\underline{\alpha}, \beta)$

Implication Elimination: in this case π is the proof

$$
\dfrac{
\begin{array}{cc}
\begin{array}{c} A_1, \ldots, A_k \\ \vdots\ \pi_1 \\ B \end{array} &
\begin{array}{c} A_{k+1}, \ldots, A_n \\ \vdots\ \pi_2 \\ B \rightarrow C \end{array}
\end{array}
}{C}\ \rightarrow\mathrm{E}
\tag{13}
$$

$$
F_\pi(\underline{\alpha}) = F_{\pi_2}(\alpha_{k+1}, \ldots, \alpha_n)(F_{\pi_1}(\alpha_1, \ldots, \alpha_k))
$$

Contr: in this case π is the proof

$$
\begin{array}{c}
A_1, \ldots, A_n \\
\vdots\ \pi_1 \\
\dfrac{B \wedge \neg B}{C}\ \mathrm{Contr}
\end{array}
\tag{14}
$$

$$
F_\pi(\underline{\alpha}) = \gamma \text{ where } \gamma \text{ is any element in } \lceil C \rceil
$$

¬¬-**Introduction**: in this case π is the proof

$$A_1, \ldots, A_n$$
$$\vdots \pi_1$$
$$B$$
$$\frac{}{\neg\neg B} \ \mathrm{I}\neg\neg \qquad (15)$$

$$F_\pi(\underline{\alpha}) = F_{\pi_1}(\underline{\alpha})$$

The function F_π is defined similarly for the case corresponding to the rule E¬¬.

$\Box$-**Introduction**: in this case π is the proof

$$A_1, \ldots, A_n, [\neg B]$$
$$\vdots \pi_1$$
$$C \wedge \neg C$$
$$\frac{}{\Box B} \ \Box\mathrm{I} \qquad (16)$$

$$F_\pi(\underline{\alpha}) = 0.$$

The function F_π is defined similarly for the case corresponding to the rule I¬$\Box$.

Rule KP$_\Box$: in this case π is the proof

$$A_1, \ldots, A_n, [\Box B]$$
$$\vdots \pi_1$$
$$C \vee D$$
$$\frac{}{(\Box B \rightarrow C) \vee (\Box B \rightarrow D)} \ \mathrm{KP}_\Box \qquad (17)$$

$$F_{\pi_1}(\underline{\alpha}) = \begin{cases} (1, \lambda x.\beta) & \text{if } F_{\pi_1}(\underline{\alpha}, 0) = (1, \beta) \\ (2, \lambda x.\gamma) & \text{if } F_{\pi_1}(\underline{\alpha}, 0) = (2, \gamma) \end{cases}$$

The main properties of the function F_π associated with a proof $\pi \in \mathcal{ND}$ are given by the following result.

Theorem 1. *Let $\pi : \{A_1, \ldots, A_n\} \vdash B$ be a proof of the calculus $\mathcal{ND}$ and let*

$$F_\pi : \lceil A_1 \rceil \times \cdots \times \lceil A_n \rceil \rightarrow \lceil B \rceil$$

be the function associated with π. For all $\alpha_1 \in \lceil A_1 \rceil, \ldots, \alpha_n \in \lceil A_n \rceil$, and for every eventually stable waveform V:

(i). *$\alpha_1, V \models A_1, \ldots, \alpha_n, V \models A_n$ implies $F_\pi(\alpha_1, \ldots, \alpha_n), V \models B$.*

(ii). *$\alpha'_1 \sim_{A_1} \alpha_1, \ldots, \alpha'_n \sim_{A_n} \alpha_n$ implies $F_\pi(\alpha'_1, \ldots, \alpha'_n) \sim_B F_\pi(\alpha_1, \ldots, \alpha_n)$.*

(iii). *α_1 exact for V and $A_1, \ldots, \alpha_n$ exact for V and A_n implies $F_\pi(\alpha_1, \ldots, \alpha_n)$ exact for V and B.*

Proof. We prove the assertion by induction on the structure of the proof π. If π only consists of an assumption introduction (the base case), then F_π is the identity on $\lceil A \rceil$ and the assertions trivially follow. The induction step goes by cases according to the last rule applied in π; here, we only consider some representative cases.

$\vee$-*elimination.* If the last rule applied in π is a $\vee$-elimination, π has the structure described in Point (11).

(i). Let us suppose that $\alpha_1, V \models A_1, \ldots, \alpha_n, V \models A_n$. By induction hypothesis on π_1, $F_{\pi_1}(\alpha_1, \ldots, \alpha_k), V \models B \vee C$. Let us assume that $F_{\pi_1}(\alpha_1, \ldots, \alpha_k) = (1, \beta)$; then $\beta, V \models B$. Now, let us consider the subproof $\pi_2 : \{A_{k+1}, \ldots, A_l, B\} \vdash D$ of π; by induction hypothesis, $F_{\pi_2}(\alpha_{k+1}, \ldots, \alpha_l, \beta), V \models D$, from which (i) follows. The case $F_{\pi_1}(\alpha_1, \ldots, \alpha_k) = (2, \gamma)$ is similar.

(ii). Suppose that $\alpha_1' \sim_{A_1} \alpha_1, \ldots, \alpha_n' \sim_{A_n} \alpha_n$ and $F_{\pi_1}(\alpha_1, \ldots, \alpha_k) = (1, \beta)$. By induction hypothesis on π_1, $F_{\pi_1}(\alpha_1', \ldots, \alpha_k') = (1, \beta')$ with $\beta' \sim_B \beta$. By induction hypothesis on π_2, $F_{\pi_2}(\alpha_{k+1}', \ldots, \alpha_l', \beta') \sim_D F_{\pi_2}(\alpha_{k+1}, \ldots, \alpha_l, \beta)$, hence $F_\pi(\alpha_1', \ldots, \alpha_n') \sim_D F_\pi(\alpha_1, \ldots, \alpha_n)$.

(iii). Let α_1 be exact for V and $A_1, \ldots,$ let α_n be exact for V and A_n. Let us suppose that $F_{\pi_1}(\alpha_1, \ldots, \alpha_k) = (1, \beta)$; by induction hypothesis, $(1, \beta)$ is exact for V and $B \vee C$, therefore, by definition, β is exact for V and B. By the induction hypothesis on π_2, $F_{\pi_2}(\alpha_{k+1}, \ldots, \alpha_l, \beta)$ is exact for V and D, and this concludes the proof.

$\rightarrow$-*introduction.* In this case π has the structure described in Point (12). First of all we must check that f is well-defined, i.e., that $\beta \sim_B \beta'$ implies $f(\beta) \sim_C f(\beta')$. If $\beta \sim_B \beta'$, by the induction hypothesis (ii) applied on π_1, $F_{\pi_1}(\alpha_1, \ldots, \alpha_n, \beta) \sim_C F_{\pi_1}(\alpha_1, \ldots, \alpha_n, \beta')$, which implies $f(\beta) \sim_C f(\beta')$.

(i). Let us suppose that $\alpha_1, V \models A_1, \ldots, \alpha_n, V \models A_n$ and let $f = F_\pi(\alpha_1, \ldots, \alpha_n)$; we prove that $f, V \models B \rightarrow C$. Let us take $\beta \in \lceil B \rceil$ and $t \in \mathbf{N}$ such that $\beta, V^t \models B$. We also have $\alpha_1, V^t \models A_1, \ldots, \alpha_n, V^t \models A_n$; since V^t is eventually stable, by induction hypothesis on π_1 we can conclude that $f(\beta), V^t \models C$.

(ii). Let $\alpha_1' \sim_{A_1} \alpha_1, \ldots, \alpha_n' \sim_{A_n} \alpha_n$, $f = F_\pi(\alpha_1, \ldots, \alpha_n)$, $f' = F_\pi(\alpha_1', \ldots, \alpha_n')$. Suppose $\beta \sim_B \beta'$; by induction hypothesis $f(\beta) \sim_C f(\beta')$, hence $f \sim_{B \rightarrow C} f'$.

(iii). Let α_1 be exact for V and $A_1, \ldots, \alpha_n$ be exact for V and A_n; we prove that $f = F_\pi(\alpha_1, \ldots, \alpha_n)$ is exact for V and $B \rightarrow C$. To this aim, let us take $\beta \in \lceil B \rceil$ such that β is exact for V and B. By induction hypothesis, it follows that $f(\beta)$ is exact for V and C, and this concludes the proof.

$\rightarrow$-*elimination.* In this case π has the structure described in Point (13).

(i). Suppose that $\alpha_1, V \models A_1, \ldots, \alpha_n, V \models A_n$; let $\beta = F_{\pi_1}(\alpha_1, \ldots, \alpha_k)$ and $f = F_{\pi_2}(\alpha_{k+1}, \ldots, \alpha_n)$. By induction hypothesis, we have both $\beta, V \models B$ and $f, V \models B \rightarrow C$, hence $f(\beta), V \models C$ and (i) is proved.

(ii). Let us suppose $\alpha_1' \sim_{A_1} \alpha_1, \ldots, \alpha_n' \sim_{A_n} \alpha_n$ and let $\beta = F_{\pi_1}(\alpha_1, \ldots, \alpha_k)$, $\beta' = F_{\pi_1}(\alpha_1', \ldots, \alpha_k')$, $f = F_{\pi_2}(\alpha_{k+1}, \ldots, \alpha_n)$, $f' = F_{\pi_2}(\alpha_{k+1}', \ldots, \alpha_n')$. By induction hypothesis we have both $\beta \sim_B \beta'$ and $f \sim_{B \rightarrow C} f'$, and this implies that $f(\beta) \sim_C f'(\beta')$.

(iii). Suppose α_1 to be exact for V and $A_1, \ldots, \alpha_n$ to be exact for V and A_n;

let $\beta = F_{\pi_1}(\alpha_1, \ldots, \alpha_k)$ and $f = F_{\pi_2}(\alpha_{k+1}, \ldots, \alpha_n)$. By induction hypothesis, β is exact for V and B, f is exact for V and $B \to C$; this implies that $f(\beta)$ is exact for V and C.

$\Box$-*introduction.* In this case π has the structure described in Point (16).
(i). Suppose $\alpha_1, V \models A_1, \ldots, \alpha_n, V \models A_n$. Since V is eventually stable, there is $t \in \mathbf{N}$ such that either $t, V \Vdash B$ or $t, V \Vdash \neg B$. Suppose that $t, V \Vdash \neg B$. By Proposition 1, there is $\beta \in \lceil \neg B \rceil$ such that $\beta, V \models \neg B$; by induction hypothesis on π_1, $F_{\pi_1}(\alpha_1, \ldots, \alpha_n, \beta), V \models C \wedge \neg C$, which implies (by Proposition 1) $t', V \Vdash C \wedge \neg C$, where $t' \in \mathbf{N}$, a contradiction. It follows that $t, V \Vdash B$, therefore $0, V \models \Box B$.
The proof of Points (ii) and (iii) is trivial. $\Box$

We remark that the assumption that V is eventually stable is essential to treat the cases of $\Box$-introduction and $\neg\Box$-introduction.

Summarizing, we have shown how to define, for every proof

$$\pi : \{A_1, \ldots, A_n\} \vdash B$$

a function F_π associating with $V \in \text{ESTABLE}$ and every n-upla of stabilization bounds $\alpha_1, \ldots, \alpha_n$ for $A_1, \ldots, A_n$ such that α_i is exact for A_i and V, an exact stabilization bound for B and V. We remark that the main advantage of our approach is given by Point (iii) of Theorem 1; indeed the logical approaches to timing analysis of [1,2,5,7,8] do not allow us to compute exact time bounds.

4.2   Application to the XOR Circuit

In this subsection we apply Theorem 1 to compute the exact stabilization bounds for the XOR circuit of Figure 1. To this aim, firstly we describe the formal correctness proof

$$\Pi \ : \ \mathcal{C}_{\text{XOR}} \vdash \text{XOR}(a, b, g)$$

in the calculus $\mathcal{ND}$, then we show how to construct the function F_Π.
   The proof can be constructed as follows:

$$\Pi \equiv \cfrac{\overset{\Gamma_3}{\underset{\pi_3}{\vdots}}}{(a \wedge \neg b) \vee (\neg a \wedge b) \to g} \quad \cfrac{\overset{\Gamma_6}{\underset{\pi_6}{\vdots}}}{(a \wedge b) \vee (\neg a \wedge \neg b) \to \neg g}}{\text{XOR}(a, b, g)} \ \text{I}\wedge$$

where the structure of the proofs π_3 and π_6 is described below.

$$\pi_3 \equiv \cfrac{\cfrac{[(a \wedge \neg b) \vee (\neg a \wedge b)] \quad \cfrac{[a \wedge \neg b], \Gamma_1}{\vdots \, \pi_1} \quad \cfrac{[\neg a \wedge b], \Gamma_2}{\vdots \, \pi_2}}{\neg e \vee \neg f}}{\neg e \vee \neg f \ \text{E}\vee} \quad \cfrac{\neg e \vee \neg f \quad \text{NAND}(e, f, g)}{\neg e \vee \neg f \to g} \ \text{E}\wedge_2}{\cfrac{g}{(a \wedge \neg b) \vee (\neg a \wedge b) \to g} \ \text{I}\to} \ \text{E}\to$$

where $\Gamma_3 = \Gamma_1 \cup \Gamma_2 \cup \{NAND(e,f,g)\}$.

$$\pi_6 \equiv \cfrac{\cfrac{[(a \wedge b) \vee (\neg a \wedge \neg b)] \quad \cfrac{\begin{array}{cc} [a\wedge b],\Gamma_4 & [\neg a \wedge \neg b],\Gamma_5 \\ \vdots\,\pi_4 & \vdots\,\pi_5 \\ e \wedge f & e \wedge f \end{array}}{e \wedge f}\,\mathrm{E}\vee}{e \wedge f} \qquad \cfrac{\cfrac{NAND(e,f,g)}{e \wedge f \to \neg g}\,\mathrm{E}\wedge_1}{}}{\cfrac{\neg g}{(a \wedge b) \vee (\neg a \wedge \neg b) \to \neg g}\,\mathrm{I}\!\to}\,\mathrm{E}\!\to$$

where $\Gamma_6 = \Gamma_4 \cup \Gamma_5 \cup \{NAND(e,f,g)\}$.

$$\pi_1 \equiv \cfrac{\cfrac{\cfrac{a \wedge \neg b}{\cfrac{a \wedge \neg b}{a}\,\mathrm{E}\wedge_1}}{} \quad \cfrac{\cfrac{\cfrac{a \wedge \neg b}{\neg b}\,\mathrm{E}\wedge_2 \quad \cfrac{INV(b,c)}{\neg b \to c}\,\mathrm{E}\wedge_2}{c}\,\mathrm{E}\!\to}{}}{\cfrac{\cfrac{a \wedge c}{a \wedge c}\,\mathrm{I}\wedge \quad \cfrac{NAND(a,c,e)}{a \wedge c \to \neg e}\,\mathrm{E}\wedge_1}{\cfrac{\neg e}{\neg e \vee \neg f}\,\mathrm{IV}_1}\,\mathrm{E}\!\to}$$

where $\Gamma_1 = \{INV(b,c), NAND(a,c,e)\}$.

$$\pi_2 \equiv \cfrac{\cfrac{\cfrac{\neg a \wedge b}{b}\,\mathrm{E}\wedge_2}{} \quad \cfrac{\cfrac{\neg a \wedge b}{\neg a}\,\mathrm{E}\wedge_1 \quad \cfrac{INV(a,d)}{\neg a \to d}\,\mathrm{E}\wedge_2}{d}\,\mathrm{E}\!\to}{\cfrac{\cfrac{b \wedge d}{b \wedge d}\,\mathrm{I}\wedge \quad \cfrac{NAND(b,d,f)}{b \wedge d \to \neg f}\,\mathrm{E}\wedge_1}{\cfrac{\neg f}{\neg e \vee \neg f}\,\mathrm{IV}_2}\,\mathrm{E}\!\to}$$

where $\Gamma_2 = \{INV(a,d), NAND(b,d,f)\}$.

$$\pi_4 \equiv \cfrac{\cfrac{\cfrac{\cfrac{a \wedge b}{b}\,\mathrm{E}\wedge_2 \quad \cfrac{INV(b,c)}{b \to \neg c}\,\mathrm{E}\wedge_1}{\cfrac{\neg c}{\neg a \vee \neg c}\,\mathrm{IV}_2}\,\mathrm{E}\!\to \quad \cfrac{NAND(a,c,e)}{\neg a \vee \neg c \to e}\,\mathrm{E}\wedge_2}{e}\,\mathrm{E}\!\to \quad \cfrac{\cfrac{\cfrac{a \wedge b}{a}\,\mathrm{E}\wedge_1 \quad \cfrac{INV(a,d)}{a \to \neg d}\,\mathrm{E}\wedge_1}{\cfrac{\neg d}{\neg b \vee \neg d}\,\mathrm{IV}_2}\,\mathrm{E}\!\to \quad \cfrac{NAND(b,d,f)}{\neg b \vee \neg d \to f}\,\mathrm{E}\wedge_2}{f}\,\mathrm{E}\!\to}{e \wedge f}\,\mathrm{I}\wedge$$

where $\Gamma_4 = \{\mathrm{INV}(a,d), \mathrm{INV}(b,c), \mathrm{NAND}(a,c,e), \mathrm{NAND}(b,d,f)\}$.

$$\cfrac{\cfrac{\cfrac{\neg a \wedge \neg b}{\neg a}\,E\wedge_1}{\pi_5 \equiv \neg a \vee \neg c}\,IV_1 \quad \cfrac{\mathrm{NAND}(a,c,e)}{\neg a \vee \neg c \to e}\,E\wedge_2}{e}\,E\to \qquad \cfrac{\cfrac{\cfrac{\neg a \wedge \neg b}{\neg b}\,E\wedge_2}{\neg b \vee \neg d}\,IV_1 \quad \cfrac{\mathrm{NAND}(b,d,f)}{\neg b \vee \neg d \to f}\,E\wedge_2}{f}\,E\to}{e \wedge f}\,I\wedge$$

where $\Gamma_5 = \{\mathrm{NAND}(a,c,e), \mathrm{NAND}(b,d,f)\}$.

Now, by definition the function associated with Π has the following form:

$$F_\Pi : \lceil\mathrm{INV}(b,c)\rceil \times \lceil\mathrm{INV}(a,d)\rceil \times \lceil\mathrm{NAND}(a,c,e)\rceil \times \lceil\mathrm{NAND}(b,d,f)\rceil \times \lceil\mathrm{NAND}(e,f,g)\rceil$$
$$\to \lceil\mathrm{XOR}(a,b,g)\rceil$$

In general we can associate with every formula in $\mathcal{C}_{\mathrm{XOR}}$ a different stabilization bound, however, we assume that:

- All the instances of the formula $\mathrm{INV}(x,y)$ have the same stabilization bound $\iota = (\iota^-, \iota^+)$;
- All the instances of the formula $\mathrm{NAND}(x,y,z)$ have the same stabilization bound $\eta = (\eta^-, \eta^+)$.

With these assumptions, we can simply write $F_\Pi(\iota, \eta)$ instead of $F_\Pi(\iota, \iota, \eta, \eta, \eta)$; we do the same for the other functions defined hereafter.

To construct the function F_π we have to consider the case of Conjunction Introduction in Point (8). We get:

$$F_\Pi(\iota, \eta) = (\ F_{\pi_3}(\iota, \eta),\ F_{\pi_6}(\iota, \eta)\ ) \in (\mathbf{N}^2 \oplus \mathbf{N}^2 \to \mathbf{N})^2$$

where F_{π_3} and F_{π_6} are the functions associated with the subproofs π_3 and π_6. The construction goes on as follows:

- $F_{\pi_3}(\iota, \eta)$ is a function $f : \mathbf{N}^2 \oplus \mathbf{N}^2 \to \mathbf{N}$ such that:

$$f((1, (t_1, t_2))) = \eta^+(\ F_{\pi_1}((t_1, t_2), \iota, \eta)\ )$$
$$f((2, (t_1, t_2))) = \eta^+(\ F_{\pi_2}((t_1, t_2), \iota, \eta)\ )$$

- $F_{\pi_1}((t_1, t_2), \iota, \eta) = (\ 1,\ \eta^-((t_1, \iota^+(t_2)))\ ) \in \mathbf{N} \oplus \mathbf{N}$.
- $F_{\pi_2}((t_1, t_2), \iota, \eta) = (\ 2,\ \eta^-((t_2, \iota^+(t_1)))\ ) \in \mathbf{N} \oplus \mathbf{N}$.
- $F_{\pi_6}(\iota, \eta)$ is a function $g : \mathbf{N}^2 \oplus \mathbf{N}^2 \to \mathbf{N}$ such that:

$$g((1, (t_1, t_2))) = \eta^-(\ F_{\pi_4}((t_1, t_2), \iota, \eta)\ )$$
$$g((2, (t_1, t_2))) = \eta^-(\ F_{\pi_5}((t_1, t_2), \iota, \eta)\ )$$

- $F_{\pi_4}((t_1, t_2), \iota, \eta) = (\ \eta^+((2, \iota^-(t_2))),\ \eta^+((2, \iota^-(t_1)))\ ) \in \mathbf{N} \times \mathbf{N}$.
- $F_{\pi_5}((t_1, t_2), \iota, \eta) = (\ \eta^+((1, t_1)),\ \eta^+((1, t_2))\ ) \in \mathbf{N} \times \mathbf{N}$.

Now, given a concrete stabilization bound for the INV and the NAND gates we can compute the resulting stabilization bound for the XOR circuit. Here we consider the stabilization bounds for INV and NAND given in Points (4) and (5); hence $\iota = (f_{INV}, f_{INV})$ and $\eta = (f^-_{NAND}, f^+_{NAND})$ where

$$f_{INV}(t) = t + \delta_I$$
$$f^-_{NAND}((t_1, t_2)) = \max\{t_1, t_2\} + \delta_N \quad \text{and} \quad f^+_{NAND}((i, t)) = t + \delta_N$$

We get:

$$F_\Pi(\iota, \eta) = (F_1, F_2)$$
$$F_1((i, (t_1, t_2))) = \begin{cases} \max\{t_1, t_2 + \delta_I\} + 2\delta_N \text{ if } i = 1 \\ \max\{t_2, t_1 + \delta_I\} + 2\delta_N \text{ if } i = 2 \end{cases}$$

$$F_2((i, (t_1, t_2))) = \begin{cases} \max\{t_1, t_2\} + \delta_I + 2\delta_N \text{ if } i = 1 \\ \max\{t_1, t_2\} + 2\delta_N \qquad \text{if } i = 2 \end{cases}$$

As an example, let us suppose that $V(a)$ stabilizes to 1 at time 10 and $V(b)$ stabilizes to 0 at time 20 (see Figure 3). The formula $(a \wedge \neg b) \vee (\neg a \wedge b) \to g$ states that $V(g)$ must stabilize to 1, and the stabilization time is given by the exact stabilization bound t for V and g. By Theorem 1, t corresponds to the value of F_1 on the exact stabilization bound $(1, (10, 20))$ for V and $(a \wedge \neg b) \vee (\neg a \wedge b)$; therefore $t = F_1((1, (10, 20))) = 20 + \delta_I + 2\delta_N$.

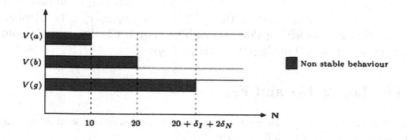

Fig. 3. A possible behavior of the XOR circuit

To conclude this section, we show that Theorem 1 essentially depends on the calculus $\mathcal{ND}$ and does not hold for proofs of Classical Logic. Indeed, let us consider the formulas $XOR(x, y, z)$ of (3) and its disjunctive normal form

$$XOR'(x, y, z) = (\neg x \wedge \neg y \wedge \neg z) \vee (\neg x \wedge y \wedge z) \vee (x \wedge \neg y \wedge z) \vee (x \wedge y \wedge \neg z)$$

Clearly, $XOR'(x, y, z)$ is classically equivalent to $XOR(x, y, z)$ and $XOR'(x, y, z)$ represents the boolean function $xor : \mathbf{N}^2 \to \mathbf{N}$. Moreover, it is easy to find a proof

$$\Pi' : \mathcal{C}_{XOR} \vdash XOR'(a, b, g)$$

in the natural deduction calculus $\mathcal{ND}_{Cl}$ for Classical Logic (see [12] for the description of such a calculus). On the other hand, as we show hereafter, there is no $\gamma \in \lceil XOR'(x, y, z) \rceil$ satisfying Point (i) of Theorem 1.

First of all, we remark that the set of stabilization bounds for $XOR'(x, y, z)$ is isomorphic to $(\mathbf{N}^3 \oplus \mathbf{N}^3 \oplus \mathbf{N}^3 \oplus \mathbf{N}^3)$, hence a stabilization bound of this set can be written as $(i, (t_1, t_2, t_3))$ with $i \in \{1, \dots, 4\}$ and $t_1, t_2, t_3 \in \mathbf{N}$. Now, let us consider the following stabilization bounds for the formulas of $\mathcal{C}_{XOR}$:

- Let $\iota = (\iota^-, \iota^+)$ be the stabilization bound for all the instances of the formula INV(x, y), where $\iota^-(t) = \iota^+(t) = 0$ for every $t \in \mathbf{N}$;
- Let $\eta = (\eta^-, \eta^+)$ be the stabilization bound for all the instances of the formula NAND(x, y, z), where $\eta^-((t_1, t_2)) = 0$ for every $t_1, t_2 \in \mathbf{N}$ and $\eta^+((i, t)) = 0$ for $i = 1, 2$ and for every $t \in \mathbf{N}$.

Now, let us assume that $F_{\Pi'}(\iota, \eta) = (1, (c_1, c_2, c_3))$ for some $c_1, c_2, c_3 \in \mathbf{N}$. Let us consider the stable waveform V such that $V(a) = V(b) = V(e) = V(f) = 1$ and $V(c) = V(d) = V(g) = 0$. It is easy to check that

$$\iota, V \models INV(a, d) \qquad \iota, V \models INV(b, c)$$
$$\eta, V \models NAND(a, c, e) \quad \eta, V \models NAND(b, d, f) \quad \eta, V \models NAND(e, f, g)$$

while

$$(1, (c_1, c_2, c_3)), V \not\models XOR'(a, b, g)$$

since $(c_1, c_2, c_3), V \not\models \neg a \wedge \neg b \wedge \neg g$. Similar conclusions can be obtained considering $F_{\Pi'}(\iota, \eta) = (j, (c_1, c_2, c_3))$ with $j = 2, 3, 4$ and $c_1, c_2, c_3 \in \mathbf{N}$. Hence, there in no function $F_{\Pi'}$ satisfying Point (i) of Theorem 1. Finally, we point out that there is no proof in $\mathcal{ND}$ of $\mathcal{C}_{XOR} \vdash XOR'(a, b, g)$.

5   The Logics $\mathbf{L_{Ef}}$ and $\mathbf{F_{Cl}}$

In this section we briefly discuss the logical properties of our semantics. Let $\mathbf{L_{Ef}}$ be the logic semantically defined as follows:

$$\mathbf{L_{Ef}} = \{A \ : \ \exists \alpha \in \lceil A \rceil \ \forall V \in \text{ESTABLE} \quad \alpha, V \models A \}$$

where we recall that ESTABLE is the set of all the eventually stable waveforms. It can be shown that $\mathbf{L_{Ef}}$ is a *non-standard intermediate logic*, that is $\mathbf{Int} \subseteq \mathbf{L_{Ef}} \subseteq \mathbf{Cl}$, where $\mathbf{Int}$ ($\mathbf{Cl}$) denotes the set of the intuitionistically (classically) valid formulas of $\mathcal{L}_{\mathbf{S}}$ and $\mathbf{L_{Ef}}$ is closed under *modus ponens*. We emphasize that, differently from *standard* intermediate logics, $\mathbf{L_{Ef}}$ is not closed under arbitrary substitutions of propositional variables with formulas, but only under substitutions associating a formula of the kind $\Box A$ with every propositional variable. Moreover, $\mathbf{L_{Ef}}$ has the *disjunction property*, that is $A \vee B \in \mathbf{L_{Ef}}$ implies $A \in \mathbf{L_{Ef}}$ or $B \in \mathbf{L_{Ef}}$.

As a consequence of Theorem 1, every formula provable in the calculus $\mathcal{ND}$ (of Table 1) belongs to $\mathbf{L_{Ef}}$. This means that $\mathcal{ND}$ is a correct calculus for $\mathbf{L_{Ef}}$;

on the other hand we do not know if it is complete for $\mathbf{L}_{\mathrm{Ef}}$ and, as far as we know, no axiomatization for $\mathbf{L}_{\mathrm{Ef}}$ is known.

Another logic that emerges from our semantical setting is $\mathbf{F}_{\mathrm{Cl}}$, a well-known axiomatizable non-standard intermediate logic which has strong connections with $\mathbf{L}_{\mathrm{Ef}}$. In [10,11] $\mathbf{F}_{\mathrm{Cl}}$ has been characterized as the smallest set of formulas closed under modus ponens containing $\mathbf{Int}$, all the instances of $\mathrm{KP}_\square$ and all the instances of $\mathrm{At}_\square$, where:

- $\mathrm{KP}_\square = (\square A \to B \vee C) \to (\square A \to B) \vee (\square A \to C)$ is the axiom schema obtained by translating the well-known Kreisel and Putnam Principle [3] into the language $\mathcal{L}_\mathbf{S}$, and corresponds to the rule $\mathrm{KP}_\square$ of Table 1;
- $\mathrm{At}_\square = \square a \to a$ with $a \in \mathbf{S}$.

A valid and complete natural calculus for $\mathbf{F}_{\mathrm{Cl}}$ is the calculus $\mathcal{ND}_{\mathbf{F}_{\mathrm{Cl}}}$ obtained by adding to $\mathcal{ND}$ the rule:

$$\frac{\square a}{a} \ \mathrm{E}\square\mathrm{AT} \quad \text{with } a \in \mathbf{S}$$

In [10,11] it is proved that $\mathbf{F}_{\mathrm{Cl}}$ is a non-standard intermediate logic with the disjunction property. Moreover, $\mathbf{F}_{\mathrm{Cl}}$ meets some important proof-theoretical properties; indeed it is interpolable and enjoys a Normal Form Theorem that can be used to reduce provability in $\mathbf{F}_{\mathrm{Cl}}$ to provability in Classical Logic. In the above quoted papers it is also illustrated the relationship between $\mathbf{F}_{\mathrm{Cl}}$ and *Medvedev Logic of Finite Problems* [6,10].

To characterize $\mathbf{F}_{\mathrm{Cl}}$ in our semantical setting, let

$$\mathrm{STABLEAT}_t = \{V \mid V \text{ is a waveform such that } V^t \text{ is stable}\}$$

It can be shown that

$$\mathbf{F}_{\mathrm{Cl}} = \{A \ : \ \exists \alpha \in \lceil A \rceil \ \forall V \in \mathrm{STABLEAT}_t \quad \alpha, V \models A \}$$

From the above semantical characterization it is immediate to check that $\mathbf{L}_{\mathrm{Ef}} \subseteq \mathbf{F}_{\mathrm{Cl}}$; on the other hand, $\mathbf{L}_{\mathrm{Ef}} \neq \mathbf{F}_{\mathrm{Cl}}$ since $\mathrm{At}_\square$ does not hold in $\mathbf{L}_{\mathrm{Ef}}$.

Also from proofs of $\mathcal{ND}_{\mathbf{F}_{\mathrm{Cl}}}$ we can extract exact stabilization bounds. Here we describe how to associate with every proof $\pi : \{A_1, \dots, A_n\} \vdash B$ of $\mathcal{ND}_{\mathbf{F}_{\mathrm{Cl}}}$ a function $F_\pi^\tau : \lceil A_1 \rceil \times \cdots \times \lceil A_n \rceil \to \lceil B \rceil$ where τ is a parameter in $\mathbf{N}$ needed to treat the rule $\mathrm{E}\square\mathrm{AT}$. The function is defined by induction on the structure of π. For the rules occurring in $\mathcal{ND}$, the function is defined according to Points (7)-(17) (the parameter τ plays no role), while the rule $\mathrm{E}\square\mathrm{AT}$ is treated as follows:

Rule $\mathrm{E}\square\mathrm{AT}$: in this case π is the proof

$$\frac{\begin{array}{c} A_1, \dots, A_n \\ \vdots \ \pi_1 \\ \square a \end{array}}{a} \ \mathrm{E}\square\mathrm{AT} \tag{18}$$

$$F_\pi(\underline{\alpha}) = \tau$$

The main properties of the function F_π^t associated with a proof $\pi \in \mathcal{ND}_{\mathbf{F}_{Cl}}$ and with $t \in \mathbf{N}$ are given by the following result.

Theorem 2. *Let $\pi : \{A_1, \ldots, A_n\} \vdash B$ be a proof of the calculus $\mathcal{ND}_{\mathbf{F}_{Cl}}$, let $t \in \mathbf{N}$ and let*

$$F_\pi^t : \lceil A_1 \rceil \times \cdots \times \lceil A_n \rceil \to \lceil B \rceil$$

be the function associated with π and t. For all $\alpha_1 \in \lceil A_1 \rceil$, $\ldots$, $\alpha_n \in \lceil A_n \rceil$, and for every waveform $V \in \text{STABLEAT}_t$:

(i). $\alpha_1, V \models A_1$, $\ldots$, $\alpha_n, V \models A_n$ *implies* $F_\pi^t(\alpha_1, \ldots, \alpha_n), V \models B$.

(ii). $\alpha_1' \sim_{A_1} \alpha_1$, $\ldots$, $\alpha_n' \sim_{A_n} \alpha_n$ *implies* $F_\pi^t(\alpha_1', \ldots, \alpha_n') \sim_B F_\pi^t(\alpha_1, \ldots, \alpha_n)$.

(iii). α_1 *exact for V and A_1*, $\ldots$, α_n *exact for V and A_n implies* $F_\pi^t(\alpha_1, \ldots, \alpha_n)$ *exact for V and B.*

6   Conclusion

In this paper we have shown how we can get a timing analysis with data-dependent valuation of exact delays by a specialization of evaluation forms semantics [11]. There are several interesting aspects we aim to investigate in our future work.

As for the semantics here considered, we want to examine thoroughly the kind of delay information related to different formulas representing the same boolean function. As an example we remark that the $\Box$ operator can be used to avoid the timing analysis of the subformulas to which it applies. It is easy to see that there exists a proof

$$\Pi' : \mathcal{C}_{\text{XOR}} \vdash \Box\text{XOR}(a, b, g)$$

in $\mathcal{ND}$, and this proof guarantees (according to Definition 1) the correctness of the input/output behavior of the XOR circuit of Figure 1. On the other hand the stabilization bounds for $\Box$-formulas give no information about the delays. At the same way, using $\Box$ in front of a formula representing a component of the circuit, we can abstract from the temporal behavior of such a component.

As for the expressiveness of our language, we observe that the *nand* function, we described by means of the formula $\text{NAND}(x, y, z)$ of Point (2), can also be represented by different formulas, e.g.,

$$\text{NAND}'(x, y, z) \equiv (x \wedge y \to \neg z) \wedge (\neg x \to z) \wedge (\neg y \to z)$$

Actually, $\lceil \text{NAND}(x, y, z) \rceil \neq \lceil \text{NAND}'(x, y, z) \rceil$, however accomplishing the analysis of the XOR circuit using $\text{NAND}'(x, y, z)$ we obtain essentially the same results, e.g., also in this case we obtain the diagram of Figure 3.

Another aspect we aim to investigate is the extension of our language by other modal operators as the Lax operator of [8].

Finally, we remark that the semantical setting of evaluation forms supports a variety of specializations that preserve the Soundness Theorem, that is the fundamental result to compute stabilization bounds with proofs. In this paper we have studied a specialization of evaluation forms semantics directly inspired by [7,8]; our aim is to investigate other specializations of evaluation forms semantics and their relation with timing analysis models.

References

1. D.A. Basin and N. Klarlund. Automata based symbolic reasoning in hardware verification. *Formal Methods in Systems Design*, 13(3):255–288, 1998.
2. J. Brzozowski and M. Yoeli. Ternary simulation of binary gate networks. In J. M. Dunn and G. Epstein, editors, *Modern Uses of Multiple-Valued Logic*, pages 41–50. D. Reidel, 1977.
3. A. Chagrov and M. Zakharyaschev. *Modal Logic*. Oxford University Press, 1997.
4. C.T. Gray, W. Liu, R.K. Cavin III, and H.-Y. Hsieh. Circuit delay calculation considering data dependent delays. *INTEGRATION, The VLSI Journal*, 17:1–23, 1994.
5. S. Malik. Analysis of Cyclic Combinational Circuits. In *IEEE/ACM International Conference on CAD*, pages 618–627. ACM/IEEE, IEEE Computer Society Press, 1993.
6. Ju.T. Medvedev. Interpretation of logical formulas by means of finite problems and its relation to the realizability theory. *Soviet Mathematics Doklady*, 4:180–183, 1963.
7. M. Mendler. A timing refinement of intuitionistic proofs and its application to the timing analysis of combinational circuits. In P. Miglioli, U. Moscato, D. Mundici, and M. Ornaghi, editors, *Proceedings of the 5th International Workshop on Theorem Proving with Analytic Tableaux and Related Methods*, pages 261–277. Springer, LNAI 1071, 1996.
8. M. Mendler. Characterising combinational timing analyses in intuitionistic modal logic. *Logic Journal of the IGPL*, 8(6):821–852, 2000.
9. M. Mendler. Timing analysis of combinational circuits in intuitionistic propositional logic. *Formal Methods in System Design*, 17(1):5–37, 2000.
10. P. Miglioli, U. Moscato, M. Ornaghi, S. Quazza, and G. Usberti. Some results on intermediate constructive logics. *Notre Dame Journal of Formal Logic*, 30(4):543–562, 1989.
11. P. Miglioli, U. Moscato, M. Ornaghi, and G. Usberti. A constructivism based on classical truth. *Notre Dame Journal of Formal Logic*, 30(1):67–90, 1989.
12. D. Prawitz. *Natural Deduction*. Almquist and Winksell, 1965.
13. R.H. Thomason. A semantical study of constructible falsity. *Zeitschrift für Mathematische Logik und Grundlagen der Mathematik*, 15:247–257, 1969.

Author Index

Lecture Notes in Computer Science

For information about Vols. 1–2302
please contact your bookseller or Springer-Verlag